In the form of a critical anthology, this book interlaces an
of seminal articles by leading figures in the theory and practice of
digital design with a series of original theoretical texts. It develops
a meta-theory of the emerging interactions of media technologies
and design in architecture. This theory is promoted as a foundation of transformations in design methods as well as a basis for the
evolution of new forms of design thinking.

The development of an explication of emerging concepts in the
form of a new taxonomy is an important contribution in any form
of discourse analysis. *Theories of the Digital in Architecture*
attempts to develop such a conceptual orientation for the growing
impact of the integration of digital media technologies in design.
It locates these conceptual structures within a historical perspective that identifies the coming into being of a new epistemology
of the digital in architecture.

Rivka Oxman is a distinguished researcher in the field of design
research. Her current work explores the impact of emerging digital
media and technologies on design. She is a Fellow of the Design
Research Society and one of the editors of the international journal
for design research, *Design Studies*.

Robert Oxman is an author and researcher in the history and
theory of architecture and design. His most recent book is *The New
Structuralism*, 2010, written in collaboration with Rivka Oxman.

...⌐ ⌐
RIES
OF THE
DIGITAL
IN
ARCHI-
TEC-
TURE

THEORIES OF THE DIGITAL IN ARCHITECTURE

RIVKA OXMAN AND ROBERT OXMAN

Routledge
Taylor & Francis Group

LONDON AND NEW YORK

First published 2014
by Routledge
2 Park Square, Milton Park, Abingdon, Oxon OX14 4RN

and by Routledge
711 Third Avenue, New York, NY 10017

Routledge is an imprint of the Taylor & Francis Group, an informa business

Cover image credit: Pnewna, 2012. From the *Imaginary Beings* series Centre Georges Pompida (Permanent Collection). Designed by Neri Oxman in collaboration with Prof. W. Craig Carter (MIT) and Joe Hicklin (The Mathworks), fabricated by Stratasys. Photo credit: Yoram Reshef, Statasys

British Library Cataloguing in Publication Data
A catalogue record for this book is available from the British Library

Library of Congress Cataloging in Publication Data
Theories of the digital in architecture / Rivka Oxman and Robert Oxman.
    pages cm
  Includes bibliographical references and index.
  1. Architecture—Philosophy.   2. Architectural design—Technological
  innovations.   I. Oxman,   Rivka, editor of compilation.
  II. Oxman, Robert, editor of compilation.
  NA2500.T49 2013
  720.1—dc23

                                                                2013010795

ISBN: 978–0–415–46923–4 (hbk)
ISBN: 978–0–415–46924–1 (pbk)

Typeset in Frutiger
by RefineCatch Limited, Bungay, Suffolk

Printed and bound in Great Britain by
TJ International Ltd, Padstow, Cornwall

For Neri and Keren from whom we continue to learn

LIST OF SOURCES

Chapter 1: Frederic Migayrou. Originally published in *Architectures Non-Standard*, 2003; new introduction, 2012.

Chapter 2: John Wiley and Sons. Originally published in *Folding in Architecture*, revised edition 2004.

Chapter 3: De Gruyter, formerly Birkhäuser. Originally published in *Digital Culture in Architecture*, 2010.

Chapter 4: Riverside Architectural Press. Originally published in *Animate Form*, 1999.

Chapter 5: John Wiley and Sons. Originally published in *Mathematics of Space*, 2011.

Chapter 6: Spon Press. Originally published in *Performative Architecture: Beyond Instrumentality*, 2005.

Chapter 7: Spon Press. Originally published in *Architecture in the Digital Age: Design and Manufacturing*, 2003.

Chapter 8: John Wiley and Sons. Originally published in *The New Structuralism: Design, Engineering and Architectural Technologies*, 2010.

Chapter 9: John Wiley and Sons. Originally published in *Patterns of Architecture*, 2009.

Chapter 10: Routledge. Originally published in *Elements of Parametric Design*, 2010.

Chapter 11: John Wiley and Sons. Originally published in *Scripting Cultures: Architectural Design and Programming*, 2011.

Chapter 12: Routledge. Originally published in *Emergent Technologies and Design: Towards a Biological Paradigm for Architecture*, 2010.

Chapter 13: Routledge. Originally published in *Emergent Technologies and Design: Towards a Biological Paradigm for Architecture*, 2010.

Chapter 14: Elsevier. Originally published in *Design Studies*, volume 33, 2012.

Chapter 15: Louisiana Museum of Modern Art. Originally published in *Frontiers of Architecture 1: Cecil Balmond*, 2007; revised 2012.

Chapter 16: Lars Spuybroek and V2_Publishing. Originally published in *Transurbanism*, 2001.

Chapter 17: John Wiley and Sons. Originally published in *Versioning: Evolutionary Techniques in Architecture*, 2002.

Chapter 18: John Wiley and Sons. Originally published in *The New Structuralism: Design, Engineering and Architectural Technologies*, 2010.

Chapter 19: New material, 2012.

Chapter 20: New material, 2012.

Chapter 21: New material, 2013.

Chapter 22: Riverside Architectural Press. Originally published in *Responsive Architecture: Subtle Technologies*, 2006.

Chapter 23: NAi Publishers. Originally published in *Towards a New Kind of Building: a Designer's Guide for Non-Standard Architecture*, 2011.

Chapter 24: John Wiley and Sons. Originally published in *The New Structuralism: Design, Engineering and Architectural Technologies*, 2010; revised 2012.

Chapter 25: Princeton Architectural Press. Originally published in *Form + Code in Design, Art and Architecture*, 2010.

Chapter 26: John Wiley and Sons. Originally published in *Scripting Cultures: Architectural Design and Programming*, 2011.

CONTENTS

NOTES ON CONTRIBUTORS

Martin **Bechthold**

Martin Bechthold is Professor of Architectural Technology at the Graduate School of Design, Harvard University, director of the Design Robotics Group, and co-director of the GSD's Master in Design Studies Program. Bechthold's research on material system innovation pursues computer-aided design and manufacturing applications in architecture, with a focus on broadening design scope through construction automation and industrial robotics. His current research investigates workflow and fabrication automation strategies for architectural ceramics and for other construction systems. He collaborates with the Wyss Center for Biologically Inspired Engineering on the development of adaptive micro-material systems. Bechthold is the co-author of *Structures* and *Computer-Aided Design and Manufacturing* as well as the author of *Innovative Surface Structures*.

Philip **Beesley**

Philip Beesley is a professor in the School of Architecture at the University of Waterloo. A practitioner of architecture and digital media art, he was educated in visual art at Queen's University, in technology at Humber College, and in architecture at the University of Toronto. At Waterloo, he serves as Director for the Integrated Group for Visualization, Design and Manufacturing, and as Director for Riverside Architectural Press. Beesley's Toronto-based practice, PBAI, is an interdisciplinary design firm that incorporates industrial design, digital prototyping, and mechatronics engineering. His work is widely cited in the rapidly expanding technology of responsive architecture.

Klaus **Bollinger** and Manfred **Grohmann**

Klaus Bollinger has studied Civil Engineering at the Technical University Darmstadt and taught at Dortmund University. Since 1994 he has been assigned Professor for Structural Engineering at the School of Architecture/ University of Applied Arts at Vienna and since 2000 guest professor at the Städelschule in Frankfurt. He is currently Head of Architecture at the University of Applied Arts, Vienna.

Manfred Grohmann has studied and taught Civil Engineering at the Darmstadt Technical University. Since 1996 he has been assigned Professor for Structural Design at Kassel University, since 2000 guest professor at the Städelschule in Frankfurt, and since 2007 at the ESA – École d'Architecture in Paris.

In 1983 Klaus Bollinger and Manfred Grohmann established the practice Bollinger + Grohmann, now located in Frankfurt am Main, Vienna, Paris, Oslo and Melbourne with around 100 employees. For years they have been collaborating successfully with numerous internationally recognized architects and strive to always provide the best solution through their creativity and technical excellence.

Mark **Burry**

Professor Mark Burry has published internationally on three main themes: the life and work of the architect Antoni Gaudí in Barcelona, putting theory into practice with regard to 'challenging' architecture, and transdisciplinary design education and practice. He has also published widely on broader issues of design, construction and the use of computers in design theory and practice. He is the founding Director of RMIT University's *Design Research Institute* (DRI) and founder and former Director of RMIT's state-of-the-art *Spatial Information Architecture Laboratory* (SIAL). Since 1979, Professor Burry has been a Principal Architect with the design team *Sagrada Família Basilica* based on site in Barcelona.

Mario **Carpo**

Mario Carpo teaches architectural history and theory at the School of Architecture of Yale University, and at the École d'Architecture de Paris-La Villette. Carpo's research and publications focus on the relationship among architectural theory, cultural history, and the history of media and information technology. His *Architecture in the Age of Printing* (2001) has been translated into several languages. His most recent books are *The Alphabet and the Algorithm,* a history of digital design theory (2011), and *The Digital Turn in Architecture, 1992–2012*, an AD Reader.

Fabio **Gramazio** and Matthias **Kohler**

Fabio Gramazio and Matthias Kohler are architects with multi-disciplinary interests ranging from computational design and robotic fabrication to material innovation. In 2000, they founded the architecture practice Gramazio & Kohler and realized numerous award-wining designs. This includes the Gantenbein vineyard façade, the Tanzhaus theatre for contemporary dance, the Christmas lights for the Bahnhofstrasse Zurich, the sWISH* Pavilion at the Swiss National Exposition Expo.02 and the Private House in Riedikon. Founding also the world's first architectural robotic laboratory at the Swiss Federal Institute of Technology ETH Zurich, the academic work of Gramazio & Kohler ranges from 1:1 prototypical installations to the design of robotically fabricated high-rise buildings. Gramazio & Kohler were awarded the Swiss Art Awards, the Global Holcim Innovation Prize and the Acadia Award for Emerging Digital Practice. Their work has been published in a large number of academic journals, further contributing to numerous exhibitions around the world, such as the Architecture Biennale in Venice (2008), the Storefront Gallery for Art and Architecture (2009) New York, and Flight Assembled Architecture at the FRAC Orléans (2011).

Sachiko **Hirosue**

Sachiko Hirosue works as a researcher at the interface of biomaterials and lymphatic physiology in the Institute of Bioengineering, School of Life Sciences, École Polytechnique Fédérale de Lausanne, Switzerland. Her interest in bio art derives from the encounter at the Subtle Technologies Festival (Toronto, Canada), which she co-chaired from 2005–2008.

Martin **Kemp**

Martin Kemp was trained in Natural Sciences and Art History at Cambridge University and the Courtauld Institute, London. He held the post of Professor of the History of Art at St Andrews, and then also, at the University of Oxford. Books include, *The Science of Art* (Yale), and *The Human Animal in Western Art and Science* (Chicago). He has published extensively on Leonardo da Vinci, including *Leonardo da Vinci: the Marvellous Works of Nature and Man*. His most recent book is *Christ to Coke: How Image Becomes Icon* (Oxford).

Branko **Kolarevic**

Branko Kolarevic is a professor at the University of Calgary Faculty of Environmental Design, where he also holds the Chair in Integrated Design. He has taught architecture at several universities in North America and Asia and has lectured worldwide on the use of digital technologies in design and production. He has authored, edited or co-edited several books, including *Manufacturing Material Effects* (with Kevin Klinger), *Performative Architecture* (with Ali Malkawi) and *Architecture in the Digital Age*. He holds doctoral and master's degrees in design from Harvard University and a diploma engineer in architecture degree from the University of Belgrade.

Greg **Lynn**

Greg Lynn was born in 1964. He won a Golden Lion at the Venice Biennale of Architecture, received the American Academy of Arts & Letters Architecture Award and was awarded a fellowship from United States Artists. Time Magazine named him one of 100 of the most innovative people in the world for the 21st century and Forbes Magazine named him one of the ten most influential living architects. He graduated from Miami University of Ohio with Bachelor of Environmental Design and Bachelor of Philosophy degrees and from Princeton University with a Master of Architecture degree. He is the author of seven books.

Chandler **McWilliams**

Chandler McWilliams is an artist and writer living in Los Angeles. He has studied film, photography, and political science; and completed graduate work in philosophy at The New School For Social Research in New York City. He has taught at schools and workshops around the world, and most recently in the Design Media Arts program at UCLA. McWilliams is the co-author of *Form + Code in Design, Art, and Architecture* (Princeton Architectural Press, 2010). Currently, McWilliams is an MFA candidate in the Program in Art at the California Institute of the Arts where he works with sculpture, text, and performance to cope with ideas of ethics, space, perception, and thought.

Achim **Menges**

Achim Menges, born 1975, is a registered architect and professor at University of Stuttgart where he is the founding director of the Institute for Computational Design (since 2008). In addition, he has been Visiting Professor in Architecture at Harvard University's Graduate School of Design (2009–10), at the AA School of Architecture in London (2009-current) and at Rice

University in Houston (2004). He graduated with honours from the AA (2002) where he subsequently taught as Studio Master of the Emergent Technologies and Design Program (2002–09) and as Unit Master of Diploma Unit 4 (2003–06). His projects and design research have received many international awards, have been published and exhibited worldwide, and form parts of several renowned museum collections.

Frédéric **Migayrou**

Frédéric Migayrou is Deputy Director, since 2007, and Chief Curator of Architecture and Design, since 2000, of the National Museum of Modern Art (MNAM-CCI), Centre Pompidou in Paris. In addition since 2011, he is Chair of Architecture and the Bartlett Professor at the Bartlett School of Architecture in London. After studies in philosophy (Doctorat 3eme cycle), he became full professor of the aesthetics and history of art (1983–1990) and was active as a critic and curator of art & architecture. As a Councellor of the Ministery of Culture (1990–2000), he reorganised the FRAC Center in Orleans and initiated a unique collection devoted to experimental architecture (Yona Friedman, Daniel Libeskind, Rem Koolhaas, Morphosis, Eric Owen Moss, Zaha Hadid . . . .) and published monographic texts and catalogues (Steven Holl, Diller & Scofidio, Jeff Wall, James Coleman . . .). In 1996 he was curator of the French Pavilion at the Venice Biennale with an exhibition "Bloc, Le monolithe fracturé" devoted to André Bloc and Claude Parent and organised an international exhibition on "Radical Architecture". Introducing in the FRAC collection many works of architects of the youngest generation who have turned to computation, he curated with Marie Ange-Brayer since 1999, *Archilab*, an annual exhibition devoted to advanced prospective architecture. Appointed in 2000 at the Pompidou Center, he curated "Non Standard Architecture" with 12 architects working on the "from file to factory" paradigm. Since this time he has curated various exhibitions including, Morphosis (2006), Pol Abraham (2008), Claude Parent Architect (2009), Large Scale Metropolises (2009), Dominique Perrault (2009), De Stijl-Mondrian (2010), La Tendenza (2012). He is currently preparing a new Archilab, "Naturalising Architecture", with Marie-Ange Brayer (2013), and monographic exhibitions on Bernard Tschumi (2014) Centre Pompidou, and on Frank Gehry (Fondation LVMH, Paris, 2014).

Kas **Oosterhuis**

Professor Kas Oosterhuis studied architecture at the Delft Technical University. In 1987–1988 he taught as Unit Master at the AA in London and worked / lived one year in the former studio of Theo van Doesburg in Paris together with visual artist Ilona Lénárd. Their design studio was in 2004 renamed *ONL* [Oosterhuis_Lénárd]. As from 2007 Kas Oosterhuis is a registered architect in Hungary, executing as General Designer the CET project. From 2000 Oosterhuis is appointed Professor of Digital Design Methods at the Delft Technical University and is currently leading a staff of 12 researchers at *Hyperbody*, the Knowledge Center for Nonstandard and Interactive Architecture at the TU Delft. He is Director of the *proto*SPACE Laboratory and is member of the Dutch Building Information Council [BIR]. He has lectured worldwide at numerous universities, academies and international conferences since 1990.

In his most recent book *Towards a New Kind of Building, a Designer's Guide to Nonstandard Architecture* [NAi Publishers 2011] Oosterhuis reveals the fundaments of his personal design universe, which embraces the paradigm shift from standard to nonstandard structures and from static to dynamic buildings as the initial condition.

Neri **Oxman**

Architect and Designer Neri Oxman is the Sony Corporation Career Development Professor and Assistant Professor of Media Arts and Sciences at the MIT Media Lab, where she founded and directs the Mediated Matter design research group. The group explores how digital design and fabrication technologies mediate between matter and environment to radically transform the design and construction of objects, buildings, and systems. A principle objective is to enhance the relationship between the built and the natural environments by employing design principles inspired by nature and implementing them in the invention of novel digital technologies. Neri Oxman received her PhD in design computation as a Presidential Fellow at MIT, where she developed the theory and practice of Material-based Design Computation. In 2006 she founded the research-oriented design firm, Material Ecology, that is engaged in experimental practices of material design and fabrication inspired by natural processes. Oxman was named to ICON's list of the top 20 most influential architects to shape our future (2009), and was selected as one of the 100 most creative people by FASTCOMPANY (2009). In 2008, she was named "Revolutionary Mind" by SEED Magazine. Her work has been exhibited at MoMA (NYC), the Centre Georges Pompidou (Paris, France), the Smithsonian Institute (Washington, DC), the Museum of Science (Boston, MA), the FRAC Collection (Orleans, France), and the 2010 Beijing Biennale.

Rivka **Oxman**

Rivka Oxman is Associate Professor in the Faculty of Architecture and Town Planning. She holds the B.Sc., M.Sc., and D.Sc. degrees from the Technion Israel Institute of Technology. Among recent academic appointments, she has been Vice Dean for Teaching. Rivka Oxman held appointments of Visiting Professor at Stanford University; Delft University of Technology; and Salford University. She held visiting appointments at Harvard, MIT, Berkeley and the University of Sydney. She is an associate editor of Design Studies – the international journal of Design Studies and is a member of the scientific and editorial boards of leading international journals and conferences. Rivka Oxman was appointed as a Fellow of the Design Research Society (FDRS) for her contributions and established record of achievement in design research, and the attainment of international peer recognition as a researcher of professional standing and competence.

Her research focuses on digital models of design and their applications in experimental design and design pedagogy. Her research relates to the contribution of digital media and material technologies to the emergence of digital design models and paradigms. She has been invited to deliver keynote lectures in leading universities and conferences around the world. In 2010 Rivka and Robert Oxman co-authored the publication, *The New Structuralism: Design, Engineering and Architectural Technologies*, Architectural Design (AD), Wiley Publications.

Robert **Oxman**

Robert Oxman is Professor and Dean Emeritus at the Faculty of Architecture and Town Planning, Technion Israel Institute of Technology. He has recently been Professor of the History and Theory of Design and Architecture and Dean of Graduate Studies at the Shenkar College of Engineering and Design. In the past he has held the Chairs of CAD and Design Methods at the Technical University, Eindhoven, the Netherlands. His field of studies is the history and theory of architecture and design, the role of theory in design, and the implications of technology upon design.

Antoine **Picon**

Antoine Picon, is the G. Ware Travelstead Professor of the History of Architecture and Technology at Harvard Graduate School of Design where he also co-chairs the doctoral programs. He holds simultaneously a research position at the Ecole Nationale des Ponts et Chaussées. He has published numerous books and articles mostly dealing with the complementary histories of architecture and technology, among which: *French Architects and Engineers in the Age of Enlightenment, Claude Perrault, L'Invention de L'ingénieur moderne, La ville territoire des cyborgs*, and *Les Saint-Simoniens: Raison, Imaginaire, et Utopie*. Published in 2010, Picon's recent book, *Digital Culture in Architecture* proposes a comprehensive interpretation of the changes brought by the computer to the design professions. In 2013, Wiley published his new book: *Ornament: The Politics of Architecture and Subjectivity*, which discusses the signification of the contemporary "return" of ornament.

Helmut **Pottmann**

Helmut Pottmann received a PhD in mathematics from the Vienna University of Technology (TU Wien) in 1983. Since 1992 he is professor at TU Wien and head of the 'Geometric Modeling and Industrial Geometry' research group. He is currently director of the KAUST Geometric Modeling and Scientific Visualization Center, Saudi Arabia. His recent research concentrates on Geometric Computing for Architecture and Manufacturing.

Casey **Reas**

Casey Reas lives and works in Los Angeles where he is a Professor at UCLA's Department of Design Media Arts. His software, prints, and installations have been featured in numerous solo and group exhibitions at museums and galleries. Casey co-founded *Processing* in 2001 while studying with John Maeda in MIT's Media Lab.

Jim **Ruxton**

Jim Ruxton received his M.A. Sc. in Electrical Engineering at the University of Ottawa in 1988. Between 1988 and 1991 he worked as an engineer designing various satellite communication devices. In 1991 he went to the Ontario College of Art and Design to explore combining electronics and art. In 1993 he graduated with an A.O.C.A. and was chosen as a medal recipient.

Since 1993 he has worked in Toronto as an engineer/artist bringing electronics into various fields of the arts. He is the sole proprietor of *Cinematronics*, a company created to service the film special effects industry. His electronic props and special devices have been used in numerous films and TV series. As well as creating his own installation art, he collaborates in the areas of dance, theatre and film to create interactive kinetic environments, allowing the viewers or performers to alter the space.

Fabian **Scheurer**

Fabian Scheurer is founding partner of designtoproduction and leads the company's office in Zurich. After graduating from the Technical University of Munich with a diploma in computer science and architecture, he worked as assistant for the university's CAAD group, as software developer and new media consultant in Munich and Zurich. From 2002 until 2006 he studied the use of artificial-life methods in architectural construction as a member of Ludger Hovestadt's CAAD group at the ETH Zurich. In 2005 he co-founded *designtoproduction* as a research group at ETH to explore the connections between digital design and fabrication. At the end of 2006 designtoproduction teamed up with architect Arnold Walz and became a commercial consulting practice, since then having implemented digital planning and production chains for projects like the Hungerburg-Funicular in Innsbruck (by Zaha Hadid), the Rolex Learning Center in Lausanne (by SANAA), the Centre Pompidou in Metz (by Shigeru Ban) and many others. Fabian Scheurer has taught as guest lecturer/tutor at the AA in London and the IAAC in Barcelona. Since 2012 he is lecturing on Digital Modeling and Production at HTW Chur (Switzerland).

Patrik **Schumacher**

Patrik Schumacher is partner at Zaha Hadid Architects. He joined the firm in 1988 and has since been the co-author of many key projects. Together with Zaha Hadid he built up Zaha Hadid Architects to become a 400 strong global architecture brand. Patrik Schumacher studied philosophy, mathematics, and architecture in Bonn, London and Stuttgart, where he received his Diploma in 1990. In 1999 he completed his PHD at the Institute for Cultural Science, Klagenfurt University. In 1996 he founded the "Design Research Laboratory" at the Architectural Association in London and continues to teach in what has become one of the world's most prestigious architecture programs.

Dennis R. **Shelden**

Dennis R. Shelden is a Founder and Chief Technology Officer of Gehry Technologies, a building industry technology company formed in 2001 by the research and development team of Frank Gehry Partners. He joined Gehry Partners in 1997 and became Director of Computing in 2000, where he was responsible for the management and strategic direction of the firm's technology efforts. Prior to joining Gehry Partners, he performed structural engineering, energy systems and technology development work at firms including Arup, Consultants' Computation Bureau and Cyra Systems.

He is concurrently an Associate Professor of the Practice in Computation and Design at the Massachusetts Institute of Technology, where he lectures and conducts research in building industry process advancement, parametric building information modeling, computational geometry, and design cognition. He holds a Bachelor of Science in Architectural Design, a Master of Science in Civil and Environmental Engineering, and a Ph. D. in Computation and Architectural Design from MIT. He is a licensed Architect in the State of California.

SHoP/Sharples, Holden, Pasquarelli

Located in Lower Manhattan, SHoP was founded in 1996 by five principals: Christopher Sharples, Coren Sharples, William Sharples, Kimberly Holden, and Gregg Pasquarelli. The practice has grown over the past sixteen years to an office of ninety. In 2007 they formed a sister firm, SHoP Construction, managed by a sixth Principal, Jonathan Mallie; and in 2012, they welcomed their seventh Principal, Vishaan Chakrabarti, Director of CURE, the Center for Urban Real Estate, at Columbia University's Graduate School of Architecture, and former Manhattan Director for the New York Department of City Planning.

SHoP's educational and professional experience encompasses architecture, fine arts, structural engineering, finance, and business management. They work on many project types, from multi-story housing to academic buildings to master plans. SHoP has won numerous awards, including the 2009 National Design Award for Architecture Design by Smithsonian's Cooper-Hewitt National Design Museum. SHoP's work has been published and exhibited internationally, and is in the permanent collection of the Museum of Modern Art.

Lars **Spuybroek**

Lars Spuybroek has been researching the relationship between art, architecture and computing since the early 1990s. He received international recognition after building the *HtwoOexpo* in 1997, the first building in the world that incorporates new media and consists of a continuous geometry. With his Rotterdam-based office NOX he built the *D-Tower*, an interactive structure changing color with the emotions of the inhabitants of a city (in collaboration with Q. S. Serafijn), and the *Son-O-House*, a public artwork that generates music by visitors exploring the space (in collaboration with Edwin van der Heide). In Lille, France, he built a cluster of cultural buildings (*Maison Folies*) in 2004. He published his monograph with Thames & Hudson, *NOX: Machining Architecture* (2004), and the first fully theoretical account of his work titled *The Architecture of Continuity* with V2_NAI publishers (2008).

Lars Spuybroek has won several prizes and has exhibited all over the world, among them presentations at the Venice Biennale, the Centre Pompidou in Paris, the Victoria & Albert in London and the Guggenheim Bilbao. He taught at many different universities such as Columbia University in New York, the Bartlett in London, ESARQ in Barcelona and from 2001 to 2006 he was Professor of Digital Design Techniques in Kassel, Germany.

Since 2006 he is Professor of Architecture at Georgia Institute of Technology in Atlanta and held the Ventulett Distinguished Chair until 2011. As Ventulett chair he started the Research & Design book series with *The Architecture of Variation* (Thames and Hudson, 2009) and *Textile Tectonics* (NAI Publishers, 2011), publications that combine theoretical with methodological research and design. His latest book titled *The Sympathy of Things: Ruskin and the Ecology of Design* is a theoretical revisiting of the ideas of John Ruskin within the framework of both historical and contemporary thought.

Oliver **Tessmann**

Since 2012 Oliver Tessmann has been assistant professor in the School of Architecture and the Built Environment, KTH, Stockholm. His teaching and research revolves around computational design and digital manufacturing in architecture. He has been a guest professor at Staedelschule Architecture Class (SAC) and worked with the engineering office Bollinger + Grohmann in Frankfurt. In 2008 Oliver Tessmann received a doctoral degree at the University of Kassel. He conducted research in the field of "Collaborative Design Procedures for Architects and Engineers". His architectural work has been published and exhibited in Europe, Asia and the US.

Michael **Weinstock**

Michael Weinstock is an Architect, currently Director of Research and Development, and Director of the Emergent Technologies and Design programme in the Graduate School of the Architectural Association School of Architecture in London. Born in Germany, lived as a child in the Far East and then West Africa, and attended an English public school but ran away to sea at age 17 after reading Conrad. Years at sea in traditional wooden sailing ships, with shipyard and shipbuilding experience. Studied Architecture at the Architectural Association and has taught at the AA School of Architecture since 1989 in a range of positions from workshop tutor, Intermediate and then Diploma Unit Master, Master of Technical Studies and through to Academic Head.

Over the last decade his published work has arisen from research into the dynamics, forms and energy transactions of natural systems, and the application of the mathematics and processes of emergence to cities, to groups of buildings within cities and to individual buildings. Whilst his principal research and teaching has been conducted at the Architectural Association, he has published and lectured widely, and taught seminar courses, studios and workshops on these topics at many other schools of Architecture in Europe and in the united States. He has made a significant contribution to the theoretical discourses of architecture, to the pedagogies of the discipline, and to practice. He has been a leader in bringing awareness and under-standing of natural systems and the historical and current impacts of complexity, climatic and ecological changes on human architectures at all scales, and of the natural and human dynamics that are currently driving changes in all the systems of nature and civilisation.

He is the author of the book, *The Architecture of Emergence: The Evolution of Form in Nature and Civilisation*, Wiley 2010, and has co-edited and conti-buted articles over many years to AD, including 'The Evolutionary Dynamics of Sentience in Cities' 2013, 'The Metabolism of the City: The Mathematics of Networks and Urban Surfaces'. 2011, and 'Metabolism and Morphology' 2008.

Hugh **Whitehead**

Hugh Whitehead graduated from Liverpool University where he wrote a thesis on optimization techniques in architecture. He was a site architect on overseas projects for Shankland Cox before joining YRM where he became an associate. He won awards for animations and his work was featured on television and exhibited at the Royal Academy. In 1998 he was invited to join Foster + Partners to set up the Specialist Modelling Group and in 2001 was a founder of SmartGeometry. Through presentations and publications he has promoted the uptake of new design technologies which have played a part in delivering significant buildings.

Jan **Willmann**

Jan Willmann graduated at Oxford Brookes University with a Master of Architecture with Distinction in the unit of Prof. Andrew Holmes and Prof. David Greene (Archigram). To establish his interest in linking architectural theory with advanced architectural design, he has been research associate at the Chair of Architectural Theory in Innsbruck (Prof. Bart Lootsma) where he received his Ph.D. with Honours. Along with gaining working experience in various architectural practices, he participated in a number of international research and publication projects, approaching the digital age in architec-ture as a composed computational and material score. Jan has lectured and taught at numerous universities and institutions, such as Die Angewandte in Vienna, the Staatliche Akademie der Bildenden Künste in Stuttgart and the University of Pennsylvania (U. Penn). Since 2011, Jan has held a position as a senior assistant at the Professorship for Architecture and Digital Fabrication (Prof. Fabio Gramazio, Prof. Matthias Kohler) at the ETH Zurich.

Andrew J. **Witt**

Andrew Witt is a designer currently based in Los Angeles, California. He is currently Director of Research at Gehry Technologies (GT). He was previously a director at GT's Paris, France office, where he consulted on parametric design, geometric approaches, new technologies, and integrated practice for clients including Gehry Partners, Atelier Jean Nouvel, UN Studio, and Coop Himmelb(l)au. Trained as both an architect and mathematician, Witt has a particular interest in a technically synthetic and logically rigorous approach to form. His work and research have been published in Surface, Space, Linear Algebra and its Applications, and Linear and Multilinear Algebra, and shown at Storefront for Art and Architecture. He has taught courses on digital design at École Speciale d'Architecture and Sci-Arc, and has lectured at MIT, ETH, EPFL, and Angewandte. He received an M.Arch (with distinction, AIA Medal, John Thayer Scholarship) and an M.Des (History and Theory, with distinction) from Harvard GSD.

Robert **Woodbury**

Robert Woodbury is a Professor at Simon Fraser University. He is the Director, Art and Design Practice of the Canadian Graphics, Animation, and New Media Network. His research is in computational design, visual analytics, and human-centered systems for sustainable living. He holds a PhD and MSc from Carnegie Mellon, and a BArch from Carleton. He has over 150 publications, including his book *Elements of Parametric Design*. In 2009 he chaired Team North, a Canadian entry to the 2009 Solar Decathlon. In 2008 he was awarded the Innovative Research Award from the Association for Computer Aided Design in Architecture and the Tee Sasada Award from the Association for Computer-Aided Architectural Design Research in Asia.

PREFACE

The discourse of the digital in design
Theoretical foundations towards a new architecture

There is a specter haunting design culture. Like the development of perspective during the fifteenth century, digital design technology is today imposing a cultural shift of pervasive immanence and ubiquity. The *digital shift* has moved the institutions of design in its various disciplines in the framework of an epochal order of change. This means that for a discipline such as architecture, the professional episteme of which is centuries old, the bases of knowledge, the interdisciplinary relationships, the technological foundations of the design and engineering professions, and the very logic of thinking, doing and making design are shifting.

Although the evolution of these ideas can be periodized within the scientific and technological developments of the information age of the last half-century, it is within the last decade that digital technologies have begun to constitute a powerful ensemble of affordances that are together transforming design. Concomitant with the development of this body of technologies, the digital in architecture has begun to foster a new set of methods that can be most precisely characterized as *the materialization of architecture*. That term defines the return of architecture to its material content as one of the foundations of the design process. Along with the return of architecture to its priorities in making that have come about with the advance of *digital fabrication* technologies, there are emerging new characteristics of form, process and content that might be thought of as *digital architecture*.

The objective of this work is to exemplify the rise of a body of theoretical foundations for the establishment of *a theory of the digital in architecture* and to identify how these theoretical foundations might relate to the issue of whether there are emerging distinctive architectural characteristics that might constitute *a digital architecture*.

The digital in architecture has become a dominant scene of architectural theoretical writings. Navigating the groundswell of theoretical literature of recent decades is a complex undertaking. One direct way of recording the emergence of a theory of the digital in architecture is to historically trace the transformation of architectural institutions. For example within the last decade there have developed new academic and professional institutions such as the *Smartgeometry* conferences and the *Design Modeling* series of conferences in Berlin that have contributed immensely to the elevation of both practice and discourse in the field. Within these and other scientific conference series (CAAD Futures, ECAADE, ACADIA, SIGRADI, etc.) academic research and education have become fomenters of the new digital culture, and leading academics and designers have become major figures in both the theoretical discourse and new practices of digital architecture. The academic and the professional have discovered a new symbiosis as the field and its theory becomes formulated.

The development of the body of theory has been further advanced by the existence of new venues of publication of both professional and theoretical production. Among other sources, the British journal *Architectural Design* (AD), particularly under the editorship of Helen Castle, has been a significant venue for fostering this discourse for the past two decades. The Princeton Architectural Press and the smaller press, Actar of Barcelona have been particularly creative in supporting innovative writing and publication in the field. The Swiss press, Birkhaüser, for example in its early publication of the series of books entitled *The IT Revolution in Architecture*, and our publisher, Taylor & Francis, in the publication of the series of books by Branko Kolarevic and collaborators, have been significant in the past two decades for providing an international forum for this cultural shift.

Our objective has been to establish a conceptual schema – an *episteme* – for the digital shift in the technologically – the *techne* – and methodologically formative period of the past decade. Thus the writings were openly selected from a large variety of sources for their prescience in identifying and defining certain of the important conceptual and theoretical contributions to *a conceptual schema of the materialization of architecture*.

The *new materialization* is becoming a dominant model of architecture's changing orientation to computational processes that support an approach to *material before form* in design. With the new orientation to the design of *digital material* (smart materials, hybrid materials, etc.), tectonic processes of the formation of *material systems* are replacing and amplifying traditional processes of shape generation in architecture. *Integrative dependencies* between structure, material and form are now embedded in the logic of the integration of generative material design and fabrication. Digital design is now emerging as a holistic integrated process from conceptualization to materialization to fabrication.

The advancement of fabrication and robotics technologies is producing a new logic of *material tectonics* in design – a *digital materiality. Informed tectonics* is proposed as a term that describes the informed linkage between form, structure and material within the design production logic of fabrication technologies.

In the past decade the theories and methods of digital design have contributed new meaning to the term tectonics. This new *digital tectonics* is transforming priorities between architectural and structural elements. Digital tectonics denotes the methods for the representation, generation and modulation of tectonic material elements in *digital morphogenesis*. These processes constitute what we have termed digital materiality.

Similar to the evolutionary and adaptive capacity of natural systems, tectonic materialization is a set of digitally linked generative processes from conception to materialization within the logic of fabrication. It is the emergence of this continuous thread of integrated processes including generation, materialization and fabrication that is among the foundations of the new design in architecture.

The art and methods of digitally generated materiality, digital morpho-genesis and fabrication design are the foundations of the new epistemology of the digital in architecture. As an objective of this work we have attempted to define this new epistemology, its new conceptual vocabulary and its theo-retical foundations.

ACKNOWLEDGMENTS

The ambience of celebrating the cultural values of architecture and environmental design characterizes our experience of the Harvard Graduate School of Design. This book was researched and developed during a sabbatical leave from the Technion Israel Institute of Technology that was spent at the at Harvard GSD in Cambridge, MA. We thank the Technion for the opportunity to devote ourselves to research and writing in this unparalleled cultural environment and to the GSD for hosting us for a year and a half of intellectual endeavor. Professor Mohsen Mostafavi, the Dean of the GSD, is a longtime friend from both the GSD and the AA. He has provided insightful leadership to both of these great institutions and we appreciated the opportunities that we had to discuss our work with him during this period. Our host at the GSD was Martin Bechthold, Professor of Architectural Technology, Director of the Design Robotics Group and Co-Director of the GSD's Master of Design Studies Program. He and his group provided many opportunities to question and discuss the emerging influence of digital technologies upon professional practice and education.

Of many colleagues at the GSD who were engaging partners in the discourse of architectural and design theories we would like to particularly thank Professor Antoine Picon for discussions on the emerging role of the digital in practice; his extensive writings on the impact of technology on architecture were important background for this work. Michael Hayes was another important influence and the opportunity to discuss the relationship between theory and design was very meaningful. Among many other colleagues at GSD Professors Picon and Hayes represented the interaction between technology, theory and design practice that was the focus of this book. Preston Scott Cohen was well known to us from the competition for the Tel Aviv museum: we benefitted from insightful conversations with him and from his many lectures.

The Loeb library proved to be a rich resource for research and we are grateful to all of the staff of librarians for their warmth and generosity in letting us share their broad knowledge of this wonderful library and its collections.

Among other friends and colleagues in Cambridge from whom we have benefitted through conversations and lectures, Nader Teherani, architect, educator and theoretician welcomed us to MIT and to his professional office; Larry Sass spoke with us regarding his original work on fabrication at MIT; with Jose Duarte, a former colleague from MIT and now a professor of architecture in Portugal, we maintained correspondence on subjects relevant to the book.

The intellectual family of the international journal *Design Studies* led by Nigel Cross has been a long-term influence on our thought and research. John Gero and Mary Lou Maher are also colleagues and friends of long duration from whom we learned and continue to learn about design theory and research.

Manfred Grohmann of Bollinger + Grohmann, Frankfurt, was one of the first to actually demonstrate to us the impact of digital technologies upon design and collaboration between the architect and engineer. B+G have, as have many leading international structural engineers, transformed both the practice of engineering and the processes of professional collaboration through exploitation of the design affordances of digital systems. It was the emerging technologies and practices of Design Engineering that led to our work with Helen Castle on the book, *The New Structuralism*, that appeared as a special edition of *Architectural Design* on the influence of digital practices on the emergence of "a new tectonics." We are deeply grateful to Helen for the opportunity that she provided us and for how much we learned from her during the process of producing the book. She and the medium of *AD* have long been a force and a milieu for the development of a theoretical discourse on the digital in architecture.

Among other European colleagues and friends with and through whom we have expanded our knowledge and understanding of design and education, Alfred Jacoby, the founder and Director of the Dessau Institute of Architecture has provided us with many challenging meetings in Dessau; our long friendship has also provided introductions to his rich world of colleagues whose conversation and discussion has been important for our own development: among many others, Lars Lerup, Neil Leach and Arie Graafland have provided outstanding experiences in their lectures and conversations.

Yehuda Kalay, the Dean of the Faculty of Architecture and Town Planning of the Technion, has provided constant support for this research and writing. His own work has long been a model for design research, architectural education and the study of the meaning, the implications, and the intellectual content that is evolving through "architecture's new media." The undergraduate and graduate students at the Technion who participated in our seminars on the conceptual and taxonomic content of the digital in design and on the revolution of design thinking and design practices deserve credit for their many contributions to the advancement of our own thinking about the subject of the digital in architecture.

In the interdisciplinary environment of the great technological university that is the Technion, we have many colleagues from whom we have learned and expanded our knowledge of design and design education, and regarding the role of design as an interdisciplinary core of engineering. Among those who have contributed through conversations and discussions are Moshe Spitalni of the Faculty of Mechanical Engineering and Yerach Doytscher of the Faculty of Civil Engineering. We would also like to express our gratitude to Dr. Ayal Nir and to Dr. Yasha Grobman, who are among younger colleagues at the Technion who have a direct interest and rich background in digital design and research in digital systems. Limor Goldhaber is a recent graduate student at the Technion who particularly contributed to our understanding of the potential and complexities of building architectural parametric systems for design. We are continuing research with Limor and anticipate a brilliant future for her.

At Tel Aviv University we have benefitted from discussions with and lectures of Hanna Naveh, the Dean of the Faculty of Arts and Dr. Eran Neumann, the head of the Azrieli School of Architecture.

Dr. Ning Gu is a colleague from Australia with whom Rivka Oxman has begun to explore the frontiers of design thinking of the digital in architecture. This experience of distributed research collaboration through the Internet has been wonderfully successful due to Ning's intellectual approach to design and the theoretical issues of the digital.

The twenty-five individual and group contributors to this book are the stars of this intellectual endeavor. We are grateful for their interest and collaboration in helping us to define the new conditions of the profession of architecture and of its knowledge and emerging practices.

To Francesca Ford, the Commissioning Editor of Taylor & Francis and to Laura Williamson, our architectural editor, we would like to express our deep gratitude for their devotion to this project and for their perseverance in the production of this book; we wish also to express our deep gratitude to our production editor, Kyle Duggan for his commitment, knowledge and expertise in guiding us in moving the manuscript to reality. We believe that the subject of this book, the emerging role of the digital in architecture, is changing the nature of both architectural practice and design thinking. We are proud that Taylor & Francis/Routledge has committed to the promotion of these ideas in this volume which now joins their distinguished catalogue of recent works on the subject.

INTRO-DUC-TION

Rivka Oxman and Robert Oxman

Within the last decade the appearance and evolution of the digital in architecture in integration with new digital technologies have begun to produce what might be termed a *Vitruvian effect*. In synthesizing material culture and technologies within the expanding relationship between the computer and architecture, this phenomenon defines a digital continuum from design to production, from form generation to fabrication design. This new continuity transcends the merely instrumental contributions of the man–machine relationship to praxis and has begun to evolve as a *medium that supports a continuous logic of design thinking and making*. As such, the digital in architecture has begun to enable a set of symbiotic relationships *between the formulation of design processes and developing technologies*. In order to accommodate these developments, a new and comprehensive domain of architectural theories is beginning to emerge in the intersection between science, technology, design and architectural culture.

> Theory: Beyond Representation

The prehistory of a comprehensive architectural theory of the digital in architecture resides in the roots of architectural culture's attempt to divest itself of the *representational* as the dominant logical and operative mode of formal generation in design. This fundamental revision, influenced by the disciplinary interest in the relevance of Deleuzeian concepts for architectural theory during the 1990s, was encapsulated in the theoretical presence and the pioneering conceptual territorialization of Lynn's *Folding in Architecture* (1993). Although Lynn's essays (collected in Lynn, 1998) had previously critiqued the *linguistic analogy* as a formal theory of design, several of the articles in *Folding* including Lynn's and Kipnis' went beyond this to present *Folding* as a shift of both theory and practice.

The decade following *Folding* is presented in Lynn (2004) as a period of discursive shift. As with any situation of cultural transformation, the age of the emergence of the digital as encompassing both architectural *and* design phenomena was complex and non-monotonic. However, it was an age of epochal threshold events. Gehry's Guggenheim in Bilbao was the dominant iconic architectural design of the end of the century transformation of the modernist ethos. The building was analog in design and digital in production; decontructionist in mood, but managing also to urbanistically satisfy certain of the conditions of *Folding* as "a more fluid logic of connectivity" (Lynn, 1993, p. 26), a contextual inte-gration that distinguished *Folding* for Lynn as an antithesis to Deconstruction in architecture. The Guggenheim shared, at least in detail of the surfaces, a preference for curvilinear surface and volume that was becoming the charac-teristic determinant of much experimental architecture of the period.

Lynn, in his revisiting of *Folding* in 2004, showed some ambivalence about abandoning formal indicators of digital practice even while criticizing his formalist predecessors. Despite the fact that he was now beyond the mathematics of the curvilinear, the new post-*Folding* recognition of *intricacy* as a morphological state of the digital in design is still essentially formal. While referring to *intricate compositions* as organic, he describes one aspect of post-*Folding* as the "drift from monolithic objects to infinitesimally scaled components." (Lynn, 2004, p. 11)

The theoretical foundations of a digital architecture appear in a rich flowering of exhibitions and publications at the beginning of the new millen-nium. By this time writings of the digital in architecture had become the *de facto* locus of architectural theoretical discourse. Among representative publications are Schmal and Flagge (2001); Migayrou (2003); Hadid and Schumacher (2003); Kolarevic (2003); Rosa (2003); and Leach, Turnbull and Williams (2004).

> Form Generation: Towards Topologic Material Practice

The introductory article by Migayrou for the *Non-Standard Architecture* exhibition of 2003–2004 foregrounded certain important concepts in the development of a theory of the digital in architecture. Migayrou shifted the emphasis of a digital architecture distinguished by complex, non-Euclidean geometry to a new set of conceptual points more Deleuzean in origin. Referring to the mathematics of non-standard analysis of Abraham Robinson and the topological theories of René Thom, Migayrou formulated a theory of architectural design as the inherent mutations of matter in which geometry and production are in an integrated process of variable actualization. Morphogenetic processes provide conditions of "multiple singularities" in a "continuum in perpetual evolution."

Referring to the new digital continuity of morphogenetic conception, generation and material production as a *digital chain*, the idea of the non-standard is less a reference to "mass customization" than it is a predictive vision of the theoretical fit between developmental biology, topology, parametric design and the coming of age of new fabrication media and technologies of production. This again suggests a Vitruvian interpretation of architectural theory as a continuum of design to production, an integrated set of natural principles, as a characteristic condition of the digital in the new architecture. Here, at last, and by definition, complex "free-form" geometry is de-emphasized as a theo-retical precondition, and viewed as one possible formal result.

In effect, *formation precedes form*, and design becomes the thinking of architectural generation through the logic of the algorithm. This is truly the shift towards a topological logic independent from formal and linguistic models of form representation. Coming one digital generation after *Folding, Non-Standard* presented a position that more easily accommodated the recognition of computational processes and emerging technologies of materialization. This can now occur in a continuous logic of morphogenesis and materiality in generative processes.

> Parametric Design

Late in this post-*Folding* period, parametric design began to emerge as a seminal medium of digital design. Beyond being merely a design technology, parametric design is a new form of the logic of *digital design thinking*. Parametric design thinking focuses upon a logic of associative and dependency relationships between objects and their parts-and-whole relationships. By changing the values of parameters within a schema of relationships (a *parametric schema*) such as geometric relationships, a multiplicity of variable instances can be created. Parametric systems enable the writing of rules, or algorithmic procedures, for the creation of variations. Thus parametric design in architecture develops as a new form of design logic (see Reas, McWilliams, and LUST, 2010, and Burry, 2011, both in this volume).

Parametric design as a facility for the control of topological relationships enables the *creation and modulation of the differentiation of the elements of a design*. The capability to create and modulate differentiation in various scales such as the gradation of elements in building façades or in urban schemes has begun to be exploited as a characteristic enabling facility of parametric design. Patrik Schumacher has defined this capability as a distinguishing characteristic of contemporary digital architectural form that he designates by the term, *parametricism* (see Schumacher, 2009, this volume).

> Parametric and Performative

During the last decade, innovative technologies have become a driving force in the formulation of theories as well as producing a new wave of tectonic and material creativity. By the early years of the new millennium parametric design, supported by the appearance of new and popularly available software, began to become the preferred design environment for a new generation of scripting-enabled design thinkers and researchers. The personalized set of media skills of this generation revolves about the form-generation capabilities of modelers based on Non-Uniform Rational B-Splines (NURBS) such as *Rhino* and the later appearance of integrated parametric modelers such as *Grasshopper*.

In conjunction with the growing sophistication of a truly *mediated architectural design* capable of a high level of *generative variability*, there is simultaneously emerging a generation of integrated simulation software for energy and structural calculations. The growing capability for scripting the algorithms of a mediated variability that can be selectively studied for performative behaviors such as energy and structural performance provided a new creative professional profile. This produced an emerging generation of *digerati* in the cutting-edge architectural schools. Their computational design skills were to be later honed in the atmosphere of digital experimentation that characterized many leading professional practices and structural engineering offices whose practices had become digital and experimental (Oxman and Oxman, 2010).

Swiss Re and The London City Hall, both by Foster Associates and both completed in 2003, are examples of the power of the linkage between parametric modelers and their scriptable mediated variability and performance simulation software (see Whitehead, 2003, this volume). The digital linkage also established an advanced environment for interactive digital generation and performance simulation as a paradigm of collaborative design between the architect and the engineer (for example, see Sasaki, 2007).

> Scripting: Disciplinary Knowledge and Research by Design

By 2004, emerging digital technologies were supporting the formation of new theory, and "the critical discourse was on procedural design and scripting and away from compositional and representational theorizing" (Carpo, 2004). This tendency for a younger generation of architects to rely upon the scripting of algorithms as a medium for research-based experimental design, was also encouraged by the experimental parametric design of designated research units within professional practices such as the AGU (Advanced Geometries Unit) of Arup under the leadership of Cecil Balmond. Among the iconic designs of the period was the 2002 Serpentine Pavilion by Toyo Ito and Balmond, a design that eloquently demonstrated the aesthetic and tectonic possibilities of the algorithmic (Sakamoto and Ferré, 2008, pp. 36–43.

This is the age of the emergence of *research by design*. It is the period during which many of the leading architectural and structural engineering practices, particularly in the UK, Germany and Japan, began to form their own internal multidisciplinary research units that developed expertise in exploiting computational geometry in the mediated generation and analysis of digital designs. Noted among such research units were Arup's AGU and Foster's Specialist Modelling Group. Many iconic architectural designs were produced from 2003 onward employing these powerful digitally integrated performative design environments in which form is driven by performance.

> Tectonics of Material Systems

The ability to *model the structures of material systems as tectonic systems* (Oxman and Oxman, 2010) has enabled the mediated manipulation of material systems as a significant contribution to contemporary research-based design in architecture. This shift to material design as a significant part of the architectural design process has redefined architecture as a material practice and provided the media to modulate *digital materiality* in design (Willmann, Gramazio and Kohler, this volume).

The *modeling of material as a tectonic system* has provided a powerful paradigm for material design in architecture as well as for the performative design of material systems. This process has promoted and enabled *material design* to become an integral part of the digital architectural design process continuum. It has renewed the architect's traditional role as the master builder empowered with the understanding and ability to digitally create in the material realm. Material is again in the purview, knowledge sphere and institutional control of the architect. This cultural technological shift has also renewed a strengthened creative collaborative design relationship between the architect and the structural engineer as united in the practice of research by design.

This has interesting theoretical sources within the modernist discourse on transparency. It characterizes the transition to an architecture of a *new transparency and materiality*, and *surfaces of complex material systems*. The phenomena were among those first identified by Terrence Riley in the exhibition *Light Construction* of 1995. Subsequently the design of material systems through experimentation with the modeling of the tectonic potential of new materials including *hybrid materials, smart materials, extreme textiles* and others has became a design research problem during the last decade. The modeling of *textile tectonics* including studies of weaving, knitting, braiding and knotting, with *craft phenomena projected as material technologies*, were among the research fields that emerged at the intersection of parametric design and material systems.

> Digital Materiality and Material Fabrication

As part of this emerging of a *digital materiality* in design there have developed new linkages between conception and production through "file to factory" and CNC (computer numerically controlled) fabrication. Digital design information can be used in fabrication driving rapid prototyping and CNC machinery. *Fabrication design* has now emerged as a leading technological and design issue of digital research and design.

Within this renewed interest in materialization and fabrication, the concept of digital materiality has given new meaning to the contemporary definition and discourse on the role of a *digital tectonics* in design. On the one hand the discourse is characterized by Frampton's concern that contemporary design culture is losing its capacity to accommodate tectonic expression as a "poetics of construction"; and assuming that this implies the ability to develop form on the basis of a relationship between structural forces and formal expression. The integration of digital materiality and performative analysis now theoretically enables such a potential for a contemporary tectonic expression to be derived from the technologies of material design and fabrication. Thus a new technology of digital materiality may resolve the conflicts that Frampton originally identified in his critique of the *virtual materiality* of digital design.

> The Digital Continuum: Form Generation, Performance, Morphogenesis, Tectonics, Materialization, Fabrication

Form generation informed by *performative design, tectonic models* and *digital materiality* are emerging as *integrated processes* in digital design. In seeking to investigate and to develop systems in which there is an integral relationship between these models and concepts, a great source of knowledge exists in the design principles of nature. Researchers and pioneers of design modeled on nature such as d'Arcy Thompson, Gaudí and Frei Otto have become the models for a new generation of theoreticians and designers (see Weinstock, 2010, and Menges, 2010, this volume).

The definition and formalization of biomimetic principles of design is potentially a significant contribution to design knowledge. *Digital morphogenesis* can combine the tectonics of digital material and performative simulation to create naturally ecologic systems. It is in the computational modeling of natural principles of performative design of material systems that we can potentially create a *second nature*, or a sounder architecture with respect to *material ecology* (Oxman, 2012).

> Theories, Concepts and Models of Digital Design in Architecture

The emerging structure of a new ontology of digital design in architecture has evolved in the last decade and continues to develop. The following represent elements and relationships of a linked schema of theories, concepts and models of the digital in architecture.

Ontology
Theory

Computational Processes
Form and Generation
Performative Design
Parametrics

Concepts and Models
Morphogenesis
Tectonics

Technologies
Materialization
Fabrication
Responsive Technology

Epistemology
Disciplinary Knowledge

> The Digital in Architecture

There is an important distinction that must be drawn between *digital design* and *digital architecture* (Oxman, 2006). While the digital in architecture does support the emergence of certain distinctive geometric preferences and aesthetic effects it cannot be said to be deterministic with respect to architectural form. Beyond blobs (binary large objects) and the commitment to the curvilinear as a sign of the avant-garde, and the preference for non-orthogonal geometries that characterized the experimentalism of the former decade, the formal tendencies of a new architecture have become much more subtly attuned to the differentiating potential of topological and parametric algorithmic thinking and the tectonic creativity innovation of digital materiality.

It is the coincidence of scripting as a new paradigm of design thinking in a view of "scripting as a driving force for 21st century architectural thinking" (Burry, 2011, p. 17) and its interaction with the design potential of material fabrication technologies that are creating the characteristic stylistic preferences and expression that we are beginning to recognize as *digital architecture*. Schumacher, among others, has come to identify the *potential for differentiation* as a major attribute of parametric algorithmic design (Schumacher, 2009, p. 431). Material experimentation and innovation in such differentiated fields includes the ability to modulate conditions of the porosity of material surfaces, the potential control of light penetration and so on. These concepts are the basis for ecological design in response to environmental conditions.

Working within the variability of parametric algorithmic design and the tectonic richness of the material shift of the last decade, the integration with performance analysis software is seminal. This is producing the *digital linkage of form generation and performative form finding* that is the significance of digital design informed by performance. As this digital linkage becomes better developed and supported by digital systems (see for example, Sasaki, 2007; Oxman and Oxman, 2010; Whitehead, 2003, this volume), we can expect that *digital morphogenesis* will emerge as a prominent model of *informed performative design* in architecture.

Digital morphogenesis is the edge of theory in relationship to emerging digital design and technology. As informed performative design evolves to include *generative architectural schema* within parametric algorithmic design *then design thinking will actually produce digital architectural form in response to environmental context*. We can already see this beginning to occur in new examples of *fabrication design* (N. Oxman, 2010, this volume) in which contextual forces and material attributes combine to *generate form*.

The *material shift* and *fabrication design* were among the dominant contributions of the evolution of digital architecture in the first decade of the new millennium; biological influence may be the great inventive scientific moment of the second decade. *Natural design* is more than imitating the appearance of the organic. It is learning from natural principles of design how to produce form in response to the conditions of the environmental context. This is an age in which digitally informed design can actually produce a *second nature*.

Burry, Mark (2011), *Scripting Cultures: Architectural Design and Programming*, AD Primer, John Wiley and Sons, West Sussex, UK

Carpo, Mario (2004), "Ten Years of Folding," in Lynn, Greg, ed., *Folding in Architecture*, Revised Edition (original 1993), AD (*Architectural Design*), Wiley-Academy, 2004, West Sussex, UK, pp. 14–19

Hadid, Zaha and Schumacher, Patrik (2003), *Latent Utopias: Experiments within Contemporary Architecture*, Princeton Architectural Press, New York

Kolarevic, Branko (2003), "Digital Morphogenesis," in Kolarevic, Branko, ed., *Architecture in the Digital Age: Design and Manufacturing*, Spon Press, New York and London, pp. 11–28

Leach, Neil (2004), "Swarm Tectonics," in Leach, Neil, Turnbull, David and Williams, Chris, eds., *Digital Tectonics*, Wiley-Academy, West Sussex, UK, pp. 70–77

Lynn, Greg, ed. (1993), *Folding in Architecture*, AD (*Architectural Design*), Wiley-Academy, West Sussex, UK

Lynn, Greg (1998), *Folds, Bodies and Blobs, Collected Essays*, La Lettre Volée, Brussels

Lynn, Greg (2004), "Introduction" to Lynn, Greg, ed., *Folding in Architecture*, Revised Edition (original 1993), AD (*Architectural Design*), Wiley-Academy, West Sussex, UK

Menges, Achim (2010), "Material Systems, Computational Morphogenesis and Performative Capacity," in Hensel, Michael, Menges, Achim and Weinstock, Michael, *Emergent Technologies and Design: Towards a Biological Paradigm for Architecture*, Routledge, Oxford, pp. 44–61

Migayrou, Frédéric (2003), "The Orders of the Non-Standard," in *Architectures Non Standard,* Centre Pompidou, Paris, pp. 26–33. Revised with new introduction, 2012

Oxman, Neri (2010), "Structuring Materiality: Design Fabrication of Heterogeneous Materials," in Oxman, Rivka and Oxman, Robert, eds., *The New Structuralism: Design, Engineering and Architectural Technologies*, AD (*Architectural Design*), July/August, 2010, pp. 78–85

Oxman, Neri (2012), "Programming Matter," in Menges, Achim, ed., *Architectural Design, Material Computation: Higher Integration in Mophogenetic Design*, Vol. 82, Issue 2, March/April, pp. 8–95

Oxman, Rivka (2006), "Theory and Design in the First Digital Age," *The International Journal of Design Studies*, Vol. 27, No. 3, pp. 229–265

Oxman, Rivka and Oxman, Robert, eds. (2010), "The New Structuralism: Design, Engineering and Architectural Technologies," AD (*Architectural Design*), Profile No. 206, Vol. 80, No. 4, July/August

Reas, Casey, McWilliams, Chandler and LUST (2010), *Form and Code in Design, Art and Architecture*, Princeton Architectural Press, New York

Riley, Terrence (1995), *Light Construction*, Museum of Modern Art, New York

Rosa, Joseph (2003), *Next Generation Architectures: Folds, Blobs and Boxes*, Rizzoli, New York

Sakamoto, Tomoko and Ferré, Albert (2008), *From Control to Design: Parametric Algorithmic Architecture*, Actar, Barcelona

Sasaki, Mutsuro (2007), *The Morphogenesis of Flux Structures*, AA Publications, London

Schmal, Peter C. and Flagge, Ingeborg (2001), *Digital Real-Blobmeister: First Built Projects*, Birkhäuser, Basel

Schumacher, Patrik (2009), "Parametric Patterns," in Garcia, Mark, ed. *Patterns of Architecture*, AD (*Architectural Design*), Vol. 79, No. 6, November/December, pp. 28–41

Weinstock, Michael (2006), "Self-Organization and Material Constructions," in Hensel, Michael, Menges, Achim and Weinstock, Michael, eds., *Techniques and Technologies in Morphogenetic Design*, AD (*Architectural Design*), Profile No. 180, Vol. 76, No. 2, March/April, pp. 26–33

Weinstock, Michael (2010), "Evolution and Computation," in Hensel, Michael, Menges, Achim and Weinstock, Michael, *Emergent Technologies and Design: Towards a Biological Paradigm for Architecture*, Routledge, Oxford, pp. 26–41

Whitehead, Hugh (2003), "Laws of Form," in Kolarevic, Brank, ed., *Architecture in the Digital Age: Design and Manufacturing*, Spon Press, New York and London, pp. 81–100

Willmann, Jan, Gramazio, Fabio and Kohler, Matthias (2012), "Towards an Extended Performative Materiality – Interactive Complexity and the Control of Space"

THEORY

A Universe of Discourse

Rivka Oxman and Robert Oxman

Since the early integration of computation and design in the 1960s, the evolution of theories has proceeded through a period of revolutionary technological and cultural transformation. The theoretical position of this book is that since the early years of the new millennium, theories of the digital in architecture are again undergoing transformative change.

If theories of the digital in architecture are in a process of contemporary evolution, they are also in a process of constant renegotiation of their discursive *interrelationships*. Architectural computing is continuously looking outward to relate to traditional and new inter-disciplinarities in order to formulate the nature of the digital discipline and its epistemology. The measure of these cultural intellectual practices as well as the way in which we formulate them experimentally is the substance of theoretical production. In doing so we postulate the new set of concepts and conceptual structures that define and explain emerging models and methods of design.

These interlacing processes of architectural theoretical discourse are one of the foundations of experimentalism, and they are today producing a new periodization of theories of the digital in architecture. We consider the first years of the millennium as a period of significant theoretical consolidation after *Folding in Architecture* (Lynn, 1993, 2004) with a flow of theoretical writings during the late twentieth and early twenty-first centuries. This period has been rich in theoretical writings defining the coming of a new architecture. This theoretical foundation has also contributed in the past decade to a period of expansion in both theory and practice that has been strongly influenced by emerging technologies. This is an age of the technological inspiration of new theories of architectural praxis. It is the age of natural computation, the coming of age of material computing, the flowering of fabrication and the coming period of bio-inspired design. It is a transformative period of architecture as regenerated by new technologies and new procedures of digital design (Reas, McWilliams and LUST, 2010).

As Carpo (2004) has argued, Lynn's *Folding in Architecture* of 1993 occupied a pivotal position as a watershed of theoretical production. On the one hand *Folding* attempted to provide both a theoretical and operative alternative to one of the then dominant bodies of theory in practice, *Deconstruction*, particularly as formulated by Johnson and Wigley in the

Deconstructivist Architecture exhibition and catalogue of MoMA in 1988. *Folding* attempted to function as an antithesis to *Deconstructivism*. On the other hand, *Folding* also attempted to formulate a theory of the digital in design as a prominent locus of architectural design theory.

This process of *centering* the digital in theoretical discourse occurred in stages. During the first stage, occupying approximately the first decade after *Folding*, there emerged a body of theoretical writings that attempted to explicate theories of digital practice in architecture up to the early years of the new millennium. This period is strongly characterized by discursive interrelationships with philosophy and mathematics, and the attempt to characterize *the new architecture* that was being produced. The intersection of theory and practice was significantly oriented to the formal and geometric nature of a developing set of phenomena that might be termed digital architecture.

This discourse produced a particular florescence of publication including Lynn (1999) and peaking in approximately 2003–2004. For example, see Leach (2002), Migayrou (2003); Hadid and Schumacher (2003); Kolarevic (2003); Rosa (2003), and Leach, Turnbull and Williams (2004). That is, the first period after *Folding* attempted to characterize the digital in architecture as producing *a new architecture*, the characteristics and the formal attributes of which were unique and capable of classification and explanation.

Following this post-*Folding* period of theorizing, the last decade has been characterized by the attempt to theorize a new body of concepts related to emerging *technological possibilities* in the field of the digital in architecture and their influence upon *design processes*, as opposed to formal characteristics. These are producing a unique body of theory related to the digital in architecture. The architectural and design influence of *parametric design, fabrication, digital material*, and *digital processes of ecological* and *biomimetic* design are among these theoretical developments. It is the explication of this second generation of digital theories, of the emergence of a body of theories of *the digital in architecture* as a *set of integrated digital processes* that is the subject of this book.

We can look more closely at how certain of these conceptual arguments unfolded. Lynn originally proposed that *Folding* as a theory of architectural design provided a paradigmatic alternative to prior theories such as Deconstructivism and other formal linguistic models that were, in design, based upon the manipulation of formal representations. As such the digital logic and processes that constituted the design phenomena of *Folding* in architecture were *anti-representational*. The new objective was to define "compositional complexity" beyond "collage aesthetics" (Lynn, 2004). In addition to stochastic and emergent processes, complexity can also be defined mainly by "*intricacy*" or "*intricate assemblages*" derived from non-linear mathematical models of complexity. Lynn's definition of intricacy includes the complex assemblage of elements in continuous wholes produced either by stochastic computational procedures or computational procedures of continuous structures such as weaving and folding. This new reliance upon *digital generative procedures* were still at this point devoted to the description and characterization of form generation as opposed to theorizing the differences between *linguistic* and *procedural design* as differing *paradigmatic models* of design.

In his retrospective analysis of *Folding* in 2004, Carpo recognizes the significance of digital technologies for the development of architectural theories. The topological variability of digital formulations, the potential for morphing forms and dynamic continuities in time was the prime motivation of the conceptual structure of the fold in design. How then to develop theory beyond the fold? The shift of dominant theory after the theoretical consolidations of 2003–2004, moves in the direction of a more scientific, computational and technological discourse. There is an attempt to move beyond the primarily formal and form generative nature of the discourse regarding "continuities" (of the fold) versus "fracture" (of Deconstructivism) in order to begin to accommodate the growing digital and technological empowerment of the period. These include *parametric design*, new concepts of *digital tectonics* with potential for *ecological and sustainability, CNC technologies, robotics, material design* and others. Folding as a metaphor for continuous and multiplicitous generation became replaced by digital subdomain theories. These were theories of *procedural processes, integrated information, performative design, new technologies of materialization and fabrication*, and *attempts to formulate computational models of natural design*.

Speaks (1995) in his introduction to Cache (1995) brings forward arguments regarding the Deleuzian *Fold* that define the important Deleuzian distinction between the "realization of the possible" and the "actualization of the virtual." These (the possible versus the virtual) present two kinds of multiplicity. In the first, *realization*, as in typological design, there is generation on the basis of givens. While in the actualization of the virtual, generation does not operate by resemblance and representation as in typology, but produces true creation through *differentiation*. These are among the conceptual distinctions that in post-*Folding* produce an emphasis upon theories that emerge from new methods and design procedures of practice. These are also, in turn, strongly the products of *emerging digital technologies*.

Non-Standard Architectures (2003) is the different theoretical path of Frédéric Migayrou along many of these same philosophical and scientific routes that produces new concepts. It also perhaps produces the predisposition to scientific theories of complexity theory that has become so formative for today's theories of digital design. The concern for dealing with "mutations of matter" in which geometry and production begin to occur simultaneously is part of Migayrou's contribution to the post-*Folding* discourse towards new projective practices of parametric digital design. The openness towards mathematical models, the nature of *singularities* achieved through *differentiation processes*, the complexities of natural morphogenesis, these are all part of a conceptual *denoument* of *Non-Standard Architectures* that break a path to the new projective experimentation of the current and future generations. In the 4th International Deleuze Studies Conference in Copenhagen in 2011, Migayrou states that, "the architectonic takes place in the extreme tension between the algebraic and the organic." This suggests the emergence today of a new operative digital architectonic that encompasses the complexity of *natural design* and is part of the new theoretical agenda of current architectural discourse.

Picon (2004, 2010) has identified various root questions of the post-*Folding* theorization of architecture. Among these is the attempt to define the distinctions of digital representation. Is digital representation a new class of design that distances us from the conventions of the traditional definition of practice and of the traditional bodies of knowledge? Or should we view this symbiosis as a "new pairing" of man and machine? Within this search for the new problematic of the digital in architecture, Picon (2004, pp. 117–18) centers the theoretical discussion on tectonics (Has a gap developed between digital representation and traditional tectonics?) and upon materiality: is there a loss or weakening of architecture's traditional relationship between tectonics and material? Are there, in fact, new classes of representational elaboration that are now emerging in the relationship between design and the digital?

Emerging theories are attempting to answer such questions about the ways in which the traditional content and processes of the discipline are now changing as a result of the impact of the digital in architecture. Among current theories (for example, Picon, 2010; Burry, 2011; Schumacher, 2011), there is emerging a new schema of concepts and issues that are building towards a comprehensive theory. We have postulated such a schema, or mapping, of emerging theories of the digital in architecture. These elaborate an ongoing shift in the theory and practice of architecture.

Allen, Stan (1997), "From Object to Field," in Davidson, Peter and Bates, Donald L., eds., *Architecture After Geometry*, AD (*Architectural Design*), Profile No. 127, Vol. 67, No. 5/6, pp. 24–31

van Berkel, Ben and Bos, Caroline (1999), "Techniques: Network Spin; Diagrams," in Braham, William W. and Hale, Jonathan A., eds., *Rethinking Technology: A Reader in Architectural Theory*, Routledge, New York, pp. 384–387

Cache, Bernard (Speaks, Michael, ed.) (1995), *Earth Moves: the Furnishing of Territories*, MIT Press, Cambridge MA

Carpo, Mario (2004), "Ten Years of Folding," in Lynn, Greg, ed., *Folding in Architecture*, Revised Edition (original 1993), AD (*Architectural Design*), Wiley-Academy, West Sussex, UK, pp. 14–19

DeLanda, Manuel (2004), "Material Complexity", in Leach, Neil, Turnbull, David and Williams, Chris, eds., *Digital Tectonics*, Wiley-Academy, London, pp. 14–21

Eisenman, Peter (1999), "Visions Unfolding: Architecture in the Age of Electronic Media," in Galofaro, Luca, *Digital Eisenman: An Office of the Electronic Era*, Birkhäuser, Basel, pp. 84–89. Original publication *Domus*, No. 734, 1992

Hadid, Zaha and Schumacher, Patrik (2003), *Latent Utopias*, Princeton Architectural Press, New York

Kalay, Yehuda E. (2004), *Architecture's New Media: Principles, Theories and Methods of Computer-Aided Design*, MIT Press, Cambridge, MA

Kubo, Michael and Salazar, Jaime (2004), "A Brief History of the Information Age," in Ferré, Albert, Kubo, Michael, Prat, Ramon, Sakamoto, Tomoko, Salazar, Jaime and Tetas, Anna, eds., *Verb Matters*, Actar, Barcelona, pp. 2–19

Leach, Neil, ed. (2002), *Designing for a Digital World*, Wiley-Academy, London

Leach, Neil, Turnbull, David and Williams, Chris, eds. (2004), *Digital Tectonics*, Wiley-Academy, London

Lenoir, Timothy and Alt, Casey (2003), "Flow, Process, Fold," in Picon, Antoine and Ponte, Allesandra, *Architecture and the Sciences: Exchanging Metaphors*, Princeton Architectural Press, New York, pp. 314–353

Lynn, Greg (2004), "Introduction" to Lynn, Greg, ed., *Folding in Architecture*, Revised Edition (original 1993), AD (*Architectural Design*), Wiley-Academy, West Sussex, UK

Mertins, Detlef (2004), "Bioconstructivisms," in Spuybroek, Lars, *Nox: Machining Architecture*, Thames and Hudson, New York, pp. 360–369

Migayrou, Frédéric (2003), "The Orders of the Non-Standard," in *Architectures Non Standard*, Centre Pompidou, Paris, pp. 26–33. Revised with new introduction, 2012

Migayrou, Frédéric (2011), "Non-Standard Architecture: Between Mathesis and Immanence," Fourth International Deleuze Studies Conference, Copenhagen Business School, Copenhagen, Denmark. Available online: https://conference.cbs.dk/index.php.deleuze/conf/paper/view/1337

Oxman, Rivka (2006), "Theory and Design in the first Digital Age," *The International Journal of Design Studies*, Elsevier, Vol. 27, No. 3, pp. 229–265

Picon, Antoine (2004), "Architecture and the Virtual: Towards a New Materiality," in Reeser, Amanda and Schafer, Ashley, eds., *New Technologies/New Architectures*, Praxis 6, pp. 114–121

Picon, Antoine (2010), "The Seduction of Innovative Geometries," in Picon, Antoine, *Digital Culture in Architecture*, Birkhäuser, Basel, 2010, pp. 60–72

Schumacher, Patrik (2011), "From Space to Field," in *The Autopoesis of Architectures: A New Framework for Architecture*, John Wiley and Sons, West Sussex, UK, pp. 421–433

Speaks, Michael (1995), "Folding Toward a New Architecture," in Cache, Bernard (Speaks, Michael, ed.) (1995), *Earth Moves: the Furnishing of Territories*, MIT Press, Cambridge, MA, pp. xii–xviii

Tierney, Therese (2007), "Biological Networks: On Neurons, Cellular Automata, and Relational Architectures," in Burke, Anthony and Tierney, Therese, eds., *Network Strategies: New Strategies in Architecture and Design*, Princeton Architectural Press, New York, pp. 78–99

Wigley, Mark (2007), "The Architectural Brain," in Burke, Anthony and Tierney, Therese, eds., *Network Strategies: New Strategies in Architecture and Design*, Princeton Architectural Press, New York, pp. 30–53

> List of Key Concepts

anti-representational
biomimetic design
differentiation
digital architecture
digital design
digital material
digital representation

digital tectonics
ecological design
emerging technologies
epistemology of digital design
fabrication design
Folding
formal representation

integrated design procedures   ontology of digital design
inter-disciplinarities   parametric systems
intricacy   periodization of theories
linguistic models   post-*Folding*
material design   procedural models
multiplicity   singularity
natural design   theoretical centering

Behind the title "Non Standard Architecture", the exhibition in 2003 recovered different goals, trying to change the critical dialogue with a traditional understanding of rationalism, rationalisation, technicism, engineering, and to find a most accurate apprehension of the mutation of the processes of conception and production of architecture imposed by the new homogeneity of the computation tools from "file to factory" on the other side. The generalisation of new software opened a generative domain, an algorithmic culture opened to the potentialities of complex morphogenesis and complex geometries. The first level of interpretation came from the field of American neo-structuralism still influenced by the Italian scene of the seventies, which turned to a unilateral linguistic transcription of architecture in terms of typologies and morphologies. The logicisation of the space defined by this neo-rationalism confronted a spatial hermeneutic where the algorithmic and the variate were assimilated as an ultimate state of ontological difference. The dynamic field of morphogenesis was formalised through computation as an homogeneous geometric domain, mathematically encoded. The quest of an ontological anchorage defined by ultimate spatial metaphors (spacement, difference, chora, deterritorialization, folds, diagrams . . .) preserved the idealistic notion of a genetic of forms. The Husserlian reduction was reified in a translation of the variations in a suspended system of notations. NSA tried to redefine the source of the morphogenesis and to refuse the logic of deconstruction muted in a generic economy of sequenciation. Through an emergence approach, the singularities were defined by their pure capacity of integration under a continuum (topologic) which opened a new economy of the manifold. In this way the multiplicities have a capacity of mutation where a contraction, a part, an element, supposed a complete mutation of the entire structure, including the geometry.

Edmund Husserl tried to define those "vague morphological entities" and the conditions of a singularisation (a thing, a form, an object . . .) apart from all the onto-theological interpretations as a dynamic of relations where the structure was not reduced to the system. This dynamic understanding of morphogenesis imposed a naturalist genealogy of structuralism where a radical materialism is related to an absolute discretisation. The Husserlian distinction between formal and material, between a formal ontology working on the ultimate structures organising the reality and the division in sectors of different material ontologies (physics, biology . . .) opened the way to a radical logicisation of ontology. This transfiguration of formal ontology as an algebra, this radical shift between physicalism and phenomenology, between the emergence of singularities and their mathematisation displaced

1

The Orders of the Non-standard

Towards a critical structuralism

Frédéric Migayrou

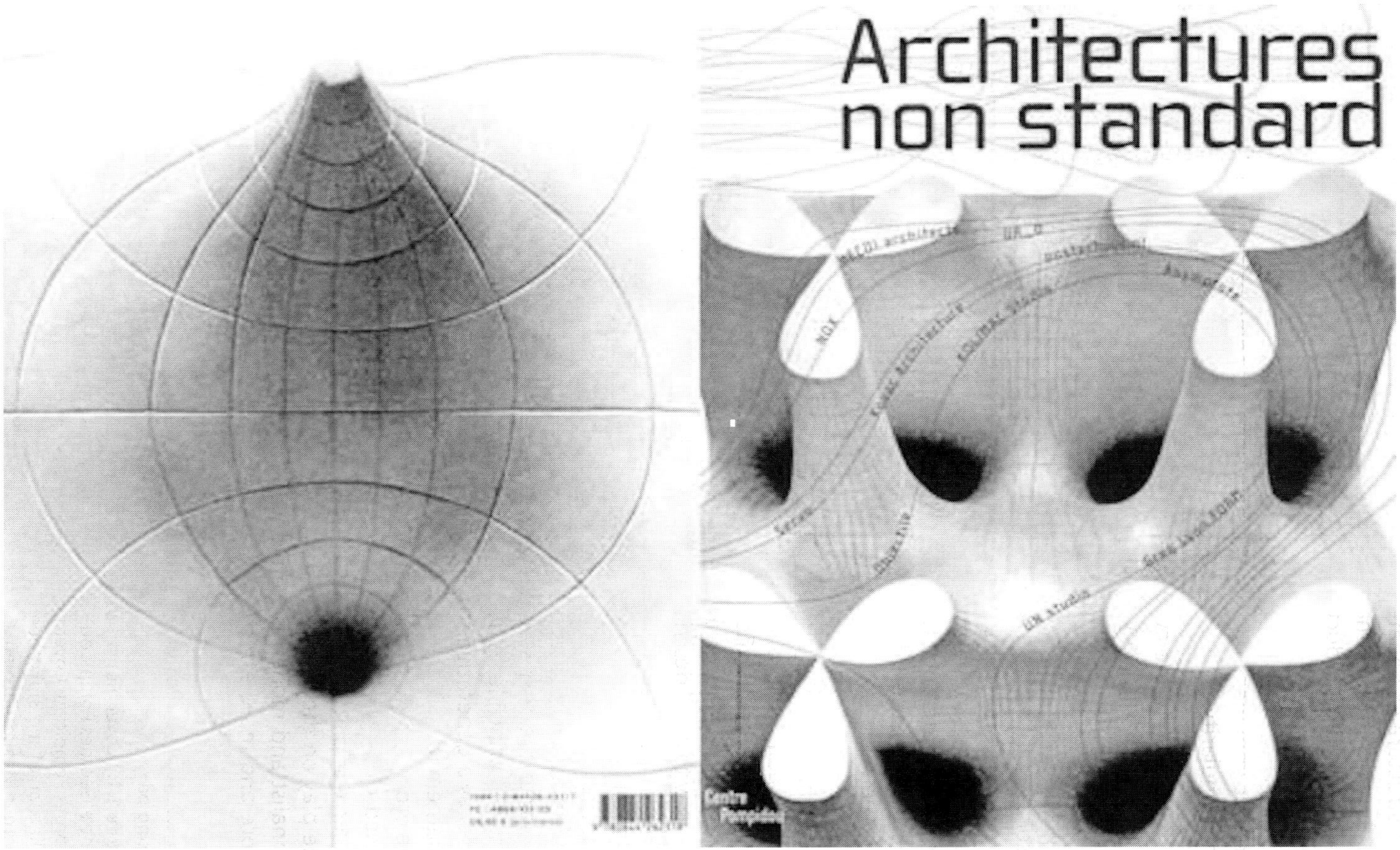

Figure 1.1

the structuralist debate. For Alain Badiou the ontology of the manifold was anchored in the axiomatic theory (Theory of Set-Group of Zemerlo-Franenkel . . .) as a radical reduction of the physical to mathematic, to a pure mathematical ontology. For Gilles Deleuze his theory of multiplicities was bound to a mathematisation defined from differential calculus. The valuation of a generic immanence imposed a new understanding of the singularisation, of the singularity:

- inherent to the event in the extensive materialism of Badiou;
- more a trajectory through the permanent reconfiguration of variable proximities for Deleuze.

The limit of those two ontologies, of those two aspects of the material – in itself for Badiou, at the end assimilated to the organic for Deleuze – reside in the status of the mathematic and the interpretation of the infinite. The reference to set theory was overawed by non-standard set theories and the Deleuzian reference to the non-standard was mainly assimilated to the epistemology of the differential calculus (in topology) through the distinction between axiomatic and problematic. As a disciple of Abraham Robinson and Georges Reeb, René Thom affirmed a more adequate relationship between mathematics and nature, a dynamic understanding of morphogenesis, where non-standard analysis was the tool, through the integration of infinite in the numbers to define the singularisation of a form or a motive. The singularity, conceived as a bifurcation along the progression of an algorithm, opened the way to a full description of the physical world, to the full discretisation of reality. This qualitative science of interaction between attractors that define relations between differential varieties which was descriptive of physical manifestation became a tool of simulation applied in physics or in biology and extensively to ecological systems. Non Standard Architecture tried to overtake the first step of the generalisation of computation, the "file to factory" principle, to radicalise the homogenisation of the simulation processes as a generative tool. The appearance of non-standard-based software (Mathematica, Processing . . .), where the modelling of the processes becomes the process itself, introduced through cellular automatons a material-design-based computation, an agent-based architecture which creates bridges to other disciplines (physics, biology, material-based ontologies . . .). Beyond the play on the word standard, standardisation and the critique of its functionalist and modernist reference, Non Standard Architecture seems today more and more effective as a domain of research around an agent-based

---

Facing page

Figure 1.1: "Cover illustrations of the *Architectures Non Standard* exhibition catalogue, Centre Georges Pompidou", 2003. Image credit: Courtesy Frédéric Migayrou, Centre Georges Pompidou. Cover image: Karl Weierstrass, "Maquette de la Fonction", 1952. Collection of the Bibliothèque de l'Institut Henri Poincaré, Paris. Photography credit: Georges Meguerditchian. Cover design: Laurent Pinon.

architecture and its immediate repercussions on the material aspect of construction.

***

Non-standard. Can one specify or define non-standard architecture? The term "non-standard" has meaning in two fields of knowledge, both of which upon first inspection appear totally heterogeneous. In its very formulation, the idea of 'non-standard' obviously evokes, on the one hand, a refusal of normalization, of widespread standardisation as a fundamental factor of industrialization, as a determining principle of Modernism in that it endeavours to deploy standardized mass production. Beyond architecture, this trend has given birth to a one-sided world culture of production and products. But 'non-standard' also refers to mathematics, more specifically to *Non-Standard Analysis*, the title of Abraham Robinson's 1961 publication.[1] Robinson conceived and laid out the theoretical foundations of this new branch of mathematics dealing with the development of infinitesimal calculus. Indeed, according to Robinson, infinitesimal figures can be assimilated into usable numbers in all operations of logic and fundamental mathematics. Robinson completes the hypothesis sketched out by G.W. Leibniz, who thought that the opposition finite/infinite was not absolute but relative. Non-standard analysis opposes the formalism of mathematical language, focused on its own objectivity, by introducing open, infinitesimal models, genuine tools of approximation that presuppose the nature of an external, constructive mathematical reality.[2] Beyond a mere debate between mathematical formalism and intuitionism, non-standard analysis posits a dynamic structuralism, an abstract semantics that underpins the interrelation between phenomena and meaning. It is the establishment of a general and "formal hermeneutics" that can become directly involved at the core of an overall physics of phenomena. If this domain of mathematical analysis found immediate applications in so many disciplines (physics, biology, economics and of course in the field of computing) it was because this "theory of models" goes well beyond the formal logic of the Vienna Circle to induce an implemented physics of meaning. René Thom, founder of this structuralism with morphogenesis, an a priori formalization of mutations in matter, spoke of a "semiophysics". Inferring the idea of a morphogenetic continuity in abstracto revolutionizes the very condition of the appearance of singularities, of the definition of form and of its meaning. Thus, reductionist theories, in which phenomena are restricted to descriptive systems, as well as phenomenology, which would remain at a descriptive distance, were brushed aside. The mathematical modelling of morphogenesis proposed by René Thom does not offer a description of general principles of physics, but the establishment of a differential model, a priori intended to bring to light the singularities in a process.[3]

In taking stock of contemporary architectural research, one is forced to acknowledge that the development of digital design applications has resulted in the widespread idea of a style, a type of rendering in which sequencing and kinetics have fostered the rise of a topological under-standing. The vulgate of a geometry that is both critical of projective geo-metry as well as its Euclidean origins, carried forward by algorithmic systems, has developed into so many formalized themes, super-surfaces, hyper-surfaces, attempting to seize a topological vocabulary: folds, loops, nodes, layers . . . Architectural design and the capacity for "generative modelling" – a genuine, real-time, analytical tool that allows the form and the organization of the architectural programme seemingly to spring from a mere choice made from among a broad selection of other possibilities – may have become indissociable. What is more, the self-organization of these generative forms has widely developed into an organic understanding in which biological structures seem to embody new unities, a differential state of the architectural object. Comprehension of what non-standard architec-ture can be hinges on the specification of this change in status, of this iden-tifying and component principle of architectural unity. Behind the flurry of publications, colloquia and the multiplication of exhibitions, all striving mainly to tackle the issues of representation or projection posed by the virtual nature of this digital space and by the generalization of a zone where cyberspace fosters an ultimate/new metaphysics of space, the tectonic shift in the founding order, in what can be the constituent logic of a new architec-tural singularity, seems to go unnoticed. Conversely, the hasty assertion of the advent of a "virtual" architecture bears its own contradiction within itself. Morphogenesis, topologies: the architecture to come is the object of widespread suspicion. It is tirelessly denounced as formalist in that, precisely because it reveals itself as a generator of infinite forms, it resists by its very essence any decree from an external order. The paradoxical tension between digital architecture, which carries with it the aura of dematerialization and the return of hylomorphism, in which the same models for matter could define the models of a built architecture, remains unresolved, if one insists solely on a critical questioning of form. By relying on fractal theories or those of morphogenesis, which pepper numerous articles of architectural criticism, thinkers are seeking to define how a singularity organizes itself within a dynamic system. Just like D'Arcy Thompson's biomorphic models, "catas-trophe theory" is seemingly exploited to elaborate a meta-geometry of matter founded on the idea of genetic mutation. Though the fields of biology and, closer to architecture, geography[4] already rely heavily on these types of modelling, for architecture they remain frozen in a descriptive approach, always assuming an external phenomenon that must be placed into a logical framework of comprehension.

For non-standard architecture this is precisely the issue, i.e. to go beyond the bounds of any assumptions about form, any anteriority or exteriority of a determining principle, of the elaboration of form. Architecture must therefore live up to its intrinsic capacity to specify, to bring singular elements to light. It must forcefully challenge an architectural tradition that has historically decided its language and syntax for the representation of an external normative principle, of a rigid restriction to orders, by counting solely upon its own structural capacities. This issue of canon, a question going back to the essence of architecture, underpins and goes beyond all relation to form. The definition of orders, of a plan in perspective, which organizes the principles of construction through the use of measure and proportion, architecture has always been nurtured by questioning its foundation: the fiction of classicism on the evocation of a forgotten origin, the earliest architecture of Marc-Antoine Laugier, the rational normative principles of J.N.L. Durand, though the elucidation of the conditions of this legal establishment has remained elusive. Even the transition from the classical field's codifying to the institution of industrial norms, to the genuine legal status conferred upon standardization, was no longer subjected to the question *quid juris, as* if the modulation of standards caught up in the flow of industrial production did not impose a rupture, another idea of architectural identity. It is in these terms that the philosopher Gilles Deleuze, in reference to an earlier text by Bernard Cache, *L'Ameublement du Territoire*,[5] defines the domain for practising a properly non-standard architecture: "It is a very modern notion of the technological object: it does not even refer back to the first wave of industrialization when the idea of a standard still retained a semblance of essence and imposed a law of constancy ('the object produced by and for the masses'), but refers rather to our current situation when the fluctuation of the norm replaces the permanence of the law, when the object positions itself in a continuum through variation, when automated digital production or the digitally operated machine replaces die stamping. The object's new status is no longer compared to a spatial mould, i.e. a relationship of form/matter, but rather to a temporal modulation that involves being continuously placed in a variation of matter as much as in a continuous development of form".[6] Thus, Deleuze confers a legal as much as an ontological dimension upon this new standard of variability, echoing an ambivalence in the works of Leibniz vis-à-vis the foundation of Modernism within the baroque, which within the logic of the baroque distinguishes a structural field, the one with the monads defining the figures and the qualities, from the chaotic world of flows. To the distance maintained by the rational subject with regard to the object – a distance that conditioned all geometric relations of the system of perspective at the beginning, notably of the organization and ordering of the field of architecture – is opposed a correlation between the subject and the object where the point of view is maintained by the variation. The object exists only in the variation of its profiles and refers to a transformation that is a component of the subject. This is precisely the dynamic that Gilles Deleuze refers to as "objectile".

The "objectile" assumes that the 'point of view' is caught up in the movement of variation, carried by continuous inflection and, as such, is a component of the subject. Perspective is interconnected with this following of modulation. The point of view is no longer defined by determining a distance, but rather through the range of all possible determinations. If, according to Deleuze, the "objectile" merges with the 'geometric', this is because inflection imposes itself as the primordial genetic element, a perpetually cursive point that generates intrinsic singularities, resisting the establishment of pure and exact figures. The repeated mention of the active line, as Paul Klee called it, this "non-dimensional point", "between the dimensions", always refers to the ordering of the entire world, the cosmos, which the artist contrasts to the indeterminacy of chaos. A line is ordered because it is carried by inflection; for Klee *(Formation of the Black Point*, 1925), as for Wassily Kandinsky *(Drawing for Point Line Plane*, 1926), inflection is most often expressed by drawing arrows indicating the component of tension, according to the idea of "material-force", to use Deleuze's term, returning to its baroque essence. This "perspectivism" without distance, this relativism that is not a variation of the truth or of the normative principle according to the subject, whose source Deleuze finds in Leibniz, Friedrich Nietzsche or Alfred North Whitehead,[7] echoes an understanding of the baroque that remains largely hidden by classicism. The same is true for the serpentine, which for William Hogarth *(The Analysis of Beauty*, 1753) organized the codification of the body's movements in dance as well as in drawing, or coming more directly from the differential geometry of Girard Desargues *(Rough Draft for Invasion of Privacy of the Events Concerning the Encounters of a Corte with a Plane*, 1639), from the order that allowed arabesques in the gardens of André Le Nôtre or the anamorphic perspectives of Jean-François Niceron *(La Perspective Curieuse*, 1651). This infinite line of inflection, which Deleuze designates as a fold, is a virtual quality that differentiates itself unceasingly to self-actualize in a conscious event, a "subjectile", or to realize itself in matter as an "objectile". Inflection is the indissociable composition of these two vectors, and intrinsically defines the principle of a legal mooring perpetually renewed, of a codification that does not reveal itself, which is beyond all representation of the law, a 'differentiation' of the norm. Bernard Cache, in a chapter of his essay entitled "Subjectiles and Objectiles: Towards a Non-standard Mode of Production", takes up the issue of the generalization of parametric functions in the software applications managing machining, which make it possible to manufacture one-of-a-kind objects industrially, each one of the same series having a different shape, and questions this historic evolution of architectural order as it transits from codification to standardization. Although the rise of the standardized object did lead to the idea of variability, this notion remained limited to a repetition of type, a mismatch between the real aesthetic determination of variation circumscribed by the avant-gardes and industrial production limited by the Taylorism of the series. This norm, always in the process of being defined and always deferred, is transcribed into "objects fluctuating on the variable curves of new industrial series . . . There are no longer pre-established functions requiring a form; we have only the occasional functions of fluctuating forms.[8]

However, one cannot so easily confront standard with non-standard in an antinomian mode, as if the ensuing deregulation established the new terrain of free expression. It is less a question of a normative system for Modernism than reconsidering its critical and aesthetic sources, ill served by a one-sided reading that believed it was moving beyond the modern moment by denouncing its formalism and its abstraction. The perpetual contradiction between the requirements of the industrial series and the preservation of architectural diversity, which form the basis of the earliest discourses on Modernism by John Ruskin or William Morris and which seemed fulfilled with the Bauhaus, was never interpreted in terms other than those of production, of an insoluble contradiction between the commercial constraint of repeating the some object the greatest possible number of times and that of industrially manufacturing different objects. This tension, which to this day animates the play between market forces and fashion trends, masks the critical return to the notion of the standard, the *Typisierung,* a questioning of the genesis, the identifying status of the "type" of the idealization of the norm in an ultimate codification determined by use, raising the *Bauentwurfslehre* (Elements of Construction Projects, 1936) by Ernst Neufert to the rank of a legal manual. Yet, it is indeed the very idea of a singularity defined by the order of its qualifications that leads to Henry Van de Velde's earliest thoughts, to his struggling in the essay "Die Linie"[9] to define the new industrial style. The line is not a decorative element, as a hasty reading of the *Jungendstil* might conclude, but is indeed a 'dynamographic' system: "A line is a force that functions in a way similar to all elementary forces: if a number of contradictory lines are assembled, they will exert effects similar to those produced by the interaction of elementary contradictory forces. When I say that a line is a force, for me, this is an observation of fact; the line derives its energy from the person who traces it. In this way, nothing is lost of the energy or the force".[10] Here, the line is invested with an anthropomorphic quality, inscribing itself like a metaphor of the inflexion and energy of the body in movement, thus echoing the Nietzschean body described in *The Will to Power* as "a differential of qualified force". This line, which condenses both the body's energy and the dynamic of cognition, springs forth in arabesques in the *Danse Serpentine* of Loie Fuller (1902), but obviously rendered more technical, swept up in the sequential process of the machine by Etienne-Jules Marey. The body is transfigured into a cinematic object, going forth reciprocally by optimizing the dynamic: a diagrammatic line endowed with a prescriptive function, like the apparatus of Lillian and Frank W. Gilbreth, allowing for a rationalization of the body's movements at work or those of a housewife in her kitchen tending to her domestic chores. The Taylorism of the Gilbreths does not assert a simple mechanization of the body; it is, to use the words of Siegfried Giedion, 'the intervention of the machine in the very substance of both the organic and inorganic".[11] It is in fact Siegfried Giedion who, seeking to understand the new space/time assumed by mechanization and, reflecting on the interchangeable nature of the elements that enable standardization, compares the "pure form" of the movement engendered by mechanization to the experiments of artists in their quest for a spiritual and conceptual space, an enhanced space that could go beyond the geometric field. He shows, in a few well-known pages, the same concern that animated Bergson's lecture at the Collège de France in

1900, '*Le Mécanisme cinématographique de la pensée*', and the work of the Gilbreths, Etienne-Jules Marey or Muybridge, and by referring to the *Nu descendant un escalier* by Marcel Duchamp as well as the inflected lines of Paul Klee or Wassily Kandinsky.

The entire understanding of the field of Modernism hinges on this problem of assimilating the new legal order flowing from this generic capacity for inflexion. This limitation of criticism is analysed by Detlef Mertins when he compares the still neo-Kantean aesthetic positioning of Siegfried Giedion with that of Emil Kaufmann. Whereas in *Space, Time & Architecture* (1941), Giedion unceasingly emphasizes the component of ambiguity in a mutual mediation of the subject and the object, where space is determined in a dialogue with the subject – pursuing the theories on Raumgestaltung initiated by August Schmarzow and then taken up by Theo Van Doesburg and Làszló Moholy-Nagy – he remains enclosed in a neo-Kantean framework: "The failure of the historical theories of Giedion and Kaufmann are symptomatic: the Modernist quest for a new normativity goes beyond the Kantean spirit without relying on the metaphysics of movement and differential that stirred the heart of all of Modernism's polemics".[12] Then the crisis of the "free line" occurred, following the exhibition "*Line and Form*" (Linie und Form) held at Krefeld by Henry Van de Velde, first founder of a school of applied arts in Weimar and whose mission was precisely to initiate new relationships between art and industry, i.e. a new logic for design. During this exhibition, which presented the photographs of a military boat, the critics, reacting in a climate of nationalism, seized upon the Yachting Style, on this call for fluidity. Along with the foundation of the Werkbund in 1907, the debate over relations between architecture and the world of industrial production became more radical, through a *sachlich* approach to design with clearly asserted production. The issue of the Typisierung involved two individuals in a virulent polemic: Henry Van de Velde and Hermann Muthesius, the first considering the standard as a dead and abstract system of norms, and the other asserting the type as the domain of shared conventions. The two parties born of this scission, one comprising Van de Velde, Bruno Tout and August Endell and the other including Hermann Muthesius, Peter Behrens and Walter Gropius, reflect this ambivalence attached to the standard, which was to leave its mark on all the architecture of the twentieth century. The back-and-forth confrontation between the two groups fostered the legal mutation of the very idea of "conception", the fact that the formation, the "in-formation" of the object, or the *Gestaltung*, to use the word that anticipates the contemporary definition of "design", is established as the conceptual approach directly articulated on the tools of production. For the evocation of a new style, still defended in 1902 by Hermann Muthesius in his famous work *Stilarchitektur und Baukunst*,[13] is substituted the assertion of an objective art (*sachlich*), freed from its last expressionist manifestations. "Behind the apparent opposition separating Van de Velde and Muthesius, it is the internal duality of their conception of *Gestaltung* that prevails, seeking to reconcile and preserve a dynamic of creation at the heart of the new industrial aesthetic. Through the notion of *Typisierung*[14] one seeks this difficult reconciliation".

Though the term *Gestaltung* became popular from 1903 onward, it was nevertheless overly determined by geometric "normativity", which defines at once an abstract structuring of experience, space and material forms organizing space, structuring where the experience is connected to the internal requirements of materials and function. This new normativity, which dealt with the design of the house, furnishings and the applied arts, was achieved by 1919 with the publication of the review *Die Form*, by Walter Riezler, and thereafter with the exhibition "*Die Form Ohne Ornament*", which attempted to bring to light types and constants of industrial production. It is of course no longer a question of discrediting ornament, as Adolf Loos advocated (*Ornament und Verbrechen*, 1908), but rather of limiting the spiritual field of the mechanical era. Walter Gropius, in the *Arbeitsrat fur Kunst* anticipating the Bauhaus project, calls for a genuine constructivist programme: "We have all become builders whose purpose is to edify a cathedral of the future that will unify under a single Gestalt architecture, sculpture and painting".[15] Against all formalist interpretations of Modernity, the review G[16] – G for *Gestaltung* – will remain the authentic manifesto in the legal establishment of this new differential singularity, this abstraction carried forward by its physical achievement, to borrow from the phenomenological notion of *Einfühlung* of Wilhelm Worringer. In a remarkable analysis of the development of the concept of *Gestaltung*, Detlef Mertins indicates it is a process, the attempt to become form, to the becoming-form's linking without distinction to the spiritual domain, organic life or artistic and industrial production. "This orientation inherited from vitalism, shared by all the key contributors, was formalized in the most empathetic and esoteric terms by Raoul Hausmann. He suggested that each form was a frozen moment-image participating in the creative aura of the atmosphere (*fluidum*), a component idea for Hugo Häring, Mies van der Rohe and Le Corbusier as well, that had to contain the entirety of the normative immobility of the type and an opening to vitalism."[17] The exigencies of a concrete, objective art, the search for a *Neue Sachlichkeit*, led the architects to resolve the antithesis between an abstract space, a space of mastery of geometric and even mathematical conception and a spatiality given over to the equally important dynamic component of the body. Pursuing a detailed exposé of the notion of *Gestaltung*, Stanford Anderson highlights this lineage between the installation of one of Maillol's sculptures by Peter Behrens at the Mannheim exhibition of 1907 and the permanent recurrence of sculptural bodies in geometric spaces of Mies van der Rohe (*Project for a House with Courtyard*, 1934, which also contained the sculpture *Méditerranée by* Maillol). "Behrens and Mies, when they would debate issues of materials or architecture, seized on a basic mathematical conception, most often inadapted to the material form: points, lines, planes cannot be built. The De Stijl artists (and Mies van der Rohe in his works inspired by De Stijl) speak of lines and planes but allow for ambiguities in their assembly to complete the forms that neither their words, nor those of a mathematician can adequately describe."[18]

This mathematization that enables one to keep *Gestaltung* within a rational and geometric framework flows directly from J.L.M. Lauweriks. Influenced, just like Piet Mondrian, by the theosophist philosophy of Dr M. Schoenmakers, Lauweriks was searching for a geometric transcription of the world inspired by this doctrine and trying to elaborate in progressive spatial diagrams the laws of spatial composition. His incessant research on the grid, as pattern or spatial object, which Peter Behrens, Mies van der Rohe or J.J.P. Oud later claimed directly, is less the effect of a mastery of the plan through separations than a game of geometric progression. Lauweriks thus was seeking to formalize an order of movement and inflection also present in his drawings portraying the turbulence of war, entitled *Weltkriegsdenkmal*, 1915.[19] This rational quest, most often interpreted unilaterally according to a Euclidean geometry, later led many architects back to classical composition, an idealistic, formalistic and abstract order, which was nevertheless in contradiction with the dynamic of the Gestaltung. The development of a historical view of Modernism even seems to be limited by this return to order. Literature dedicated to the Bauhaus, notably Hans M. Wingler's work, eschews any reference to Henry Van de Velde concerning the first school in Weimar and his relationship with Gropius, while the expressionist origins of the Werkbund are greatly diminished. Graver still, two logics of the *Sachlichkeit* are distinguished here: that of the artists, open in a way to experimentation, and that of the architects, supposedly aiming only for the rationalization of the products of industrialization, and substituting the notion of "good form" (Die gute Form) for that of Gestaltung. And yet, many artists and architects tried to open geometric space to a spiritual dimension, an issue that was even at the very foundation of twentieth-century avant-gardes. The repercussions of the *Analysis Situs* by Henri Poincaré would have a very important impact on all fields of creation. Beyond the abstract fascination for the fourth dimension and its representations, those of Charles Sirato and his *Manifeste Dimensioniste* (1936), for example, it is indeed the comprehension of a mathematical continuum of this type, of the possible formalization of a new cognitive domain that would bring together Marcel Duchamp, Theo Van Doesburg, Piet Mondrian, Kasimir Malevich, El Lissitzky, Richard Buckminster Fuller and others. From the exhaustive historical indexation undertaken by Linda Dalrymple Henderson in *The Fourth Dimension and Non-Euclidien Geometry in Modern Art*,[20] the central idea it proposes is that the issue does not lie in the definition of a new spatiality, an extended geometry, but in the approach to this "continuum", which transgresses the contingent structure of space. As Henri Poincaré insists in *Le Continu Mathématique* (1893), it is about going beyond the order of representation while simultaneously asserting that geometry with X dimensions does indeed have a real object. Poincaré, giving as an example the change in the state of an object or a body in motion, seeks to define a priori the relationship between the intuitive and the analytical continuum, and he does so by using infinitesimal models. Beyond the emblematic *Nu descendant un escalier* (1912) of Marcel Duchamp, the numerous studies on the body in motion, the photographic prints, on inflexion, the organic forms, which mark the research of the avant-garde with so many milestones, are never limited to a quest for new forms. Lâszló Moholy-Nagy demanded proximity, the immediacy of phenome-nality, by reconfiguring the position, tasks and competencies of the "designer". "The sea rolls up onto the beach, the waves fold the sand. The point on a wall cracks, its surface becoming a web of lines. A car moves in the snow, the tyres leave deep traces. A rope falls, it creates short curves on the ground. A board is cut, it allows the traces of the saw to appear. All these phenomena, caused by these varied processes, can be thought of as diagrams in space representing forces acting upon the different materials as well as the resistance of these materials to the drive of these forces. If elements, forces and processes partici-pate in an optimum coincidence, one can speak of an "objective" quality. This indicates that 'optimum' and 'objectivity' never constitute a rigid formula."[21]

Though all the artistic currents flowing from the avant-gardes preserved this internal contradiction of *Gestaltung* by understanding their form as an "in-formation", it is nevertheless surprising that a neo-rationalist contempo-rary architecture should have so meticulously gone about erasing the genealogy of the concept to rely only on geometric formalism where the architectural order had to limit itself to measures and proportions. The minimalist craze, an architecture of reduction, obviously owes nothing to Mies van der Rohe and one has trouble understanding how the questioning of standardization or normalization of production never reappeared, either with the postmodernist wave or with the protagonists of deconstruction, as if the identifying status of the standard, the type, remained an unquestion-able a priori of industrialization. How was it possible that a rigged-together historical reading submitted to the revision of the Werkbund, the Bauhaus, made no mention of the platform of the Circle group, Moholy-Nagy's influence in New York or the publication of works by Gyorgy Kepes, which served as school manuals for several generations of students? Why is there no curiosity about this internal contradiction that riddles the work of Max Bill, who, after his time at the Bauhaus, developed research on the elements of prefabrication? All of his work stands in this tension between an art and a concrete geometric architecture, also claimed by many minimalist architects, a deep study of the conditions for production of industriai design with the foundation of the Technische Hochschule fur Gestaltung in Ulm, and, on the other hand, the incessant research on topology, with the rings of Móbius to lean on. All of this is to forget that *Gestaltung* also extends to and speaks of *Gestalt*, this pre-phenomenological current undertaken by Franz Brentano, in which he refers to the long tradition of the idea of *empathy* as formulated by Theodor Lipps – to which Peter Behrens refers as much as Hermann Muthesius – to then be largely taken up by German aesthetics – one thinks especially of Konrad Fiedler and August Schmarzow – and to end with its theoretical fulfilment in the work by Wilhelm Worringer, *Abstraktion und Einfühlung, a* recurring reference of the modern current.[22]

Anticipating the phenomenological concept of intentionality, it is indeed a question of describing the phenomenon of the joint constitution of form and consciousness, of seizing the intertwined threads of qualitative, physical, material and biological determinations leading to a form to be established. How is the constitution of singularities rightly organized, without maintaining the representative distance of a subject or the idealist a priori of transcendental schematism? The debates and research of non-standard architecture still hang between a seemingly irreconcilable alternative of an almost materialistic immanence claimed by Gilles Deleuze and the semiophysics of René Thom, open to all applications in the domain of computing. "The fold not only affects the materials, which thus become material for expression, according to different scales, speeds, vectors (mountains and waters, paper, fabrics, living tissue, the brain), but it also determines and makes the form appear, it makes it a form of expression, *'Gestaltung'*, the genetic element of the infinite line of inflection, the curve of a unique variable".[23] For the philosopher, the fold is obviously not a topological figure; it is not an issue of abstracting levels of structures, but of plunging into the heart of the general phenomenon of self-organization. In a decisive article dealing with the specification of the notion of structure, Deleuze appeals directly to the mathematical concept of singularity as it is specified within the framework of differential calculus. Structure unfolds as process: "a system of differential relationships of singularities corresponding to these relationships and tracing the space of the structure".[24] When Jean Petitot draws a parallel between the approach of Gilles Deleuze and that of René Thom, he is attempting to formulate what a "theory of morphogenesis might be *in abstracto*, purely geometric, independent of a substrate of forms and the nature of the forces that create them", claiming "a physics of meaning."[25] Thus, non-standard logic appears as a tool for this formalization, this substantivization of indeterminate objects. It enables one to elaborate an autonomous, virtual, structuralist domain, capable of actualizing and validating any model of interpretation according to a new general hermeneutics. The entire American current of "formal ontology" draws its inspiration directly from the *Gestalt* of Franz Brentano so as to update the laws of objective associations in the cognitive domain.

This "associativity" allows the person engendering it to dispose of a genuine topology of meaning, a "mereology", whose formalization through non-standard models found an effective application in the field of artificial intelligence, then, by extension, in all the fields of biology, geography and sociology, ending up with the creation of diagnostic software programs as well as expert design systems.[26] The formal hermeneutics Jean-Michel Salanskis claims, beyond the semiophysics of René Thom, the extension of a "non-standard constructivism", goes beyond the latest phenomenological forms of description, to focus on tackling only the rationalization coming from mathematical continuity, to the a priori material relationships. Referring to the non-standard analysis of Georges Reeb, he insists that the theory of models intervenes "like a representative additive with regard to complexity ... The mathematics of continuity teaches how to understand from the approximate approach of the hyperfinitary excess of the discrete".[27] The questioning that this opens up brings ambiguity, however, since it is confined to an unprecedented rationalism presiding over the logic of the constitution of the real rendered in a generalized domain of computing. Thus, the issue of a "naturalization of phenomenology" is an ineffective screen for the project of logicization of intentionality.[28]

Non-standard architecture is connected at the edge of this redefinition of *Gestaltung*, where digital tools and their capacity for algorithmic calculation allow one to enter on a solid footing into the domain of a continuous formal schematism revolutionizing the logic of architectural design. Here, form becomes a morphogenetic a priori, the forms chosen to embody architecture being in a state for defining a singularity only in a continuum in perpetual evolution. And this is indeed what Greg Lynn means when he proposes the idea of inflection *(curvature)* as a method for integrating different forces, an idea that refers directly to the notion of the mathematical continuum: "Producing a geometric form based on a differential equation is problematic without a differential approach to series and repetition. There are two kinds of series, one discrete, one of repetitive series, and the other continuous, the one of iterative series. The difference between each object in a sequence is an individuated state critical for each repetition."[29] Here again one finds the schematism of the continuous, which René Thom uses as a tool for interpreting mutations of life, those of embryogenesis, translating them geometrically as "salience" or "pregnancy", a return to the relationship of the objectile and the subjectile, demonstrative of the movement to "singularization" and "individuation."[30] There is nothing organic about the architecture of Greg Lynn or that of Lars Spuybroek; no form is transposed from the description of living states. Architecture is specifiable only through the structural breakdown of the space of the forms to which it belongs; it is self-actualizing only in the permanent gap between the movement that differentiates it and the always inadequate definition of its own position. Non-standard architecture can thus be broadened to the principle of continuity with the full procedural field of architectural production. It is indeed because it seemingly denies any reality of representation, of any objectivity, but by asserting a priori its use of algorithmic calculators that it engenders confusion as to the state of "virtuality", a theme endlessly renewed by the said virtual architecture. The imagery produced by architects who would enter into a contradiction with the reality of the principles of construction is not "virtual". What is virtual is the a priori of a schematic domain of the non-standard, which can be self-actualized, or not, in the genetic definition of singularity. All of the literature on the virtual is thus subject to caution, precisely the caution that supports the traditional idea of a sphere of representation. Therefore, one must be wary of the idea of dematerialization, of a belief in the "immaterial"[31] which supposedly accounts for the transition from the world of objects to the world of media, and which confuses within it all logic of production with the one of a technical mediation, or to follow Jean-François Lyotard, a language whose interplay constitutes the last refuge of an intentional normativity.

Non-standard architecture, by contrast, has established itself as a domain of unprecedented materialization because it takes form in the very heart of a formal schematism that today drives all sectors of human activity. Behind the popular representation of the generalization of all things digital is the actual implementation of a theory of models articulated with non-standard logics that animate a computational space that now stretches from the economy to politics, industry, knowledge production ... However, by accepting this widespread mathematization, must one also reconstitute a last normative sphere that would define the central point of this schematism, the last figures of an order, those of a morphological type and those of the structures for a formal semantics? The issue of positivism should be clearly stated, beyond formal ontology, and its optimization of artificial intelligence should renew the closed world of a rationalism whose purpose would limit itself to the unilateral quest for performance and optimization. How then can one imagine an open normativity, always anchored to the heart of the singular derivation? How can one build norms that only self-organize their intrinsic capacity of never shifting into the representation of their own order and, therefore, norms that would only retain from their own effectiveness their capacity perpetually to delegate their identification? This proposition, which could introduce a genuine structure for a discourse on architectural policy, a policy of a perpetually renewed effectiveness, already determines the programmes that are recomposing the growing diversity of architectural trades. To produce architecture, therefore, is to accompany and transfigure the data of a situation; it is to make, beyond any notion of programme, a moment of resolution appear, a singular field that organizes its requirement for a generic interrelation with a genuine semiophysics of context. It is in this sense that the diagram is claimed by many architects as a method of deriva-tion, under the same unity, of the qualitative and informational elements of a most heterogeneous kind. The diagram returns to the function given to it by Deleuze, to a principle of singuiarization, an "abstract machine", detached from any morphogenetic understanding of a physical order of matter. Ben van Berkel and Caroline Bos clearly identify this genetic character, which in the interplay of inflection mixes the two faces of the objectile and subjectile. "The diagrams, rich in meaning, filled with the potential of movement, are carried by the structure, outside any specific spatial positioning. Understood as activators and triggers for construction, they are no more objective than subjective, no more anterior than posterior to theory, not more conceptual than contextual. The diagram is positioned in the operational, inter-subjective and process field where meanings form and transform themselves interactively."[32]

The internal logic of non-standard architecture cannot conform to an order other than the pursuit of a rigid orientation established by the play in the diagram, organizing, on one level, the necessity of the diagnosis and, on another level, the methods for realizing the architectural project. Architecture transfigures its unity, its synthetic capacity to gather together the two faces of the architectural project: the diagnosis on the one hand, the design on the other. The diagrammatic method takes up these two dimensions under the syntactical unity offered by the language of algorithms. On the one hand, the diagram provides inflection of a hermeneutic capacity, and this outside of any contextual sociology (which could be called deconstruction), and grants it, on the other hand, constructive capacity where the engineering resolves itself in digital translatability, which hybridizes all the tools of production. Indeed, any non-standard project can be immediately developed into variations of industrial production because it is subject to automatic translation, to conversion into an immediate feasibility at every step of the digitized chain (what Bernard Cache defines as "associativity", by comparing architecture's current situation with the digital revolution in the publishing industry and book fabrication). This idea of a differential norm, of a "normativity" that constantly shifts the principle of its representation, suggests a new set of principles, doubtless more relevant, for understanding Modernism's foundation. Le Corbusier, who worked for several months with Peter Behrens (1910–1911) and who was unable to avoid the polemics of the Werkbund and also claimed the spirit of *Sachlichkeit*[33] never allowed himself any abstract representation of the norm. Normativity remained riddled with the relativism of the *Gestaltung*, which perhaps allows us to restore the post-war work of Le Corbusier to this continuity, i.e., of Ronchamp or the *Poème Électronique* and the *Philips Pavilion*. "The standard is established on solid foundations, not arbitrarily, but in the secure knowledge of things motivated and logic controlled by analysis and experimentation".[34]

1   Abraham Robinson, 'Non-standard Analysis', in *Proceedings of the International Congress of Mathematicians*, Amsterdam, North Holland Publishing Co., 1961, pp. 432–40. Abraham Robinson, Non-Standard *Analysis*, Amsterdam, North Holland Publishing Co., 1966.
2   Abraham Robinson's work had a strong, immediate and international impact, especially in France, where the mathematician Georges Reeb understood straight away its significance. Joseph Warren Dauben, *Abraham Robinson*, The Creation of Non-Standard Analysis: A Personal and Mathematical Odyssey, preface by Benoît B. Mandelbrot, Princeton, Princeton University Press, 1995, pp. 374–75.
3   René Thom, *Modèles mathématiques de la morphogenèse*, Paris, Christian Bourgois, 1974; and René Thom, *Stabilité structurelle et morphogenèse*, Paris, InterEditions, 1977.
4   Gilles Richtot, *Essai de géomorphologie structurale*, Laval, Presses de l'Université de Laval, 1974. Gaetan Desmarais and Gilles Richtot, *La Géographie structurale*, Paris, L'Harmattan, 2000.
5   Bernard Cache, 'L'Ameublement du territoire', manuscript, published *first* in the US under the title *Earth Moves*, Cambridge, Mass., The MIT Press, then in France as *Terre meuble*, Orléans, HYX, 1997.
6   Gilles Deleuze, *Le Pli*, Paris, Minuit, 1988, p. 26.
7   Ibid., p. 27.
8   B. Cache, *Terre meuble*, op. cit., p. 68.
9   Henry Van de Velde, 'Die Unie', *Die Zukunft*, no. 49 (Berlin), 6 September 1902. The text was reprinted in *Der Neuer Stil*, Weimar, Carl Steinert, 1906. On this analysis, see Kary Jormakka (Dir.), *Form & Detail*, Henry Van de Velde Bauhaus in Weimar, Universitätsverlag Weimar der Bauhaus Universität, 1997, pp. 68–69.
10 G. Deleuze, *Nietzsche et la philosophie*, Paris, PUF, 1973, p. 59: 'Nietzsche calls the will to power the element of the genealogy of force. Genealogical means genetic

differential. The will to power is the differential element of forces, i.e. the element of production of the difference in quantity.' Henry Van de Velde, at the time close to Nietzsche, later designed the layout for the second edition of *Thus Spake Zarathustra* as well as the building housing the Nietzsche Archives in Weimar in 1903.

11   Siegfried Giedion, *Mechanization Takes Command: A Contribution to Anonymous History*, New York, Oxford University Press, 1948; French edition, *La Mécanisation au pouvoir*, translated by P. Guivarch, Centre Georges Pompidou-Centre de Création Industrielle, Paris, 1980, p. 58. Curiously, Siegfried Giedion, who in this work achieves a synthesis of the development of the concept of *Gestaltung*, makes the indissociable link between determination of standardisation and the mechanization of movement and initiates a genuine archaeology of inflexion.

12   Detlef Mertins, 'System and Freedom: Siegfried Giedion, Emil Kaufmann and the Constitution of Architectural Modernity', in R.E. Somol (Dir.), *Autonomy & Ideology: Positioning an Avant-Garde in America*, New York, The Monaccelli Press, 1997, p. 230.

13   Hermann Muthesius, *Stilarchitektur und Baukunst. Wandlungen der Architektur im XIX Jahrundert und ihr heutiger Standpunkt*, Mülheim-Ruhr, K. Schimmelpfeng Verlag, 1902. Little by little the notion of style becomes problematic and there was a search for a more sachlich vocabulary. The word '*Baukunst*' began to be used in place of the word 'architecture'.

14   Lothar Kühne, 'Henry Van de Velde und der Typisierungsstreit', *Form und Zweck*, no. 4, 1978, p. 39.

15   Walter Gropius, 'Mlas ist Baukunst?', *Flugblatt zur Ausstellung für unbekonnte Architektur*, 1919, published in Hartmut Probst and Christian Schüdlich (eds), Walter Gropius, *Ausgewiihlte Schriften, vol. 3*, Berlin, Ernst & Sohn, 1988, pp. 58–59.

16   The review *G: Material* zur elementaren *Gestaltung* was edited by Hans Richter and Mies van der Rohe. The six issues published from 1923 to 1926 define a cross-disciplinary editorial policy gathering dadaists, surrealists, constructivists and neo-plasticiens. One finds in its pages El Lissitzky, Theo Van Doesburg, Walter Benjamin, Hans Arp, Friedrich Kiesler, Antoine Pevsner . . . Detlef Merlins, who was preparing another edition of this review, emphasizes the coherence of the commitment of such a diversity of creatures: "The first issue included 'Realist Manifest' by Pevsner and Gabo of 1920, who declared that art should give form to expressions of life in space and time; the *Proun Room* of El Lissitzky for the 1923 exhibition in Berlin 1923, updated by Werner Grüff with a new generation of engineers capable of going beyond 'machinism' through intuition; and the creation of the project by Mies for a concrete office building in 1923 accompanied by his famous manifesto on the art of building pure presence" (Detlef Mertins, introduction to Walter Curt Behrendt, *The Victory of the New Building Style*, transl. from the original, *Der Sieg der neuen Baustils* [1927], Los Angeles, Getty Research Institute, 2000, p. 49).

17   Detlef Merlins, op. cit., p. 50.

18   Stanford Anderson, *Peter Behrens and a New Architecture for the Twentieth Century*, Cambridge, Mass., The MIT Press, 2000, p. 90.

19   Nic Tummers, *Der Hagener Impuls: J.L.M. Lauweriks Werk und Einfluss ouf Architektur und Formgebung um 1910*, Hagen, Unnepe Verlagsgesellschaft, 1972, p. 88.

20   Linda Dalrymple Henderson, *The Fourth Dimension and Non-Euclidean Geometry in Modern Art*, Princeton, Princeton University Press, 1983.

21   Làszló Moholy-Nagy, *Vision in Motion*, New York, Paul Theobald & Co., 1947; 1968 edn, p. 36.

22   One returns here to the important collection of texts on empathy in the German aesthetic of the end of the nineteenth century: Robert Vischer, Harry Francis Mallgrave and Eleftherios Ikomonou, *Empathy, Form & Space: Problems in German Aesthetics, 1873–1893*, Los Angeles, Getty Centre Publications Programs, 1994.

23   Gilles Deleuze, *Le Pli*, op. cit., p. 49.

24   Gilles Deleuze, 'À quoi reconnaît-on le structuralisme?', in François Châtelet (Dir.), *Histoire de la philosophie, idées, doctrines. Le XXe siècle*, Paris, Hachette Littérature, 1973, pp. 309–10.

25   Jean Petitot, *Morphogenèse du sens*, Paris, PUF, 1985 (see pp. 66–74). Jean Petitot, 'Rappels sur l'analyse non standard', in Hervé Barreau, Jacques Harthong (eds), *La Mathématique non standard*, Paris, Editions du CNRS, 1989.

26   Barry Smith (ed.), *Parts and Moments: Studies in Logic & Formal Ontology*, Munich, Philosophia, 1982. Barry Smith and Chris Welty, *Formal Ontology in Information Systems*, Proceedings of the International Conference on Formal Ontology in Information Systems, Ogunquit, Maine, ACM Press, 2001.

27   Jean-Michel Salanskis, *Le Temps du sens*, Orléans, HYX, 1997, p. 278. See also Jean-Michel Salanskis, *L'Herméneutique formelle. L'infini, le continu, l'espace*, Paris, Editions du CNRS, 1991, and *Le Constructivisme non standard*, Paris, Presses Universitaires du Septentrion, 1999.

28   Jean Petitot, Francisco J. Varela, Bernard Pachoud, Jean-Michel Roy, *Naturalizing Phenomenology*, Stanford, CT, Stanford University Press, 2000.

29   Greg Lynn, *Animate Form*, Princeton, Princeton Architectural Press, 1999, p. 33.

30   René Thom, *Esquisse d'une sémiophysique*, Paris, Interéditions, 1988. See the first chapter, 'Saillance et prégnance', pp. 16–34.

31   Jean-François Lyotard, *Les Immatériaux*. Album, Centre Georges Pompidou/Centre de création industrielle, Paris, 1985. Lyotard proposes to substitute the idea of a figure-image for the figure-matrix. The message is no longer independent from the means; matter is 'in-formed': 'With the "immaterials" the assignment of an identity (thing, class, mind . . .) to a structural pole seems an error. The same identity can occupy different poles of the structure' (p. 17).

32   Ben Van Berkel and Caroline Bos, 'Diagrams, interactive instruments in the opération', *Any, Diagram Works*, no. 23, New York, 1998, p. 23.

33   'Having placed architecture in this purely spiritual *event* of composition, I can easily understand *why the* doctrines of the *Sachlichkeit* are so inaccessible to my arguments . . . We didn't feel the imperious necessity of being sachlich in architecture by respecting the objective conditions of the plastic' (Le Corbusier, 'Défense de l'architecture', *L'Architecture d'aujourd'hui*, special issue 'Le Corbusier', no. 10, Paris, 1934, p. 61). On Le Corbusier and the influence of the Werkbund on the conception of standardization, see Winfried Nerdinger, 'Standard et type. Le Corbusier et l'Allemagne, 1920–27', in Rut Foehn (ed.), *L'Esprit nouveau, Le Corbusier et l'industrie*, 1920–25, Berlin, Ernst & Sohn, pp. 44–65.

34   Le Corbusier-Saugnier *Vers une architecture*, Paris, Editions Crés, 1923, p. 108.

Folding in Architectre, first published in 1993 as a "Profile" of *Architectural Design*, ranks as a classic of end-of-millennium architectural theory.[1] It is frequently cited and generally perceived as a crucial turning point. Some of the essays in the original publication have taken on lives of their own, and have been reprinted and excerpted—out of context, however, and often without reference to their first appearance in print. This ahistoric approach is characteristic of all works in progress: so long as a tradition is still active and alive, it tends to acquire a timeless sort of internal consistency, where chronology does matter. In Antiquity and in the Middle Ages such phases could last for centuries. But we have been living in times of faster change for quite a while now—we even had to invent a new philosophy of history in the nineteenth century to take this into account—and ten years are quite a stretch in Internet time. This is one reason why the editors of the revised 2004 edition decided that the original 1993 issue of *Folding in Architecture* should be reprinted in facsimile, verbatim and figuratim, complete and unabridged: only some typographical errors have been edited out. Indeed, *Folding in Architecture* is now a classic—not a timeless one, however, but time specific.

More than would be customary in other trades and professions, many architects and architectural historians still believe in historical progress and in the pursuit of innovation. Any reasonable architectural thinker of our days, if asked, would disparage such a primitive theory of history, but theory and practice are here curiously at odds. Regardless of much discourse on long durations, the directionlessness of time, time warps, the end of time, and perhaps even the death of the author, it is a fact that events and people are still banally and routinely singled out to acquire historical status in architecture when they are thought to have started something. *Folding in Architecture* is no exception. In the common lore, this publication is now seen as seminal because it was the catalyst for a wave of change that marked the decade and climaxed towards the turn of the millennium, when, for a short spell of time, the new avant-garde that evolved out of it came to be known as "topological", and was regarded as the quintessential architectural embodiment of the new digital technologies that were booming at the time.

Art historians, sociologists and psychologists will at some point reconstruct the story of architectural folding in the nineties and, as art historians frequently do, they will not fail to identify a trend towards curvilinearity that reversed a preceding trend towards angularity of form. Indeed, forms have a tendency to swing from the angular to the curvilinear, from parataxis to syntax, and art historians, following a pattern inaugurated in 1915 by Heinrich Wölflin, have since brought this interpretive model to bear in a

Figure 2.1

number of circumstances.[2] Obviously, the nineties started angular and ended curvilinear.[3] By the end of the decade, with few exceptions, curvilinearity was ubiquitous. It dominated industrial design, fashion, furniture, body culture, car design, food, critical theory in the visual arts, sex appeal, the art of discourse, even architecture. Admittedly one of the most influential architectural writers of the decade, Rem Koolhaas, kept designing in an angular mode, but the most iconic building of the time, Gehry's Bilbao, was emphatically curvilinear. In spite of the many varieties and competing technologies of curves that followed, curvilinear folds were and still are often seen as the archetypal and foundational figure of architecture in the age of digital pliancy. Yet, even cursory scrutiny of the essays and projects presented in this volume shows that digital technologies were but a marginal component of the critical discourse of the time. Likewise, most of the illustrations in this book feature strikingly angular, disjunctive forms. How can fractures, ridges and edges represent formal continuity? Where are the folds?

> The Formative Years: Philosophy, Flaccidity, and Infinity

At the beginning of the last decade of the century, architectural theory was busily discussing deconstructivism, and its eminently angular avatars in building. For reasons too long to explain, and perhaps inexplicable, American critical theory of the time was driving under the influence of some Parisian thinkers—some of them virtually ignored in their homeland. When Gilles Deleuze's impervious book on *The Fold, Leibniz and the Baroque* was first published in France in 1988, it failed to excite critical acclaim in the immediate surroundings of Boulevard Raspail.[4] Yet the Deleuzian fold was granted a second lease on life when Peter Eisenman—starting with the first publications on his Rebstock project in 1991—began to elaborate an architectural version of it.[5]

Deleuze's book was on Leibniz, on folds, on the baroque and on many other things as well. Most of it can be read as a vast hermeneutic of continuity which Deleuze applied to Leibniz's theory of ideas (including his notorious monadology), to Leibniz's mathematics (differential calculus in particular) and to various expressions of the baroque in the arts: the fold, a unifying figure whereby different segments and planes are joined and merge in continuous lines and volumes, is both the emblem and the object of Deleuze's discourse. Folds avoid fractures, overlay gaps, interpolate. Eisenman's reading of Deleuze's fold, in this early stage, retained and emphasized this notion of forms that can change, morph and move: a new category

---

Facing page

Figure 2.1: Cover of Folding in Architecture, AD, Revised Edition, 2004. Illustration: Peter Eisenman, Center for the Arts, Emory University, Atlanta, Concept Model. Image credit: Eisenman Architects. Photo credit: Cover image courtesy Eisenman Architects.

of objects defined not by what they are, but by the way they change and by the laws that describe their continuous variations. Eisenman also related this differential notion of objects to a new age of electronic technologies and digital images (with no reference, however, to computer-aided design: Eisenman's writings of the time frequently cite fax technology as the harbinger of a new paradigm of electronic reproducibility, alternative and opposed to all paradigms of the mechanical age and destined to obliterate the Benjaminian distinction between original and reproduction).[6]

Eisenman's essays prior to 1993 also bear witness to a significant topical shift which evolved from a closer, often literal interpretation of Deleuze's arguments (in 1991 Eisenman even borrowed Deleuze's notion of the "objectile," on which more will be said later),[7] to more architecturally inclined adaptations, including the use of René Thom's diagrams as design devices for generating architectural folds—a short circuit of sorts, as Thom's topological diagrams are themselves folds, and Thom actually itemized several categories of folding surfaces.[8] In his perhaps most accomplished essay on the matter, "Folding in Time", Eisenman dropped Deleuze's conception of the "objectile", which he replaced with the contiguous and also Deleuzian concept of "object-event": the breaking up of the Cartesian and perspectival grids of the classical tradition, prompted and promoted by the moving and morphing images of the digital age, requires architectural forms capable of continuous variation—forms that move in time.[9] Several stratagems, such as Thom's folding diagrams, may help to define them, but the "folding" process remains purely generative,[10] and it does not relate to the actual form of the end product. Forms do not fold (actually, in all Eisenman's projects featured in *Folding in Architecture* in 1993 they fracture and break), because most buildings do not move: when built, architectural forms can at best only represent, symbolize or somehow evoke the continuity of change or motion.

This stance of Eisenman's would be extensively glossed over, rephrased and reformulated in the years that followed,[11] but in the context it seems unequivocal: folding is a process, not a product; it does not necessarily produce visible folds (although it would later on); it is about creating built forms, necessarily motionless, which can nevertheless induce the perception of motion by suggesting the "continual variation" and "perpetual development" of a "form 'becoming'."[12] Again, art historians might relate such forms to a long tradition of expressionist design. Eisenman himself, at this early stage in the history of folding, defined folding as a "strategy for dislocating vision."[13]

In 1993, Lynn's prefatory essay to *Folding in Architecture* eloquently argued for continuities of all types: visual, programmatic, formal, technical, environmental, sociopolitical and symbolic. The list of suitable means to this end is also remarkably diverse: topological geometry, morphology, morphogenesis, Thom's catastrophe theory, Deleuze's theory of the fold and the "computer technology of both the defense and Hollywood film industry."[14] Nonetheless, a survey of the essays and projects featured in *Folding in Architecture* reveals some puzzling anomalies. Ten years later, many of the issues and topics that were so obviously prominent in 1993 seem to be accidental leftovers of a bygone era. Today, they simply don't register. In other cases, we can see why certain arguments were made—as we can see that from there, they led nowhere. Yet this panoply of curiosities and antiques also includes vivid anticipations of the future. That much can be said without risk, as a significant part of that future has already come to pass.

Were Henry Cobb's lanky and somewhat philistine skyscrapers the predecessors of many folds and blobs to come? How does a philosophical and almost ontological quest for continuity in motion and form relate to Chuck Hoberman's humungous mechanical contrivances: buildings that actually move with cranky hinges, sliding metal panels, pivoting bolts and rivets? Jules Verne would have loved them. Why include the translation of the first chapter of Deleuze's *The Fold*, an opaque and vaguely misleading tirade on the organic and the mechanical in the seventeenth-century philosophy of nature, and not the second chapter, on Leibniz's law of continuity, differential calculus and the mathematical definition of the fold? What do Bahram Shirdel's ridges and creases have in common with some of the earliest cucumiform epiphanies by Frank Gehry? The commentary blandly states that Gehry's irregular geometries were made possible "by 3-D computer modelling."[15] Digital technologies for design and manufacturing are mentioned by both Lynn and Kipnis as one tool among others that can help create "smooth transformations,"[16] but the one essay entirely devoted to computing, Stephen Perrella's, is on morphing and computer animation in the making of the movie *Terminator 2* (the film's special effects director is quoted as saying "we also used a programme called Photoshop").[17] Yet Lynn's presentation of Shoei Yoh's "topological" roof for the Odawara Sports Complex includes a stunningly perceptive analysis of the new tectonic, formal and economic potentials brought about by the merging of computerized design, construction and fabrication. To date, little more has been said on the topic, which remains a central issue of the now incessant debate on non-standard manufacturing.

The reason why some of the topics that emerged from the architectural discourse on folding of the early nineties now some seem so distant and outlandish, whereas others do not, is that something happened to separate them from us: a catastrophic event of sorts, a drastic environmental change followed by a typically Darwinian selection. As a result, many of these issues dropped out of sight. But those that remained thrived, and some were hugely magnified.

> Maturity: Mathematics, and the Digital Turn

Most architects in the early nineties knew that computers could easily join dots with segments. But as CAD software quickly evolved, the graphic capabilities and processing speed of the machines grew, and the price of the new technologies declined, it soon appeared that computers could just as easily connect dots with continuous lines, and sometimes even extrapolate mathematical functions from them. Conversely, given a mathematical function, computers can visualize an almost infinite family of curves that share the same algorithm, with parameters that can be changed at will. Smoothness, first defined as a visual category by theorists of the picturesque at the end of the eighteenth century, turned out also to be a mathematical function derived from standard differential calculus.[18] Topological surfaces and topological deformations are equally described by mathematical functions—a bit unwieldy perhaps for manual operations, but already in the mid-nineties well within the grasp of any moderately priced desktop computer.

In this context, it stands to reason that the original quest for ontological continuity in architectural form should take a new turn. Computers, mostly indifferent to queries on the nature of Being, can easily deliver tools for the manipulation of mathematical continuity. These could be directly applied to the conception, the representation and the production of objects. And they were. In the late nineties, Bernard Cache could conclude that "mathematics has effectively become an object of manufacture,"[19] and Greg Lynn remarked that computer-aided design had "allowed architects to explore calculus-based forms for the first time."[20] To a large extent, our calculus is still Leibniz's: Lynn also added that Leibniz's monads contained integrals and equations.[21] As Leibniz's monads famously had no windows, this is hard to prove. Yet at this point Lynn was getting significantly closer to Deleuzes's original reading of Leibniz.

The mathematical component of Deleuze's work on Leibniz, prominent but previously ignored, now sprang to the forefront—together with the realization that Leibniz's differential calculus was for the most part the language still underlying the families of continuous forms that computers could now so easily visualize and manipulate. Indeed, as Deleuze had remarked, Leibniz's mathematics of continuity introduced and expressed a new idea of the object: differential calculus does not describe objects, but their laws of change—their infinite, infinitesimal variations. Deleuze even introduced a new terminology for his new two-tiered definition of the object: he called "objectile" a function that virtually contains an infinite number of objects.[22] Each different and individual object eventualizes the mathematical algorithm, or objectile, common to all; in Aristotelian terms, as Leibniz might have used, an objectile is one form in many events. Deleuze's fold is itself a figure of differential calculus: it can be described geometrically as a point of inflection (the point that separates concavity and convexity in a curved line, or the point where the tangent crosses the line).[23] However, in good old calculus (as old as Leibniz, in fact), a point of inflection is in fact a maximum or a minimum in the first derivative of the function of the original curve. Deleuze mentions Bernard Cache with regard to both the mathematical definition of the fold and the concept of the objectile (which, however, he does not attribute to his gifted student).[24] Bernard Cache's essay, *Earth Moves*, where both notions are developed, did not appear in print until 1995—and in English. The original French manuscript is cited in the English version as having been drafted in 1983.[25]

So we see how an original quest for formal continuity in architecture, born in part as a reaction against the deconstructivist cult of the fracture, ran into the computer revolution of the mid-nineties and turned into a theory of mathematical continuity. By a quirk of history, a philosophical text by Gilles Deleuze accompanied, fertilized and at times catalyzed each of the different stages of this process. Without this preexisting pursuit of continuity in architectural forms and processes, of which the causes must be found in cultural and societal desires, computers in the nineties would most likely not have inspired any new geometry of forms. Likewise, without computers this cultural demand for continuity in the making of forms would soon have petered out and disappeared from our visual landscape. The story of folding, and in particular of the way folding went digital at a time when computers were becoming such a pivotal component of architectural design, once again suggests that only a dialectical interaction—a feedback loop of sorts—between technology and society can bring about technical and societal change: including, in this case, change in architectural form.

The notion of a direct causal correspondence between digital technologies and complex geometries (including the most general of all, topology) was built on a truism, but generalized into a fallacy. True, without computers some of those complex forms could not have been conceived, designed, measured, or built. However, computers per se do not impose shapes, nor do they articulate aesthetic preferences. One can use computers to design boxes or folds, indifferently. In fact, the story that we have been tracing indicates that the theory of folding created a cultural demand for digital design, and an environment conducive to it. Consequently, when digital design tools became available, they were embraced and adopted—and immediately put to use to process what computers in the nineties could do best and, coincidentally, what many architects at the time most needed and wanted: folds. If we look at *Folding in Architecture* now, we cannot fail to notice that digital technologies were then the main protagonist *in absentia*. Not surprisingly, they would not remain absent for long: computers are much better at generating folds than Thom's clumsy topological diagrams. In the process, folding evolved towards a *seconda maniera* of fully digital, smooth curvilinearity. Folds became blobs.[26]

> Senility? Technologists and Visionaries

As suggested above, *Folding in Architecture* contains the seeds of many developments that would mark the nineties, and issues that were prefigured there are still actively debated. As it now appears, mathematical continuity in design and in manufacturing can be the springboard for different and, in some cases, divergent endeavors. A continuous sequence of endless variations in time may be used to capture a still frame: a one-off, a synecdoche of sorts, which can be made to stand for the rest of the sequence, and evoke the invisible. This was Eisenman's stance ten years ago and, if the forms may have changed, the principles underpinning them have not. Eisenman's frozen forms were meant to suggest movement. Similar formal statements today—regardless of some rudimentary qualities of motion and interactivity that recent technologies can confer upon buildings—are more frequently read as metaphors or figurative reminders of the new modes of making things: they may give visible form to the mostly invisible logic at work, which in time will change our production and manufacturing techniques. Architects often prefigure technical change, and artistic invention may anticipate forth-coming techno-social conventions. Visionary anticipations of the future, digitally made environment were markedly smooth and curvilinear in the late nineties; and they may remain so for some time to come. Considering the technology for which they stand, this is not inappropriate: these technical objects should been seen as presentations, not as prototypes.

Yet, alongside this metaphor of technological change, which architectural invention may represent and even memorialize, real technological change is happening, although perhaps not so fast as the "irrational exuberance" of the late nineties may have led us to believe.[27] The new technological paradigm is also predicated upon continuous variations, but instead of producing one variance out of many, it posits that many variants may be produced simultaneously or sequentially. Thus, the same tools for processing mathematical continuity can be used to mass-produce the infinite variants of the same "objectile"—at no additional cost. Continuity in this case is not set in a chronological sequence, but in a manufacturing series. At a small scale, some such technologies already exist—they are in use and they produce things. How and when they might become relevant to the general process of building remains to be seen. When this happens, for the first time in the history of the machine-made environment, forms of all types (within the limits of the objectile/object paradigm) may be mass-produced on demand, indifferently, and at the same unit price. New, non-standard, custom-made and infinitely variable and adaptable forms will follow programs as never before. Better and cheaper objects and buildings will be made available to more people. And if this agenda may recall the moral ambitions of twentieth-century Modernism, the architectural forms that will come out of it will most certainly not.

In a coda to his brief presentation of Shoei Yoh's topological roofs, published in 1997 in an illustrated monograph of Yoh's work, Lynn extended his interpretation of Yoh's continuity of form obtained through a multiplicity of minor variations.[28] Yoh's structures can endlessly change, morph and adapt as they are built by the assembly of non-standard parts. Let's compare with the most eloquent example of the opposite: in any given structure, whether horizontal or vertical, Mies's I-beams were all the same size, regardless of load; hence, as many engineers are keen to point out, if one section fits the load, then all others are by necessity oversized. In contrast, each individual component in Yoh's 3-D latticed trusses is only as big as it needs to be. At

Mies's time, the waste of building materials caused by oversizing might have been compensated by the economies of scale obtained trough the mass production of identical parts: one doubts that this argument might have ever been prominent in Mies's mind, but Mies's aesthetics to some extent sublimated that technical condition. Today, digital file-to-factory production systems can generate the same economies of scale with no need to mass-produce identical beams: beams can be all different—within some limits—and still be mass-produced. Economies of scale can thus be compounded by a more economical use of materials.

As Lynn points out, Yoh's use of advanced technologies and off-site prefabrication is paralleled by his adaptation of traditional building materials and artisanal modes of production. For example, some of Yoh's buildings use wood or bamboo frames and match local building know-how with computer-based design technologies. Although Yoh himself never seems to have investigated the theoretical implications of this practice, the alliance between artisanal (pre-mechanical) and digital (post-mechanical) technologies is based on solid facts and figures. The artisanal mode of production is mostly foreign to economies of scale: two thousand identical Doric capitals, or two thousand variations of the same Doric capital, come at the same unit price, as each capital is handmade. In the digital mode, industrial economies of scale are obtained regardless of product standardization. In both cases, the result is the same: identical reproduction has no technical rationale, nor any economic justification. When pursued manually or digitally, standardization does not generate cheaper products, nor better built ones. Of course one may cherish identicality for a number of other reasons, unrelated to cost or functioning. But let's put it another way. There was a time when identical reproduction, or standardization, was eminently justified: the more identical pieces one could make, the less their unit cost would be. Standardization was then an inescapable moral and social imperative. This age of the industrial standard began with the mechanical phase of the Industrial Revolution—and ended with it.

However, as it happens, the end of the mechanical era has been proclaimed on many occasions. One of the most propitious times to proclaim the end of the first machine age was in the early thirties of the last century, and with some logic: in 1929 the machine age seemed to have imploded—spontaneously, so to speak: a sudden but natural death. In *Technics and Civilization*, first published in 1934, Lewis Mumford disparaged all that had gone wrong with the machine age that had just crashed, which he characterized as "paleotechnic," and heralded an imminent golden age of new machines, the "neotechnic" age, where the evil machines of old would be replaced by new and better ones, not hard but soft machines—organic instruments of a new biotechnic economy, where man would no longer be obliged to adapt itself to the mechanical rhythm of the machine, but machines would learn to adapt themselves to the dynamic flow of organic life.[29] Mumford's discourse was tantalizingly self-contradictory and included streaks of viscerally anti-modern propaganda, but in writing of an age of new machines, "smaller, faster, brainer [sic], and more adaptable" than those of the earlier mechanical age, he seems even more than a preacher—he sounds prophetic.[30] Around the same time, Frank Lloyd Wright—then almost on the same wavelength as Mumford, and probably inspired by him—presented his anti-European blueprint for a "disappeared city," and insisted that the industrialization of building need not result in the standardization of form: all buildings should be machine-made, but no two homes need be alike.[31]

In 1932 and 1934, respectively, Wright and Mumford were probably running a little ahead of the technology of their time. Yet it is one of the most significant legacies of the publication of *Folding in Architecture* that, since 1993, we have no reason not to be aware that this time around, non-standard production has opened for business and is here to stay.

1   *Folding in Architecture*, Greg Lynn (ed), *Architectural Design*, Profile 102, 63, 3–4 (1993).

2   In his *Principles of Art History*, first published in 1915, the historian and philosopher of art Heinrich Wölfflin defended a cyclical view of the evolution of man-made forms, which swing from classical sobriety to Baroque fancifulness, then back to reason and so on ad infinitum. Wölfflin never characterised the Baroque, either the time specific or the timeless version of it, as an age of decline or degeneracy. Instead, he used sets of oppositions (linear and painterly, plane and recession, closed and open form, etc) through which he defined classical and Baroque phases. Heinrich Wölfflin, *Kunstgeschichtliche Grundbegriffe* (1915); English translation: *Principles of Art History*, trans MD Hottinger from seventh revised German edition (1929), G Bell and Sons (London), 1932, pp 230–5. See also Michael Podro, *The Critical Historians of Art*, Yale University Press (New Haven and London), 1982, p 140.

3   Luis Fernández-Galiano has compared the 'sharp folds of the F-117 Nighthawk Lockheed's stealth fighter' and the 'undulating profile' of the later B-2 stealth fighter made by Northrop Grumman, considering the former as representative of the 'fractured forms of deconstructivism that initiated the nineties under the wings of Derrida', and the latter as representative 'of the warped volumes of the formless current that are wrapping up the decade, referring back to Deleuze or Bataille'. Luis Fernández-Galiano, 'Split-screen. La décennie numérique', *Architecture d'Aujourd'hui*, no 325 (December 1999), pp 28–31: 30. Oddly, the technical specifications – aerodynamics and the avoidance of radar detection – would have been the same for both of these fighter planes. As architectural curvilinearity has been conspicuously ebbing and flowing in recent times, the rise of architectural flaccidity in the digital environment of the late 1990s has prompted a critical reassessment of antecedents, including some that had been overlooked until very recently. For a thorough survey of preblob, space-age ovoids in the 1960s and their biomorphic and technological underpinnings (mostly related to the development of plastics technology) see Georges Teyssot, 'Le songe d'un environnement bioréaliste. Ovoïdes et sphéroïdes dans l'architecture des années soixante' in *Architectures expérimentales, 1950–2000*, Collection du FRAC Centre, Éditions HYX (Orléans), 2003, pp 39–43.

4   Gilles Deleuze, *Le pli: Leibniz et le baroque*, Éditions de Minuit (Paris), 1988; English translation: *The Fold: Leibniz and the Baroque*, foreword and translation by Tom Conley, University of Minnesota Press (Minneapolis), 1993.

5   Peter D Eisenman, 'Unfolding Events: Frankfurt Rebstock and the Possibility of a New Urbanism' in Eisenman Architects, Albert Speer and Partners and Hanna/Olin, *Unfolding Frankfurt*, Ernst and Sohn (Berlin), 1991, pp 8–18; 'Oltre lo sguardo. L'architettura nell'epoca dei media elettronici' (Visions' Unfolding: Architecture in the Age of

Electronic Media), *Domus*, no 734 (January 1992), pp 17–24 (frequently reprinted, most recently in Luca Galofaro, *Digital Eisenman: An Office of the Electronic Era*, Birkhauser (Basel), 1999, pp 84–9; and 'Folding in Time: The Singularity of Rebstock', *Folding in Architecture* (1993), pp 22–6.

6   See in particular Eisenman, 'Unfolding Events', p 9; 'Visions' Unfolding' (1992), p 21; and 'Folding in Time' (1993), p 24.

7   Eisenman, 'Unfolding Events', p 14.

8   Greg Lynn, 'Architectural Curvilinearity: The Folded, the Pliant and the Supple', *Folding in Architecture* (1993), pp 8–15. See in particular p 13 on 'the catastrophe diagram used by Eisenman in the Rebstock Park project . . . by Kipnis in the Briey project, and Shirdel in the Nara Convention Hall'.

9   Deleuze 'argues that in the mathematical studies of variation, the notion of object is change. This new object for Deleuze is no longer concerned with the framing of space, but rather a temporal modulation that implies a continual variation of matter. . . . No longer is an object defined by an essential form. He calls this idea of an object, an "object event". The idea of event is critical to the discussion of singularity. Event proposes a different kind of time which is outside of narrative time or dialectical time.' Eisenman, 'Folding in Time' (1993), p 24.

10   'These typologies, introduced into the system of the Fold, allow the Fold to reveal itself; the folding apparatus is invisible, purely a conceptual drawing, until it is activated by something cast into it.' Eisenman, 'Unfolding Events', p 16.

11   For a recapitulation of this discussion in essays by Michael Speaks, Greg Lynn, Jeffrey Kipnis and Brian Massumi, see Giuseppa di Cristina, 'The Topological Tendency in Architecture' in *Architecture and Science*, Wiley-Academy (London), 2001, pp 6–14, in particular p 10 and footnotes 15–18; Michael Speaks, 'It's Out There . . . The Formal Limits of the American Avant-garde', Hypersurface Architecture, Stephen Perella (ed), *Architectural Design*, Profile 133, 68, 5–6 (1998), pp 26–31, in particular p 29: 'Why does [Lynn's] architecture not move? . . . Why does his architecture stop moving when it is no longer design technique and becomes architecture?'

12   Eisenman, 'Alteka Office Building', *Folding in Architecture* (1993), p 28.

13   'Folding is only one of perhaps many strategies for dislocating vision.' Eisenman, 'Visions' Unfolding', (1992), p 24.

14   Lynn, 'Architectural Curvilinearity', p 8.

15   Frank Gehry and Philip Johnson, 'Lewis Residence, Cleveland, Ohio', *Folding in Architecture* (1993), p 69.

16   Lynn, 'Architectural Curvilinearity', p 12; Jeffrey Kipnis, 'Towards a New Architecture', *Folding in Architecture* (1993), pp 40–9: 47.

17   Stephen Perrella, 'Interview with Mark Dippe. Terminator 2', *Folding in Architecture* (1993), pp 90–93: 93.

18   See in particular Edmund Burke, *Philosophical Enquiry* (1757); William Gilpin, *Observations . . . relative chiefly to picturesque beauty* (1782) and *Three essays: On picturesque beauty; On picturesque travel; and On sketching landscape: to which is added a poem On landscape painting* (1792). In mathematical terms, the quality of smoothness of a line or surface is defined by the function that designates the angular coefficients of the tangents to each point of it (that is, by the first derivative of the function that describes the original line or surface).

19   Bernard Cache, 'Objectile. The Pursuit of Philosophy by Other Means', Hypersurface Architecture II, Stephen Perella (ed), *Architectural Design*, Profile 141, 69, 9–10 (1999), pp 67–71: 67.

20   For centuries, architects had been drawing with algebra, but now, 'CAD software enables architects to draw and sketch using calculus' Greg Lynn, *Animate Form*, Princeton Architectural Press (New York), 1999, pp 16–18.

21   Lynn, Animate Form, pp 15–16.

22   Deleuze, *Le pli*, p 26.

23   Deleuze, *Le pli*, pp 20–5.

24   Deleuze, *Le pli*, pp 22, 26.
25   Bernard Cache, *Earth Moves. The Furnishing of Territories*, transl. by Anne Boyman, ed.
     by Michael Speaks, MIT Press (Cambridge MA and London), 1995, p iii.
26   The official date of birth of architectural blobs (of blobs defined as such) appears
     to be May 1996. See Greg Lynn, 'Blobs (or Why Tectonics is Square and Topology is
     Groovy)', ANY 14 (May 1996), pp 58–62. For a survey of blob developments in the late
     1990s see Peter Cachola Schmal (ed), *Digital Real. Blobmeister: erste gebaute Projecte*,
     Birkhäuser (Basel), 2001. On the early history of space-age ovoids in the1960s, and the
     eponymous film that popularised the blob in 1958, see Georges Teyssot, 'Le songe d'un
     environnement bioréaliste', p 40.
27   See Mario Carpo, 'Post-Hype Digital Architecture. From Irrational Exuberance to
     Irrational Despondency', *Grey Room* 14, No 14, 2004 102–115.
28   'In all of these [Shoei Yoh's] projects there is a response to the shift in the economies
     and techniques of construction from one of assembly-line production of a standard
     to the assembly-like production of a series of singular units. These projects articu-
     late an approach to standardisation and repetition that combines a generic system
     of construction with slight variations of each member. This attribute is reminiscent
     of historic methods of craftmanship where every element could be generic in some
     regard while given a distinct identity in each instance . . . Through both manual
     construction and industrial fabrication [these projects] exploit the economy of what
     is often referred to as "custom assembly-line production".' Greg Lynn, 'Classicism and
     Vitality' in Anthony Iannacci (ed) *Shoei Yoh*, L'Arca Edisioni (Milan), 1997, pp 13–16: 15.
     See also Lynn's 'Odawara Municipal Sports Complex' in *Shoei Yoh*, pp 67–70; and 'Shoei
     Yoh, Odawara Municipal Sports Complex', *Folding in Architecture* (1993), p 79.
29   Lewis Mumford, *Technics and Civilization*, George Routledge and Sons (London) and
     Harcourt, Brace and Co (New York), 1934, especially Chapter VIII, sections 1 ('The
     Dissolution of "The Machine"') and 2 ('Toward an Organic Ideology'), pp 364–72.
30   'In the very act of enlarging its dominion over human thought and practice, the
     machine [Mumford here means the earlier, 'paleotechnic' machine] has proved to a
     great degree self-eliminating . . . This fact is fortunate for the race. It will do away
     with the necessity, which Samuel Butler satirically pictured in Erewhon, for force-
     fully extirpating the dangerous troglodytes of the earlier mechanical age. The old
     machines will in part die out, as the great saurians died out, to be replaced by smaller,
     faster, brainer [sic], and more adaptable organisms, adapted not to the mine, the
     battlefield and the factory, but to the positive environment of life.' Mumford, *Technics
     and Civilization*, p 428.
31   Frank Lloyd Wright, *The Disappearing City*, William Farquhar Payson (New York), 1932,
     pp 34, 45.

What is digital architecture? Is it legitimate to apply the term to any design made with the assistance of a computer, or should it be reserved to productions that put to real use the capacity of the machine to be more than a drawing tool? For the past ten to fifteen years, in order to distinguish the term from the rapidly increasing use of computer-aided design, digital architecture has been often characterized by an experimental dimension more pronounced than in mainstream production. As a result, there has been a tendency to confuse digital and experimental. Because of this tendency, noticeable in exhibitions like ArchiLab or the Venice Biennale, many innovative practices that undoubtedly belonged to the latter category have been deemed digital.[1] But if the term is certainly appropriate for the productions of designers like Ali Rahim, Benjamin Aranda and Christopher Lasch, who rely heavily on the computer, does it truly capture what is arresting with the projects of Preston Scott Cohen or Jesse Reiser? Is it appropriate to interpret recent features of Jacques Herzog and Pierre de Meuron's architecture, like the accent put on surface and ornament, in relation to the rise of digital culture? The vagueness of the term has been further increased by the series of offices that have pioneered the use of computer-aided design, where the senior partners have little actual familiarity with the machine. In these offices, programs are usually run by younger designers who have benefited from an early exposure to computer culture. To what extent is their production, which closely follows the intuitions and ideas of their employers, really digital? The question has been raised by the architecture of Frank Gehry. In Gehry's office, the use of Catia (Computer-Aided Three-Dimensional Interactive Application) CAD software remains external to the core of a highly personal design process that relies on traditional means like sketches, cardboard and wood models.[2]

However, the ambiguity is not as problematic as it might appear at first glance. As we have stressed it, digital architecture, in the narrow sense of a production using the computer in an experimental perspective, is inseparable from broader trends at work in the contemporary architectural world. Because they express some of these trends with a special clarity, Cohen, Reiser, but also Herzog & de Meuron have their full place in the discussion of what digital architecture is about. As for the argument based on the generation gap between architects trained before and after the spread of digital tools, its relevance is undermined by the enduring character of the relation between architecture and computer culture. For almost half a century, this connection has influenced theorists and practitioners beyond the mere use of software.

Despite the diversity of research directions revealed by this half-a-century-long history, the architectural uses of the computer

3

The Seduction of Innovative Geometries

Antoine Picon

Figure 3.1

in an experimental perspective have generally privileged form: the investigation of shapes in complete contrast with the limited vocabulary of modern architecture. The result has been a proliferation of alternative geometries that are calling for new criteria of evaluation. However, this focus on form should not lead to the reduction of the quest to a mere stylistic obsession. As we will see throughout this chapter, digital architecture's formalist orientation is inseparable from a series of broader concerns, like the ambition to be in tune with the general march of the world's economy. Above all, formalism is to be understood here as synonymous with an inquiry regarding the mechanisms of formation, or to put it like Sanford Kwinter, "the processes by which discernible patterns come to dissociate themselves from a less finely-ordered field."[3] The desire to understand form in terms of formation is one of the reasons for the attention that digital architects pay to recent scientific developments, for instance in dynamic systems theory or genetics that put an emphasis on the property of emergence conceived as a capacity of auto-organization at work throughout nature.

In the long history of the connections between digital culture and architecture, the postmodern turning point with its formalist dimension stands clearly as a key to present developments. Taking up Robert Venturi's appeal to complexity and contradiction exposed in his 1966 eponymous essay,[4] postmodernism proper was followed by a deconstructionist phase in which architectural form was meant to express the conflicting logics of its surroundings by resorting to heterogeneity and fragmentation. Completed in 1989, Peter Eisenman's Wexner Center in Columbus, Ohio, was in that respect one of the most paradigmatic projects of the time with its colliding grids. Although the smooth forms of contemporary digital architecture are in complete contrast with deconstructionist violence, they have inherited from them the project to address with lucidity heterogeneous and often conflicting conditions.

Typical forms of digital architecture are, above all, indebted to the reaction against deconstruction that arose in the early 1990s. One of the most telling episodes of this reaction was the enthusiasm for folding – understood sometimes literally, most of the time as a metaphor – that characterized a whole range of architectural productions around that period, especially in the United States. The use of the term was triggered by the translation of French philosopher Gilles Deleuze's essay, *Le Pli (The fold)*, into English.[5] A study of Leibniz's metaphysics, *The Fold* insisted on one of its aspects: the possibility to envisage complexity in other terms than discontinuity and frontal collision. For architects like Peter Eisenman, the book opened new perspectives on the question of complexity. These perspectives were theorized in an influential collection of essays edited by Greg Lynn. Published in

---

Facing page

Figure 3.1: "'Lightfall', Herta and Paul Amir Wing, Tel Aviv Museum of Art, Preston Scott Cohen, Architect. Image credit: Courtesy of the office of Preston Scott Cohen.

1993 as a special issue of *Architectural Design,* "Folding in Architecture" suggested an alternative to deconstruction and its cult of fracture based, to use one of Lynn's expressions, on "smooth transformation involving the intensive integration of differences within a continuous yet heterogeneous system."[6] Advocating curvilinearity, pliancy, gentle blending and of course folding, Lynn's prose was evocative of the geometric developments that would soon follow using the computer. Interestingly, computers remained marginal among the sources of inspiration he evoked such as topological geometry, morphology and catastrophe theory. They were only mentioned en passant, dealing with the defense industry and Hollywood's early morphing effects. Thus, the folding trend was announcing the formal investigations of digital architecture while remaining extraneous to early computer-aided architectural experiments. There is perhaps no better illustration of the necessity to interpret digital design within the broader frame of contemporary architectural evolution than this convergence that technology cannot explain by itself. As historian Mario Carpo puts it in his retrospective assessment of the episode, "computers *per se* do not impose shapes, nor do they articulate aesthetic preferences. One can use computers to design boxes or folds, indifferently."[7]

Although in his introduction to "Folding in Architecture", he insisted on the potential of the new approach to deal more efficiently with increasingly conflicted urban and cultural contexts, Lynn mostly retained the possibility to chart a new formal territory marked by continuity and smooth transitions. From the mid-1990s on, the computer became an essential tool in this exploration. Lynn himself soon became an enthusiastic proponent of the machine and one of the most influential theorists of the new design principles it seemed conducive to.

Based on continuity, these principles were at odds with the common perception of the digital as fundamentally discontinuous. More generally, digital architecture is often based on an idiosyncratic interpretation of the scientific and technological principles it claims as a source of inspiration. Its use of topology represents another instance of this idiosyncratic interpretation. Whereas for mathematicians topology corresponds first and foremost to the study of invariants, architects tend to give precedence to the geometric discontinuities it reveals. In other words, for designers invariance does not matter so much as dramatic change. There is perhaps no better illustration of the autonomy of digital design vis-à-vis the scientific and technological principles and tools it uses, beginning with the computer, than this type of divergence.

The machine has been nevertheless instrumental in the direction taken by digital architecture. Since the early developments of computer-aided design, all sorts of new and spectacular forms have appeared on screens. Some of these forms have even begun to transform the built environment. Among them, a special mention must be made of the smooth volumes, strongly reminiscent of organic life, that have appeared in the wake of the orientations pointed out in "Folding in Architecture". To designate them,

Greg Lynn coined the term "blob", the acronym for Binary Large Object.[8] If the name was supposed to be merely technical, a direct reference to Blob modeling, a module in the Wavefront software used by the architect, it was subsequently often interpreted in relation to the 1958 eponymous film in which an amoeba-like alien made of a gelatinous substance terrorizes a small American town.[9] Between technicality and monstrosity, the term reflected the ambivalent reception that computer-produced forms encountered among architects, beyond the small numbers involved in their early exploration. Visually unsettling for eyes trained in the appreciation of modern architectural vocabulary, they could indeed appear as the result of an outré cult for the new and trendy. Despite this mixed reception, blobs rapidly became a built reality. Revealingly, blob architecture associated young Turks of digital design like Lars Spuybroek with historical figures of the 1960s and 1970s experimental architecture such as Peter Cook, a former Archigram member, or Jan Kaplický of Future Systems.[10] Spuybroek's studio, Nox, opened the way with its 1993–1997 Water Pavilion. A few years later, Cook and Kaplický gave prototypical examples of blob architecture with the Kunsthaus of Graz and the Selfridges Department Store in Birmingham. That the blob trend was so easily adopted by Cook or Kaplický is telling of how, beyond the postmodern and folding episodes, digital architecture inherited from the researches of former experimental architecture, beginning with Archigram's various pods and bubbles.

Blobs were not the only direction taken by digital architecture, far from it. For a start, they were part of a broader inquiry regarding the topological properties of surfaces and volumes and their link to geometric operations that could be modeled on the computer. Of special appeal were in that respect those topological singularities which René Thom had called catastrophes.[11] As geometric analogues to events, they seemed to translate time into space while challenging some fundamental assumptions regarding the latter. The Moebius strip and the Klein bottle questioned for instance the boundary between exterior and interior and more generally the notion of clear-cut thresholds between spatial and functional sequences. Whereas blob architecture has stalled in recent years for reasons we will evoke later in this chapter, these singularities have retained their appeal. Ben van Berkel and Caroline Bos' 1998 Moebius House is echoed by the recently completed Klein Bottle House of the Australian practice McBride Charles Ryan.

Moreover, just like folding, the smoothness that digital designers were looking for could be understood either literally or metaphorically. Taking it metaphorically allowed for a broader range of shapes than the amoeba-like blobs. Hence the presence of projects that did not look smooth at all with their angular, almost deconstructionist features, like Michele Saee's early production. However, like blobs, they contrasted with mainstream geometry, thus reinforcing the tendency to confuse digital and experimental.

The development of digital architecture has undoubtedly benefited from the seduction exerted by forms that were impossible to obtain using prior design tools. Until the early 1990s, sophisticated geometric researches were generally synonymous with the presence of paraboloids or hyperboloids, like those used for concrete shells or tensile structures, or with the smooth but loosely defined forms of plastic casts and pneumatic structures.[12] The spread of the computer has changed that, allowing digital architects to expand dramatically the range of their formal vocabulary. What is new is not only the variety of the shapes themselves, but also the possibility to define them rigorously using computer modeling.

This change is inseparable from the development of a wide array of geometric modeling techniques. Beside wire frame and solid modeling, a special mention must be made of NURBS – the acronym for Non-Uniform Rational B-Splines – that are available in software like Maya or Rhino. More than other techniques, they allow designers to interact with curves, surfaces and volumes in a highly intuitive way, to produce and visualize complex deformations as easily as if they were compressing, elongating, twisting or pinching real objects in space. In this regard, despite their limitations, NURBS are emblematic of the creative space opened up by modeling.

Even more emblematic is the recent development of parametric design that coordinates the different aspects of a project so that all sorts of modifications become easy, even with an extremely intricate geometry. In a presentation given for the 2008 Venice Biennale, Patrik Schumacher, partner at Zaha Hadid Architects, hailed what he called "parametricism" as the new defining moment for architecture enabling designers to reach a complete fluidity at all stages and all scales, from initial sketches to construction, from single building to major urban compositions.[13] If such a vision is certainly simplistic insofar that it minimizes the various technological and economic obstacles that designers have still to address in their everyday practice, parametric design makes nevertheless geometric complexity manageable.

If "computers *per se* do not impose shapes", they have certainly contributed to broaden the range of possibilities offered to designers. On a stylistic standpoint, the consequence of this freedom has been often assimilated to a new baroque condition because of the dynamic appearance of projects and the importance taken by deformations. Indeed, many projects suggest the idea of a frozen flow or wave somewhat reminiscent of the undulations of Bernini's or Borromini's walls. At different scales, from the modesty of the Water Garden for Jeffrey Kipnis's house in Columbus to the gigantic West Side competition entry for New York, the architecture of Jesse Reiser and Nakano Umemoto provides various examples of the frozen flow concept. Other digital productions are more reminiscent of the complex, almost fractal play of volumes and light in Guarini's cupolas. Daniel Libeskind's extension to the Victoria and Albert Museum in London suggests a similar play. Presented by its author as an investigation using Leibniz as a key to gain access to some fundamental structures of baroque metaphysics and culture, Gilles Deleuze's analysis of the fold has added another layer to the analogy. Claiming inspiration from the philosopher, folded and fractal surfaces have been interpreted not only as distant cousins of baroque undulations but as expressions of an intellectual kinship based on notions such as complexity, multiplicity and movement. For a designer like Preston Scott Cohen, the relation to the spirit of mannerism and baroque follows, however, a totally different path based on the use of sophisticated projective geometry and on the interest taken in optical constructions like anamorphoses.[14] Despite the prevalence of Deleuze-based readings, there are various ways to relate digital architecture to baroque today. But the parallel, as we will see in a moment, must not be taken too far, for significant differences remain between the baroque approach to Form finding and the morphological explorations that are currently going on.

1   See for instance Marie-Ange Brayer, Frédéric Migayrou (eds.), ArchiLab. Orléans 1999 *(Orléans: Mairie d'Orléans, 1999),* and more volumes of the yearly meeting in Orléans; Kurt Forster (ed.), Metamorph 9. International Architecture Exhibition *(*Venice: Fondazione La Biennale di Venezia, 2004).
2   Cf. Bruce Lindsey, *Digital Gehry* (Basel, Berlin, Boston: Birkhäuser. 2001).
3   Sanford Kwinter, *Far from Equilibrium. Essays on Technology and Design Culture* (Barcelona, New York: Actar, 2008), p. 146.
4   Robert Venturi, *Complexity and Contradiction in Architecture* (New York: Museum of Modern Art, 1966).
5   Gilles Deleuze, *The Fold: Leibniz and the Baroque* (Paris: 1988, English translation Minneapolis: University of Minnesota Press, 1993).
6   Greg Lynn, "Architectural Curvilinearity: The Folded, the Pliant and the Supple", in Greg Lynn (ed.), *Folding in Architecture,* Architectural Design (London: 1993, revised edition London: Wiley-Academy, 2004), pp. 24–31, p. 24 in particular.
7   Mario Carpo, "Ten Years of Folding", in *Folding in Architecture,* pp. 14–19, p. 16 in particular.
8   See for instance Greg Lynn, *Folds, Bodies & Blobs: Collected Essays* (Brussels: La Lettre Volée, 1998).
9   Irvin Yeaworth (director), *The Blob,* 1958. On the connection with early digital architecture, see John K. Waters, *Blobitecture: Waveform Architecture and Digital Design* (Gloucester, Massachusetts: Rockport Publishers, 2003), pp. 8–11 in particular.
10 The notion of experimental architecture was formalized by Peter Cook in his book *Experimental Architecture* (New York: Universe Books, 1970).
11 René Thom, *Mathematical Models of Morphogenesis* (Paris: 1974, English translation New York: Halsted Press, 1983).
12 Cf. Antoine Picon (ed.), *L'Art de l'Ingénieur: Entrepreneur, Constructeur, Inventeur* (Paris: Centre Georges Pompidou, Le Moniteur, 1997).
13 Patrik Schumacher, *"Parametricism as Style – Parametritist Manifesto",* 2008, http://www.patrikschumacher.com/Texts/Parametricism%20as%20Style.htm (visited on 20 January 2009).
14 Preston Scott Cohen, *Contested Symmetries and Other Predicaments in Architecture* (New York: Princeton Architectural Press, 2001).

FORM

From
Composition to
Generation

Rivka Oxman
and
Robert Oxman

Traditional architectural logic defines architectural form as "the shape or morphology of building; it is the configuration of its physical matter, apart from its actual material properties" (McLeod, 2003, p. 50). The traditionally configurative nature of form and space representation has now become procedural and generative in emphasis. Beyond the consideration of form as formal composition, *form-generation procedures* now frequently precede and underlie spatial configuration.

This shift from the spatial/configurative definition of form and formal knowledge to the material/procedural definition of the sources of form generation in architecture may be seen, for example, in FOA's approach to the "breeding of architecture" (Zaero-Polo, 2003, p. 56). "For me, the real essence of the practice of architecture is the process of organizing materials in such a way that the form and program of a building become consistent. . . . Architectural types are assemblages of form and program." Further, with respect to design as form generative processes, he states, "A coherent practice might emerge from a phylogenetic process in which a few seeds proliferate across different environments over time, generating distinct yet consistent results." This conception of design knowledge postulates "a consistent reservoir of architectural species that will proliferate, mutate and evolve in the years to come." Such "seeds" are now beginning to establish the knowledge base of digital processes of formation and generation.

With respect to *design generation*, Kwinter (1994, pp. 96–97) distinguishes *formalism* in design similar to the definition generally given in science as:

> the mechanisms of *formation* . . . the processes by which discernible patterns come to dissociate themselves from a less finely-ordered field. . . . What I call true formalism refers to any method that diagrams the proliferation of fundamental resonances and demonstrates how these accumulate into figures of order and shape.

So the interpretation of formalism is *procedural*. Zaero-Polo's phylogenetic interpretation of architectural *formal types* as *generative orders* is an example of the genetic seeds bearing their own generative formalisms. These two components – the *genetic matter of generation* in combination with *algorithmic processes* – are the foundations of form generation in digital design.

Underlying the transition to generative processes has been the growth of geometric empowering that has derived from the technical evolution of late-generation calculus-based (NURBS-based) modeling systems. With the emergence in the nineties of powerful and popular design modeling systems and their later evolution to parametric systems in the last decade this has established the preconditions for the broad design cultural developments of the last half decade.

The earliest theoretical explication of the future of architectural design media and their implications for the revolutionary change of the formal vocabulary of architecture as well as the transformation of the nature of architectural designing can be found in the early writings of Greg Lynn published between 1992 and 1996. Lynn in *Greg Lynn: Folds, Bodies and Blobs: Collected Essays* (1998) transitions between the exhilaration of the new geometric and formal potential and the formally dominated discourse of a prior generation. This cultural ambivalence ends with *Animate Form* (1999) which is a theoretical treatise that attempts to project both the alignment of the theory and form of a new architecture as well as to elucidate theoretically the architectural formal implications of the new media.

While there is a strong residue of geometric exhilaration for the curvilinear in this work, it is, however, the most prescient statement of the changed orientation of procedural design and the revolutionary transformations that it is capable of producing. *Animate Form* postulates form generation with architecture as "the co-presence of motion and force at the moment of formal conception . . . and as a participant immersed within dynamic flows."(Lynn, 1999, p. 11.) Architecture has departed from an age of autonomous purity to one of contextual specificity. Animated architecture is not dynamic, but rather the product of a virtual dynamism in which there is continuous temporal change through multiple states. Thus the nature of generation involves the *trace* of becoming in a sequenced serial process. Conceiving of a field of context containing time, motion and force, design is creation within "a numerically controlled multi-type that is flexible, mutable and differential." (Lynn, 1999, p. 13.)

This condition of the continuity of *evolutionary form* may be seen as a series of multiple states created by the computational properties of topology, time and parameters. *Continuity, mutability* and *differentiation* are the three attributes of animation as a model of *computational design generation*. From the point of view of a new method of becoming that is unique, *multiplicity* becomes a key concept. "A multiplicity is neither one nor many, but a continuous assemblage of *heterogeneous singularities* that exhibits both collective qualities of continuity and local qualities of heterogeneity" (Lynn, 1999, p. 23).

Architecture's new digital media changed the way that architects thought and designed, changed the interpretation of architectural form both geometrically and with respect to topological design, and transformed many of the root concepts of Modernist architectural thinking such as endless space to concepts such as *continuous evolution* or *multiplicitous creativity*.

Shelden and Witt (2011) point to the last half decade as the site of the emergence of a radical expansion of the potential vocabularies of architectural form due to the discovery of new geometries. Prominent among these developments are the culture-changing potential inherent in *procedural logics* and *parametric associative geometries*. While recognizing and explicating these new geometric systems and their architectural potential, they transcend the purely geometric to link the procedural logic to an emerging ontology of architectural form that might link form to material to fabrication in an *informed topology*. They state this potential future as follows: "What we need are richer descriptions of topology that embed also implicit logics of construction and concurrent local discretization that emerge organically from the global typology itself" (p. 40).

The broad professional dissemination of *parametric systems* as design environments is a phenomenon of the past decade with software such as *GenerativeComponents* introduced in 2003 and *Grasshopper* more recently. *Associative modeling* of *parametric schema* has become a frequently employed model of design and a medium for generation and test procedures particularly in performative design (see Bollinger, Grohmann and Tessmann; and Whitehead, both in this volume). The *Smartgeometry* series of annual conferences has been instrumental in the teaching and dissemination of these models of design.

Parametric design has been so productive for architectural research and design that it is now possible to speak of *parametric form*, or the formal attributes intrinsic to form generation and management with parameters. Parametric form is characterized by *variability, continuity* and the potential for local *differentiation*. Variability is a general attribute of parametric control and modulation. The algorithmic production of variability is responsible for those *parametric propagation processes* so effectively employed in research-based practices. See, for example, Whitehead, this volume.

The complex curvilinear and undulating surfaces of projects such as the *Aegis Hyposurface* (Goulthorpe, 2008) enable both the geometric complexity of surfaces and volumes. Lynn (2003) has developed a theory of *intricacy* as a generative property rather than a formal attribute. According to Lynn, "Intricacy's visual sensibility emerges from technique rather than figuration or content." It produces a monolithic complexity of continuous form that includes "compositional practices of weaving folding and joining." This would include contemporary experimental work on *aggregates* and *assemblages* and on *self-organizing systems* in what Lynn terms "the logic of fused ecologies."

One of the most distinctive phenomena associated with parametric design is the potential for local or global *differentiation* (Mertins, 2003). Differentiation is the result of a "deterritorialization" that "corrodes sameness and promotes difference." Schumacher (this volume) has employed the term *parametricism* to connote *differentiation* processes such as gradients within the tectonic patterns of architectural systems and the urban fabric of urban systems.

The pairing of theory and form is an essential dualism in design generation. The creative multiplicity of parametric design environments is such that technology may be seen to be emerging as a generator of design theory. Six models of digital design theory and computational methods are presented below that have emerged as dominant models of form generation.

Mathematical Form Generation is the exploitation of mathematical formulae as the basis of generative procedures. Such was the design process of the *WaterCube*, the National Swimming Center built for the 2008 Beijing Olympics. The *WaterCube* is based upon the Weaire-Phelan foam geometry of repeating polyhedra. This is a mathematical model of the natural phenomenon of soap-bubble formation. In this case the model was employed to produce the continuous structural envelope and enclosure system. See Burry and Burry (2010) for this and other case studies.

Tectonic Form Generation is closely related to mathematical generation. It employs *tectonic pattern* as the basis for form generation. Both of these methods of form generation are frequently employed in the work of the Advanced Geometry Unit (AGU) of Arup. These methods were developed and exploited in the 2002 Serpentine Pavilion in London by Toyo Ito and Cecil Balmond, as well as the Serpentine Pavilion, 2005 by Alvaro Siza, Edouardo Souto de Moura and Cecil Balmond. For these and other case studies in tectonic generation and parametric/algorithmic architecture, see Sakamoto and Ferré (2008); Leach, Turnbull and Williams (2004).

Material Form Generation is a type of tectonic generation based upon three-dimensional models of material structures. Among such structures of integrally assembled materials are procedures for folding, braiding, knitting and weaving, or various traditional methods for creating interlaced material systems. Graphic interlacing is based upon two-dimensional patterns while craft methods of knitting and weaving are based upon three-dimensional interlacing methods. Textile modeling as a basis for parametric form generation has become of research interest in architecture in recent years; Spuybroek refers to this field as *Textile Tectonics*

(Tremontin, 2006). This work is based upon computational modeling of three-dimensional textile interlacing material structures that can be modulated parametrically. With respect to the relationship between theory and the generative design of material structures, Spuybroek states that "Architectural design is not about having ideas, but about having techniques, techniques that operate at a material level. It's about making matter think and live by itself" (Tremontin, 2006, p. 53).

Natural or *Neo-Biological Form Generation* is the exploitation of a natural form, phenomenon, process, procedure or biological principle as the basis for a model of form generation in architecture. Frei Otto's design research is noted for the investigation of natural forms such as branching and the study of biological systems as a form of research for design. There is a significant relationship between the study of natural systems and biological systems as a basis for morphogenetic design theories (see articles by Menges and Weinstock in this volume). In current design research there is a developing interrelationship between these first four models of design generational procedures and the growing knowledge base of digital design generational procedures. There is a large body of literature on the communality and compatibility of these procedures. See Sakamoto *et al.* (2008); Hwang, *et al.* (2006); Ferré, *et al.* (2004).

Fabricational Form Generation is the use of fabrication design logic and technique as the basis for the development of procedural models of design. Given the inherent coordination between digital processes of fabrication and design, this is rapidly emerging as a major field of modeling of design generation. As fabrication techniques expand in their scale capabilities as well as their generality of application we can expect that this field will have a significant impact on the future of the digital in architecture. For current architecture produced by fabrication logic see Jurgen Mayer's *Metropol Parasol* in Seville. The field is presented in this volume as a new frontier of the integration of various approaches to the digital in architecture; it is represented by various articles, among others: N. Oxman; Scheurer; and Willmann, Gramazio and Kohler. For a survey and classification of fabrication models, see Iwamoto (2009); for a general review of the state of the art, see Glynn and Sheil (2011).

Performative Form Generation is the concluding model of this series. In performative generation ecological factors such as the physical data of the context provide input for the design process in which a parametric schema is modulated to achieve a solution balancing performance with other desired objectives. Performative generation is the computational unison of generation and analysis. In this volume, see N. Oxman, and Bollinger, Grohmann and Tessmann. For the application of computational techniques in architectural structural engineering in the collaborative design of Toyo Ito with Mutsuro Sasaki, see Sasaki (2007).

We have seen that in the relationship between form generation and digital techniques in architecture there is a complex interrelationship between idea and technique; between theoretical positions and the potential and influence of techniques and technologies of the digital in architecture. If there is, or can be, a general theory of the digital in architecture it must be one that can accommodate this duality between concepts and technologies.

Burry, Jane and Burry, Mark (2010), *The New Mathematics of Architecture*, Thames and Hudson, London

Ferré, Albert, Kubo, Michael, Prat, Ramon, Sakamoto, Tomoko, Salazar, Jaime and Tetas, Anna, eds. (2004), *Verb Matters*, Actar, Barcelona

Glynn, Ruari and Sheil, Bob, eds. (2011), *Fabricate: Making Digital Architecture*, Riverside Architectural Press, London

Hwang, Irene, Sakamoto, Tomoko, Ferré, Albert, Kubo, Michael, Sadaranganie, Noorie, Tetas, Anna, Ballesteros, Mario and Prat, Ramon (2006), *Verb Natures*, Actar, Barcelona.

Iwamoto, Lisa (2009), *Digital Fabrications: Architecture and Material Techniques*, Princeton Architectural Press, New York

Kwinter, Sanford (1994), "Who's Afraid of Formalism," in Kubo, Michael and Ferré, Albert, eds. (2003), in collaboration with FOA, *Phylogenesis FOA's Ark*, Actar, Barcelona, pp. 96–99. Originally published in *Any Magazine*, no. 7/8

Leach, Neil, Turnbull, David and Williams, Chris (2004), *Digital Tectonics*, Wiley-Academy, West Sussex, UK

Lynn, Greg (1998), *Folds, Bodies and Blobs, Collected Essays*, La Lettre Volée, Brussels

Lynn, Greg (1999), *Animate Form*, Princeton Architectural Press, New York

Lynn, Greg (2003), *Intricacy*, Institute of Contemporary Art, University of Pennsylvania, Philadelphia

McLeod, Mary (2003), "Form and Function Today," in Tschumi, Bernard and Cheng, Irene, eds., *The State of Architecture at the Beginning of the 21st Century*, The Monacelli Press, New York, pp. 50–51

Mertins, Detlef (2003), "Same Difference," in Kubo, Michael and Ferré, Albert, eds., in collaboration with FOA, *Phylogenesis FOA's Ark*, Actar, Barcelona, pp. 270–279

Moussavi, Farshid (2009), *The Function of Form*, Actar, Barcelona and the Harvard Graduate School of Design, Cambridge, MA, pp. 7–36

Reiser, Jesse and Umemoto, Nanako (2006), *Atlas of Novel Tectonics*, Princeton Architectural Press, New York

Sakamoto, Tomoko and Ferré, Albert (2008), *From Control to Design: Parametric / Algorithmic Architecture*, Actar, Barcelona

Sasaki, Mutsuro (2007), *The Morphogenesis of Flux Structure*, AA Publications, London

Shelden, Dennis R. and Witt, Andrew, J. (2011), "Continuity and Rupture," in Legendre, George L., *Mathematics of Space*, AD (*Architectural Design*), Vol. 81, No. 4, pp. 36–43

Stiny, George (2006), *Shape: Talking About Seeing and Doing*, MIT Press, Cambridge, MA

Tremontin, Maria Ludovica (2006), "Interview with Lars Spuybroek," in Garcia, Mark, ed., *Architextiles*, AD (*Architectural Design*), Vol. 76, No. 6, pp. 52–59

Zaero-Polo, Alejandro (2003), "Breeding Architecture," in Tschumi, Bernard and Cheng, Irene, eds., *The State of Architecture at the Beginning of the 21st Century*, The Monacelli Press, New York, p. 56

> List of Key Concepts

aggregates
algorithmic generation
assemblages
associative modeling
configurative generation
continuous evolution
continuity
differentiation
evolutionary form
evolutionary series
form generation
formalism
formation
fabrication design generation
informed generation
intricacy
heterogeneity

material generation
mathematical generation
multiplicitous creativity
mutability
natural generation
neo-biological design
parametric associative
    geometry
parametricism
parametric schema
parametric systems
performative generation
procedural design generation
procedural logic
tectonic generation
textile tectonics
variability

Animation is a term that differs from, but is often confused with, **motion**. While motion implies movement and action, animation implies the evolution of a form and its shaping forces; it suggests animalism, animism, growth, actuation, vitality and virtuality.[1] In its manifold implications, animation touches on many of architecture's most deeply embedded assumptions about its structure. What makes animation so problematic for architects is that they have maintained an ethics of statics in their discipline. Because of its dedication to permanence, architecture is one of the last modes of thought based on the inert. More than even its traditional role of providing shelter, architects are expected to provide culture with stasis. This desire for timelessness is intimately linked with interests in formal purity and autonomy. Challenging these assumptions by introducing architecture to models of organization that are not inert will not threaten the essence of the discipline, but will advance it. Just as the development of calculus drew upon the historical mathematical developments that preceded it, so too will an animate approach to architecture subsume traditional models of statics into a more advanced system of dynamic organizations. Traditionally, in architecture, the abstract space of design is conceived as an ideal neutral space of Cartesian coordinates. In other design fields, however, design space is conceived as an environment of force and motion rather than as a neutral vacuum. In naval design, for example, the abstract space of design is imbued with the properties of flow, turbulence, viscosity, and drag so that the form of a hull can be conceived in motion through water. Although the form of a boat hull is designed to anticipate motion, there is no expectation that its shape will change. An ethics of motion neither implies nor precludes literal motion. Form can be shaped by the collaboration between an envelope and the active context in which it is situated. While physical form can be defined in terms of static coordinates, the virtual force of the environment in which it is designed contributes to its shape. The particular form of a hull stores multiple vectors of motion and flow from the space in which it was designed. A sailboat hull, for example, is designed to perform under multiple points of sail. For sailing downwind, the hull is designed as a planing surface. For sailing into the wind, the hull is designed to heel, presenting a greater surface area to the water. A boat hull does not change its shape when it changes its direction, obviously, but variable points of sail are incorporated into its surface. In this way, topology allows for not just the incorporation of a single moment but rather a multiplicity of vectors, and therefore, a multiplicity of times, in a single continuous surface.

Likewise, the forms of a dynamically conceived architecture may be shaped in association with virtual motion and force, but

4
Animate Form
Greg Lynn

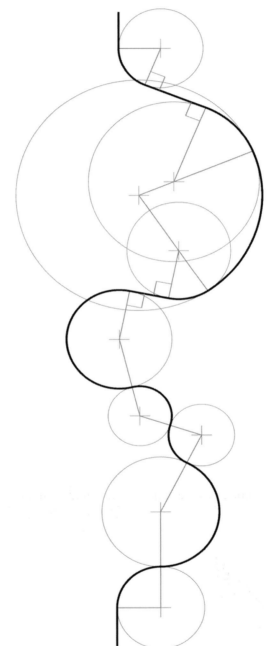

Figure 4.1

again, this does not mandate that the architecture change its shape. Actual movement often involves a mechanical paradigm of multiple discrete positions, whereas virtual movement allows form to occupy a multiplicity of possible positions continuously with the same form.

The term **virtual** has recently been so debased that it often simply refers to the digital space of computer-aided design. It is often used interchangeably with the term simulation. Simulation, unlike virtuality, is not intended as a diagram for a future possible concrete assemblage but is instead a visual substitute. "Virtual reality" might describe architectural design but as it is used to describe a simulated environment it would be better replaced by "simulated reality" or "substitute reality." Thus, use of the term virtual here refers to an abstract scheme that has the possibility of becoming actualized, often in a variety of possible configurations. Since architects produce drawings of buildings and not buildings themselves, architecture, more than any other discipline, is involved with the production of virtual descriptions. There is one aspect of virtuality that architects have neglected, however, and that is the principle of virtual force and the differential variation it implies. Architectural form is conventionally conceived in a dimensional space of idealized stasis, defined by Cartesian fixed-point coordinates. An object defined as a vector whose trajectory is relative to other objects, forces, fields and flows, defines form within an active space of force and motion. This shift from a passive space of static coordinates to an active space of interactions implies a move from autonomous purity to contextual specificity.[2] Contemporary animation and special-effects software are just now being introduced as tools for design rather than as devices for rendering, visualization and imaging.[3]

The dominant mode for discussing motion in architecture has been the cinematic model, where the multiplication and sequencing of static snapshots simulates movement. The problem with the motion-picture analogy is that architecture occupies the role of the static frame through which motion progresses. Force and motion are eliminated from form only to be reintroduced, after the fact of design, through concepts and techniques of optical procession.

In contrast, animate design is defined by the co-presence of motion and force at the moment of formal conception. Force is an initial condition, the cause of both motion and the particular inflections of a form. For example, in what is called "*inverse kinematic*" animation, the motion and shape of a form is defined by multiple interacting vectors that unfold in time perpetually and openly. With these techniques, entities are given vectorial

Facing page

Figure 4.1: "An example of a composite curve using the logic of regional definition and tangency. Each section of the composite curve is defined by a fixed radius. The connection between radial curved segments occurs at points of tangency that are defined by a line connecting the radii. Perpendicular to these lines, straight line segments can be inserted between the radial curves." Image credit: Greg Lynn Form.

properties before they are released into a space differentiated by gradients of force. Instead of a neutral abstract space for design, the context for design becomes an active abstract space that directs form within a current of forces that can be stored as information in the shape of the form. Rather than as a frame through which time and space pass, architecture can be modeled as a participant immersed within dynamical flows. In addition to the special-effects and animation industries, many other disciplines such as aeronautical design, naval design, and automobile design employ this animate approach to modeling form in a space that is a medium of movement and force.

Previous architectural experiments in capturing motion have involved the superimposition of simultaneous instances. The superimposition of a sequence of frames produces memory in the form of spatio-temporal simultaneity. This idea of an architecture in which time is built into form as memory has been a persistent theme throughout its history, but it was Sigfried Giedion in both *Mechanization Takes Command* (1948) and *Space, Time, and Architecture* (1941) who established these themes as the primary concern of twentieth-century architectural theory and design.[4] Giedion included both cubist and futurist approaches to capturing motion in form, using as examples the work of Marcel Duchamp and Umberto Boccioni. Giedion's interpretation of these cubo-futurist experiments continues to influence contemporary design and theory.[5] In both approaches, multiple static frames of an object in time are captured and superimposed in the same space simultaneously, generating a temporal palimpsest.

Another model of indexical time is associated with Colin Rowe and his disciples. In Rowe's text, "Transparency: Literal and Phenomenal," co-authored with Robert Slutzky, the idea of a formal, or phenomenal, transparency is proposed along with literal transparency.[6] Phenomenal transparency is the tracing or imprinting of a deeper formal space on a surface. Similarly,

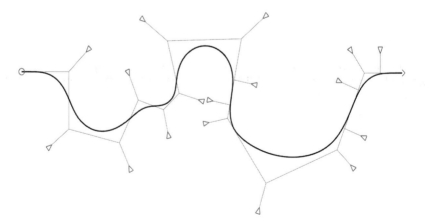

Figure 4.2: "A similar curve described using spline geometry, in which the radii are replaced by control vertices with weights and handles through which the curved spline flows." Image credit: Greg Lynn Form.

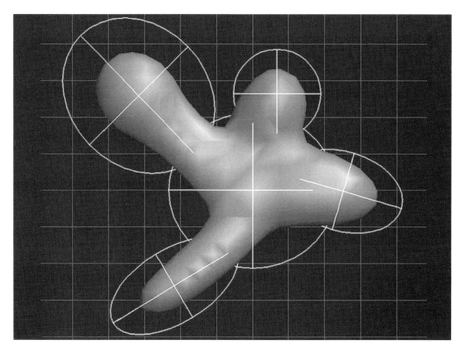

Figure 4.3: "Isomorphic polysurface with primitives fused into a single surface." Image credit: Greg Lynn Form.

examples of formal or phenomenal time include *"shearing," "shifting,"* and *"rotating"* operations. Superimposed snapshots of motion imply time as a phenomenal movement between frames or moments. For instance, Kenneth Frampton's description of Charles Gwathmey's early work as *"rotational"* is one such example of time being used to describe the movement between superimposed, formal moments.[7] Another example is that of the *"trace,"* a term that has emerged in the last twenty years as a graphical notation of time and motion in architecture.[8] In such projects, a design process of sequential formal operations is recorded in the building's configuration through colors, alignments, imprints, additions and subtractions. One such example is the simultaneous presence of multiple historical ground conditions at a single moment. The intervals between the moments that are superimposed generate irresolute conditions which are exploited for their destabilizing effect on the present.

In all of these indexical responses to time, a superimposition or sequence of static forms is put into relation such that the viewer resolves multiple states through the initiation of optical motion. Although form is thought in series and motion in these examples, movement is something that is added back to the object by the viewer. This involves a dialectic definition of motion that assumes that matter is inert while our experience of it involves movement. Statics becomes the condition of matter without force and dynamics becomes the condition of matter acted on by force. Both positions assume that force is something which can be added or subtracted from matter.

The modeling of architecture in a conceptual field populated by forces and motion contrasts with these previous paradigms and technologies of formal stasis. Stasis is a concept which has been intimately linked with architecture in at least five important ways, including (1) permanence, (2) usefulness, (3) typology, (4) procession, and (5) verticality. However, statics does not hold an essential grip on architectural thinking as much as it is a lazy habit or default that architects either choose to reinforce or contradict for lack of a better model. Each of these assumptions can be transformed once the virtual space in which architecture is conceptualized is mobilized with both time and force. With the example of permanence, the dominant cultural expectation is that buildings must be built for eternity when in fact most buildings are built to persist for only a short time. Rather than designing for permanence, techniques for obsolescence, dismantling, ruination, recycling and abandonment through time warrant exploration. Another characteristic of static models is that of functional fixity. Buildings are often assumed to have a particular and fixed relationship to their programs, whether they are intersected, combined or even flexibly programmed. Typological fixity, of the kind promoted by Colin Rowe for instance, depends on a closed static order to underlie a family of continuous variations. This concept of a discrete, ideal, and fixed prototype can be subsumed by the model of the numerically controlled multi-type that is flexible, mutable, and differential. This multi-type, or **performance envelope**, does not privilege a fixed type but instead models a series of relationships or expressions between a range of potentials. Similarly, independent interacting variables can be linked to influence one another through logical expressions defining the size, position, rotation, direction, or speed of an object by looking to other objects for their characteristics. This concept of an envelope of potential from which either a single or a series of **instances** can be taken, is radically different from the idea of a fixed prototype that can be varied.

Finally, static models underwrite the retrograde understanding of gravity as a simple, unchanging, vertical force. Architecture remains as the last refuge for members of the flat-earth society. The relationships of structure to force and gravity are by definition multiple and interrelated, yet architects tend to reduce these issues to what is still held as a central truth: that buildings stand up vertically. In fact, there are multiple interacting structural pressures exerted on buildings from many directions, including lateral wind loads, uplift, shear, and earthquakes, to name a few of the non-vertical conditions. Any one of these **live** loads could easily exceed the relative weight of the building and its vertical **dead** loads. The naive understanding of structure as primarily a problem of the vertical transfer of dead gravity loads to the ground excludes, for instance, the fact that lighter buildings have a tendency to uplift; the main structural concern in these cases is how to tether the roof. Of course architects and structural engineers do not ignore these other structural factors, but the primary perception of structure has always

been that it should be vertical. A reconceptualization of ground and verticality in light of complex vectors and movements might not change the expe-
diency and need for level floors, but it would open up possibilities for
structure and support that take into account orientations other than the
simply vertical.

These concerns are not merely technical as architecture presently
expresses also the cultural diagrams of stasis. Despite the popular conception
among architects that gravity is a fact, the contemporary debates about
theories of gravity could inform present discussions of architecture in the
same spirit that they have done in the past. The history of theories of
gravity are extremely nuanced, fascinating and unresolved. Since the time of
Sir Isaac Newton, gravity has been accepted as the mutual relative attraction
of masses in space. Given a constant mass, stability is achieved through orbits
rather than stasis. This distinction between stasis and orbital or dynamic
stability is important. In the case of a single, simple gravity, **stasis** is the
ordering system through the unchanging constant force of a ground point.
In the case of a more complex concept of gravity, mutual attraction generates motion; **stability** is the ordering of motion into rhythmic phases. In the
simple, static model of gravity, motion is eliminated at the beginning. In the
complex, stable model of gravity, motion is an ordering principle. Likewise,
discreteness, timelessness, and fixity are characteristic of stasis; multiplicity,
change, and development are characteristic of stability.

These differences are very apparent in the two models of gravity debated
by René Descartes and Gottfried Wilhelm Leibniz. Descartes isolated and
reduced elements in a dynamic system to their constitutive identities to
create a steady-state equation: he eliminated time and force from the equation in order to calculate a precise position. Leibniz, on the other hand,
examined components within their contextual field of influences and within
a developing temporal continuum. By retaining the creative structural role of
time and force, Leibniz determined that a position in space can only be calculated continuously as a vectoral flow.[9] The name that he attributed to any
provisionally reduced component or primitive element is that of the "*monad*."
Where Newton used calculus to replace the zero value of statics with a
"*derivative*," Leibniz formulated the concept of the "*integral*," where within
any monad there is a kernel of the whole equation in the form of the variables. Any monad has the ability to unfold a "*possible world*." Thus integral
calculus is structured on a monad logic of continuous multiplicity. The shift
from a discrete model of gravity as a force that could be eliminated from
matter, to a concept of gravity as integral and continuous with masses in
space, involves a redefinition of space from being neutral and timeless to
being temporally dynamic. Once design is posed within a Leibnizian monad-
ological space, architecture may embrace a sensibility of micro and macro
contextual specificity as a logic that can not be idealized in an abstract space
of fixed coordinates. In such an abstract active space, the statics of fixed
points in neutral space is replaced by the stability of vectors that balance one
another in a phase space.

If architecture is to approach this more complex concept of gravity, its design technologies should also incorporate factors of time and motion. Throughout the history of architecture, descriptive techniques have impacted the way in which architectural design and construction has been practiced. In the eighteenth century, the orrery came to represent not only the image of the machine but also the conceptual processes of a universe that is harmonically regulated as a closed system of circular orbits around radial center points. Because an orrery uses fixed radial points, any discrete moment in time can be calculated as a fixed point. The compass, like the orrery, has implicit in it a series of conceptual and disciplinary limits that are rehearsed with every arc that is drawn. Events such as the advent of perspective, stereometric projection, and other geometric techniques have extended the descriptive repertoire of architectural designers. In our present age, the virtual space within which architecture is conceived is now being rethought by the introduction of advanced motion tools and a constellation of new diagrams based on the computer. The geometry and the mathematics that Leibniz invented to describe this interactive, combinatorial, and multiplicitous gravity remain as the foundations for topology and calculus upon which contemporary animation technology is based. There can be little doubt that the advent of computer-aided visualization has allowed architects to explore calculus-based forms for the first time.

The sequential continuity of more than two variables interacting with one another poses a problem that only calculus can answer. First posed by Karl Weierstrass, Charles Hermite and Gosta Mittag-Lefler in 1885, the "n-body" problem was later made famous by Henri Poincare in 1889, when he was able to prove that no discrete solution for such a problem could exist. The fundamental aspect of this problem, referred to as "the Poincare three-body problem," is that the temporal and spatial position of entities cannot be mathematically calculated for a future position without sequentially calculating the positions leading up to that moment. The mathematics of form and space that architects have historically understood, involve mathematical descriptions from which time has been eliminated. In the three-body problem however, time, or more properly duration and sequence, are integral to the spatial relationships being calculated. Another aspect of this kind of relationship in which three or more objects interact, is that they often produce nonlinear behavior. The method by which these problems can be calculated is through a mathematics that is sequential and continuous: thus the invention by both Newton and Leibniz of differential calculus.

Although the mechanical, acoustic, and structural systems of buildings have been calculated and conceived using the tools of calculus, architects infrequently use calculus for the design of form. The fact that architecture is so heavily dependent on mathematics for the description of space has been a stumbling block to the use of motion and flow in the design process, as these ideas require that architects draw geometries whose underlying mathematics is calculus. The tools that architects use to draw, such as adjustable triangles and compasses, are based on simple algebra. The prevalence of topological surfaces in even the simplest CAD software, along with the ability to tap the time-and-force modeling attributes of animation software, presents perhaps the first opportunity for architects to draw and sketch using calculus. The challenge for contemporary architectural theory and design is to try to understand the appearance of these tools in a more sophisticated way than as simply a new set of shapes. Issues of force, motion and time, which have perennially eluded architectural description due to their *"vague essence,"* can now be experimented with by supplanting the traditional tools of exactitude and stasis with tools of gradients, flexible envelopes, temporal flows and forces.[10]

As architects have been disciplined to eliminate questions of flow and motion from the rigorous description of space, these qualities have been relegated to personal taste and casual definition. Because of the present lack of experience and precedent with issues of motion and force in architecture, these issues might best be raised from within the technological regimes of the tools rather than from within architectural history.[11] Through experimentation with non-architectural regimes, architects may discover how to engage time and motion in design. The computer has already proven to be useful as both a descriptive and a visualizing tool to architects, but the introduction of time and motion techniques into architecture is not simply a visual phenomenon. The visual qualities of computer-generated images may be important but it seems misguided to understand geometry in terms of style. The invention of stylistic categories risks the reproduction of the same spurious comparisons of modern architecture to boats and aircraft based on the similarity of shapes. For instance, although geodesic domes often employ triangulated surfaces and some computer programs convert vector surfaces to fixed points through the use of triangular polygon meshes, it is a very shallow comparison to equate architecture designed using topological surfaces to Buckminster Fuller simply because of the commonality of triangulated surfaces.[12]

Nonetheless, there are distinct formal and visual consequences of the use of computer animation. For instance, the most obvious aesthetic consequence is the shift from volumes defined by Cartesian coordinates to topological surfaces defined by U and V vector coordinates. Another obvious aesthetic byproduct of these spatial models is the predominance of deformation and transformation techniques available in a time-based system of flexible surfaces. These are not merely shapes but the expression of the mathematics of the topological medium.

In addition to the aesthetic and material consequences of computer-generated forms, computer software also offers capabilities as a conceptual and organizational tool. But because of the stigma and fear of releasing control of the design process to software, few architects have attempted to use the computer as a schematic, organizing and generative medium for design. The limits and tendencies of this tool, as a medium for design, must be clearly understood conceptually before they can be grasped by a systematic intuition.[13]

There are also some misconceptions about the role of computers in the design process. A precious few architectural designers and theorists, Karl Chu and John Frazer being the most lucid among them, argue for the creative capacity of computers to facilitate genetic design strategies. The genetic, or rule-based, phenomenon of computation should not be discounted. Yet at the same time, genetic processes should not be equated with either intelligence or nature. The computer is not a brain. Machine intelligence might best be described as that of mindless connections. When connecting multiple variables, the computer simply connects them, it does not think critically about how it connects. The present limits of connectionism are staggeringly complex, and the directness with which multiple entities can be related challenges human sensibility. The response has been to attempt to develop a commensurate sensibility in the machines themselves; but the failures of artificial intelligence suggest a need to develop a systematic human intuition about the connective medium, rather than attempting to build criticality into the machine. Even in the most scientific applications of computer simulations it is argued that first an intuition must be developed in order to recognize the nonlinear behavior of computer simulations.[14] Also, the computer is not nature. Although it makes shapes that are temporally and formally open to deformation and inflection, those shapes are not organic. The organic appearance of what will later be discussed as a system of interaction and curvilinearity is a result of organizational principles based on differentials. The formal organizations that result from the sequential mathematical calculation of differential equations are irreducibly open in terms of their shape. They are often interpreted as organic because of the inability to reduce these shapes to an ideal form. In contrast, the reducible, fixed forms of simple mathematics—such as spheres, cubes, pyramids, cones and cylinders—have a simplicity and purity that allows them to transcend their formal particularities.

Instead of approaching the computer as either a brain or nature, the computer might be considered as a pet. Like a pet, the computer has already been domesticated and pedigreed, yet it does not behave with human intelligence. Just as a pet introduces an element of wildness to our domestic habits that must be controlled and disciplined, the computer brings both a degree of discipline and unanticipated behavior to the design process. By negotiating the degree of discipline and wildness, one can cultivate an intuition into the behavior of computer-aided design systems and the mathematics behind them.

There are three fundamental properties of organization in a computer that are very different from the characteristics of inert mediums such as paper and pencil: **topology, time**, and **parameters**. These three properties should be discussed, beginning with the principles of topological entities, continuing with the implications that topological forms raise for the relationship between time and shape, and concluding with a discussion of statistics and parameters that can be stored in these timed surfaces.

One of the first principles of topological entities is that because they are defined with calculus they take the shape of a multiplicity; meaning they are

not composed of discrete points but rather, they are composed of a continuous stream of relative values. Historically, baroque geometries of composite
entities, such as multiple radii, have been cited as multiplicitous spaces. But
the idea that the baroque period anticipates topology in architecture is
somewhat misplaced. There is a critical difference between the discrete
geometry of baroque space—a geometry of multiple points, and the continuity of topology—a multiplicity without points. Where baroque space is
defined by multiple radii, a topological surface is defined as a flow that
hangs from fixed points that are weighted. Although baroque space is
geometrically highly continuous and highly differentiated, it does retain
multiple spatial centers. The continuous contours of baroque interiors are
composed of segments of multiple discrete radial elements (fig. 4.1). For
example, in Francesco Borromini's Quattro Fontane the complex of primitive
volumes is tangentially aligned to produce a continuous surface, giving
the space simultaneous dynamism and centrality. The relationships
between these radial primitives are often of bilateral symmetry and always
of tangency.

Instead of being defined by points and centers, topology is characterized
by flexible surfaces composed of splines (fig. 4.2). These splines are oriented
in an opposing U and V orientation to construct surfaces composed of
curve networks. Unlike lines, splines are vectors defined with direction. The
vectors are suspended from lines with hanging weights similar to the
geometry of a catenoidal curve.[15] Yet unlike a catenoidal curve, a spline can
accommodate weights and gravities directed in free space. The points, or
"control vertices," from which these weights hang, and through which the
spline flows, are located in X, Y, Z coordinate space. From a sequence of
control vertices the direction and strength of weights establishes a tension
along the hulls. Although the control vertices, hulls, and weights are defined
in a point-based, Cartesian space, the splines are not defined as points but as
flows. The spline curve is unlike a line or radius in that its shape is not
reducible to exact coordinates. The spline curve flows as a stream between a
constellation of weighted control vertices and any position along this
continuous series can only be defined relative to its position in the sequence.
The formal character of a particular spline is based on the number of control
vertices influencing a particular region of the flow. For instance, a three-
degree spline will begin at its root and determine its inflection between
every three points in a series. A seven-degree spline curve will be defined by
groups of seven control vertices, thus appearing smoother. A two-degree
spline will appear linear because it lacks smooth continuity between control
vertices. Even though the control vertices remain constant in these examples,
the particular shape changes due to the degree of relative definition of the
controlling points of the sequential flow. Similarly, without changing
the position of any one of the control vertices or the degree of the spline,
the shape will be altered when the weight or direction of any of the normals
is altered.

A change in any point distributes an inflection across regions of these entities. Because splines are vectorial flows through sequences of points they are by definition continuous multiplicities rather than discrete entities. A multiplicity is a collection of components that is neither reducible to a single entity nor to a collection of multiple entities. A multiplicity is neither one nor many, but a continuous assemblage of heterogeneous singularities that exhibits both collective qualities of continuity and local qualities of heterogeneity. In the use of topology in design, these multiplicities imply a very different approach to location, as there are no discrete points along a spline.

The two linked principles that are central to the temporal component of topology are (1) the immanent curvatures that result from the combinatorial logic of differential equations, and (2) the mathematical cause of that curvature. Because topological entities are based on vectors, they are capable of systematically incorporating time and motion into their shape as inflection. Inflection, or continuous curvature is the graphical and mathematical model for the imbrication of multiple forces in time. The shift from linearity to curvilinearity is a feature of contemporary mathematics and geometry that has been discussed elsewhere.[16] Curvilinearity is a more sophisticated and complex form of organization than linearity in two regards: (1) it integrates multiple rather than single entities, and (2) it is capable of expressing vectorial attributes, and therefore time and motion. Curvature in a temporal environment is the method by which the interaction of multiple forces can be structured, analyzed, and expressed.

The calculation of time as expressed through curvature is possible with calculus, which animates numerical snapshots at an infinite speed, simulating time. Underlying all of the contemporary animation software is a mathematics of the infinitely small interval which simulates actual motion and time through **keyframing**. These transformations can be linearly **morphed** or they can involve nonlinear interactions through **dynamics**. These sequential transformations are possible because the formal entities themselves are described using flexible topological surfaces made of vector splines rather than points.

An example of curvature as a mathematical and intuitive system can be explained by the situation of a FrisbeeTM being chased by a running dog. There are at least three contributing elements to the path of the dog and its possible intersection with the projectile. First, the FrisbeeTM has a vector for direction and speed; second, the space in which they move has a wind velocity and direction as well; and third, the FrisbeeTM has a gravitational attraction to the earth. In order to intersect with the FrisbeeTM at a future moment in time, the dog will not follow the projectile but perform a differential equation to calculate both its and the Frisbee'sTM future positions in time as vectors moving toward a moment of possible intersection. The path of the dog will inevitably be described by a curved line. The inflections of this curved line indicate the velocities, directions and timing of each of the imbricated vectors. This situation cannot be described by a straight line with endpoints because, mathematically, it is a differential equation with more than two interacting components. Likewise, any multiplicity such as this will be described by some form of curvature because multiplicities are constructed of interacting entities exerting a differential influence on one another. Curvature is a mode of integrating complex interacting entities into a continuous form. What is important about this example is that initially, the hypothetical dog might be expected to duplicate the trajectory of the FrisbeeTM and therefore it would have difficulty catching the moving object. With practice, the dog might be expected to intuit the patterns of motion of the FrisbeeTM and eventually it will follow a cut-off path in order to intersect with the FrisbeeTM. Although the dog does not actually calculate a differential equation, it perceives the motion patterns of multiple vector fields acting in space and time and can anticipate the unfolding of these patterns. By analogy, it is not necessary for architects to perform the differential equations that generate topological forms, as the equation for even the simplest spline is too complex for most architects to calculate. Instead, designers must understand the patterns of topology as they unfold dynamically with varying performance, rather than understanding them merely as shapes.

The shapes that are formed in computer-aided design are the result of decisions made using parameters. Numerical data which describe characteristics of the virtual design environment—such as temperature, gravity, and other forces—have an impact on the forms which result. For example, dynamic modeling systems are based on the interaction of multiple parameter statements calculated sequentially rather than in an instant. Numerical parameters can be keyframed and dynamically linked through **expressions** to alter the shape of objects. In addition to mere changes in shape, these parameters control gradient characteristics of fields such as directional forces, gravities, warps, and particles. Gradient parameters of decay, wave behavior, attraction, and density affect objects as numerical fields of force rather than as object transformations. The linkages between these characteristics of time, topology, and parameters combine to establish the virtual possibilities for designing in an animate rather than static space. Each of these characteristics can be used to rethink the familiar Cartesian space of neutral equilibrium as a more active space of motion and flow.

The curvilinearity which results from these multiple parameters has previously been simplistically understood as a debased form of linearity, but in fact, it is the ordering of a dynamical system of differential factors. In the early part of this century, Scottish zoolologist Sir D'Arcy Thompson analyzed variations in the morphology of animals using deformable grids, which yielded curvilinear lines due to changes in form. He compared the curvature of deformations in formal configurations to the curvature of statistical data, such as speed, temperature, and weight. Thompson was one of the first scientists to notate **gradient** forces (such as temperature) through **deformation, inflection**, and **curvature**.[17] These three terms all involve the registration of force on form. Rather than thinking of deformation as a subset of the pure, the term deformation can be understood as a system of regulation and order that proceeds through the integration and resolution of multiple inter-acting forces and fields.

Where Thompson pioneered the analyses of deformation as an index of contextual forces acting on an organism, in the late nineteenth century Étienne-Jules Marey pioneered the study of curvature as the notation of both force and time. Francois Dagognet described the project of Marey as:

> . . . showing what one could learn from a curve, which was not merely a simple 'reproduction.' It was from and with the curve that forces could initially be calculated. It was easy to obtain the mass of the body as well as the speed it was going (chronobiology); from this one could induce the force that had set it in motion, the work expended to produce this action. The trajectory always had to be questioned and interpreted. Not only were the slightest nicks and notches in the line due to certain factors, but they enabled the determination of resistances as well as impulses.[18]

Marey was one of the first morphologists to move from the study of form in inert Cartesian space, devoid of force and motion, to the study of rhythms, movements, pulses, and flows and their effects on form. These factors he termed "*motor evidence.*" In his book *Animal Mechanism* he shifted his attention from the study of internal pulses and rhythms to the external movements of animals. Unlike Muybridge and others who also employed chronophotography techniques, Marey triggered the exposures with both pneumatic and electrical sensors located on the animals. This, along with his method of attaching tiny reflecting optical disks allowed Marey to sequence the exposures with rhythms of motion. Dagognet describes Marey as pursuing "*movements not moments*" in his continuous data recordings. After exposing rhythmic sequences of images on a single plate, Marey would connect curved lines through these points to describe a continuity across the snapshots. To borrow a term used to describe the behavior of chaotic attractors, Marey produced "*phase portraits*" by describing time as a continuous curvilinear flow, rather than a divisible sequence reducible to discrete frames. This is the critical difference between Marey's traces of vector movement and the techniques of sequential traces. Marey's model for continuous time based on the inflection and curvature of motion paths and flows, is akin to computer animation.

In addition to these examples of analyzing time, movement, and trans-formation, another model that has been developed in conjunction with evolutionary theories is the idea of the fitness landscape. With the replace-ment of fixed types by temporally organized phylogenetic trees, came the model of the developmental landscape to describe the space within which organisms evolve. In mathematics the landscape model has been developed by René Thom, in physics by Stuart Kauffman and in developmental biology by Conrad Waddington. It initially appeared when Francis Galton described evolution in terms of a fitness landscape; whereby a surface represents an external environment across which a facetted sphere rolled. The facetted sphere represents an organism with its own internal constraints, and the landscape represents its potential pathways of development. This concept of a landscape of development informed Charles Darwin's evolutionary theory of speciation. Similar to any landscape model of organization is an evolutionary or developmental logic.

A landscape is a system where a point change is distributed smoothly across a surface so that its influence cannot be localized at any discrete point. Splines are the constituent element of topological landscapes. Spline surfaces have already been explained as vector sequences whose regions of inflection produce singularities on a continuous surface. The slow undulations that are built into any landscape surface as hills and valleys do not mobilize space through action but instead through implied virtual motion. The movement of a point across a landscape becomes the collaboration of the initial direction, speed, elasticity, density, and friction of the object along with the inflections of the landscape across which it is traveling. The landscape can initiate movements across itself without literally moving. The inflections of a landscape present a context of gradient slopes which are enfolded into its shape. The condition of oriented surfaces has been elaborated by Paul Virilio and Claude Parent in terms of *"oblique"* movement.[19] Likewise, any object moving across a landscape has an initial condition of speed and density that is unfolded across the landscape. This collaboration of enfolding a context and unfolding an object is a temporal, mobile, and combinatorial model for stability and organization. In this schema the object has actual force and motion, where the landscape has virtual force and motion stored in its slopes. The slope of a landscape is a gradient of motion, direction, and time. A landscape also implies a geological timescale of formation in that although it appears static at any instant, its form is the product of long historical processes of development. This class of landscape objects can be extended to include any form from which temporal development cannot be simply reduced. Topological surfaces that store force in the inflections of their shape behave as landscapes in that the slopes that are generated store energy in the form of oriented rather than neutral surfaces.

The earlier example of the boat hull is itself a micro-landscape for the movements stored in its surface shapes, across which viscous water flows. Similarly the global flows of the water and wind present a macro-landscape for the motion of the boat to flow through. Other topological landscapes include isomorphic polysurfaces (or **blobs**), **skeletons** (or inverse kinematics networks), **warps, forces**, and **particles**. Spline entities are intensively influenced by their context due to the fact that they are defined by hanging weights, gravity, and force. For example, the weights and directions pulling on control vertices in space can be affected by gradients of attractive or repulsive force in which the spline is situated. Similarly, the weights of one spline surface can effect those of another spline surface (fig. 4.3). These resulting structures are called blobs for their ability to mutually inflect one another and form composite assemblages. The blob is an alternative example of a topological surface exhibiting landscape characteristics although it does not look like a topography. These blob assemblages are neither multiple nor single, neither internally contradictory nor unified. Their complexity involves the fusion of multiple elements into an assemblage that behaves as a singularity while remaining irreducible to any single simple organization. With isomorphic polysurfaces, "meta-clay," "meta-ball," or "blob" models, the geometric objects are defined as monadlike primitives with internal forces of attraction and mass. A blob is defined with a center, a surface area, a mass relative to other objects, and a field of influence. The field of influence defines a relational zone within which the blob will fuse with, or be inflected by, other blobs. When two or more linked blob objects are proximate they will either (1) mutually redefine their respective surfaces based on their particular gravitational properties or (2) actually fuse into one contiguous surface defined by the interactions of their respective centers and zones of inflection and fusion.

Because it is not reducible to any single simple ordering principle, a blob's fusion and unification are distinct from a discrete totality or whole. In the case of the isomorphic polysurfaces, either a low number of interacting components or a regular distribution of components will yield a global form that is more or less simple. On the other hand, a high number of components and an irregular distribution of those components yields a global form that is more or less complex. The difference between simple and complex systems is relative to the number of interactions between components. In this schema, there is no essential difference between a more or less spherical formation and a blob. The sphere and its provisional symmetries are merely the index of a rather low level of interactions, while the blob is an index of a high degree of information, where information is equated with difference. Thus, even what seems to be a sphere is actually a blob without influence; an inexact form that merely masquerades as an exact form because it is isolated from adjacent forces. Yet, as a blob, it is capable of fluid and continuous differentiation based on interactions with neighboring forces with which it can be either inflected or fused. In this way, complexity is always present as potential in even the most simple or primitive of forms. Moreover, it is measured by the degrees of both continuity and difference that are copresent at any moment.

Like a natural landscape that stores the history of its geological formation in its shape, these fused topological aggregates manifest their geological conglomeration on a single surface. Time, force, and multiplicity constitute the form of a geological landscape. This structuring of time and energy through curvilinear inflections is characteristic of motion or action geometry. These inflections index both the internal combinations and relationships of elements and their deformation within a larger contextual field. When proposing the model of an internally regulated structure, there are two possibilities: the first approach posits an essential internal order that can be discovered through reductive analysis, the second is a loose binding of constraints that can be realigned and reconfigured in a proliferative and evolutionary manner. In the second category, the internal order is both activated and made legible through the unfolding of its order instigated by external forces. The relationship between a system of internal constraints, such as skeletons (inverse kinematic chains), particles, or blobs and the context in which they unfold is intensive. Just as a topological landscape or an assemblage of blobs stores various attractions and combinations in a single surface, so too can topological entities be mutually inflected by the fields in which they are situated. For instance, the space in which a surface or surfaces are located can be assigned with directional force which will inflect the normals of a surface, thus inflecting the shape of the surface based on the relative position to the point from which the force is emanated. The field in which forms are defined is not neutral but can be populated by a variety of interacting forces which establish gradients of influence in a modeling space. Gradient shapes are areas that do not have distinct contours or edges but are instead defined by dissipation from points of emission. These gradients are not measured based on points or coordinates but on fields. Like a temperature map that measures the continuous and gradual change of force across a field, these force gradients do not have edges or contours. The spatial context within which surfaces and splines are conceived then is also animate rather than static.

This possibility of an animate field opens up a more intricate relationship of form and field than has been previously possible. Rather than an entity being shaped only by its own internal definition, these topological surfaces are inflected by the field in which they are modeled. If an entity is moved in space, its shape might change based on the position within gradient space even though the definition of the entity remains constant. Thus, the same entity duplicated identically but in a different gradient space might have a different configuration. A sequence of identical entities located in a series through a gradient space would constitute both a self similarity and a difference based on the characteristics of the gradients and how they were positioned. This relationship between a force and the object which stores that force in its form is reminiscent of the insight made by Henri Bergson in his book, *Matter and Memory*, in which he argues for a nondialectical understanding of the relationship between substance and energy.[20] Bergson argued that matter could not be separated from the historical process of its becoming.

Contemporary theories of organic form, evolution, mutation and vitalism, as defined as the developmental unfolding of a structure in a gradient environment of influences, might be informative to the discussion of topology, time, and parameters as they apply to architectural design. Such discussions of organic processes often involve non-dialectical relationships between matter and information, form and time, and organization and force. This resistance to treat form, time, and motion discretely is equivalent to what might be understood as an organic tradition. The thread of "*anorganic vitalism*" that runs from Leibniz through Bergson and Gilles Deleuze could underwrite such a discussion, while replacing their natural essentialism with a revised cybernetic concept of the machine as a feedback device that creates hierarchy and organization. One of the best possible models of *"anorganic vitalism"* is the proposition of *"fused assemblages"* put forward by Lynne Margulis. The major revision to concepts of holism that Margulis introduces is from a predetermined identity to identities of becoming. Margulis formulated the evolutionary hypothesis that microorganisms evolve their complexity by incorporating simpler organisms into larger multiplicities that become capable of reproduction as a singularity.[21] Thus, organisms are seen as previously free living colonies of organs that become a fused singularity. In her schema, there is little difference between a single body and an ecology of organisms, as both exploit one another's functions and machinic behaviors through feedback and exchange. A body, Margulis suggests, is the fused assemblage of an ecosystem operating with a high degree of continuity and stability. There is no essential structure to such an assemblage that one can uncover or deduce, at either the macro or micro scale. It is a logic of differentiation, exchange, and assemblage within an environment of gradient influences. The form, or shape, most often cited in reference to such an environment is that of the landscape. The epigenetic landscape is a theoretical and analytic device used to describe the relationship between an evolving form, or organism, within its developmental field, or environment.

Producing a geometric form from a differential equation is problematic without a differential approach to series and repetition. There are two kinds of series: a discrete, or repetitive series and a continuous, or iterative series. In a continuous or iterative series, the difference between each object in the sequence is critical and individual to each repetition. If the difference is the product of three or more variables, and if those three variables are unrelated, then the change between each iteration will be nonlinear in its structure and it will therefore be difficult to predict with absolute precision. Each step is thus dependent on the precise position of each of three or more variables; meaning that the future position of the iterative series cannot be calculated outside of the series itself. In an incremental, discrete series, the differences that accompany each repetition are linear and reducible. The entire infinite set of possible futures of the series can be calculated in advance with a simple mathematical equation. In the case of the continuous series such exact definitions are impossible to determine at the beginning, as the beginning is not an origin but merely a point of departure. The future possible positions of a continuous series must be thought of as a continuum rather than as an enclosed infinity. This points to the important distinction between the infinite and the continuous, two terms which are often casually conflated. Difference and repetition, when thought of in a continuous rather than discrete manner, mandate a thinking in duration rather than in points.

This difference is crucial to an understanding of the spatial difference between the infinite and the continuous. A continuous series can be "infinitized," or reduced, through "iterative reduction," leaving a single, ideal type. In this method, a limited set of variation is organized in a series so that its continuous differences can be progressively eliminated, leaving a discrete type that can then be infinitely extended. This method of iterative reduction can be attributed to Edmund Husserl, as it is central to his invention of phenomenology.

Motion and time are similarly taken away then added back to architecture. Architectural space is infinitized by removing motion and time through iterative reduction. They are then added back typically through phenomenology. The dynamic concept of architecture, however, assumes that in any form there are inflections that direct motion and provoke and influence the forces moving through, over, under and around surfaces. The form is the site for the calculation of multiple forces. This is the case in the example of the sailboat, where on the hull's surface multiple points of sail are calculated and resolved in the form itself. The perception of the hull does not require the resolution of multiple vectors of movement as those vectors are stored in the object itself as potential energy or flow within a gradient field of forces. Moreover, the primary method of experiencing these vector effects is not optical or through aesthetic contemplation but instead through performance. The vector flows that are calculated and stored in the shape of the hull can be unfolded through both aesthetic analyses and use. Perhaps the best precedent for the unfolding of curved space is evident in the concept of Frederick Keisler's "*endlessness*" along with Adolf Loos's concept of the "*raumplan*" from which it was derived while Kiesler was working in Loos's office.[22] Although a discussion of the counter tradition of modern endless space versus the canonical modern tradition of infinite space is not possible here, the difference from the more classical and reductive models of modern form should be recognized.

The best model for the discussion of non-reducible forms of motion might be to return to the model of the landscape or the oblique ground, where motion is stored in the gradient slopes of a surface across which an object moves. Here the potential motion of an object across a surface is stored in a virtual manner as future potential energy. To return to the force discussions, the influence of a gradient space of force and energy is built into the spline networks through the inflection of their normals. A landscape is a ground that has been inflected by the historical flows of energy and movement across its surface. These historical forces manifest a geological form of development that is inflected and shaped by the flows that have moved across it. These slow transformational processes result in forms which are oriented with motion, both the virtual motion of their history and the actual motion they initiate through their slopes and valleys. This animation of slow form with the historical processes of gradual geological becoming is a paradigm of motion and time that renders substance virtually animated and actually stable. Rhythmic motion is manifest in stable-oriented form rather than in literally moving objects. In the words of Hans Jenny,

> . . . Nature reveals an abundance of sculptured forms, and all of them, it must
> be remembered, are the result of vibration. If the tome ceases, the mass
> 'freezes.' Looking at these vibrational effects, it would be no exaggeration to

speak of a true magnetocymatics with its own dynamokinetic morphology. Experiments like this based on pure empiricism stimulate the plastic imagination and develop the power to feel oneself into a space permeated by forces.[23]

The work of Hans Jenny in the 1950s and 1960s is undoubtably the best example of the study of how oscillating, fluctuating, gradient fields of forces can produce not only patterns but forms. The primary theme that runs through Jenny's writings about these experiments is the continuous character between the forms produced and the fields from which they emerged. For example, Jenny argues that in the case of *"the vibrational field it can be shown that every part is, in the true sense, implicated in the whole."*[24] His experiments consisted of the effects of vibrations on a particulate concrete medium. The concrete forms he studied were in an environment where vibration and wave phenomenon were inherent to the system of form generation and evolution. He gave these structures the name *"cymatics"* meaning the *"characteristic phenomenology of vibrational effects and wave phenomenon with typical structural patterns and dynamics."*[25] In general, Jenny pioneered the use of viscous particle flows on plates that were both vibrating and magnetized. His techniques varied from the study of iron filings on plates to the sandwiching of fluids between vibrating glass plates. Jenny also used motion pictures to capture the movement of these forms within the magnetic pathways of oscillating fields. His method was to study the motion sequences of the forms rather than their static form. Previously, particles of filings and other materials were treated as discrete elements that would form a pattern that was coincident with the geometry of the plate. By introducing viscosity to the particles thus forming a continuous semisolid flow, Jenny was able to study the shaping of form in free space rather than in two-dimensional pattern only. By varying the Reynolds numbers of these particles suspended in a fluid, he was able to develop an intuition into the morphology of forms within magnetic fields. His studies involved the familiar use of a vibrating plate that would configure iron filings into patterns. Added to this influence was the presence of magnetic fields to impose polar patterns on the filings. These forces were then thought of in terms of periodic excitement by both the vibration oscillation and the changing position of the magnet. Thus the forms that emerged were studied both in their form and in the ways in which they would follow the magnetic pathways. The play between two types of fields, magnetic and vibrational, produced form. The character of these forms were persistence and continuity, but, unlike discrete reducible forms, they remained continuous with the fields within which they were generated. Rather than making shapes through the familiar operations of a sculptor or architect, through direct manipulation of material for example, Jenny modulated form through oscillating frequencies and parameters. Jenny sculpted form through the adjustment of oscillators without forfeiting his intuition to a machine intelligence. The shift from sculptural techniques of whittling, carving, chipping, and scraping material to the modulation, oscillation, and vibration of particles does not mandate the relinquishment of creativity to machinery. Instead, it suggests the creative manipulation of a flow of parameters in time.

The use of parameters and statistics for the design of form requires a more abstract, and often less representational origin for design. The shape of statistics, or parameters, may yield a culturally symbolic form, yet at the beginning, their role is more inchoate. A return to the discussion of the orrery might supply two terms: the "*concrete assemblage*" and the "*abstract machine*." For example, in Étienne-Louis Boullée's Cenotaph to Newton, the orrery operates as both an abstract model and as a sign. The orrery, in the sense that it represents the movements and organization of a centered and harmonically regulated universe, is a concrete assemblage. To the degree that it is a diagram for centralized harmonic regulation, like a compass, it is an abstract machine. The diagram for the orrery can be seen to circulate among many institutional and symbolic regimes where it takes on many meanings. As a statement of centralized regulation, however, its abstract performance is consistent. Any abstract machine, such as an orrery, can be understood as both a technical statement and as a signifier. Neither its representational nor its technical structure can be understood independently. The difference between its abstract and representational roles can be located precisely at the moment it crosses the technological threshold from being a diagram to a concrete assemblage. The use of the term abstraction here is not intended to be confused with the purist or modern notion of visual abstraction. In those instances abstraction involves an aesthetic reduction to fixed formal essences through the paring away of differences. An alternative concept of abstraction, one that is more generative and evolutionary, involves proliferation, expansion and unfolding. This marks a shift from a modernist notion of abstraction based on form and vision to an abstraction based on process and movement. In order to define such a diagrammatic regime, it is perhaps most helpful to cite Michel Foucault's terms; "*abstract machine*" and "*diagram*." Gilles Deleuze has referred to these terms as "*asignifying concepts*." By definition, an asignifying concept is instrumental before it is representational. This model depends on the precise distinction between "*linguistic constructions*" and "*statements*." Linguistic constructions, such as propositions or phrases, can always be attributed to particular referents. Statements, on the other hand, are not initially linguistic but are machinic processes.[26] For instance, the sequence of letters **Q, W, E, R, T, Y** is distributed on a typewriter or computer keyboard to produce words. The logic of their sequential distribution is based on the control of the speed at which one can potentially type words in the English language. There is no single sentence or word that tests this distribution but rather an indefinite series of existing and future words. Because there is an open series the system must be characterized as indefinitely structured. The keyboard is an actual machine, or concrete assemblage, because it is technological. But the distribution of its letters on keys in space is a virtual diagram, or an abstract machine. Statements such as these are machinic techniques, discursive concepts, or schemata that precede the representational and linguistic effects they facilitate. Signifiers are not rejected but delayed toward the moment that they are "*found at the inter-section of different systems and are cut across by the statement acting in the role of primitive function.*"[27] Linguistic constructions are merely postponed, not abolished, and a regime of abstract, schematic statements are seen to preempt and sponsor them. From the particular discursive formation of multiple, diagonally intersecting statements, some form of expression emerges. Through the interaction of a multiplicity of abstract statements, signifiers emerge in a more dynamic manner than mere representational effects might. The shift from linguistic models to the proliferation of asigni-fying statements marks what Deleuze terms a move from the "*archive*" to the "*diagram.*"[28] The move from linguistic constructions to statements, or more properly from meaning to machine, is a necessary shift in sensibility if one is to tap the potential of abstract machines such as computational motion geometry and time-based, dynamic force simulations.

This shift is the primary explanation for the apparent alliance between certain aspects of Deleuze and Foucault's discourse and many contemporary architects now weary of representational critiques spanning from stylistic postmodernism to deconstruction. In Deleuze's interpretation of Foucault's critique of panopticism, concrete architectural form is transformed into abstract machinic instrumentality. Techniques, as opposed to technology, become an expression of cultural, social, and political relations rather than as an essential power. The effects of abstract machines trigger the formation of concrete assemblages when their virtual diagrammatic relationships are actualized as a technical possibility. Concrete assemblages are realized only when a new diagram can make them cross the technical threshold. It is the already social diagrams that select the new technologies. It is in the spirit of the abstract technical statement yet to become concrete that topologies, animation and parameter-based modeling are being explored here. In order to bring these technologies into a discipline that is defined as the site of translation from the virtual into the concrete, it is necessary that we first interrogate their abstract structure. Without a detailed understanding of their performance as diagrams and organizational techniques it is impossible to begin a discussion of their translation into architectural form. The availa-bility and rapid colonization of architectural design by computer-aided tech-niques presents the discipline with yet another opportunity to both retool and rethink itself as it did with the advent of stereometric projection and perspective. If there is a single concept that must be engaged due to the proliferation of topological shapes and computer-aided tools, it is that in their structure as abstract machines, these technologies are animate.

1   For varied and rigorous discussions of the animal as the surrogate, model and meta-phor for architecture in history, theory and design see the chapter "Donkey Urbanism" in Catherine Ingraham's book *Architecture and the Burdens of Linearity* (New Haven: Yale University Press, 1998) as well as her essay "Animals 2: The Problem of Distinction (Insects, For Example)" in *Assemblage* 14 (Cambridge, 1991), 25–29.

2   It is important to any discussion of parameter-based design that there be both the unfolding of an internal system and the infolding of contextual information fields.

This issue of contextualism is discussed more extensively in my essay "Architectural Curvilinearity: The Folded, the Pliant and the Supple," in *Architectural Design* 102, *Folding in Architecture* (London, 1993) where in the same volume it is also criticized by Jeffrey Kipnis in his essay "Towards a New Architecture."

3   There are two instances of architectural theorists and designers crossing over from models of cinema to models of animation. The first is Brian Boigon's "*The Cartoon Regulators*" in *Assemblage*, 19 (Cambridge, 1992), 66–71. The second is Mark Rakatansky's discussions of the writing and animation of Chuck Jones regarding theories of mobility, action, and gesture in *Any Magazine* 23 (New York, 1998).

4   Sigfried Giedion, *Mechanization Takes Command: A Contribution to Anonymous History* (New York: Oxford University Press, 1948). See also Giedion's *Space, Time and Architecture* (Cambridge: Harvard University Press, 1941).

5   See Sanford Kwinter's "Landscapes of Change" in *Assemblage* 19 (Cambridge, 1992), 50–65.

6   Colin Rowe and Robert Slutsky, "Transparency: Literal and Phenomenal," in *The Mathematics of the Ideal Villa and Other Essays* (Cambridge: MIT Press, c1976).

7   Kenneth Frampton, in "Frontality vs. Rotation" in *Five Architects: Eisenman, Graves, Gwathmey, Hejduk, Meier* (New York: Oxford University Press, 1975), 9–13.

8   The trace has been defined primarily by Jacques Derrida, Peter Eisenman and Bernard Tschumi. Both Bernard Tschumi and Peter Eisenman have referred to the concept of the trace as the representation of time-based processes through simultaneity and seriality. Tschumi captured movement as still frames from a story board in the cinematically inspired *The Manhattan Transcripts* (London: Academy Additions, 1981). Peter Eisenman has worked with traces for the notation of multiple archeological moments and steps in a design process throughout his career. The first method of tracing in Eisenman's work appeared in both his early houses and later in the Aronoff Center at the University of Cincinatti. Harry Cobb has argued that these traces of transformational processes constitute a new form of architectural ornament in the book *Eleven Authors in Search of a Building: The Aronoff Center for Design and Art at the University of Cincinnati,* ed. Cynthia Davidson (New York: Monacelli Press, 1996).

9   Andrew Benjamin's discussion of "*timing*" discriminates between two models of complexity; the first, associated with Descartes, is one of a complex order made of simpler orders; the other, associated with Leibniz, is a complexity of ensembles whose individual and collective order exists "*at the same time.*" "*Here the ensemble in question involves the belonging together of that which resists synthetic unity. The existence of the monad as an already existent ensemble means that the monad is an original ensemble, i.e. an ensemble in which differential plurality is not a consequence of the event, on the contrary it is constitutive of the event—the relational ensemble—itself.*" Andrew Benjamin, *The Plural Event: Descartes, Hegel, Heidegger* (London: Routledge, 1993), 125.

10 Motion and time have been understood as "*vague essences*" because they could not be dimensioned within a static system of point description. The term "*vague essences*" is meant to indicate the properties of forces, behaviors, and relationships that are inherently dynamic and indeterminate and that can not be reduced and quantified once and for all. As Luce Irigaray has argued, because of a persistent Cartesianism, there has been a historic inattention to these temporally and formally indeterminate systems of organization and sciences of vague essences. See the chapter "The Mechanics of Fluids" in Luce Irigaray's book *This Sex Which Is Not One*, trans. Catherine Porter (Ithaca: Cornell University Press, 1985), 106–118.

11 A rare insidence of a philosophical, technical, and historical treatment of topology and calculus in regard to architectural design is Bernard Cache, *Earth Moves: The Furnishing of Territories,* trans. Anne Boyman, ed. Michael Speaks (Cambridge: MIT Press, 1995).

12 This comment is made in reference to a short text co-written by the editors of *Assemblage* comparing Buckminster Fuller's use of "geodesics" with Jesse Reiser's

use of "geodetics," based on the similarity of triangulated surfaces in *Assemblage* 26 (Cambridge, 1997).

13   See Gilles Deleuze's discussion of Henri Bergson in the chapter "Intuition as Method" in his book *Bergsonism*, trans. Hugh Tomlinson and Barbara Habberjam (New York: Zone Books, 1991).

14   In conversation, Rob Shaw explained that the thousands of hours spent in front of a computer screen watching visualizations of chaotic equations was a method of training oneself to recognize those same behaviors intuitively. Rob Shaw and Doyne Farmer were the first people to map the non-periodic behavior in a dripping faucet.

15   A catenoid is a curve defined as a hanging weighted string. Catenoidal curves have been used previously by Antoni Gaudí, Frei Otto and other structural expressionists.

16   See my book *Folds, Bodies and Blobs: Collected Essays* (Brussels: La Lettre Volée, 1998).

17   D'Arcy Thompson, *On Growth and Form* (Cambridge: Cambridge University Press, 1961).

18   Francois Dagognet, *Étienne-Jules Marey: A Passion for the Trace* (New York: Zone Books, 1992), 62.

19   Pamela Johnston, ed. *AA Documents 3: The function of the oblique, The architecture of Claude Parent and Paul Virilio 1963–1969* (London: Architectural Association Publications, 1996).

20   See Henri Bergson, *Matter and Memory,* trans. Nancy Margaret Paul and W. Scott Palmer (New York: Zone Books, 1988) and also Bergson, *Creative Evolution*, trans. Arthur Mitchell, with a foreword by Irwin Edman (New York: The Modern Library, 1944).

21   LynneMargulis, and Dorian Sagan, *Microcosmos: Four Billion Years of Evolution from Our Microbial Ancestors* (Berkeley: University of California Press, 1997).

22   For a discussion of the tradition of "*endlessness*" initiated by Keisler see "Dieter Bogner, Bart Lootsma, Greg Lynn, Lars Spuybroek" in *Cahier* 6 (Rotterdam, 1997), 93–104.

23   Hans Jenny, *Cymatics: Wave Phenomena, Vibrational Effects, Harmonic Oscillations with their Structure, Kinetics and Dynamics*, vol. 2 (Basel: Basilius Press, 1974), 58.

24   Jenny, *Cymatics*, 9.

25   Jenny, *Cymatics*, 7.

26   "*Foucault gives it its most precise name: it is a 'diagram', that is to say a 'functioning, abstracted from any obstacle [. . .] or friction [and which] must be detached from any specific use. The diagram is no longer an auditory visual archive but a map, a cartography that is coextensive with the whole social field. It is an abstract machine.*" Gilles Deleuze, *Foucault,* trans. Seán Hand, foreword by Paul Bové (Minneapolis: University of Minnesota, 1988), 34.

27   Deleuze, Ibid, 39.

28   This argument has been developed more extensively in reference to the work of Ben Van Berkel and his office's use of diagramming as a strategy for beginning the design process in "Forms of Expression: The Proto-Functional Potential of Diagrams in Architectural Design" in *El Croquis* 72/73 (Madrid, 1995).

It can be argued that architecture's contemporary embrace of the geometries of modern mathematics has occurred derivative of, but largely removed from, the corresponding evolution in the foundational basis of space and shape that these advances propose. As algorithmic design has emerged through application of a collection of discrete geometric techniques, the contemporary language of form has become a disparate archipelago of geometries with unique topological signatures, collectively instantiated into space but otherwise disconnected from any unifying framework.

The project featured here is twofold. First, it seeks to reconnect the theory and discourse of contemporary architectural form to its origins in the development of modern mathematics, and in doing so bring to light the radical implications these theoretical developments offer to the epistemology of form. From the basis of this emergent theoretical foundation, a framework for the examination of form is proposed that reveals the distinct topologies of contemporary architectural form as aspects of a synthetic and unifying problematic. As a central example, the framework is applied to the oppositions of continuous and discrete topologies, and demonstrates that these apparently contrary signatures can be seen as duals, co-emerging from a common origin.

> Space and Shape

From antiquity until the present, architecture has been founded on the principles, constructs and, to no small extent, the ontologies of the Euclidean and Cartesian systems. Often used interchangeably, these systems both individually and in concert make specific assertions on the nature of geometry and its relationship to space. Euclid's *Elements*[1] establish geometry through assertions on constructions of shapes – the lines and arcs, their measurements, angles and intersections – without directly referencing a spatial medium. They establish 'shape as construction'.

The Cartesian system declares shape as an algebraic function on points in real numbered coordinate space (R^n). The fact that the Euclidian constructions hold when described as coordinates is one of the remarkable achievements of the Cartesian system. However, no less remarkably, the Euclidean axioms do not presume or require the presence of any space, real numbered or other, to be complete.

The nature of space, in which the constructions occur and the axioms hold, has been debated throughout the history of spatial ontology,[2] and specifically whether space is absolute, discrete from geometries it contains, or relational, sufficiently defined by relationships between spatial phenomena. Despite the complexity of

Figure 5.1

Descartes' position,[3] and Euclid's silence on the topic, the Euclidean/Cartesian system has become identified with geometry as functions on points in three-dimensional, real-numbered space, and of 'shape as occupancy' of three-dimensional space. This containing space is presumed Euclidean: linear, continuous, absolute and singular; there is only one such space in which all shape occurs.

Shape grammar theory, as established by George Stiny,[4] provides an important counterpoint to this largely pervasive view of design shape as occupancy of point set topology. This work re-prioritises shape over space, and re-establishes an axiomatic system of shape as an algebraic topology of shapes and their parts. As with the Euclidean elements, shape grammars form a complete system of shape description whose closure is independent of any containment space. While much of the application of this system has been concerned with developing substitution grammars of Euclidean transformations implicitly deployed in the context of a Euclidean spatial medium, the shape grammar system has demonstrated applicability to problems involving non-Euclidean elements and their transformations as well.

In the last half decade, the available descriptions of architectural form have radically expanded beyond the Euclidean to include new geometries: the non-Euclidean, the fractal, the procedural and the parametric. The existence of such geometries has been supposed over the past three centuries, but prior to digital computation they could be treated only in their most general forms and through their most simplistic examples, largely inaccessible to anyone beyond topologists. These geometries are no longer seen as monstrous or pathological, devised to challenge the limits of the Euclidean, but rather as generalisations of the classic geometries, formalisms of utility and applicability to architecture, and indeed of everyday experience. Collectively they can be seen as positing a view of 'shape as space'; moreover as connections via mappings among a disparate network of Euclidean, non-Euclidean and more general topologies.

The most visible examples are the tensor manifolds of Non-uniform Rational B-spline (NURBS) surfaces. These geometries occur as R2 x R3 mappings between two or more distinct topological spaces: an intrinsic two-dimensional parametric space, and the containing three-dimensional space outside the surface. The extrinsic space contains the shape as points of occupancy, while the intrinsic space – the space of the surface – is the basis by which its shape is described, measured and traversed, and the perspective from which its continuity emerges. Its signature as a continuous surface emerges from both its real numbered Cartesian intrinsic and extrinsic structures, and by the specific coordinate relationships defined across its

---

Facing page

Figure 5.1: A medial surface discretised by parallelepipeds. The medial surface represents a class of surfaces that synthesise global topology with local discretisation. Image credit: Dennis R. Shelden.

mapping. By extension to alternative dimensions, the two- and three-dimensional Euclidean and non-Euclidean shapes including points, lines, curves, surfaces and volumes are described. This mapping is itself a space – the product space of the intrinsic and extrinsic – and an instance in the space of the family of all similarly structured mappings. This framework extends directly to the parametric, wherein shapes are instances of geometric functions driven from spaces of discrete parametric values. The spaces are not atomic, but in turn disaggregate into subspaces of individual parameters, subshapes and their products. As shapes aggregate through their combinatorics, so do their individual connected spaces connect into larger networks. Shape exists in – and as – this network of spatial connection.

In the purely digital realm, both intrinsic and embedding spaces are by necessity Euclidian – real numbered coordinate systems within the machine. However, this manifold structuring applies in a formally rigorous manner when extended to a much wider spectrum of embedding topologies. Manifolds can be embedded into any topological space where locally continuous measurement by real numbered coordinates holds. This broad class of admissible embedding topologies includes the affine, vector and tensor spaces among many others. We can in fact rigorously consider manifolds that bridge from the digital into the 'worldly' topologies and transformations of physical space. The measurements and mappings, historically the realm of craft, are now conducted through increasingly sophisticated machines providing direct and continuous transformation between numerical coordinates and physical location.

What emerges is a view of space and shape that is a radical expansion of the Cartesian system. Space and shape are no longer distinct, but synonymous. Shapes emerge from, within and as a system of spatial networks of heterogeneous dimension and signature, no longer inert but active and dynamic, continuously created, connected and destroyed by design. Within this system, Euclidean geometries and spaces take a natural place as the restricted class of linear transformations in the more general class of differentiable mappings. The Euclidean re-emerges locally within the network as a regularising structure wherever Cartesian product spaces of independent real variables and their linear transformations occur.

In the context of such an expanding constellation of interconnected space, the notion of a singular and privileged containing space loses hold as a necessary or even relevant construct. Special relativity dictates that the container view of space cannot hold, but we do not need to recourse to the very large, very small or very fast to witness the efficacy of the relational space–time view. At the scale of human experience, we may arbitrarily select a containing Euclidean space worldview – of specific dimensionality, measured by a specific coordinate system, etc., and normalise shape by its embedding into this arbitrarily privileged frame. But this reductionism erases the syntactic structure of shape that can only be seen through its nature as the connective tissue in and among the relational spaces in which shape participates, both generating and inhabiting.

This evolution of the spatial fabric presupposed by contemporary geometry, of shape as space, and of space as relational, localised and connected, is arguably the central ontological advance of contemporary form making and associated architectural description. Most significant for design is the migration of form's locus, which emerges not simply as the occupancy of any specific Cartesian space, nor its numerical description, but resides in and as the connection between spatial frames – the intrinsic and the extrinsic, the Euclidean and non-Euclidean, the continuous and the discrete, the digital and the physical.

> Continuous Maps and their Epistemic Limits

The new geometries are uneasily classified as either continuous or discrete, a dichotomy whose simple and axiomatic distinction in the classical view – between the real and the integer – no longer so simply holds. The non-Euclidean shapes are intrinsically continuous, but can demonstrate folds and singularities in the embedding space. The procedural shapes of subdivision surfaces may be extrinsically continuous but arise out of discrete intrinsic operations. Parametric shapes may be both continuous in state space and their extrinsic instantiation, but may exhibit singularities in either, and no longer maintain any topological similarity between intrinsic and extrinsic views.

The impulse to equate continuous maps to complete definitions of architectural elements is compelling because it has proven so germane to problems of constructability, rationalisation and parametric control. If one understands the surface as a purely functional space, problems of design rationalisation become more precise and tractable. Unfortunately the lure of such problems has kept recent applications of mathematical approaches within architecture focused on technical problems of surface resolution and modularisation, rather than on broader questions of spatial structure and design coherence. Fascinating as issues of surface differential geometry are, the more fundamental formal issues play out at the scale of the global surface – that is, how surfaces enclose and partition spaces, how one circulates among them, and resolution of spatial connectedness and separation. How can we bridge the gap between the mathematics of continuous discretisation and the syntax of architectural spaces?

To answer, we must consider why the functional definition of surface geometry has become so distinct from the topological one. It follows from the axiomatisation of mathematics in the nineteenth century. During this time the mathematician Felix Klein was preoccupied with the question of unifying a multiplicity of theoretical geometries. Klein's ambition was to classify the varieties of surfaces through the sets of maps or functions that left these surfaces invariant.[5] Continuous maps themselves form a space which can be transformed, and these second-order sets of transformations can themselves also be transformed, and so on, creating an infinitely nested sequence of continuous function sets that indirectly describe the properties of the first set of surfaces. Klein's proposal for a unified classification of surfaces through their nested invariant functional meta-behaviour is known as the Erlangen programme.

While the Erlangen programme opened profound new understandings in the mathematics of geometric group theory, it also effectively divorced geometry from spatial intuition: since facts about commutative algebra became facts about the surface itself, spatial visualisation became super-fluous to the mathematical study of surfaces. By distancing geometry from visualisation, Klein's Erlangen Program lay the seeds of the divorce between geometry and design.

This split is fundamental because continuous mathematical functions, algebraically expressed, often obscure rather than reveal spatial or topological facts. The local, closed, analytic representation of the surface does not commu-nicate its key spatial properties – the moments of self-intersection, self-tangency, the way it partitions space. Consider, for example, the functional expression of the tangent developable surface $s(u,v)=c(u) + v(c'(u))$.[6] The function is by defini-tion continuous, but it is difficult, a priori, to observe that such a surface has a singularity, precisely at the curve of its generation. Thus for designers, a purely functional approach obscures as much as it illuminates.

What designers need are descriptors of shape and space that encompass, but move beyond, notions of functional continuity to include singularities, ruptures and exceptional conditions. What we need are richer descriptions of topology that embed also implicit logics of construction and concurrent local discretisation that emerge organically from the global topology itself. Of course the tools we have are new, but this synthetic ambition for deductive relationships of local parts to global whole is a fundamental tension within the project of design itself.

> Continuous Maps and the Topological Exceptions of the Gothic

The dialectic between global continuity and local discontinuity forms a clear thread within design history, emerging from material laws of aggregation and deformation. Certain designers strive for perfect and unobstructed continuity, and others for punctuated discontinuity. The tension is illustrated in the topological exceptions of Gothic vaults – moments where continuity is frustrated by ruptures in the logic of module propagation itself. Gothic builders attempted to build complex vault surfaces with modules – bricks – with no explicit mathematical relationship to the vault geometry. The diver-gence of each successive row of aggregation from the ideal design surface accumulated to the point of system rupture – the necessary introduction of a distinct material and module. As the logic of discrete material confronts the desire of global continuous expression, the need for more integrated descrip-tors of shape emerges.

> Semantic Descriptors of Global Ruptures

Mathematics seduces with its promise of rigorous synthesis to otherwise contradictory systems of rules. To control the logic of ruptures, architects need a semantic set of descriptors that are not merely parametric but topological, which represent, essentialise and make operative the basic tensions of contrary and contested conditions in design. In this context we mention two constructs – the curve skeleton and the medial surface – that suggest generative topological tools and semantic descriptors of shape.

Architecture is the design of a felicitous relationship of parts to whole, a synthetic project of multi-objective invention. The promise of mathematics is that those diverse relationships and constraints can be made conceptually or notationally explicit, and their manipulation can be precise.

Computer vision scientists began the search for such semantic descriptors to distil shapes to their computer-readable fundamentals. In the 1960s, interest in syntactic structure for the human senses produced operators that would take any shapes and automatically generate information about their fundamental spatial or topological configuration. A pioneer among these researchers was Harry Blum, of the US Air Force Research Laboratories. During the 1960s, Blum devised a construct which, given a particular shape, would generate a second encoded shape that would distil the key formal features of corners, changes in curvature and general configuration. This second, encoded shape often indirectly revealed features of the first shape that were difficult to detect directly. Blum called his shape descriptor the 'curve skeleton'.[7]

The significance of Blum's curve skeleton for design is that one can deductively calculate the topological singularities of a broad range of shapes, surfaces and spaces from a non-analytic description of global shape. Instead of operating on the functional notation of the shape, it operates on the shape itself, regardless of its notational representation. The curve skeleton appears in many contexts – as a diagram of circulation, as an aid to smooth subdivision, as an emergent property of circle and shape packings.

The urban form of Paris is an example of the surprising uses of the curve skeleton. In post-Haussmann Paris, designers pack regularly shaped apartments into irregularly shaped city blocks. This quasi-uniform packing – not unlike the packing of stones in a Gothic vault – must be reconciled with the irregular block shapes of the global urban plan. The solution is remarkable: the curve skeleton, this essential diagram of shape, appears not as a planned structure but as an emergent trace, an inevitable consequence of uniform packing within a non-uniform boundary.

Curve skeletons can be generalised from planimetric to surfacial constructs. Applying the logic of the curve skeleton to a collection of curves in space produces a surface wall between each pair of curves in the set; a configuration called a 'medial surface'. The medial surface is the precise surface that would induce a given set of circulation paths around and through it.

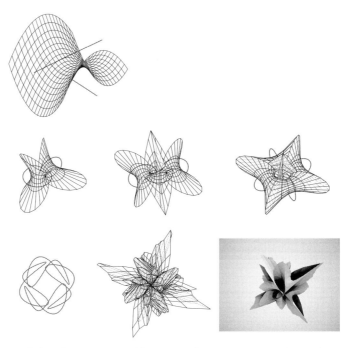

Figure 5.2: Medial surfaces generated from sets of curves. Image credit: Andrew Witt.

The curve skeleton, and to some extent the medial surface, are nearly self-dual: they can represent either circulation paths, or the surfaces and walls that enclose circulation paths. From wall boundaries the skeleton describes a circulation path through them. Conversely, from a circulation path the skeleton will describe walls that induce that circulation. The curve skeleton thus represents something fundamental about space and circulation, a reciprocity between the singularities that structure both.

What is more, for medial surfaces there is post-rational surface discretisation; their definition guarantees that they are rationalisable in a quad-dominated way. In fact, there is an elegant connection between the global and local forms of these medial surfaces since the joint lines between different surfacial domains extend continuously from one to the next. Medial surfaces thus represent a sort of synthesis of continuity and rupture, in one simple descriptor.

With these curve skeleton diagrams and medial surfaces, the topological properties of space – connectivity, passage, edge and rupture – follow directly from the connective paths of the designed promenade. These surfaces represent a deductive relationship between parts and whole. Our contemporary opportunity is to broaden the connection of mathematics

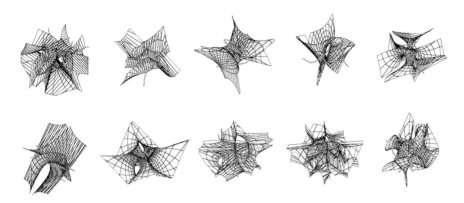

Figure 5.3: Medial surfaces generated from sets of curves. Image credit: Andrew Witt.

to architecture beyond intensive application of continuous surface functions to a disciplinary project that is more synthetic and spatially specific. In short, we can broaden our vision beyond analysis and generative procedures to design.

> Conclusion

Architecture is the design of a felicitous relationship of parts to whole, a synthetic project of multi-objective invention. The promise of mathematics is that those diverse relationships and constraints can be made conceptually or notationally explicit, and their manipulation can be precise. A logic of continuous maps is an aspiration towards that comprehensive quality – a precise description of the local, topologically global and structurally recursive. But these maps, limited as they are by the semantics of their symbolic notation, hold the seed of their own rupture, particularly when iteratively applied. Continuous maps can fold, intersect with themselves, exhibit singularities; what is continuous from one point of view or notational representation may not be so from another. The identification of these ruptures, both at the local scale and at the global, topological scale, becomes key to understanding space itself and the descriptive, analytic and designed project of architecture – the description of the thing itself, beyond its multiple notational representations. In particular, architecture can begin to move beyond empty ideological distinctions that rest on notational distinctions, beyond simple dichotomies between pre-rationalisation and post-rationalisation, towards a more profound and codetermined logic of space. What is required is a more synthetic approach of global–local reciprocity, and an embedded logic of mathematical design.

1   TL Heath, *Euclid: The Thirteen Books of The Elements*, Dover Publications (New York), 1956.

2   GV Leroy, *Die philos. Probleme in dem Briefwechsel Leibniz und Clarke*, Giessen, 1893.

3   N Huggett, 'Cartesian Spacetime: Descartes' Physics and the Relational Theory of Space and Motion', *British Journal for the Philosophy of Science* 55(1), 2004, pp 189–93.

4   G Stiny, *Shape: Talking about Seeing and Doing*, (MIT Press (Cambridge, MA), 2008.

5   F Klein, *Elementary Mathematics from an Advanced Standpoint: Geometry*, Dover Publications (New York), 2004.

6   E Kreysig, *Differential Geometry*, Dover Publications (New York), 1981.

7   Harry Blum, 'A Transformation for Extracting New Descriptors of Shape', in W Wathen-Dunn, *Models for the Perception of Speech and Visual Form*, MIT Press (Cambridge, MA), 1967, pp 362–80.

PERFORMANCE/ GENERATION

From Analysis
to Informed
Synthesis

**Rivka Oxman
and
Robert Oxman**

Performance-based design relates to a set of concepts engaging the analysis and understanding of how the environmental context may inform complex processes of design synthesis.

Simulation is one of the seminal concepts of *performance-based design* (redefined as performative design when integrated with generation). In contemporary design practice simulation involves an instrumental toolset that enhances analytical procedures. Beyond simulation, environmental design is built upon a *posteriori* techniques of analysis such as types of post-occupancy evaluations that determine what a building or environment *does* and how it makes effects rather than merely the descriptive content of what it is and how it is perceived (Leatherbarrow, 2005).

With this definition, the complexity of the concept of performance is demonstrated. Both temporally (when in the cycle of life of a building, a settlement, or a landscape do we evaluate the performative behavior?) and content-wise (what do we in fact measure, including physical factors or human-centered behavioral qualities?), performance is contingent upon multivariate parameters. In any multivariate design environment the integration and balance of the various factors frequently becomes a theoretical problem. Even if we limit simulation techniques to physical and environmental parameters such as structure, climate and acoustic factors, multivariate performance-based design methods are complex.

Beyond simulation and the definition of performance evaluation parameters considered, the third of the seminal concepts of performance-based design relates to evaluative criteria, how they are formulated and how they are applied in design. The term and the techniques most frequently associated with performance-based models and techniques are *optimization*. Optimization is not necessarily the dominant value and operative principle of natural systems, in which redundancy frequently supplants optimization as an operative technique of survival under the dynamic conditions of natural and evolutionary processes (Weinstock, 2006).

Form finding is a significant concept that changes the traditional meaning of performance by integrating formation and generation processes (Oxman, 2008). Among the canonic precedents of performance techniques applied in design are the *form finding* experiments of Gaudí, Otto, Isler and others. These works are almost universally monotonic in their emphasis upon structural design and in involving large spans, or the special conditions of lightweight structures, or minimal surface design. Otto is an exception among this body of pioneer designers. He consistently engaged multiple conditions of diverse functions and problems as they related to approaches to *analog modeling* as a technique of performative experimental design.

These then are the source concepts and contradictions that come into play in current theories and methods of *digital performance-based design*. Design engineering in archi/structural design is one of the leading fields in the advancement of such design techniques (Oxman and Oxman, 2010). Their applications and development over the past decade in the works of such leading structural designers as Balmond (Arup), Sasaki, Bollinger + Grohmann, Happold, AKT and others have pioneered the processes and techniques of performance-based design. They have developed these techniques as both a *digital generative method* and a *collaborative medium*.

The introduction in design research of topics such as evolutionary processes in natural systems with an emphasis upon morphogenesis as an evolutionary and adaptive process in natural systems has made intellectual and operative contributions in the last decade (Hensel, Menges and Weinstock, 2006). The purpose of this introduction is to clarify this intricate thread of conceptual relationships as they form the field of *digital performative design*.

In performative design, projected building performance becomes the guiding principle of the logical progression of the design process. The coordination of multiple design parameters currently still requires the agency of design team collaborators in the form of consultants. In digital performance-based design (performative design) digital models of the projected design are the basis for analytical processes of evaluation. Generally the digital toolset differs by type of design area (structural, climatic, acoustic, sustainability, costs, etc.). Structural analyses such as FEM and energy analyses have become very sophisticated and effective. Gaussian analyses for degree of curvature are among other classes of analytical procedures that are having an impact on the ability to modulate geometry in response to production rationalization.

Current digital analytical toolsets (Malkawi, 2005) are mainly analytical; they do not yet provide both analysis and synthesis. The most well used toolsets are essentially *single domain toolsets* (for structure, climate, etc.) packages each of which may analyze multiple parameters within the domain. The interoperability and integrated systems of *multiple domain tools* exists, but is less well developed. Toolsets may integrate *optimization techniques* that support the exploration of the design space through the evolutionary modeling of Generative Algorithms (GA). These provide recursive processes of generation-evaluation-modification integrated with a morphing module. Finally, most current toolsets provide a *visual interface* of a model representation as well the provision of data which provides for visual evaluation.

Many of these toolsets are customized in project-driven environments (Whitehead, 2003). Whitehead points out that in order for performance analysis to be useful in the processes of design and manufacturing, a very exact control of project geometry, along with its potential for contributing to the geometric and topological variation of the project, is required. In modulating the evolutionary processes of performative design a high level of knowledge of architectural geometry has become a necessity. This is among the functions and knowledge base of "research-based design," undertaken in large offices by specialist multidisciplinary research groups such as the SMG: Specialist Modelling Group of Foster, or the AGU: Advanced Geometry Unit of Arup.

Whitehead, in his description of the form-related integrated energy solution of the London City Hall, explains how the energy-related design process was supported by the research group's provision of a parametric setup for each project that typically included a set of "variational templates." The variational setup of the project (geometry + topology + material considerations) must also relate to a "project tectonics." Thus the *evolutionary potential of tectonic systems* is becoming an additional form of architectural knowledge. It is also potentially an important new medium for the future development of digital generative performative design environments.

We have defined form finding as the use of physical models in the experimental design of structures. In *digital form finding* the designer, rather than creating a one-off design, designs an ad hoc "project generative system," a modeling system that includes parametric digital morphing of the topological design space of the model. The results of analytical procedures support critical assessment on the part of the design team and modifications to the model in a time-based iterative process. The toolset can aid in the *generate/evaluate/moderate cycle* of digital design while not yet being able to add fully automatic moderation and regeneration to the cycle.

Digital tectonic modeling is particularly suited to the instrumentation and evaluation of the performative capabilities of the *self-organization of material systems* under contextual loadings of various classes. Thus research into the *tectonics of material systems* is one of the forms of foundational knowledge for future design environments of digital performative generative design. This knowledge provides for the modeling of material formative processes.

Morphogenesis studies and morphogenetic design processes are relevant to performance-based design in that they introduce various significant concepts and bodies of knowledge. The study of natural and biological developmental processes provides knowledge relevant to the development of digital performative systems. Furthermore, the field of *biomimicry* introduces issues related to the characterization of principles of "natural design" and their implications for human design. Among these, the concepts of genome and phenome in developmental biology are significant for the understanding of adaptive evolutionary modeling as a basis for the formalization of emergent behaviors. The structural morphologies of material systems and their evolutionary adaptive behavior offer the theoretical foundation for a *material tectonics* and a *digital material tectonics*. These are the potential future media for performative generative systems. Finally, morphogenesis studies provide insights into the application of morphological differentiation and heterogeneity (cf. standardization and repetition) and redundancy as strategies for adaptation versus optimization (Weinstock, 2006).

Digital generative processes in *performative generative design* are still mainly experimental. They are generally based upon a generative algorithm such as Genetic Algorithms, L Systems, or Shape Grammars and may also include optimization techniques. The modification process begins with a predesigned schema and continues to modify it until defined performance criteria are achieved. The generative algorithm serves to maintain the topology of the solution space while enabling geometric modification. Most current generative systems are still rather explicit and deterministic with respect to the linkage between geometry and typology. Consequently, there are still serious limitations with respect to the generality of generative systems and their degree of potential for finding "innovative" design solutions. Given such current limitations to performative generative design, the search for new knowledge bases in architectural geometry as well as in material tectonics may eventually contribute to the future potential of performative generative systems by integrating generative tools with digital tectonic systems. That is, without the formulation of a well-founded theory of digital (material) tectonics, we cannot expect significant advancement in performative generative design media.

Performance-based generative design in practice is a highly iterative and interactive process (Bollinger, Grohmann and Tessmann, 2008, 2010) involving multiple digital feedback loops of synthesis and evaluation, as "evolutionary algorithms generate and manipulate character strings that serve as genotypes, or entire populations of structures." (Bollinger, Grohmann and Tessmann, 2010, p. 36.) The genotype of the structural model enables the construction of a set of parametric modules that are the phenotypes in the process of digital form finding. The VOxEL building, designed with LAVA Architects, went through a digital evolutionary cycle of two hundred such iterations. The goal was not necessarily structural optimization so much as achieving equilibrium between the multiple parameters of the design. The logic of the *continuous digital workflow* in digital performative generative design must also include material systems and construction procedures. In this highly interactive set of iterative processes the analytical data provides feedback to the generative material model (the project-specific generative material tectonic) for form generation and refinement.

Linkages to emerging CAM technologies are providing the possibility for the exploration of material tectonics. Beyond project-specific material tectonic systems, we require a general theory of material tectonics in order to eventually be able to achieve the design of generative performative systems.

Bollinger, Klaus, Grohmann, Manfred and Tessmann, Oliver (2008), "Form, Force, Performance: Multi-Parametric Structural Design," in Hensel, Michael and Menges, Achim eds., *Versatility and Vicissitude: Performance in Morpho-Ecological Design*, AD (*Architectural Design*), Profile No. 192, Vol. 78, No. 2, pp. 20–25

Bollinger, Klaus, Grohmann, Manfred and Tessmann, Oliver (2010), "Structured Becoming: Evolutionary Processes in Design Engineering," in Oxman, Rivka and Oxman, Robert eds., *The New Structuralism: Design, Engineering and Architectural Technologies*, AD (*Architectural Design*), Profile No. 206, Vol. 80, No. 4, July/August, pp. 34–39

Hensel, Michael (2004), "Finding Exotic Form," in Hensel, Michael, Menges, Achim and Weinstock, Michael, eds., *Emergence: Morphogenetic Design Strategies*, AD (*Architectural Design*), Profile No. 169, Vol. 74, No. 3, May/June, pp. 26–33

Hensel, Michael and Menges, Achim (2006), "Differentiation and Performance: Multi-Performance Architectures and Modulated Environments," in Hensel, Michael, Menges, Achim and Weinstock, Michael, eds., *Techniques and Technologies in Morphogenetic Design*, AD (*Architectural Design*), Profile No. 180, Vol. 76, No. 2, March/April, pp. 60–63

Malkawi, Ali M. (2005), "Performance Simulation: Research and Tools," in Kolarevic, Branko and Malkawi, Ali M., *Performative Architectures: Beyond Instrumentality*, Spon Press, New York and London, pp. 85–96

Oxman, Rivka (2008), Performance-Based Design: Current Practices and Research Issues, *International Journal of Architectural Computing*, Vol. 6, No. 1, pp. 1–17

Oxman, Rivka (2009), "Performative Design: a Performance-Based Model of Digital Architectural Design," *Environment and Planning (B): Planning and Design*, Vol. 36, pp. 1026–1037

Oxman, Rivka and Oxman, Robert, eds. (2010), *The New Structuralism: Design, Engineering and Architectural Technologies*, AD (*Architectural Design*), Profile No. 206, Vol. 80, No. 4, July/August

Weinstock, Michael (2006), "Self-Organisation and the Structural Dynamics of Plants," in Hensel, Michael, Menges, Achim and Weinstock, Michael, *Techniques and Technologies in Morphogenetic Design*, AD (*Architectural Design*), Profile No. 180, Vol. 76, No. 2, March/April, pp. 26–33

Weinstock, Michael and Stathopoulos, Nikolaos (2006), "Advanced Simulation in Design," in Hensel, Michael, Menges, Achim and Weinstock, Michael, *Techniques and Technologies in Morphogenetic Design*, AD (*Architectural Design*), Profile No. 180, Vol. 76, No. 2, March/April, pp. 54–59

Whitehead, Hugh (2003), "Laws of Form," in Kolarevic, Branko, ed., *Architecture in the Digital Age: Design and Manufacturing*, Spon Press, New York and London, pp. 81–100

> List of Key Concepts

adaptive systems
archi/structural design
differentiation
digital form finding
digital performativity
ecological performance
emergence
evolutionary systems
form finding
generation/evaluation (generate
    and test)
generative performative design
integrated performance
material ecology
morpho-ecologies

multivariate performance factors
multivariate performative design
optimization
performance
performance analysis
performance-based design
performance behavior
performance factors/parameters
performative ecologies
performative generation
performative materiality
performativity
redundancy
simulation
simulation tools/techniques

In avant-garde contemporary architectural design, various digital generative and production processes are opening up new territories for conceptual, formal and tectonic exploration, articulating an architectural morphology focused on the emergent and adaptive properties of form.[1] In a radical departure from centuries-old traditions and norms of architectural design, digitally generated forms are not designed or drawn as the conventional understanding of these terms would have it, but they are calculated by the chosen generative computational method. Instead of working on a *parti*, the designer constructs a *generative system* of formal production, controls its behavior over time, and selects forms that emerge from its operation. The emphasis shifts from the "making of form" to the "finding of form," which various digitally based generative techniques seem to bring about intentionally.

The new, speculative design work of the digital avant-garde, enabled by time-based modeling techniques, is provoking an interesting debate about the possibilities and challenges of the digital generation of form (i.e. the *digital morphogenesis*).[2] There is an aspiration to manifest formally the invisible dynamic processes that are shaping the physical context of architecture, which, in turn, are driven by the socio-economic and cultural forces within a larger context. According to Greg Lynn, "the context of design becomes an active abstract space that directs from within a current of forces that can be stored as information in the shape of the form."[3] Formal complexity is often intentionally sought out, and this morphological intentionality is what motivates the processes of construction, operation and selection.

This dynamic, time-driven shift in conceptualization techniques, however, should not be limited to the issues of representation, i.e. formal appearance, only. While we now have the means to visualize the dynamic forces that affect architecture by introducing the dimension of time into the processes of conceptualization, we can begin to qualify their effects and, in the case of certain technical aspects, begin to quantify them too. There is a range of digital analytical tools that can help designers assess certain *performative* aspects of their projects, but none of them provide dynamic generative capabilities yet.

> Performance-based Design

The aesthetics of many projects of the digital avant-garde, however, are often sidetracking the critical discourse into the more immediate territory of formal expression and away from more fundamental possibilities that are opening up. Such possibilities include the emergence of *performance-based design*, in which

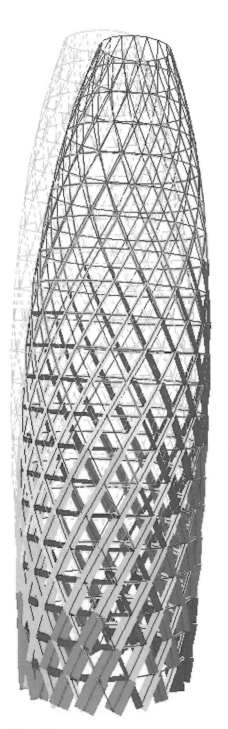

Element list: "Skin"

Scale: 1:1.101E+3

Deformation magnification: 25

Axial Force, Fx: 2.000E+3 kN/

1.056E+3 kN
754.2 kN
452.5 kN
150.8 kN
-150.8 kN
-452.5 kN
-754.2 kN
-1.056E+3 kN

Case: 4 :"Wind X"

Figure 6.1

building performance becomes a guiding design principle, considered on a par with or above form making.

The current interest in building performance as a design paradigm is largely due to the emergence of sustainability as a defining socio-economic issue and to the recent developments in technology and cultural theory. Within such an expansive context, building performance can be defined very broadly, across multiple realms, from financial, spatial, social and cultural to purely technical (structural, thermal, acoustical, etc.). The issues of performance (in all its multiple manifestations) are considered not in isolation or in some kind of linear progression but *simultaneously*, and are engaged early on in the conceptual stages of the project, by relying on close collaboration between the many parties involved in the design of a building. In such a highly "networked" design context, digital quantitative and qualitative performance-based simulations are used as a technological foundation for a comprehensive new approach to the design of the built environment.

It is important to note that performance-based design should not be seen as simply a way of devising a set of practical solutions to a set of largely practical problems, i.e. it should not be reduced to some kind of neo-functionalist approach to architecture. The emphasis shifts to the processes of form generation based on performative strategies of design that are grounded, at one end, in intangibilities such as cultural performance and, at the other, in quantifiable and qualifiable performative aspects of building design, such as structure, acoustics or environmental design. Determining the different performative aspects in a particular project and reconciling often conflicting performance goals in a creative and effective way are some of the key challenges in performance-based design.

> Calculating Performance Then

The performative design thinking, framed by a broadly defined performance agenda and supported by a range of digital performance analysis and simulation tools, as outlined briefly above, was envisioned decades ago. Back in the late 1960s and early 1970s, a group of researchers led by Thomas Maver at ABACUS (Architecture and Building Aids Computer Unit Strathclyde) at the University of Strathclyde's Department of Architecture and Building Science, proposed that the building design be directly driven and actively supported by a range of integrated "performance appraisal aids" running on computer systems.[4]

Facing page

Figure 6.1: FEA analysis of stress for the Swiss Re building, London, 1997-2004, by Arup, architect Foster + Partners. Image credit: Computer model and analysis by Arup. Courtesy of Branko Kolarevic.

Digital building performance "appraisal aids" and performance-based design were at the center of computer-aided building design research for more than three decades — many of the essential concepts and techniques were pioneered in the late 1960s and early 1970s. For example, the first use of computer graphics for building appraisal was in 1966, the first integrated package for building performance appraisal appeared in 1972, the first computer-generated perspective drawings appeared in 1973, etc.[5] The 1970s resulted in the "generation of a battery of computer aids for providing the designer with evaluative feedback on his design proposals," enabling architects to "obtain highly accurate predictions of such building performance measures as heat loss, daylight contours, shadow projections and acoustic performance."[6]

One of the first digital performance analysis tools to emerge was PACE (Package for Architectural Computer Evaluation), developed at ABACUS and introduced in 1970 as a "computer-aided appraisal facility for use at strategic stages in architectural design," (Maver, 1971, p. 207) which, unlike many of the efforts at the time, focused "not on optimization of a single parameter but on production of a comprehensive and integrated set of appraisal measures."[7] PACE was written in FORTRAN and run on a time-sharing system; the "conversational interaction" was through a teletypewriter terminal. The program measured costs, "spatial," environmental and "activity" performance. The "spatial performance" component measured site utilization (plot ratio) and plan and mass compactness. Computing the environmental performance resulted in "plant sizes which [would] give adequate environmental conditions," (Maver, 1971, p. 214) while taking into account the heat gain and loss. The "activity performance" module measured "the degree to which the relationships input under activity information are satisfied by the proposed scheme." (Maver, 1971, p. 210.)

The program would instruct the designer how to change geometrical or constructional information, i.e. how to modify the design concept to improve performance and then submit the modified design for "reappraisal." In the end, the "repetitive man/machine interaction" would lead to "convergence of an 'optimum' design solution." A particularly interesting aspect of the program was its built-in capacity to "learn:" if the designer was satisfied with the scheme, the program would update the stored mean values used in assessments.[8]

As is often the case with visionary ideas, much of the early work in digitally driven, performance-based design was far ahead of its time both conceptually and technologically. But its time has now come, as performance-based design is slowly but steadily coming to the forefront of architectural discourse.

> Simulating Performance Now

Today, digital quantitative and qualitative performance-based simulation represents the technological foundation of the emerging performative architecture described earlier. Analytical computational techniques based on the finite element method (FEM), in which the geometric model is divided into small, interconnected mesh elements, are used to accurately perform structural, energy and fluid dynamics analyses for buildings of any formal complexity. These quantitative evaluations of specific design propositions can be qualitatively assessed today thanks to improvements in graphic output and visualization techniques. By superposing various analytical evaluations, design alternatives could be compared with relative simplicity to select a solution that offers desired performance.

Future Systems, a design firm from London, used computational fluid dynamics (CFD) analysis in a particularly interesting fashion in its Project ZED, the design of a multiple-use building in London (1995). The building was meant to be self-sufficient in terms of its energy needs by incorporation of photovoltaic cells in the louvers and a giant wind turbine placed in a huge hole in its center. The curved form of the façade was thus designed to minimize the impact of the wind at the building's perimeter and to channel it towards the turbine at the center. The CFD analysis was essential in improving the aerodynamic performance of the building envelope.

The original blobby shape of Peter Cook and Colin Fournier's competition winning entry for the Kunsthaus Graz, Austria, was altered somewhat after the digital structural analysis by consulting engineers Bollinger + Grohmann from Frankfurt revealed that its structural performance could be improved with minor adjustments in the overall form, by extracting the isoparametric curves for the envelope definition not from the underlying NURBS geometry but from the structural analysis. Likewise, Foster + Partners' design for the main chamber of the London City Hall had to undergo several significant changes after engineers from Arup analyzed its acoustical performance using in-house developed acoustic wave propagation simulation software.

In Gehry's office, Gaussian analysis is used to determine the extent of curvature of different areas on the surface of the building. That way the designers can quickly assess the material performance, i.e. whether the material can be curved as intended, as there are limits to how much a particular material with a particular thickness can be deformed. More importantly, the curvature analysis provides quick, visual feedback about the overall cost of the building's "skin," as doubly curved areas (shown in red) are much more expensive to manufacture than the single-curved sections (shown in green and blue tones).

As these examples demonstrate, the feedback provided by visualization techniques in the current building performance simulation software can be very effective in design development. The software, however, operates at the systemic level in the same *passive* fashion as two or three decades ago. "Computer-aided appraisal" now and back in 1980, as described by Thomas Maver, has consisted of four main elements: representation, measurement, evaluation and modification:

The designer generates a design hypothesis which is input into the computer (representation); the computer software models the behaviour of the hypothesized design and outputs measures of cost and performance on a number of relevant criteria (measurements); the designer (perhaps in conjunction with the client body) exercises his (or their) value judgement (evaluation) and decides on appropriate changes to the design hypothesis (modification).[9]

As noted by Maver, "if the representation and measurement modules of the design system can be set up and made available, the processes of evaluation and modification take place dynamically within the design activity as determinants of, and in response to, the pattern of explorative search," (Maver, 1971, pp. 207–14) which is a fairly accurate description of how performance analysis ("appraisal") software is being used today.

> Challenges

Designing buildings that perform (i.e. "which work — economically, socially and technically") is a central challenge for architects, as observed by Thomas Maver back in 1988.[10] He called for the development of "software tools for the evaluation of the technical issues which are relevant at the conceptual stages, as opposed to the detailed stages, of design decision-making."[11]

The challenges of developing such software, however, are far from trivial. Most of the commercially available building performance simulation software, whether for structural, lighting, acoustical, thermal or airflow analysis, requires high-resolution, i.e. detailed, modeling, which means that it is rarely used in conceptual design development. This shortcoming, and the lack of usable "low-resolution" tools, is further compounded by the expected degree of the user's domain knowledge and skills. Another frequently encountered problem is that certain performance aspects can be analyzed in one environment while other performative analyses must be performed in some other software, often resulting in substantial and redundant remodeling. Providing a certain degree of *representational integration* across a range of "low-resolution" performance simulation tools is a necessary step for their more effective use in conceptual design.

Assuming that analytical and representational integration can be achieved, and that intuitive "low-resolution" performance simulation tools can be developed, additional challenges are presented by the need for *active* design space exploration. Instead of being used in a passive, "after-the-fact" fashion, i.e. after the building form has already been articulated, as is currently the case, analytical computation could be used to actively shape the buildings in a dynamic fashion, in a way similar to how animation software is used in contemporary architecture.[12] In other words, the performance assessment has to be *generative* and not only *evaluative*. For that to happen, however, a fundamental rethinking of how the digital performance simulation tools are conceptualized is required.

Ulrich Flemming and Ardeshir Mahdavi argued in 1993 for the close "coupling" of form generation and performance evaluation for use in conceptual design.[13] Mahdavi developed an "open" simulation environment called SEMPER, with a "multidirectional" approach to simulation-based performance evaluation.[14] According to Mahdavi et al., SEMPER provides comprehensive performance modeling based on first principles, "seamless and dynamic communication between the simulation models and an object-oriented space-based design environment using the structural homology of various domain representations," and bidirectional inference through "preference-based performance-to-design mapping technology."

> Performance-based Generative Design

As Kristina Shea observed, "generating new forms while also having instantaneous feedback on their performance from different perspectives (space usage, structural, thermal, lighting, fabrication, etc.) would not only spark the imagination in terms of deriving new forms, but guide it towards forms that reflect rather than contradict real design constraints."[15] As a structural engineer, she cites the form finding techniques used in the design of tensile membrane structures (pioneered by Frei Otto) as the nearest example of performance-driven architectural form generation, in which the form of the membrane is dynamically affected by changing the forces that act on the model. She notes that the form finding techniques in structural engineering are generally limited to either pure tensile or pure compression structures, and she promotes the need for developing digital tools that can generate mixed-mode structural forms.[16]

According to Kristina Shea, a generative approach to structural design requires a design representation of form *and* structure that encodes not only (parametric) geometry but also a design *topology* based on the connectivity of primitives.[17] The experimental software she developed, called *eifForm*, is based on a structural shape grammar that can generate design topology and geometry, enabling the transformation of form while *simultaneously* maintaining a meaningful structural system. Primitives and their connectivity are added, removed and modified with a built-in *randomness* in design generation, directed by a *non-deterministic, non-monotonic* search algorithm based on an optimization technique called "simulated annealing," analogous to the "crystallization processes in the treatment of metals."[18] The software develops the overall form of a structure dynamically, in a time-based fashion, "by repeatedly modifying an initial design with the aim of improving a predefined measure of performance, which can take into account many different factors, such as structural efficiency, economy of materials, member uniformity and even aesthetics, while at the same time attempting to satisfy structural feasibility constrains." The end product is a triangulated pattern of individually sized structural elements and joints.

In a similar vein, I have proposed in a recent paper[19] the development of generative tools based on performance evaluation in which, for example, an already structured building topology, with a generic form, could be subjected to dynamic, metamorphic transformation resulting from the computation of performance targets set at the outset. Such a dynamic range of performative possibilities would contain at its one end an unoptimized solution and at the other an optimized condition (if it is computable), which might not be an acceptable proposition from an aesthetic or some other point of view. In that case, a suboptimal solution could be selected from the in-between performative range, one that could potentially satisfy other non-quantifiable performative criteria.

This new kind of analytical software will preserve the topology of the proposed schematic design but will alter the geometry in response to optimizing a particular performance criteria (acoustic, thermal, etc.). For example, if there is a particular geometric configuration comprised of polygonal surfaces, the number of faces, edges and vertices would remain unchanged (i.e. the topology does not change), but the shapes (i.e. the geometry) will be adjusted (and some limits could be imposed in certain areas). The process of change could be animated, i.e. from the given condition to the optimal condition, with the assumption that the designer could find one of the in-between conditions interesting and worth pursuing, even though it may not be the most optimal solution.

In this scenario, the designer becomes an "editor" of the morphogenetic potentiality of the designed system, where the choice of emergent forms is driven largely by the project's quantifiable performance objectives and the designer's aesthetic and plastic sensibilities. The capacity to generate "new" designs becomes highly dependent on the designer's perceptual and cognitive abilities, as continuous, dynamic processes ground the emergent form, i.e. its discovery, in qualitative cognition. Even though the technolog-ical context of design is thoroughly externalized, its arresting capacity remains internalized. The generative role of the proposed digital techniques is accomplished through the designer's simultaneous interpretation and manipulation of a computational construct (topological configuration subjected to particular performance optimizations) in a complex discourse that is continuously reconstituting itself — a "self-reflexive" discourse in which graphics actively shape the designer's thinking process.

> Conclusion

In conclusion, the new "performative" approach to design requires, at a purely instrumental level, yet-to-be-made digital design tools that can provide dynamic processes of formation based on specific performative aspects of design. There is currently an abundance of digital analytical tools that can help designers assess certain performative aspects of their projects *expost-facto*, i.e. after an initial design is developed, but none of them provide dynamic generative capabilities that could open up new territories for conceptual exploration in architectural design. More importantly, the emergence of performance-based generative design tools would lead to new *synergies* between architecture and engineering in a collaborative quest to produce unimaginable built forms that are *multiply performative*.

1   Branko Kolarevic, Chapter 2 "Digital Morphogenesis" in B. Kolarevic (ed.), *Architecture in the Digital Age: Design and Manufacturing*, London: Spon Press, 2003, pp. 11–28.
2   Ibid.
3   Greg Lynn, *Animate Form*, New York: Princeton Architectural Press, 1999, p. 11.
4   Thomas W. Maver, "PACE 1: Computer Aided Design Appraisal" in *Architects Journal*, July, 1971, pp. 207–214.
5   Thomas W. Maver, "Predicting the Past, Remembering the Future" in *Proceedings of the SIGraDi 2002 Conference*, Caracas, Venezuela: SIGraDi, 2002, pp. 2–3.
6   Nigel Cross and Thomas W. Maver, "Computer Aids for Design Participation" in *Architectural Design*, 53(5), 1973, p. 274.
7   Maver, "PACE 1," op. cit.
8   The program also offered eight perspective views of the scheme, which were drawn on a "graph plotter" driven by the paper tape produced by the program. That was a "revolutionary" technological development back in 1970s!
9   Thomas W. Maver, "Appraisal in Design" in *Design Studies*, 1(3), 1980, pp. 160–165.
10 Thomas W. Maver, "Software Tools for the Technical Evaluation of Design Alternatives" in *Proceedings of CAAD Futures '87*, Eindhoven, Netherlands, 1988, pp. 47–58.
11 Ibid.
12 Kolarevic, op. cit.
13 Ulrich Flemming and Ardeshir Mahdavi, "Simultaneous Form Generation and Performance Evaluation: A 'Two-Way' Inference Approach" in *Proceedings of CAAD Futures '93*, Pittsburgh, USA, 1993, pp. 161–173.
14 A. Mahdavi, P. Mathew, S. Lee, R. Brahme, S. Kumar, G. Liu, R. Ries, and N. H. Wong, "On the Structure and Elements of SEMPER, Design Computation: Collaboration, Reasoning, Pedagogy" in *ACADIA 1996 Conference Proceedings*, Tucson, USA, 1996, p. 72.
15 Kristina Shea, "Directed Randomness" in N. Leach, D. Turnbull and C. Williams (eds), *Digital Tectonics*, London: Wiley-Academy, 2004, p. 89.
16 Ibid, p. 89.
17 Ibid, p. 93.
18 Ibid. Simulating annealing is described by Shea as "a stochastic optimisation technique that tests a batch of semi-random changes generated by the structural shape grammar, measures their performance and then chooses one that is near the best. The amount of deviation from the best is gradually reduced throughout the process, but not necessarily from one design to the next." (Shea, 2004, p. 93)
19 Branko Kolarevic, "Computing the Performative in Architecture" in W. Dokonal (ed.), *Digital Design, Proceedings of the ECAADE 2003 Conference*, Graz, Austria, 2003.

Foster and Partners is a practice well known for its many completed buildings, but this chapter will focus more on the process of design, which is less often described, and in particular on the work of the Specialist Modelling Group. The chapter aims to convey some of the atmosphere of working in the Foster studio and, as such, it is a personal view rather than a corporate one.

The Specialist Modelling Group (SMG) was established in 1998 and, to date, has been involved in 63 projects. We have had the opportunity to see many of them progress from concept design through to fabrication and on-site construction. The group currently consists of four people, who support approximately 400 architects in the studio – a demanding ratio, but one that provides a stimulating source of new challenges. All the members of the group share a common architectural or engineering background, but have very different specialities and diverse interests, which range from aeronautical engineering to air-supported structures.

The SMG's brief is to carry out research and development in an environment that is intensely project-driven. This provides a sharp focus for development, while forcing us to examine fundamental, or even philosophical, questions. For example, we must decide whether geometry is really the essence of form, or just a convenient means of description. Producing a form that can be built requires definition of the relationship between geometry and form in terms of a particular medium. Therefore, it is significant that designers in the studio work with many different materials and in a wide range of media.

The use of digital media has an influence that could be described by analogy. One of the best materials for sculpting is clay, but the results are free form and have no descriptive geometry. However, when clay is placed on a potter's wheel, it inherits geometry from the mechanism that drives the wheel and a highly geometric form is produced. Digital techniques are also mechanistic and can have a similar effect. At the same time, they enable us to cross the boundaries between different media, while expressing the same design intent. The use of rapid prototyping technology closes the loop in a digital design process by recognizing the fact that key decisions are still made from the study of physical models.

Analytical studies, on the other hand, are becoming an increasingly important part of our work. This discussion features two projects, *City Hall* (1998–2002), London, and the *Chesa Futura* (2000–03), St Moritz, in both of which analytical studies have had a profound effect on our methodology.

7

Laws of Form

Hugh Whitehead

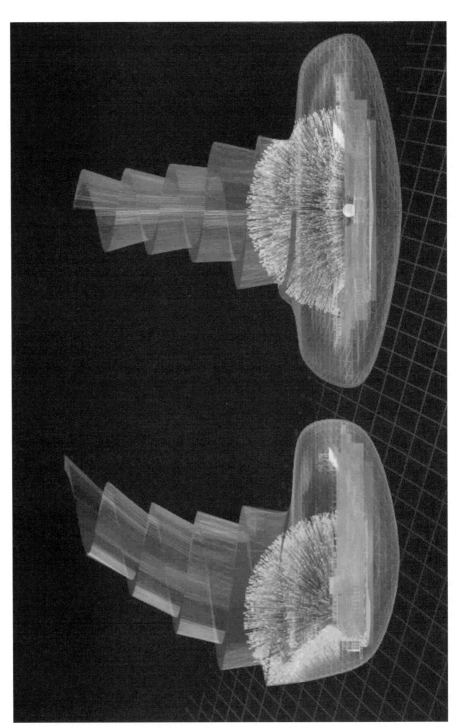

Figure 7.1

> Panelization Theory

Foster and Partners has designed a number of buildings in recent years that were based on toroidal geometry. Each has extended the envelope of design and increased our knowledge of how to construct buildings based on sculptural forms. The following projects illustrate that radically different architectural expressions can be generated from the same simple geometric principle: the *American Air Museum*, the *Dubai Cultural Centre*, the *Sage Music Centre*, *Albion Riverside* and the *Headquarters for Swiss Re*.

In order for comparative performance studies to inform the design process, we required very precise control of geometry. As a result, we became particularly interested in exploring different combinations of torus patch constructions as an approach to the panelization of curved surfaces. A torus is a solid ring of circular section, generated by revolving a circle about an axis outside itself but lying in its plane, such as a donut or a tire. A torus patch is interesting from an architectural point of view because it has a natural flat panel solution, due to the fact that a constant section revolved around a constant centre produces a surface without twist. As ongoing research, we continually explore other constructions, such as ruled surfaces or hyperbolic paraboloids, which produce surfaces with natural flat panel solutions. While a curved surface can always be triangulated to produce flat panels, this approach does not offer any repetition of panel types and creates difficulties with partitioning and space planning requirements.

The two projects described in detail – *City Hall* and the *Chesa Futura* – have required radical new solutions to the control of geometry and the architectural expression of curved surfaces. In this respect "radical" is an appropriate word because it literally means "back to the roots." The idea that returning to "first principles" is the only way to be original has always been part of the Foster design culture.

> CITY HALL, LONDON

Soon after the SMG was formed, the studio entered the competition to design *City Hall* in London, which occupies a strategic position on the south bank of the River Thames adjacent to Tower Bridge and directly opposite the Tower of London – a World Heritage Site. The brief presented an opportunity to produce an iconic, signature building that would be

---

Facing page

Figure 7.1: Digital models and acoustical analysis of alternatives for the London City Hall debating chamber. Image credit: Computer model and analysis by Arup; architect: Foster + Partners. Courtesy of Branko Kolarevic.

sensitive to environmental issues while making a statement about public involvement in the democratic process. Having won the competition, the team was encouraged to extend the conceptual boundaries during the development of the scheme.

Three years later the building has just been completed. It houses the assembly chamber for the 25 elected members of the London Assembly and the offices of the Mayor and 500 staff of the Greater London Authority (GLA). It is a highly public building, bringing visitors into close proximity with the workings of the democratic process. The building is set within the new Foster-designed *More London* masterplan on the south bank of the Thames, bringing a rich mix of office buildings, shops, cafés and landscaped public spaces to a section of the riverside that has remained undeveloped for decades.

A large sunken outdoor amphitheatre paved in blue limestone leads to a public café at the lower ground level, beyond which is an elliptical exhibition space directly below the assembly chamber. From this space, a half-kilometer-long, gently rising public ramp coils through all ten stories to the top of the building, offering new and surprising views of London, and glimpses into the offices of the GLA staff. The ramp leads past the Mayor's Office to a public space at the top of the building known as "London's Living Room." This day-lit space, with external viewing terrace, can be used for exhibitions or functions for up to 200 guests.

> Design Studies

In retrospect, one of the most interesting aspects of the *City Hall* project was how the design evolved from the initial ideas at the competition stage to become a form that had an integrated energy solution and a rationale which would enable it to be built. Originally, the concept was to create a large "lens" looking out over the river, with a set of floor plates attached at the back in a serrated profile, which resulted in a "pine cone" glazing effect. At first sight, the inspiration for the form may seem somewhat arbitrary, which was, in fact, how it began; as the team started work on the project one of the partners was heard to say, "We are doing something by the river. I think it is a pebble."

We took up the idea and attempted to create a "parametric pebble." The problem we faced was how to formulate a "pebble" in descriptive geometry. Our first thoughts were to start with a sphere, which has a minimal ratio of surface area to volume, and then explore how it could be transformed. This could have been achieved using animation software, but we chose to develop it in Microstation, the office standard computer-aided design (CAD) system, because the results could immediately be passed to the team for use as a design tool. Having first derived a "minimal control polygon" for a sphere, we connected it to a parametric control rig, so that the form could be adjusted by using proportional relationships (figure 7.2(a), 7.2(b), 7.2(c)). The creation of a set of variational templates for direct use by the design team

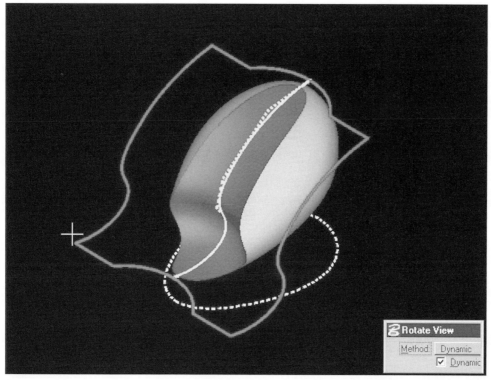

Figure 7.2 (a)

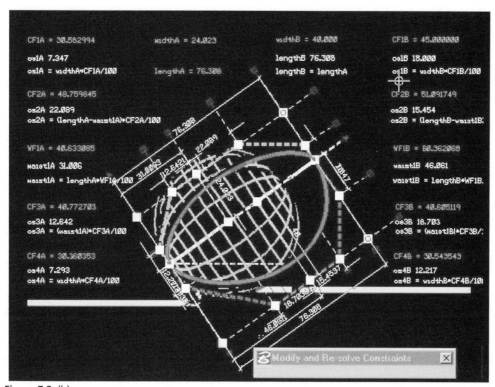

Figure 7.2 (b)

(*Continued*)

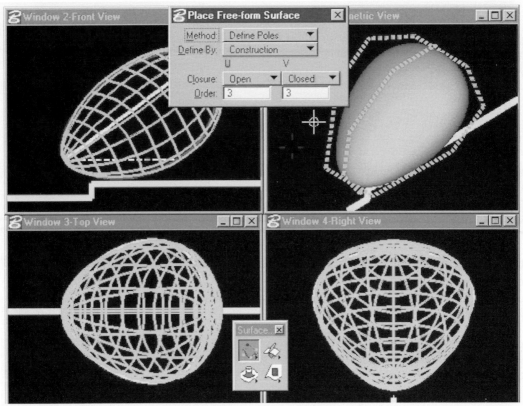

Figure 7.2 (c)

Figure 7.2: "Parametric Pebble", London Town Hall, Foster and Partners. Image credit: Foster + Partners.

has now become a typical part of our brief. While it may take several hours for our group to produce a custom-built parametric model, it is often used for several months by the team to produce alternatives for testing during design development.

A proportional control mechanism allows designers to dynamically fine-tune curves by hand and eye, while the system precisely records dimensions. Once an appropriate shape is found, the control polygon is extracted and used to produce a solid model for further development. The pebble-like form, created in this way for *City Hall*, had some remarkable properties. If the main axis is oriented towards the midday sun, the form presents a minimal surface area for solar gain, which became very important as the design progressed. The side elevations were also curved, presenting a minimal area to the east and west, where the façades face a low sun angle. The resulting form, as seen from the north, has an almost circular profile, exploiting views across the river.

Behind the giant "lens" is an atrium, a spectacular plunging void that descends to a debating chamber that is open to the public. The initial shape of the atrium was created using simple curve manipulations to generate a trimming surface, which was then used in a Boolean operation to cut away the front of the building. Although this early solid model more closely resembled a piece of product design than a building, the form had strong aesthetic qualities and already carried special properties, which would lead to an energy-efficient solution.

By slicing the solid model with horizontal planes, a set of floor plates was extracted to be used as the basis for space planning studies, checking the brief, and computing net-to-gross ratios, with the results being fed back into the parametric model to improve performance. The slicing of floor plates revealed further interesting characteristics of the form. The floor plates were found to be elliptical, with the long axis of the ellipse shortening to become a circular floor plate, and then lengthening in the other direction in a transition towards the top of the building. Almost by accident, we had discovered something that could be used to generate the form through a rational transformation.

A number of detailed studies followed, with intense thought and effort applied to the glazing of the "lens." These studies relied heavily on the CAD system and its link to the CNC (computer numerically controlled) machine, because every one of the diamond-shaped panels would have unique dimensions. By applying a diamond grid to a torus-patch surface, the advantage had been lost because the panels inherited different twist and different dimensions. However, the team liked the appearance and saw potential in this design option. To eliminate twist, the panels could lift off the surface, which would allow the possibility of introducing vents around the sides. In order to test this geometry in a physical model, panels were cut using the CNC machine and then glued onto a frame. They all fitted perfectly, which was, in itself, a remarkable achievement. The result gave us confidence that by scaling the techniques to digital fabrication technology, the result would be deliverable as a built form.

The dialogue between the design team, the SMG, and the model shop created an information flow that raised further interesting questions, such as how to draw in non-Cartesian space. The designers dealt with that challenge in a very pragmatic way, sketching with a felt-tip pen directly on a vacuum-formed surface, which had been produced in the model shop from the computer-generated design surface. So now, when teams want to explore non-Cartesian geometry, a digital solid model is contoured to produce a tool for a vacuum form, on which the designers sketch ideas – why draw on flat paper when we can draw on any surface? CNC machines are also commonly used to cut out floor plates and to quickly assemble basic physical models; by stretching tape strips across them, the designers found they could rapidly explore ideas for panelization and glazing systems. Some designers were even more direct in their work methods – molding a piece of plasticine and then etching the surface with a pen. As these examples illustrate, a variety of

digital and non-digital means were combined during the detailed exploration of options for the diamond grid and the "lens."

> The Energy Case

Analysis of the energy studies had a major impact on the scheme development. From the earliest stage, we intended the building to be energy efficient and that its form would have special properties from an energy
point of view. Arup's engineers did a solar study of the proposed design,
and produced a remarkable image in which they color-coded the surface
according to the total amount of energy that each cladding panel
would receive during one year. They also provided irradiance figures in a
spreadsheet format, so that the distribution could be analyzed in detail.
Although these figures were informative, they did not provoke as much in
the way of design ideas as a digital fly-around sequence of the form, color-
coded with the irradiance data. From this, it was immediately clear that the
south façade was performing as expected – it was self-shading, as shown in
the image by the blue overhang areas. The east and west surfaces were
green, indicating that the oblique angles of incidence were indeed limiting
solar gain. But to the north, where the atrium glazing would be, there
was only a thin strip of light blue. The protected area was not large enough
for the "lens" that had been envisioned – there was a conflict between
the design and the outcome of the energy analysis. The solar study
showed us that the glazing system had to change and, so, in this case, the
color-coded diagram actually led to the glazing solution. The same study also
showed a very localized hotspot at the top as an ideal position to mount
solar panels.

   The final solution required a radical change, so that the design of the
glazing system would literally fit the energy analysis produced by Arup. Without
the "lens," a torus-patch solution was no longer appropriate for the atrium,
while the office cladding required flat, trapezoidal glass panels, triple-glazed
with louver systems and blinds in precisely controlled areas. The geometric
solution was to post-rationalize the surface into a stack of sheared cones.
Applying this principle, we found that by glazing between circular floor plates,
regardless of their size or offset, the panels remain planar if they follow the
shear. We then developed a software macro that enabled programmatic generation of the glazing solution using this technique. The result produced a dynamic
visual effect as the frames for the glazing fan backwards with the rake of the
building. To estimate the cost of such a solution, the original macro was extended
to lay out the glazing panels in a flat pattern, automatically scheduling all areas
of the façade, and listing panel node coordinates. This technique has become
very important in our work. When a flat-patterned drawing is given to fabricators or contractors, regardless of the complexity of the form, they immediately
recognize it as something that can be priced, manufactured and assembled
on-site.

> Form and Space

A further important element of the *City Hall* was the internal glazing to the atrium, which separates the offices from the public space. The shape of this surface resembles a glass chemical flask, with the debating chamber at the base. The building already had a strong rationale for its external geometry. The inclined form allows maximum sunlight to reach the riverfront walkway, the roof presents the minimum surface to the sun, and transparent glazing is restricted to the north-facing atrium, while the south façade is self-shading. The form of the "flask" needed to have an equally strong rationale for its definition, construction, and performance.

A digital model was created so that the shape of the flask could be transformed through a morphing sequence, allowing the team to explore the spatial requirements for the chamber. Starting with a symmetrical flask defined as a surface of revolution, the plan shape was transformed from a circle into an ellipse. The centre of gravity was moved down towards the bottom of the flask, while the neck of the flask was gradually bent to fit the curve of the north façade. The morphing sequence was produced by "key framing" the three different transformations, so that they could be executed in parallel to produce a wide range of alternatives. By setting up two extremes, the sequence was used to generate intermediate versions and so find the most appropriate blend of characteristics. For example, in a time-based morphing sequence of 100 frames, i.e. different states, the designer could choose number 67 as the preferred solution.

Arup's engineers performed an acoustic analysis of the proposed geometry of the debating chamber, and determined that this dramatic shape would be difficult to treat acoustically because all the sound reflected straight back towards the speaker. Surprisingly, the breakthrough came from a parallel study of the public circulation. The office had recently completed the *Reichstag* – the *New German Parliament Building* in Berlin, which features a spiral ramp in the glazed cupola above the debating chamber as a remarkably successful element in making politics a public process. A similar spiral ramp was wrapped around the "flask" and, as a consequence, the glazing leaned outward, causing the sound to reflect in a totally different way. Further acoustic analysis on the altered geometry of the "flask" (fig. 7.1) showed the results to be ideal. The sound performed as required – it was scattered and reflected up the neck of the "flask." It could also easily be dampened by applying a sound-absorbing surface to the soffit of the ramp.

Devising a flat-panel solution for the geometry of the "flask" proved even harder to resolve than the external cladding surface. First, the form was elliptical, second, the ellipses reduced progressively in size at varying offsets, and, third, the surface was helical. Just as we had found a solution and tested it in a physical model, another lateral shift in thinking resulted in a decision to move the ramp inside, so that the glazing could be detached and moved outwards to span simply from floor to floor.

The glazing was still inclined and had the same acoustic properties, but the ramp was no longer outside the "flask" – it had moved inside to become part of the space.

A sudden lateral shift in thinking is something that often arises when working with design teams and consultants on many different projects. As a group, we design tools, techniques and workflow, but with detachment, being interested in the process of providing solutions for other people to work with. This requires the group to integrate very closely with project teams, so that whether we work with them for a day, a month, or a year, we are part of the team. As the design evolves, a very large number of physical scale models is produced, sometimes being collected together as a "model graveyard" which shows the history of the design development.

Different alternatives are digitally analyzed for their performance, as in the solar study by Arup. Resulting images tell a very important story, because they illustrate the distribution of irradiance values for every panel. Cones show the orientation of each panel, while color is a visual code for the irradiance value. The image produced from the analysis showed the team where to focus its design effort – on the solar protection systems. These examples illustrate that the synthesis of form is considered from many different viewpoints – functional, spatial, sculptural, structural and environmental. In trying to combine all these aspects in an optimal solution, we have to build tools that cannot be found in off-the-shelf software.

Everything in the studio is done from first principles, and so even the tools we need have to be built from first principles. Custom-developed software utilities provide ways of exploring design intent by directly driving the geometry engine behind the CAD system. This is leading towards a system that supports programmable model building, and which records design history in an editable form.

> Design Rationalization

Before a building such as the *City Hall* could progress to construction, the design process had to be taken apart and reassembled as a sequence of procedures. This meant that the whole building was reanalyzed as a set of construction components. There is a concrete core, a steel structure, the ramp, the atrium, the entrance glazing, the front diagrid, and the office side cladding, resulting in a complete component model.

> Geometry Method Statement

Separate trades and different contractors were responsible for each component, so, in order to coordinate construction, we had to assist the contractors in understanding the building's geometry. A further analysis of the form was undertaken as a post-rationalization of the geometry, referred to by the team as "Nine Steps to Heaven". The final form was described as a sequence of nine dependent stages, using only rational curves for all the setting out, and this was issued as a Geometry Method Statement.

It may be asked why the reduction to arc-based geometry was necessary when computers can work easily with free-form curves and surfaces. The reason for this decision comes from extensive experience of the realities of building. Construction involves materials that have dynamic behavior, although their digital definition is static. They have real thickness that varies, and they move and deform, which requires a strategy for the management of tolerances. From a construction point of view, everything about the design, particularly the cladding and the structure that supports it, depends on the control of offset dimensions. CAD systems can work with **free-form** curves and surfaces, and produce offsets that are accurate to very fine tolerances. However, these are not precise and because the system generates more data with each successive operation, processing limits are rapidly exceeded and the system becomes overpowered. Offset dimensions can be simply controlled by specifying radii because an arc has only one center. High precision is required only in defining the coordinates for the arc centers, which leads to a dramatic reduction in problems, both in the factory and on-site.

It may seem counter-intuitive that in order to build a complex form, originally generated as a **free-form** surface, we embarked on a long and difficult process of post-rationalizing the design to arc-based geometry. However, the real benefits lay in achieving reliable data transfer between independent digital systems. By following the Geometry Method Statement issued to contractors, we were able to describe the *City Hall* geometry in terms of basic trigonometry. This was entered as a set of expressions in Excel spreadsheets, which programmatically generated cladding node coordinates for the entire building. This has now become a form of information that can be used directly by manufacturers on their production lines. However, coordinates computed in the Excel spreadsheets had first to be compared with those from the Microstation model produced by the design team.

A similar checking procedure was then used with the fabricators and contractors. They were instructed to build digital models by following our Geometry Method Statement on their own CAD system, so that coordinates could be compared by overlay and any discrepancies noted. Closing the data loop in this fashion has a number of advantages. By requiring contractors and fabricators to develop their own models from first principles, the problems that typically occur in data translation between different CAD systems were avoided. More importantly, the process transfers accountability from the design team to the suppliers, because each works with a digital model built specifically to fabricate and assemble their own components. It is a deliberate strategy of education that works for all parties; the contractors and fabricators come to understand all the subtleties of the building as a logical consequence of the underlying principles of the design.

> Tolerance Management

The construction sequence had to be ordered in a very specific way. Because the structure of the building leans backwards, it progressively deflects as it becomes loaded with additional floors. This transformation could not be predicted reliably and, therefore, it had to be monitored and measured on-site. There also had to be a strategy to deal with the implications of movement, particularly to monitor deflections and manage tolerances, so that different trades could work with each other and not clash.

Warner Land Surveys, who were appointed initially by the client to be responsible for setting out on-site, undertook this pivotal role. They were then appointed independently by the steelwork contractor to advise on all aspects of the control of steel fabrication. With a further appointment by the client to monitor the assembly of the cladding system, they effectively took control of every aspect of the delivery process, which converted complex geometry to built form. Warner is a technically advanced company, who used the latest surveying equipment to monitor deflections as the structure was progressively loaded. The way Warner used their technology integrated perfectly with our design process. Like the fabricators, they built their own digital models of the project, but their checking procedures required three different versions – the design model as a basis for comparison, a fabrication model to manage tolerances, and a construction model to monitor deflections. Owing to the eccentric loading, the deflections became increasingly significant towards the upper floors of the building, as can be seen in a Sway Diagram.

At the top of the building, there was a 50 mm sway, to which 50 mm tolerance was added, plus a further 50 mm as a minimum gap, requiring a total of 150 mm between the edge of the floor plate and the cladding. A system for attaching cladding panels was required, which could accommodate that kind of variation. In order to control positioning during construction, Warners marked every piece of steel structure with holographic targets in the factory. By recording coordinates for each target in a database, they were able to track every piece from the factory to its installation on-site. Using laser surveying equipment, XYZ coordinates could be measured during installation to an accuracy of 1 mm anywhere on the site. For example, as a beam was lowered down into position, they could precisely track its position until it was placed in its intended location.

Every cladding component was barcoded, to enable accurate tracking during both the production and the assembly process. Even cladding components that varied in size by less than a tenth of a millimeter still had different barcodes. The cladding was fixed on-site panel by panel using bespoke connections resembling a ball and socket joint, except that the ball fitted into a square box. The connection system was designed to accommodate a wide range of movements and adjustments, providing for a perfect fit of the whole system. The assembly of cladding panels was tested in the factory, where three adjacent panels were placed side by side on a rig that could be adjusted hydraulically to simulate floor-plate configurations anywhere in the building. Each panel was checked in turn before leaving the factory to ensure a proper fit on-site. Weather tests were carried out by subjecting panels to a strong wind generated by an aeroengine and destruction tests were performed by swinging large boulders at them.

The final design for the atrium glazing also required special prefabrication of the diagrid structure, which was generated from the Geometry Method Statement and used digital fabrication techniques to ensure a precision piece of engineering. The completed building was delivered on time and on budget. It attracted 10,000 visitors during the first weekend after the opening ceremony.

> ST MORITZ – CHESA FUTURA

The second project discussed also involves complex geometry and high-tech construction methods, but is different in every other respect, particularly because it is made of wood. The *Chesa Futura* apartment building is in the popular skiing resort of St Moritz in the Engadin Valley in Switzerland. It is situated among dramatic landscape at 1800 m above sea level. It fuses state-of-the-art computer design tools and traditional, indigenous building techniques to create an environmentally sensitive building. It combines a novel form with traditional timber construction – one of the oldest, most environmentally benign and sustainable forms of building.

The building is raised off the ground on eight legs and has an unusual pumpkin-like form. This is a creative response to the site, the local weather conditions, and the planning regulations. The site has a height restriction of 15.5 m above its sloping contours. If the building were built directly on its sloping site, the first two levels would not have views over the existing buildings. Elevating the building provides views over the lake for all apartments and maintains the view of the village from the road behind the building. Raised buildings have a long architectural tradition in Switzerland – where snow lies on the ground for many months of the year – avoiding the danger of wood rotting due to prolonged exposure to moisture.

By sculpting the building into a rounded form, it responds to the planning regulations. A conventional rectilinear building would protrude over the specified height. Because the ground and first floor levels are not utilized, the three elevated stories are widened to achieve the desired overall floor area, but do not appear bulky due to the building's rounded form. The curved form allows windows to wrap around the façade, providing panoramic views of the town and the lake.

> Development of the Form

The curved form resulted from responding to the potential of the site, while conforming to its constraints. The initial design sketches were interpreted and formalized as a parametric model, which the team then referenced so that changes could be tracked in both directions. A parametric version of the section went through many months of changes, which were also informed by simultaneous planning studies. The constraints were such that a two-degree rotation of the plan resulted in a 50 m² loss of floor area, while a two-degree rotation of the section reduced headroom by 100 mm at each level.

Although it appears to be a relatively simple form, for every combination of plan and section, there were endless possible approaches to surfacing techniques. The key to controlling the form was to slice it with two sloping planes at a three-degree inclination. The idea of using parallel slice planes, which separate the wall element from the roof above and the soffit below, may seem a fairly obvious proposition but it had surprising additional benefits. We started to think of the wall as a shell, which had a polar grid associated with it. The polar grid is an ideal way of locating elements, such as windows, whose positions are based on radial setting-out geometry. We defined four sectors and a number of subdivisions within each sector, so that every subdivision could be either a window location or a rib position. This gave us great flexibility and control, and also provided a convenient coding and referencing system. Having placed the window reveal surfaces as cutters, we then applied Boolean subtractions to create a perforated shell. The insertion of floor plates resulted in a form that related to the section, with a step in each floor plan to maximize the view.

The initial modeling process is described only briefly, because the interesting part of the project was the way in which the many different generations of model, both digital and physical, were used by the engineers to develop the construction process.

> Construction Strategy

Owing to the severe winter weather conditions in St Moritz, there are only six months of the year when building work can be undertaken. The planned construction sequence was therefore firstly to erect a steel table with a concrete slab, and then to prefabricate the whole wall system during the winter, when no work was possible on-site. The following spring, the frame, walls and roof could be rapidly installed, and the shell completed and made weathertight before winter, when the interiors could be finished. This became the strategy that made construction possible, but meant that precise phasing of the work was absolutely critical.

> Information Strategy

In order to rationalize the geometry of the shell and develop it as a parametric model, we explored the idea of relating plan to section as if on a drawing board, but generating constructions by using software macros. The macro uses a "ruler," driven by the polar coordinate system, to scan the sectors of the plan drawing and record measurements projected onto track curves on the adjacent section. This, in turn, builds parameter sets, which are passed to a rule-based wall section, causing it to adapt to any location on the shell. The macro has two modes of operation: it can output a design surface shell as a solid model with associated ribs for the structural frame, or a matrix of drawing templates to be used for detailing or shop drawings.

As the design progressed, each team member became responsible for a different set of parametric offsets, determined by the thickness of materials used in construction. One team member would work on the roof, another was in charge of structure and finishes, a third was in charge of the wall zone with battens, fireproofing and plywood cladding, while a fourth was responsible for all the window details. By having access to the same parametric templates, the team was able to respond to design direction and to coordinate development of the project, each making their own changes while responding to the implications of changes made by others.

As with *City Hall,* the parametric geometry was deliberately arc-based but for entirely different reasons. The prefabrication strategy required a solid model that would be capable of driving advanced CAD/CAM machinery in a factory in Germany to precision engineering tolerances. In order to use this technology successfully, we had to understand the solid modeling process at the level of the underlying mathematics used by the software. Although the surface has free-form characteristics, it is, in fact, an analytical surface made up of patches, which have perfect tangency across boundaries that are always arcs.

An analytical surface is ideal for working with most solid modeling kernels – the software is able to calculate offsets with precision, giving results that are fast, clean and robust, which is particularly important during intensive design development. The ability to make rapid and reliable surface and solid offsets without suffering any CAD problems allowed us to share digital models with our engineers in Switzerland and fabricators in Germany. Choosing to pre-rationalize the design surface by making it arc-based achieved a degree of control that allowed us to simplify and resolve many complex issues of design and production. The software macros developed could derive all the arcs from rule-based constructions and then place them in three-dimensional space, automatically generating shell, frame and rib geometry based on parameter values entered for the offsets. The result was a shell with a precise rational definition, which became the design surface that was signed off to the engineers.

At this point we made a commitment to make no further alterations to the design surface, although offsets were continually varied throughout the year as the project evolved. We could locate any component by choosing a position on the polar grid, creating a plane, and intersecting it with the design surface to determine the radial offset for placing the component. In addition to being able to accurately model and place components in space, we could generate a matrix of sections, drawn for each rib position and thus produce templates for all the shop drawings. When both the plan and section were still changing, even at a late stage in the project, we could programmatically regenerate the design surface shell in a way that was consistent and reliable. Software tools were evolved that allowed the design to become a cyclic rather than a linear process. The freedom to explore multiple iterations of a design proved to be the key to optimization.

> Assembly Strategy

In the Foster studio, most of the key design decisions are still made from the study of physical models. In fact, the CAD system was introduced initially to the studio to provide shop drawings for our model makers. Digital technology now allows us to begin with the digital models, which are then passed to the model shop for fabrication using CNC machines. There is a constant dialogue between drawings, computer models and physical models. A typical project review uses every possible medium: hand drawings, CAD models, rendered images, hidden-line models, CNC-cut models and sketch models.

The next generation of the *Chesa Futura* model was based on realistic components, designed to test the actual assembly process of building, as envisioned by Arup and developed by Toscano, the Swiss engineers. This model was created from the ground up – beginning with the steel table with hangers for the soffit, the concrete slab, the ribs and C-columns for the front balconies, then the spandrels, and finally the ring beam at the top. This corresponds to the slice plane used to define the initial geometry, which became expressed as an inclined gutter marking the change of materials from wall to roof. The windows are all identical, standard 1.4 m "Velux" sealed double-glazed units, which give the best performance in the severe local weather conditions. The reveal for each window is different and custom made, but the cost savings are far greater from the repetition of window type.

Each generation of digital model led to the next physical model, as increasing levels of detail were explored. At this stage, there was a need to study how to control the coursing of the timber shingles in relation to window openings. The coursing lines were produced by software macros as flat patterns, cut by CNC machine, and then assembled on the model. To represent timber shingles at this scale of model required a high level of precision and many hours of patient work by the model makers. There was a coursing diagram, worked out on the digital model, which showed how the skin was to be battened, because it is the timber battens that control the shingle layout on-site. The shingles were modeled in strips of etched brass, which were applied on the course lines and then painted over. Due to the level of detail achieved, this model allowed us to rehearse all the key aspects of the full-scale assembly process and to discuss points of detail with the craftsmen involved.

When it came to factory production, the full-size ribs were CNC fabricated from glue-laminated beams – thin layers of wood glued together under pressure. This is a wonderful material because it has the strength of steel, the malleability of concrete, the lightness of timber, and exceptional fabrication possibilities. The fabricators, Amann, specialize in producing remarkable buildings that use glue-laminated beams. They have a very advanced CAD/CAM machine with an impressive array of 20 tools, which descend from racks in their prescribed order to cut, drill, rout or bore at any angle, with any curvature (single- or double-curved), on a piece of laminated timber up to 40 m in length.

After designing a shell to engineering tolerances, it is a delightful irony that it will be clad with timber shingles, cut with an axe by an 80-year-old local expert, and then nailed on by hand by the rest of his family.

The final generation of building model resolved all the junction details between finishes. At this stage, a most useful technique was to illustrate details using hidden-line sectional perspectives. These are cut-away views of the solid model with architectural drawings applied to the cut surface. They successfully communicated process, assembly and final appearance in a single image.

> Full-scale Prototype

The detailed design was put to the final test in a life-size mockup of a typical part of the shell, comprising a single window with the surrounding reveals and supporting ribs. This was erected on-site and marked an important moment in the development of the project, when everybody started to believe that the building was achievable. As construction progressed on-site, it was remarkable to see how a building with such an unusual combination of form and materials sat so naturally in its context. While the skin of the building is made from a local, natural and traditional material timber shingles – the very high-tech frame that supports it, justifies the name *Chesa Futura* – House of the Future.

> EVOLUTION

There are common themes in the two projects discussed and in the way our use of technology has evolved to support them. Through the experience of

City Hall we learned the importance of being able to post-rationalize building geometry. In the case of the *Chesa Futura,* we were able to embed the rationale in the tools used to create the form. The development of customized utilities is now based on a function library, which extends with every project undertaken and is structured to allow functions to be combined by the user without having to prescribe the workflow.

Most designers already think programmatically, but having neither the time nor the inclination to learn programming skills, do not have the means to express or explore these patterns of thought. Conceptually, designers have outgrown conventional CAD packages, which in order to be useful in design terms, must now include systems for describing the structure of relationships, the behavior of physics and the effects of time.

Since its formation, the SMG has been collaborating with Robert Aish, Director of Research at Bentley Systems, to specify and test a new development platform. The results of the first evaluation cycle were shown at a research seminar at the 2002 Bentley International User Conference. This platform will be object-based and aims to use new technology to promote learning and the sharing of expertise through a more symbiotic relationship between designers and the systems they use.

Computational design techniques are changing the role of analysis tools in the collaboration of architects and engineers. Digital feedback loops of synthesis, analysis and evaluation establish a *process of becoming* in which structural solutions evolve and adapt to specific requirements. Highly differentiated constructions are possible when digital techniques are fully integrated in design and production. Klaus Bollinger, Manfred Grohmann and Oliver Tessmann discuss these novel paradigms in relation to recent projects from the engineering office Bollinger + Grohmann.

Complexity characterizes systems – sets of elements and their relations – whose behavior is hardly predictable. The system properties are not defined by individual elements, but rather emerge from intricate interaction without any top-down control.

In structural design analysis the prediction of structural behavior is complemented by synthesis which means that not only analytical but also generative strategies are required. Collaborative design of architects and engineers furthermore demands the embedding of structural design in a larger system with an increasing number of elements and relations. The resulting complexity is tackled in our practice by circular procedures regardless of whether they are digital or analog. Instead of a linear cause-effect relationship, circularity creates feedback where effectors (output) are connected to sensors (input) which act with its signals upon the effectors. The computer becomes more than a mere calculating machine. Its formalized systems are not inscribed into mechanical cogwheels and step reckoners but provided as a string of symbols based on a certain syntax. Scripting and programming help to access this layer of description where the algorithm (the machine) and the data are represented with similar symbols and syntax. These processes create the conditions for the digital mediation of design emergence through evolutionary structures, this becoming characteristic of design engineering.

8

Structured Becoming

Evolutionary Processes in Design Engineering

Klaus Bollinger, Manfred Grohmann, Oliver Tessmann

> The Complexity of Evolving Structures

Evolutionary Algorithms generate and manipulate character strings which serve as genotypes, or blueprints, of entire populations of structures. The genotype serves as input data for parametric structural models which become the phenotypes. Those structural individuals are successively analyzed and evaluated. Evaluation criteria do not necessarily originate from structural requirements but also cover architectural aspects. The goal is not an optimized structure but an equilibrium of multiple requirements. Successive generations are mainly based on the gene pool of the best solutions of the previous iteration. The individuals are

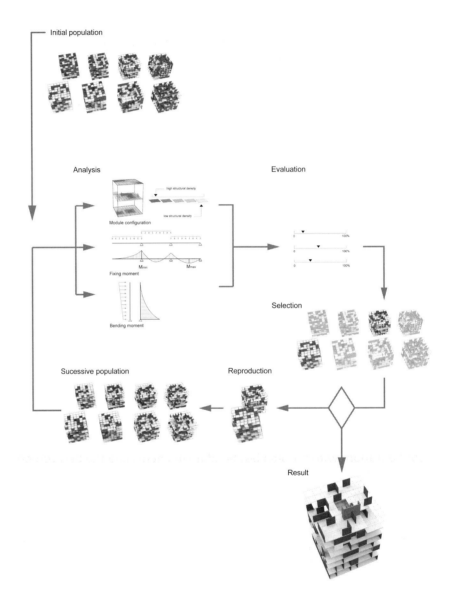

Figure 8.1

reconfigured and mutated to generate a new set of various solutions. A cyclic process which takes the previous output as the new input is established.

> VOxEL

In the competition for a new architecture faculty building in Stuttgart designed by LAVA an Evolutionary Algorithm was used. The proposal is based on a three-dimensional spatial continuum that provides a close interlocking of space, structure, voids and various functions. Beyond the 'Maison Domino' concept, the configuration offers flexibility across multiple levels.

The architectural and structural concept is based on a non-hierarchical organization of floor slabs and shear walls proliferated into a three-dimensional matrix according to functional and structural requirements. The construction can be conceived as a square-edged sponge with continuously changing porosity. The shear walls resist lateral forces and replace a conventional structural core. Thus flexibility is gained in the third dimension.

The structural system developed in an evolutionary process. In a three-dimensional grid every cell was mapped with one of two properties:

1 Cells, free from any structure to provide voids for or large spaces.
2 Cells with a higher degree of subdivisions and structural density.

Based on this preconceived setup every grid cell was subsequently populated with a structural module consisting of two, one or no shear walls to create the square-edged sponge.

An initial generation of 50 random sponge versions was generated and analyzed. Three evaluation criteria were used to rank the different solutions:

• Vertical bending moments in the floor slabs under dead load;
• Horizontal bending moments in the shear walls under lateral loads;
• The placement of shear walls in relation to the cell property.

The configurations with the smallest bending moments and the best composition of shear walls according to the cell properties were used to generate offspring. Hence, the following generation was based on previously successful solutions. The recombination of the genotype (Crossover) during reproduction and random mutation provided variation within the population.

After more than 200 generations the process yielded a system which adapted to multiple architectural criteria while at the same time fulfills the structural necessities.

Facing page

Figure 8.1: Diagram of the evolutionary algorithm. An initial population of random configurations gradually evolves until predefined properties are achieved. Image credit: Bollinger + Grohmann.

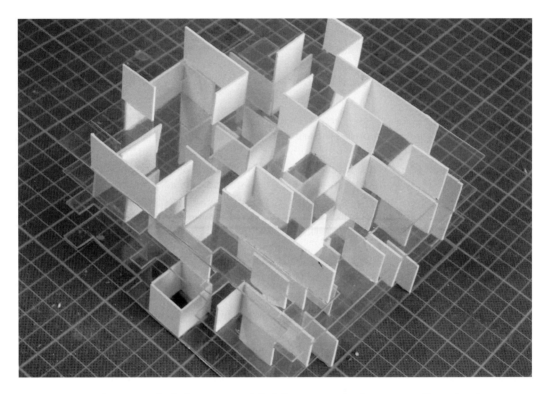

Figure 8.2: Physical concept model of the square-edged sponge configuration. Image credit: LAVA.

> The Complexity of Evolutionary Differentiation

The fact that computational design increased the complexity of geometry and computer-numerically-controlled machines are able to fabricate such a non-standard architecture is well known. But it is now imperative in design engineering that the digital logic of evolutionary structuring must also be reflected in the material systems and the construction process.

In 1959 Konrad Wachsmann perceived the principles of industrialization similar to those of mass production. The benefit of automation is only attainable through quantity in production, a principle that distinguishes industrialization from craftsmanship. To guarantee sound assembly of mass-produced objects Wachsmann introduced a system of modular coordination that defines properties and quality of products. A superior universal module coordinates the different categories of modules like geometry, tolerances, construction, etc. This industrial logic ensured constant and repeatable quality but at the same time it limited the range of what was buildable. Deviation from the idealized type, is discarded and not conceived as a possible solution.

The continuous digital workflow is comprised of similar elements of coordination but adapted to novel technological possibilities. The original within such a process is the generative algorithm. It produces data that is subsequently instantiated as g-code for milling or laser cutting, 3d printing, rendering, or drawing. Form is separated from the underlying principles which organize the relations of the different elements within the component. Every component can differ in geometry as long as the relations between its elements are correct. There is no ideal component and subsequent deviation. The two different paradigms of industrial logic and digital fabrication became very obvious during the development of glass fixings for the roof of the Hungerburgbahn stations. The connection of the steel structure and the double-curved glazed skin required a solution which embodies the logic of digital design and manufacturing.

> Hungerburgbahn by Zaha Hadid

Four new stations of the cable railway connect the Innsbruck city centre with the surrounding mountains. Every station is comprised of a free formed glazed roof and solid concrete plinths. Although different in geometry all stations create a family with a highly recognisable formal language. The architectural goal was the creation of continuous, homogeneous surfaces without obtrusive joints and fixings. Only glass provided the desired surface qualities and thermal standards.

The double-curved float glass was coated from the inside with polyurethane resin, which accounts for the colour, as well as ensures a residual load-bearing strength in the event of breakage. The load-bearing structure consists of 8 and 12mm vertical steel ribs with a depth of up to three metres. The structure follows a series of cross sections of the skin with a spacing of 60mm in-between the two.

A large effort was expended in the design of the glass-steel connection. The structural ribs were conceived as "two-dimensional" elements with a free-formed perimeter, but the glass fixings had to follow the double curvature of the skin. The problem was at first approached with the logic of serial production. Brackets with flexible joints were proposed but the solution proved to be unfeasible. Such a joint serves very well in absorbing tolerances, but here every joint would have had to be adjusted into a position that represents a three-dimensional coordinate and a tangential surface direction on the double-curved skin.

The advantage of 18 000 similar brackets would have turned into a time-consuming disaster on-site. The finally realised solution was provided by a simple continuous polyethylene profile which acts as linear support for the glass panels. The profile is slotted and bolted to the steel ribs.

Since the upper face follows the double curvature of the glass skin every single profile had to be milled individually. A continuous digital chain and a five-axis mill helped to cut the profile from sheet material and minimize costs. The CNC data could be automatically derived from the 3d model through specially developed software by DesignToProduction. The same custom application provided information for bolted connections, segmentation and nesting of profiles on the sheet material. Compact T-shaped sheet-metal elements were used for fixing the glass. Tight-fit screws could be placed anywhere on the polyethylene profiles which speeded up the assembly.

The material polyethylene in combination with digital design tools, specific software development and CNC fabrication proved to be most suitable to fulfill the demands of the project.

> The Complexity Beyond Typology: Non-linear Structures and Evolutionary Design

The glass fixing system of the Hungerburgbahn is an example for a typology which is derived from the entire population of elements rather than from a single condition. The aggregate-level concept of population thinking migrated into fabrication through the use of digital technologies. The VOxEL project refers to a paradigm shift in structural design driven by a conceptual use of digital techniques in every phase of design and construction. The finite element method allows the examination of structures beneath the scale of parts which dissolves traditional structural engineering typological building blocks. Structural behavior relies more on a network of interconnected elements than on simple structural typologies. Such an engineering approach improves the collaboration with architects and their surface models. Analysis data is fed back into the generative model and serves as design driver rather than the basis for mere post-rationalization. Thus the application of the phrase *design engineering* to designate a highly interactive process of form generation and refinement between architect and engineer as diverse requirements are mediated between them is, in fact, a new and unique emerging paradigm of engineering design.

PARAMETRICS

The Design of Multiplicities

Rivka Oxman and Robert Oxman

Parametric design is an approach to digital design founded upon relational, or associative, modeling. It operates under conditions of constraints to exploit parametric modifications as a means to generate variability of an object, or system, under design. The *malleability of parametric systems* resides in the powerful generative potential of infinite topological variations mediated by modifications of parameters. This process, termed "parametric design" in architecture and other configurative/geometric disciplines, generally operates together with the presentation and simultaneous modification of a visual model of the object under design. The processes of parametric variations are updated simultaneously in the display. Given that various current software packages also provide a level of interactivity, parametric design has become the keystone design methodology/technology of both research and practice in architecture.

Thinking *parametric design logic* as a new form of digital design thinking (Burry, 2011) promises to continue to influence future developments in theories and technologies of design media. From a historical and theoretical point of view this conceptual and operative leap may truly be considered paradigmatic. The mature and popular use of parametric modeling systems such as *GenerativeComponents* and *Rhino/Grasshopper* are post-millennium systems. They became broadly available in architecture in the middle of the last decade. Thus the wide professional acceptance of parametric design is a relatively recent phenomenon. Much of the early work in parametric design systems occurred in design experimentation with free-form exterior envelopes and the mediation of planar and curved surfaces referred to as *hypersurfaces*.

Parametric design as a form of *digital design thinking* requires acquiring a basis for understanding the *logic of topology* as a basis for the *design of multiplicities*. Starting with the explicit *parametric schemata* of a design solution, the designer establishes the associative relationships by which parts are defined and relate to one another and by which they can support the *topological variability* of a family of solutions. In order to master *parametric modeling*, there is importance to the sequential construction of the object and the topological relationships of its elements. The mathematics of the object, the graph of its relationships between parts, and geometric constraints must be defined in order to produce a framework for multiplicity of solutions and, ultimately, multivariate behavior. It is this intellectual content that characterizes designing with a logic of parametric models to support the mediation and management of the processes of *parametric mutations* that control variations.

Rule-based *algorithmic design* can produce multiple, parallel design solutions. This facilitates a variety of design results that can be compared/evaluated relative to desired constraints and design objectives. This particular logic of design requires the ability to achieve a suitable definition of the problem, develop its abstract representation as a schemata, and its mathematical description. Making explicit the intellectual content of designs and their configurative potential through rule-based operations is the residual design knowledge that is the experience acquired in parametric design. Though much of this knowledge (e.g. geometric knowledge) is today built in to software packages, the basic logic of design is a new form of design thinking that must be learned and can be taught.

In architecture one significant component of creative design is mastery of tectonic knowledge. The knowledge and understanding of tectonics and tectonic patterning must encompass the mathematics and three-dimensional morphology of tectonic patterns. Parametric design implies the ability (knowledge as well as digital skills) to mediate tectonic knowledge. Much of this knowledge falls within the purview of commercial software systems. But creativity involves the ability to create new parametric schemata and to control their parametric behaviors.

There are currently three important domains of parametric architecture: *differentiation* as a medium of form generation; *informed tectonics*; and *continuities* from design to digital production. These are briefly discussed below.

Differentiation is the local distortion, or unique modulation, of a continuous tectonic model in order to accommodate local requirements. This capability of differentiation of local modulations within a general tectonic model is a distinguishing performative characteristic of parametric design systems. The ability to locally differentiate material structures can produce unique effects to the point that various contemporary designers consider this capability as among the hallmarks of contemporary design (see Schumacher, 2010, in this volume). The ability to achieve local differentiation is also a characteristic of natural systems. Any designer who might aspire to emulate natural design must understand the malleable tectonics of natural material systems as well as the craft of their parametric modeling.

Integrated Parametric Systems and Informed Tectonics (N. Oxman, 2011) is the exploitation of parametric mutations as the operative basis for performance-based design. The integration between tectonic design, performative evaluations and generative procedures is an important area of development. Integrations between parametric modeling environments and analytical simulation packages such as *Ecotect* already exist and are among the foundations of creative collaborations between architects and design engineers (Sasaki, 2007).

Material-based Design and Continuity from Design to Production is the situation in which information flow works continuously in both directions from design to production. This implies that the tectonic schemata and its parametric logic are continuously updated throughout the design process. Furthermore, it implies that the logics of material and fabrication-production can be encoded in the parametric system (see Willmann, Gramazio and Kohler, 2012; and Scheurer, 2010, both in this volume).

Parametric Digital Form finding is the experimental development of systems of form generation based upon the above three principles. It is an approach to parametric design that emulates natural design in the capability of supporting adaptability naturally through the design emergence of parametrically adaptive systems.

From a research point of view, digital research has shifted strongly in the direction of the research issues of parametric design. How do we define parametric schemata? Can they be reusable code modules in various problems? Can parametric schemata become collective knowledge? These are among the contemporary issues that are providing both theoretical and operative challenges to a new generation of digital researchers.

Patrik Schumacher's series of articles on *Parametricism* (Schumacher, 2009, this volume; Schumacher, 2011) are part of his work on a general theory of architecture and a new ontology of design. Among the characteristics of this theory is the emphasis upon architecture as complex variegated order in which all elements of architecture are parametrically malleable in order to achieve continuity and differentiation. Emphasis is placed upon formal malleability of parametric systems as well as performative capability that is potentially inherent in *parametrically mediated architecture*.

Parametric design is presented as a new way of thinking about creative design that possesses the complex intricacy of self-organizing natural models. Schumacher attempts to define parametricism as a design paradigm beyond a formal style. This paradigm, according to Schumacher, includes the replacement of repetition with differentiated orders in order to achieve such effects as parametric tectonic patterning of the surfaces of exterior wall systems; and performative articulation of tectonic texture for 3-D adaptable environmental screening. These environmentally adaptive façades reflect his interest in *parametric figuration* as a means of articulating surface relief for the control of environmental conditions such as light control. Architectural patterning realized as parametric surfaces developed from work on tessellations for doubly curved surfaces; these lead to the potential for intelligent differentiated surfaces in which data drives parametric adaptation.

Woodbury's work provides one of the principal contemporary resources for a design methodological exposition and scientific presentation of parametric design (Woodbury, 2010). He stresses the importance of considering the requisite educational demands for understanding and acquiring the logic and expertise of *parametric thinking*. These include abstraction, graph design, schema design, math, scripting and the mathematical definition of parametric models. As the importance of parametric design increases, its role in architectural education is expanding and demanding change of curricula. This constitutes a theoretical as well as an operative challenge. He raises questions regarding the meaning of architecture and the need to reformulate and restate values in the light of changing design paradigms. Parametric design is presented as a "learnable craft," and the intellectual challenges of this craft require new approaches to education and practice. The selection presents many of the basic definitions and terms of the field as well as well-known examples such as Grimshaw's Waterloo International Train Terminal. Among the discussion of knowledge, Woodbury presents the constituents of parametric mastery in the understanding of parametric knowledge combined with the requisite skill to produce good code.

Burry's recent book (2011) offers personal insight into the evolution of the role of parametrics in design as it developed within the frontier of research-related design practice in Europe. His work then became extended and broadened through the academic research center that Burry established in Melbourne. Threaded into his theoretical exposition of a conceptual structure for research-related practice is the remarkable achievement of his long-term relationship with the recreation of the design geometrical logic of Gaudí's Sagrada Familia through the exploitation of parametric design and architectural geometry.

The symbiosis of the knowledge of architectural geometry in relation to parametric design developed as singularly important in the emergence of the (geometric) design research facilities with the important architectural and design engineering practices. Within research groups such as Foster's *Specialist Modelling Group* (SMG) parametric design matured as a medium of research-based design generation in such projects as the Swiss Re Tower.

Burry's professional and academic work have extended a conceptual taxonomy of parametric design. In his work with Goulthorpe on the *Aegis Hyposurface* he began to characterize an ontology of design problems in relationship to parametrics, for example, in the use of surface perturbation algorithms in that project. The *Paramorph* research dealt with creation through generation and parametric knowledge generation through the classification of genotypes (schema) and phenotypes (variations) relationships. The use of "scripting overlays" began to function as the operative medium in the inculcation of the designer's logic upon the software package. Current work in his research group extends this theoretical emphasis in the exploration of parametric schemata as a basis for collaborative design and collaborative knowledge.

Beyond these research frontiers, and related to them, is the issue of the knowledge of the architectural designer. Is this design paradigm defining a new body of knowledge including architectural mathematics and geometry and programming/scripting skills that must be addressed in the education of designers? Is this body of specialist knowledge now becoming so extensive that we are witnessing the rise of new design specializations as well as new roles for digital designers who possess both the ability to engage with parametric design systems as well as to exploit their unique logic in the service of new paradigms of design?

Cheon, Janghwan, Hardy, Steven and Hemsath, Tim (2011), *Parametricism*, ACADIA Regional Conference Proceedings, College of Architecture, University of Nebraska-Lincoln

Reas, Casey, McWilliams, Chandler and LUST (2010), "Parameterize," *Form + Code in Design, Art and Architecture*, Princeton Architectural Press, New York, pp. 93–116

Sakamoto, Tomoko and Ferré, Albert (2007), *From Control to Design: Parametric Algorithmic Architecture*, Actar, Barcelona

Sasaki, Mutsuro (2007), *Morphogenesis of Flux Structures*, AA Publications, London

Schumacher, Patrik (2009), "Parametricism, A New Global Style for Architecture and Urban Design," in Leach, Neil, ed., *Digital Cities*, AD (*Architectural Design*), Vol. 79, No. 4, July/August, p. 17

Terzidis, Kostas (2006), *Algorithmic Architecture*, Architectural Press/Elsevier, Oxford

Williams, Chris (2004), "Design by Algorithm", in Leach, Neil, Turnbull, David and Williams, Chris, *Digital Tectonics*, Wiley-Academy; West Sussex, UK, pp. 78–85

> List of Key Concepts

associative geometry
associative modeling
differentiation
evolutionary parametric design
informed tectonics
integrated parametric systems
multiplicities
parametrically mediated
    architecture
parametric design logic
parametric figuration
parametric form finding

parametricism
parametric model
parametric mutations
parametric schemata
performative design
relational modeling
rule-based parametric design
scripting
scripting overlays
tectonic schemata
topological variations
topology

Patterns are explored here in the narrow sense of designed patterns that spread across all sorts of surfaces, including architectural surfaces.[1] They have been covering architectural surfaces since time immemorial, in the same way that they have been spread all over man-made objects. The human body was perhaps the first surface to receive designed patterns. Architectural patterns thus have a broad and deep lineage, and one should not expect them to have any well-defined, unitary function. As patterns evolve they acquire new functions and lose their prior functions, or new functions are superimposed upon older ones. Patterns might serve purposes of decorative enhancement, feature accentuation, camouflaging, totemic identification, semiotic differentiation, or any combination of these.

There are two general terms from traditional architectural theory that cover the different practices referred to here: 'ornament' and 'decoration'. To oppose ornament or decoration to function would be a fallacy. In classical architectural theory, decoration was the complimentary term of a fundamental distinction and was considered within an overall tripartite division of architecture's teachings: distribution, construction and decoration, the three fundamental tasks of architectural design. This division of architectural knowledge was established in French architectural theory by Augustin-Charles d'Aviler in his *Cours d'architecture* (1691–93), a standard reference work throughout the whole of the eighteenth century. The triad of distribution, construction and decoration is also found in Jacques-François Blondel's opus magnum *Cours d'architecture* (1771–77), and Karl Friedrich Schinkel (1805) refers to it in his (unfinished) architectural treatise. According to Schinkel:

> The purposefulness of any building can be considered from three principle perspectives: purposefulness of spatial distribution or of the plan, purposefulness of construction or the joining of materials appropriate to the plan, purposefulness of ornament or decoration.[2]

Schinkel's conception, once more, shows that the later (modern) opposition between decoration and function is false.

In place of the classic triad referred to above, the distinction between 'organisation' and 'articulation' could instead represent the two central dimensions of the task of architectural design. The aspect of construction has been largely outsourced to the disciplines of building engineering. Organisation is concerned with the spatialisation of the social order via objective distances/proximities and via physical divisions/connections between domains. Articulation is concerned with the subjective comprehension of the spatialised social order. Articulation cannot be dispensed with; it involves the central core competency of architecture.

9

Parametric Patterns

Patrik Schumacher

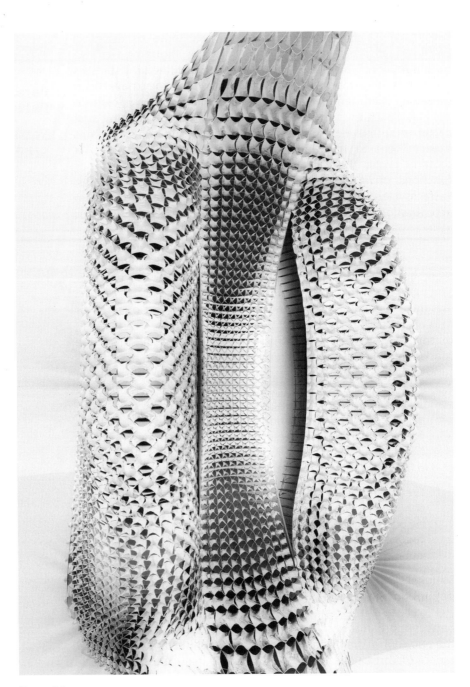

Figure 9.1

Articulation contains the differentia specifica that demarcates architecture/design from all engineering disciplines. Articulation reckons with the fact that buildings function only via the user's active 'reading' of their spatial organisation. What things look like matters. At a certain level of social complexity, adequate spatial organisations can only become effective if their ordering operations can enlist the user's capacity to actively 'read' the urban/architectural environment. Only on the basis of articulate organisations will users be enabled to navigate, and collectively utilise, the built environment to its fullest potential. The reference problem for the task of articulation is orientation. Articulation should facilitate orientation by making the spatial organisation, and the social order within it, legible. Orientation also implies the steering of expectations about the social scenarios that might unfold within a space and about the conduct that is appropriate within that space.

The distinction of articulation versus organisation cannot be aligned with the distinction of form versus function: the two intersect each other. Both organisation and articulation have functional as well as formal aspects. Both organisational diagrams and strategies of articulation need to be selected on the basis of their social functionality, and both are dependent on the availability of a pertinent formal repertoire.

Architectural patterns are a potent device for architectural articulation. For instance, in classical architecture ornamental patterns (mouldings) often emphasise a building's ordering symmetry axes. Typical ornamental motifs are also used to distinguish typical functions. Traditionally, the concepts of 'character' and 'expression' were deployed as mediating terms to explain how decoration is to be related to a building's purpose. These were taken from the theatre and were first introduced into architectural theory by Germain Boffrand in his *Livre d'architecture* of 1745:

> Architecture . . . its component parts are so to speak brought to life by the different characters that it conveys to us. Through its composition a building expresses, as if in the theatre, that the scene is pastoral or tragic; that this is a temple or a palace, a public building destined for a particular purpose or a private house. By their planning, their structure and their decoration, all such buildings must proclaim their purpose to the beholder. If they fail to do so, they offend against expression and are not what they ought to be.[3]

It is noteworthy here that all three terms of the classical tripartite division – planning (distribution), structure (construction), decoration – are together involved in expressing the character of the building. Boffrand goes on:

> If you are setting out to build a music room, or a salon in which to receive company, it must be cheerful in its planning, in its lighting, and in its manner

Facing page

Figure 9.1: Accentuating deployment of façade relief. Hadid Masterclass, University of Applied Arts, Vienna. Image credit: University of Applied Arts, Vienna.

of decoration. If you want a mausoleum, the building must be suited to its use, and the architecture and decoration must be serious and sad; for Nature makes us susceptible to all these impressions, and a unified impulse never fails to touch our feelings.[4]

The unified impulse that touches our feelings might be best translated into our contemporary language as the 'atmosphere' of a space. Jacques-François Blondel referred to 'imperceptible nuances' in connection with the concepts of character and expression:

> It is by the assistance of these imperceptible nuances that we are able to make a real distinction in the design of two buildings of the same genre but which nevertheless should announce themselves differently: preferring in one a style sublime, noble and elevated; in the other a character naïve, simple and true. Distinct particular expressions . . . that need to be felt . . . contribute more than one ordinarily imagines in assigning to each building the character that is proper to it.[5]

Ornamental patterns that convey atmospheric values are received semiconsciously. In fact, architectural articulation in general operates largely via patterns that are perceived in passing, in a mode of 'distraction'[6] rather than

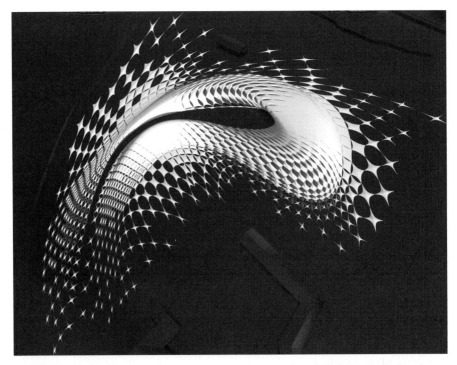

Figure 9.2: Architecture as a pattern of continuously transforming components, Randers Art Museum Competition, London 2009, Zaha Hadid Architects. Image credit: Image courtesy of Zaha Hadid Architects.

focused attention. The information processing that is relevant for the quick, intuitive orientation of users is largely unconscious. In this way articulated spaces achieve the behavioural priming appropriate for the respective social setting.

The concept of decoration does not carry the full intent and emphasis of what the agenda of articulation involves today. Architectural projects are now often confronted with unique briefs and institutional arrangements that require solutions of unprecedented novelty. Reliance on a handful of given character types can no longer exhaust the task of articulation. Articulatory strategies have to be devised that order the visual field and guide the eye to recognise abstract configurations and the focal moments or key distinctions within them. However, the traditional concept of decoration did go beyond its current connotations of superficial and arbitrary beautification. As demonstrated above, decoration, in classical architectural theory, was linked to the twin concepts of character and expression. Decoration was seen as a necessary ingredient of architecture, as it was a necessary ingredient of all artefacts. A building without decoration was unfinished, unable to enter the social world, just as it was impossible to join society naked, or without sufficient behavioural decorum. Decoration, expressing the appropriate character of a space, was linked to propriety within a sophisticated system of social distinctions. Today spaces seem more neutral, encounters are less ritualised and decorum seems less conspicuous. But have these registers of social coding disappeared altogether?

The decorative patterning of surfaces was still taken for granted all the way through the nineteenth century until, suddenly, Modernism opted for the clean, white wall – in the footsteps of the clean, white shirt. The first examples of unadorned, naked architecture were causing public scandals, most notoriously Adolph Loos' Haus am Michaelerplatz (1898) in Vienna. However, Loos soon won the argument. The re-evaluation of values was extreme: ornament signified backwardness. According to Loos, the evolution of culture is synonymous with the removal of ornament. His famous polemic compared ornamentation with the tattoos of criminals, and his reasoning goes as follows: 'Primitive men had to differentiate themselves by various colours; modern man needs his clothes as a mask. His individuality is so strong that it can no longer be expressed in terms of items of clothing.'[7]

Loos' allusion to modern individuality is pertinent here. However, the demise of traditional ornament does not imply the demise of articulation. The accelerating and intensifying fashion system bears witness against his account. The end of ornamentation is not synonymous with the end of design's expressive function, neither does it spell the end of the phenomenon of style, as Loos presumed, nor the final demise of surface patterning.

The modern denigration of overt ornament cannot be accounted for by the mere fact that industrialisation overtook handicraft production. It was only after nearly a hundred years of industrialisation, after the social revolutions that followed in the aftermath of the First World War, that the pure Sachlichkeit of 'White Modernism' succeeded. To be sure, this radical rejection of what had been taken for granted for thousands of years was a heroic act of iconoclasm fully consistent with the revolution and with the general emancipation of creative potentials that the Modern movement delivered. The traditional orders and regimes of ornamentation stood in the way of unfettered design research. They had to go. Thus, if we now call for a vigorous return to the deployment of patterns in architecture and design, this does not imply that unadorned, Modernist architecture was a mistake. Equally, the fact that Modernism as a whole went into crisis also does not imply that it was a mistake – Modernism delivered a huge material step forward – but it does imply that it would be a mistake to continue the Modernist paradigm and to prolong its strictures against ornament/decoration. On the back of Modernism's achievements a new, more complex and versatile societal formation has evolved that poses new challenges for the task of architectural organisation and articulation. Today's 'White Minimalism' is indeed a historical mistake.

Modernist strictures against ornament/decoration were first challenged by Postmodernism. Although historical motifs were brought back in a mode of playful eclecticism, there was no engagement with systematic articulatory patterning. Notwithstanding Minimalism's historical fallacy, it was from within this movement that the return to patterns, and the attendant new embrace of ornament, was initiated during the 1990s. The seminal project in this respect was Herzog & de Meuron's 1993 Ricola Storage Building in Mulhouse-Brunstatt, France. The introduction of different surface effects, like different material textures, had already happened within the later phases of Modernism, but artificial, quasi-graphic techniques of surface treatment and surface patterning were now being deployed. These moves signal the enrichment of the formal repertoire of architecture, without falling back on traditional regimes of adornment and their meanings. Instead, new atmospheres with new associations and nuances could be projected and elaborated. However, from the vantage point of today, Minimalist pattern deployment had obvious limitations: the underlying spatial organisation of its compositions was exceedingly simple and the surfaces that received patterning were simple, flat planes. Patterns were repetitive and were applied like wallpaper.

In the meantime, the avant-garde that had followed on from Deconstructivism under the heading of 'folding in architecture'[8] was at first focusing only on (complex) geometry, though the initially faceted surfaces soon evolved into smooth NURBS surfaces. Towards the end of the 1990s, new possibilities of patterning were discovered by applying the technique of texture mapping onto warped NURBS surfaces, and such effects were achieved on built projects by projecting video images onto curvilinear surfaces, or by embedding digital display systems within the surfaces. In 1998, AD published Hypersurface Architecture,[9] a whole programmatic issue dedicated to these new possibilities. Architectural patterning had arrived within the avant-garde movement that we now – both in retrospect and in anticipation of more exciting explorations to come – promote as the style of parametricism.[10]

The technique of texture mapping has since been replaced by scripting, and mapping only survives as an initial shortcut to test or illustrate effects that are then to be implemented by scripts. Early examples of NURBS surface articulations that were not just arbitrary mappings or projections emerged with the introduction of CNC milling. Bernard Cache and Greg Lynn both experimented with effects like heightened contour lines and tool paths, producing a contemporary translation of the idea of 'faktura' (the deliberate deployment of the visual traces of the manufacturing process). At the same time, the question of how NURBS surfaces could be tessellated became an issue. The need for tessellation became an opportunity for articulation, and the difficulty of devising both feasible and elegant tessellations for double-curved surfaces was the occasion that brought parametric modelling and scripting to the fore.

The problem of fitting panels onto a complex surface has also been driving the development of Bentley Systems' GenerativeComponents (GC) associative and parametric modelling system with its central idea of populating a complex host surface with computationally self-adapting elements. The classical GC setup involves the design of an inherently variable component that is defined across a range of surface parameters. To ensure perfect fit, each instantiation is parametrically adapted to its unique position on the host surface. The result might be called a 'parametric pattern'. However, in this classical setup the curvature variation of the surface provides the data set that drives the parametric adaptation of the component with the aim of keeping the pattern as even and homogeneous as possible. The aim is to maintain component identity by compensating for the underlying surface differentiation.

Parametricism transforms this technique of parametric pattern design into a new and powerful register of articulation. The crucial move that inaugurates 'parametricist patterning' is the move from adaptive compensation to the amplification of differences. The underlying surface variability is utilised as a data set that can drive a much more radical pattern differentiation. The underlying surface differentiation is thus amplified and made much more conspicuous, and this strong emphasis on conspicuous differentiation is one of the hallmarks of parametricism.

Differentiation might also be introduced wilfully, by 'painting' the surface with any pattern or image that then becomes the data set to drive component differentiation. In the current phase of technique exploration and formal experimentation, this arbitrary play with differentiation might be tolerated. Ultimately, however, such an injection of differentiation should be rejected; it is 'ornamental' in a rather questionable sense. The differentiation of the surface should serve as a medium of articulation, and it can do so only if it is correlated with the geometric or functional aspects of the space the surface constructs. A strong emphasis on correlation is a second hallmark of parametricism. The articulation by means of correlative surface differentiation is free to take on any relevant data set of the overall spatial construct within which the respective surface is situated. Significant correlates might include the underlying primary structure. The surface articulation might correspond to structural flow lines or stress distribution.

Correlates might further include the apertures that are set into the surface. Patterns might accentuate apertures, a surface might be made to correlate with the furnishings within a space, and the expected pattern of occupation might also be utilised as a data set driving a corresponding surface differentiation. A sophisticated setup should be able to cater for multiple data sets simultaneously.

Another powerful opportunity is the adaptive differentiation of facades with respect to environmental parameters that vary widely according to the orientation of the surface. Here, functional and formal variation go hand in hand. The gradual variation of sunlight intensity on a curved surface translates into a gradient transformation of the component formation. Within parametricism, such functional exigencies are heightened into an artistic concept.

It is important to note that parametricism, as a style, constitutes an artistic agenda that embodies a will to form. Appearances matter, but they matter as part of performance. The ethos of this artistic agenda is one of articulation that stands against a mere formalism. Appearances are revealing an otherwise invisible performativity, or accentuate and make conspicuous what might otherwise get lost in an unarticulated visual chaos.

Figure 9.3: Dynamic observer-dependent articulatory, pattern. Louis Vuitton Store, Macau. Zaha Hadid Architects. Image credit: Image courtesy of Zaha Hadid Architects.

The following specific registers of surface articulation might be distinguished: relief, seaming, material, texture, colour, reflectivity and translucency. Potentially, all of these registers should be not only utilised but choreographed via correlating scripts. Surface relief is of particular interest here because it makes the surface sensitive to both changing light conditions and changing view angles.

In order to take the conditions described above into account, parametric design must extend its attention beyond the consideration of object parameters to include both ambient and observer parameters. The systematic work with such parameters enhances the sense of animation that can be achieved with respect to the articulation of architectural surfaces. The manipulation of lighting conditions, and shifts in observer position might trigger dramatic shifts in the appearance and understanding of a surface or space. Patterns might be set up in such a way that key parameters become Gestalt sensitive, so that a small variation in a critical parameter – object, ambient or observer – triggers a surprising Gestalt switch. This design agenda has been referred to as 'parametric figuration'.[11] For architectural surface patterns to participate in this agenda a certain degree of surface depth is required. Parametric figuration is perhaps the most ambitious form of architectural articulation and to become really effective it would need to go beyond merely visual effects. The Gestalt switches would need to be correlated with the changing events scenarios that would benefit from a shift in understanding and orientation. Only at that stage would we be able to talk about dynamic, high-performance ornaments.

Figure 9.4: Cultural Cenre, Baku, 2007–2011, Zaha Hadid Architects. Image credit: Image courtesy of Zaha Hadid Architects.

1   Patterns in the more profound application of patterns of spatial organisation that structure urban and architectural space have been treated in the author's article 'Parametricism: A new global style for architecture and urban design', in Neil Leach (ed), *AD Digital Cities*, Vol 79, No 4, July/August 2009.

2   Karl Friedrich Schinkel, *Das Architektonische Lehrbuch*, Deutscher Kunstverlag (Munich/Berlin), 2001, p 22. The text from 1805 remained an unpublished fragment during Schinkel's time.

3   Germain Boffrand, *Book of Architecture Containing the General Principles of the Art*, Ashgate Publishing (Aldershot), 2003, pp 21–22; French original, *Livre d'architecture* (1745), excerpt in Harry Francis Malgrave (ed), *Architectural Theory*, Blackwell Publishing (Oxford), 2006, p 193.

4   Boffrand, op cit.

5   Jacques-Francois Blondel, *Course of Architecture*, 1771, excerpt in Malgrave, op cit, p 198. Blondel goes on to utilise the distinction of male versus female as an analogical character distinction applicable to buildings. The male character entails massiveness, firmness, grandeur, should be sparse in the detail of its ornament, show simplicity in general composition and feature projecting bodies that throw large shadows.

6   Walter Benjamin, 'The Work of Art in the Age of Mechanical Reproduction', in Walter Benjamin, *Illuminations: Essays and Reflections*, Schocken Books (New York), 1969.

7   Adolf Loos, *Sämtliche Schriften 1897–1930*, Herold Druck- und Verlagsgesellschaft (Vienna), 1962.

8   See Greg Lynn (ed), *AD Folding in Architecture*, Vol 63, No 3–4, 1993.

9   See Stephen Perrella (ed), *AD Hypersurface Architecture*, Vol 68, No 5–6, 1998.

10 Schumacher, op cit.

11 The author has been experimenting with the agenda of parametric figuration in various teaching arenas: Innsbruck University, the Architectural Association Design Research Lab (DRL), Yale University and Vienna University of Applied Arts.

This chapter sketches how parametric design work changes what designers do and what they must think about while they are doing it. The treatment is mainly descriptive. It derives from the properties of parametric systems themselves; from my own knowledge of computation and design; but mostly from working, over several years, with designers using and learning parametric systems.

10

How Designers Use Parameters

Robert Woodbury

> 1.1 Conventional and Parametric Design Tools

In conventional design tools it is "easy" to create an initial model – you just add parts, relating them to each other by such things as *snaps* as you go. Making changes to a model can be difficult. Even changing one dimension can require adjusting many other parts and all of this reworking is manual. The more complex the model, the more work can be entailed. From a design perspective, decisions that should be changed can take too much work to change. Tools like these can limit exploration and effectively restrict design.

On the other hand, erasing conventional work is easy. You select and delete. Since parts are *independent,* that is, they have no lasting relationship to other parts, there is no more work to do to fix the representation. You might well have to fix the design, by adding parts to take the place of the thing erased or adjusting existing parts to fit the changed design.

Since the 1980s, conventional tools have used the ubiquitous generic concepts of *copy, cut* and *paste*. These combine erasure and addition of parts to support rapid change by copying and repositioning like elements. Copy, cut and paste work in conventional design precisely because of part independence.

Parametric modeling aims to address these limitations. Rather than the designer creating the design solution (by direct manipulation) as in conventional design tools, the idea is that the designer establishes the *relationships* by which parts connect, builds up a design using these relationships and edits the relationships by observing and selecting from the results produced. The system takes care of keeping the design consistent with the relationships and thus increases designer ability to explore ideas by reducing the tedium of reworking.

Of course, there is a cost. Parametric design depends on defining relationships and the willingness (and ability) of the designer to consider the relationship-definition phase as an integral part of the broader design process. It initially requires the designer to take one step back from the direct activity of design and focus on the logic that binds the design together. This process

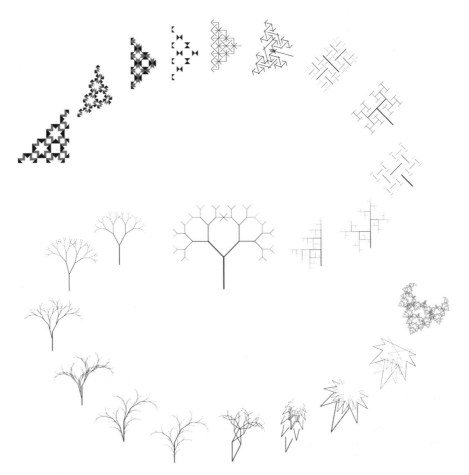

Figure 10.1

of relationship creation requires a formal notation and introduces additional concepts that have not previously been considered as part of "design thinking".

The cost may have a benefit. Parametric design and its requisite modes of thought may well extend the intellectual scope of design by explicitly representing ideas that are usually treated intuitively. Being able to explain concepts explicitly is a part of at least some real understanding.

Defining relationships is a complex act of thinking. It involves strategies and skills, some new to designers and some familiar. The following sections outline some of these strategies and connect them with what designers already have in their repertoire. The first section, entitled *New Skills,* outlines the small-scale, technical knowledge and craft in evident use by effective parametric modeling practitioners. The second section, entitled *New Strategies,* steps slightly closer to design to sketch the new tasks that designers can and do undertake with the new tools. Both sections are descriptive, not normative. By this I mean they are based on observing and working with designers using parametric modelers, not on surmising what designers might, in some sense, need to know.

> 1.2 New Skills

Drawing is a skill. Combining multiple orthographic and perspective sketches to reveal the implications of a design idea is strategy. Here are six skills held by those who know and use parametric tools. Some have analogues to historical design skills. Others are new to design. Parametric mastery requires them all.

1.2.1 Conceiving Data Flow: Caveat: The examples in Sections 1.2.1 to 1.2.4 are very simple, almost trivial. This is deliberate. Through simplicity, I hope to explain crucial principles that are easily obscured. **Reader, please bear with me**.

Data *flows* through a parametric model, from independent to dependent nodes. The way in which data flows deeply affects the designs possible, and how a designer interacts with them. This can be illustrated with a very simple example: a three-room rectangular plan drawn with lines representing walls. In the figures that follow a propagation graph represents only the dimensions of the rooms; the lines would, in turn, depend on the nodes in this graph. In Figure 10.2, room dimensions are related by open dimension chains. Figure 10.3 shows the same set of rooms, with the

---

Facing page

Figure 10.1: A single recursive structure with minor variations produces a wide range of designs. Image credit: Drawings courtesy Robert Woodbury.

additional relationship that $room_1$ is always square. Here the graph has a new link (between w_1 and h_1) and one fewer source node (h_1).

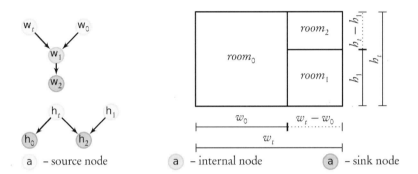

Figure 10.2: The plan has $room_{0...2}$. Each $room_i$ has a width w_i and a height h_i. The total width is w_t; the total height is h_t. Dimensions w_t and w_0 are independent. Dimensions w_1 and w_2 are dependent: $w_t \rightarrow w_0 \rightarrow w_1$ and $w_1 \rightarrow w_2$. Dimensions h_t and h_1 are independent, where as h_0 and h_2 are dependent: $h_t \rightarrow h_0$ and $h_t - h_1 \rightarrow h_2$. An increase in h_t results in $room_1$ remaining the same height: $room_0$ and $room_2$ expand to take up all of the new space. Image credit: Drawings courtesy Robert Woodbury.

Conceiving, arranging and editing dependencies is the key parametric task.

To make things more complex, dependency chains – several nodes in sequential dependency – tend to grow. Figure 10.4 expands the examples above it to include the points and lines representing the floor plan. It shows that long dependency chains are the norm, and visualizing the graph can become difficult.

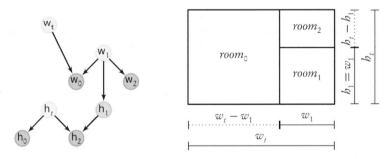

Figure 10.3: The main interactive difference between this design and that of Figure 10.1 is that $room_1$ is always square and its size is explicitly controlled. The propagation graph is distinctly different. Image credit: Drawings courtesy Robert Woodbury.

Designers use dependencies in combination to exhibit some desired aggregate form or behaviour. Dependencies may correspond to geometric relationships (for example, between a surface and its defining curves), but are not restricted to this and may in fact represent higher order (or more abstract) design decisions. Parametric approaches to design aim to provide designers with tools to capture design decisions in an explicit, auditable, editable and re-executable form.

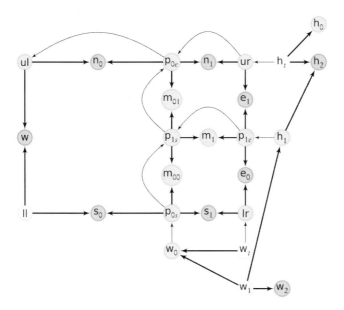

Figure 10.4: Adding the points and lines defining the floor plan increases both the length of the dependency chains, the overall graph complexity, the difficulty of inventing short, clear, descriptive names, and, especially, the challenge of achieving are adable graph layout. This diagram is based on that of Figure10.2. Image credit: Drawing courtesy Robert Woodbury.

1.2.2 Dividing to Conquer: For very good reasons, designers organize their work as *near-hierarchies,* that is, recursive systems of parts with limited interactions between parts. This is a near-universal claim, and it is easy to test. Think of a designed object that is so organized, for example, an automobile organized into body, drive train and electrical systems. Now think of a designed object that is a non-near-hierarchy in some way, either by having only one part or by having extremely complex interactions among its parts. Compare the relative difficulty of imagining each. **See?**

One of the many reasons for near-hierarchies is that the limited interactions among system parts enables a divide-and-conquer design strategy – divide the design into parts, design the parts and combine the parts into an entire design, all the while managing the interactions among the parts. The strategy works best when the interactions are simple.

Parametric modeling enables, indeed almost requires, a divide-and-conquer strategy. In building a parametric design, it is easy to keep adding nodes to the graph. A moment comes though, when the graph is too complex to fully grasp. At a much earlier moment, it becomes difficult to explain the graph to another, or to resume work on it after an inevitable interruption (in this situation, there really is "another" – it is you, after you've taken a break and come back with a different memory state). Using a divide-and-conquer strategy is to organize a parametric design into parts so that there are limited and understandable links from part to part. Directional data flow assures a hierarchical model, with parts higher in the flow typically being assemblies – organizing concepts. Parts at the bottom of the flow usually correspond to physical parts of the design.

Returning to the three-room floor plan, even this seemingly simple design could be given a hierarchical structure. Figures 10.5 and 10.6 show that a decision to model the three rooms in two *wings*, assigning each room to one of the wings, has profound effects on the plans obtainable, particularly when the number of rooms in each wing increases.

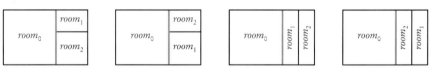

Figure 10.5: All possible arrangements into two wings with *room*$_0$ in the west wing and *room*$_1$ and *room*$_2$ in the east wing. Image credit: Drawings courtesy Robert Woodbury.

Figure 10.6: All possible arrangements into two wings with *room*$_0$ and *room*$_1$ in the west wing and *room*$_2$ in the east wing. Image credit: Drawings courtesy Robert Woodbury.

Skilled designers spend much time on developing and refining the near-hierarchical structure of their models. They arrive at parametric design as able practitioners of divide and conquer – architects usually organize designs (especially at the construction documentation phase) into technical subsystems. In conceptual design, common design schema separately play on space and tectonics. But skills transfer poorly across domains. The divide and conquer of parametric modeling requires knowledge from both the design domain and about how to structure parametric designs so that data flows from part to part in a clear and explainable manner.

1.2.3 Naming: Parts have names. This is designerly practice, not physical law. But there is a good reason for this – names facilitate communication. "The column at grid location E2:S4" is a more reliable way of identifying a particular column than "that square mark a third of the way across and halfway up the sheet".

Parametric modelers spend much time in devising and refining the names of their parts. Simply renaming the rooms and dimensions of the three-room floor plan shows why they do this. Figure 10.7 is identical to Figure 10.3 in all respects, except that the nodes and rooms have been given arbitrary names.

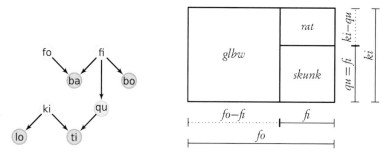

Figure 10.7: Confusion reigns with arbitrary names. Even though this figure and Figure 10.2 are identical except for names, it takes much more effort to understand this one. Image credit: Drawings courtesy Robert Woodbury.

1.2.4 Thinking with Abstraction: The word "abstraction" is laden, that is, its meaning depends on context.

Designers and computer scientists use the term differently.

An abstraction describes a general concept rather than a specific example. In common usage, abstraction is associate with vagueness; it may be hard to infer much from an abstract idea. In design, abstract ideas are often protean, that is, they are used as a base from which to generate many alternatives. In this role, both connotations of the word apply: a general concept can be realized in many ways, and a vague concept can be given many interpretations, each of which may have multiple realizations.

In computer science, abstraction has the first meaning: an abstraction describes a class of instances, leaving out inessential detail. Computer scientists (and their craftful cousins, programmers) are constantly seeking formalisms and code that apply in many situations. In fact, the utility of a computational idea is deeply linked to its generality – the more often it applies, the more useful it becomes. Designers too know and practice such abstraction. Dimensional modules, structural centre lines and standard details all are media for abstract design ideas.

To abstract a parametric model is to make it applicable in new situations, to make it depend only on essential inputs and to remove reference to and use of overly specific terms. It is particularly important because much modeling work is similar, and time is always in short supply. If part (remember divide-and-conquer?) of one model can be used in another, it displays some abstraction by the very fact of reuse. Well-crafted abstractions are a key part of efficient modeling. For example, in floor plans comprising rectangular rooms, two good abstractions are to consider the rooms and the walls respectively as nodes. Using rooms as nodes (Figure 10.8) creates two independent subgraphs in the design, one for west-to-east relations and one for north-to-south relations.

When walls are nodes, as in Figure 10.9, the graph becomes a very simple tree structure of successive subdivisions, either vertical or horizontal, dividing an overall rectangular plan. Each of the four abstractions in this section based on dimensions (Figures 10.2 and 10.3); points and line segments (Figure 10.4); rectangles (Figure 10.8); and walls (Figure 10.9) each offer advantages and disadvantages; and, sadly, each requires work to understand, develop and use. Computer scientists use the term *representation* to describe abstractions with mathematical proofs relating properties of the abstraction to properties of a class of objects.

An important form of abstraction for parametric modeling is *condensing* and *expanding* graph nodes. In any graph, a collection of nodes can be condensed into a single node; and graphs with condensed nodes are called *compound graphs*.

A condensed node can be expanded to restore the graph to its original state. Condensing and expanding implement hierarchy and aid divide-and-conquer strategies. Parametric modelers implement this strategy to create new kinds of multi-property nodes, to support copying and reuse of parts of a graph and thus to build user-defined libraries of parametric models.

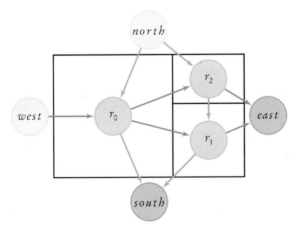

Figure 10.8: *The loosely-packed arrangement of rectangles (LOOS)* representation (Flemming, 1986, 1989). Treating each rectangle as a graph no decreases two separate subgraphs in the design (west-to-east and north-to-south). In addition to its simple graph, the LOOS representation has the benefit of being able to represent every possible layout of rectangles, and provides relatively simple operations for inserting and deleting rectangles. Image credit: Drawing courtesy Robert Woodbury.

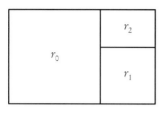 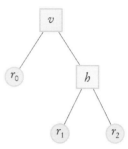

Figure 10.9: In the *subregion representation* (Kundu, 1988; Harada, 1997), the representation is a simple tree, with each square node representing both a rectangular region and either a vertical (v) or horizontal (h) wall dividing the region and each round node representing a specific rectangle. This representation is extremely simple and has an easily understood dimensioning scheme; each v and h node contains an independent parameter. Image credit: Drawings courtesy Robert Woodbury.

1.2.5 Thinking Mathematically: Whether conventional or parametric, a CAD model is a set of mathematical propositions. A line object is a statement that the segment between its end points is a part of the model. Mathematical calculations are routinely made by the system: putting new points on the active plane, placing a line tangent to a circle through a point and specifying a point as the centroid of a polygon each model basic mathematical inferences. Designers do more than make collections of propositions: they make *proofs* of their designs. By using constructions such as grids, snaps, circle intersections and tangents, they construct mathematical proofs that the designs thus specified are consequent to their base assumptions. Of course, designers seldom look at their work in this way, and mathematicians might cringe to consider such special-purpose constructions as meaningful proofs. But the analogy stands; in some sense, designers "do" mathematics. Practically though, designers *use* mathematics more than they *do* mathematics. To use mathematics is to begin with established mathematical fact and to rely on it to make a construction or, even more loosely, as a metaphor for a design move. To do mathematics is to derive theorems (new mathematical facts) by inference from prior known statements. The difference is in both intent and practice. A designer sets out to create a design, a description of a special artefact suited to purpose. A mathematician seeks to discover new and general facts from old or new paths of inference to already known facts. Design work is more like McCullough's (1998) digital craft and less like Lakatos's (1991) cycle of proof and refutation. We can quibble about how similar (or not) these two acts are, but there is an essential difference in license taken and understanding sought. Using mathematics to do design requires far less understanding than doing mathematics for its own sake. Note the word "requires". Some designers choose to delve into the mathematics of their work. Sometimes such apparent distraction becomes core to developing a body of work.

Other times it follows the time-honoured tradition of curiosity as its own reward.

Design has always had practitioners who take more than slight steps towards mathematical maturity. Gothic buildings can be understood and were evidently designed as complex sequences of geometric construction proceeding from a few key dimensions. Traditional Persian Rasmi domes result from projecting a drawing onto a predetermined dome geometry. In Persian, the verb for drawing and the word "rasmi" have the same linguistic root. Da Vinci's Vitruvian Man drawing is the centrepiece of a collection of notes on Vitruvius's *The Ten Books on Architecture* (Pollio, 2006).

Palladio (1742; 1965) expounded on and (sometimes) used proportional systems in his building plans and elevations. Antoni Gaudí limited his form finding mostly to developable surfaces, to great sculptural effect. Le Corbusier espoused *The Modular*, a manifesto on the play of the golden ratio $\emptyset = (1 + \sqrt{5})/2$, also the solution to the equation $1/\emptyset = \emptyset/(1 + \emptyset)$, and in turn the division of a line segment such that the small and large parts are in the same ratio as the large part to the whole. Canadian architect James W. Strutt based his life's work on the play of sphere and polyhedral packings and their duals. Geometric construction and visual clarity are signatures for Foster + Partners. These are statements of historical fact, not judgments on the work obtained. Valuing design for using geometry is circular reasoning at best.

Parametric systems can make such mathematics active. By coding theorems and constructions into propagation graphs and node update methods, designers can experience mathematical ideas at play. The once dry ideas of surface normals, cross products, tangencies, projections and plane equations become an essential part of the modeler's repertoire. Active and visual mathematics can become means and strategy to the ends of design.

Modern mathematics is too vast for the lifetime of a single mind. Indeed, it seems too vast for an entire industry. New geometric operators appear slowly in CAD, leaving much design possibility unexplored. For example, in 2009, the mesh subdivision and refinement techniques common in animation systems were only beginning to appear in CAD. The field of computational geometry provides such basic constructs as convex hulls, Voronoi diagrams and Delaunay triangulations that would enable new avenues of exploration were they in the CAD toolkit. Parametric modeling enables new mathematical play. Designers know something about these other fields – their demands may well push system developers to richer tools. Section 1.3.5 outlines some of the new strategies in contemporary parametric design.

1.2.6 Thinking Algorithmically: A parametric design is a graph. Its graph-dependent nodes contain either or both update methods and constraint expressions. Both are *algorithms* and can be changed by users, at least in principle. Long practice in using, programming and teaching parametric systems shows that, sooner or later, designers will need (or at least want) to write algorithms to make their intended designs.

It is useful to consider what an algorithm is. There are many definitions. Berlinski (1999) (whose book you should read!) writes on page *xix*:
An algorithm is

a finite procedure,
written in a fixed symbolic vocabulary,
governed by precise instructions,
moving in discrete steps, 1,2,3,. . .,
whose execution requires no insight, cleverness,
intuition, intelligence or perspicuity,
and that, sooner or later, comes to an end.

Berlinski's definition is less formal than those you will find in dictionaries and computer science texts, but contains all of the accepted essential elements of an algorithm. Design highlights two of its aspects. The first is "procedure": an algorithm is a process that must be specified step by step. Designers largely describe objects rather than processes. The second is "precise": one misplaced character means that an algorithm likely will not work. In contrast, designerly representations are replete with imprecision – they rely on human readers to interpret marks appropriately. It is hardly surprising then that many designers encounter difficulty in integrating algorithmic thinking into their work, in spite of over 30 years of valiant attempts to teach programming in design schools. It is even less surprising that computer-aided design relegates programming to the background. Almost all current systems have a so-called *scripting language.* These are programming languages; developers call them scripting languages to make them appear less foreboding. In almost all of these, to use the language your must remove yourself from the actual task and your accustomed visual, interactive representation. You must work in a domain of textual instructions. This is not surprising either – algorithmic thinking differs from almost all other forms of thought. But the sheer distance between representations familiar to designers and those needed for algorithms exacerbates the gap.

In both conventional and parametric systems, the scripting language can be used to make designs. The language provides functions that can add, modify or erase objects in a model. In addition, parametric systems bring the algorithm closer to design models. They do this by localizing algorithms in nodes of a graph, either as constraint expressions or as update methods. However, designers still must grasp and use algorithmic thought if they are to get the most out of such systems.

> 1.3 New Strategies

Conceiving data flow; dividing to conquer; naming; and thinking abstractly, mathematically and algorithmically form the base for designers to build their parametric craft. In this section, I describe strategies that my research group has observed over several years of running courses and workshops in parametric modeling. Our observation techniques have ranged from informal interaction and journaling to structured *participant observer* studies (Qian, Chen and Woodbury, 2007).

1.3.1 Sketching: The sketch occupies a near sacred place in the design pantheon. A library of books attests to its importance to design, extolls its protean virtues and urges students to learn this all-important skill. Toothy paper and the 2B pencil are among the saints of architectural hagiography. Irony aside, all design teachers know that the student who sketches well tends to do well in the studio; and that pencil sketching remains a vital and important tool for design. But what is a sketch? In *Sketching User Experiences*, Bill Buxton (2007) crafts a thorough argument for the qualities and uses of sketches in interaction design. In the chapter *The Anatomy of Sketching* (pp. 111–120), he posits 11 qualities of design sketches. For Buxton, sketches are (or have) *quick; timely; inexpensive; disposable; plentiful; clear vocabulary; distinct gesture; minimal detail; suggest and explore rather than confirm; appropriate degree of refinement;* and *ambiguity*. Of these, only clear vocabulary, distinct gesture and appropriate degree of refinement make any reference to the media conveying a sketch. All of the other eight (and much of these three) refer rather to the role of sketches in the design process. Buxton does not have the only or final word on sketching in design, but his voice is both recent and clear. To paraphrase his words: Designers have always sketched. It is how they do their work.

We have known since McLuhan that media and content deeply inter-twine; the carrier and carried cannot be pulled apart. Well mastered, the skill of pencil sketching meets all of Buxton's criteria. But when *taken in their own terms,* so do other media and tools. Unencumbered with the 2B religion, students use the media at hand, and today such media are mostly digital. These fresh newcomers consistently do work that meets all of Buxton's criteria. And their eyes are different. What old-timers like Buxton and I might see as overly determined and graphically definite, the new generation sees as ambiguous and free. If you don't like it, change it! The digital generation might well add the word *dynamic* to Buxton's list.

Parametric models are, by their nature, dynamic. Once made, they can be rapidly changed to answer the archetypal design question: "What if . . .?" Sometimes a single model replaces pages of manual sketches. On the other hand, parametric models are definite, complex structures that take time to create. Too often, they are not quick. A challenge for system developers is to enable rapid modeling, so that their systems can better serve sketching in design.

1.3.2 Throw Code Away: Designers do design, not media. Unless they get seduced by the siren of the parametric tool, they model just what they need to the level of confidence and completeness they need. From project to project, day to day or even hour to hour, they tend to rebuild rather than reuse. In stark contrast, much of the toolkit of computer programming (and parametric modeling is programming) aims at making clear code, reducing redundancy and fostering reuse. In the world of professional programming, these aims make eminent sense. In the maelstrom of design work, they give way to such simple devices as copying, pasting and slightly modifying entire blocks of code. Professional programmers would be horrified by such acts. Designers are delighted if the resulting model works, right now.

At the 2007 ACADIA conference, Brady Peters presented a paper on the design and construction of a roof over the courtyard of the Smithsonian Institution Patent Office Building (Peters, 2007) by Foster + Partners. During his talk, he showed some of the computer code that generated the design alternatives. It was highly repetitive. Entire blocks of almost identical code appeared again, and again. To an audience question (OK, it was from me) about why he, as a skilled programmer, would not have made his code more clear, he responded simply "I didn't need to do that." Peters wasn't being lazy or uncraftful; he was being a designer. Throw away code is a fact of parametric design.

1.3.3 Copy and Modify: Designers may throw their own models away, but will invest considerable time in finding existing models and using them in their own context. This is hardly surprising. References such as *Architectural Graphics Standards* (Ramsay and Sleeper, 2007a) and their recent digital versions (Ramsay and Sleeper, 2007b) provide exemplary details that, for much design, are the foundation for detailed work. In an engineering design domain, Gantt and Nardi (1992) report script finding and reuse as an important mode of work. Given the additional work that must go into a parametric model, we should expect to see an intellectual trade in models and techniques. As both a learning and enabling tool, existing code reduces the job of making a model. It is typically easier to edit and change code that works than it is to create code from scratch, even if what it produces differs from current intentions. The key is the word "works", that is, code that produces a result. Starting with a working model and moving in steps, always ensuring that the model works, is often more efficient than building a model from scratch.

Copy-and-modify is the flip side of throw away code. Designers show natural reluctance to invest sufficient work in making code that will be clear to others, but they are happy to use such code when it is available. This makes "good" code a treasured community resource. The copy-and-modify strategy requires a community of practice that generates the code. The World Wide Web fosters such communities. Enabled by the fact that pages are written in human-readable HTML (and other languages), web designers often mine existing pages for code snippets that show how to achieve a particular effect. In design, the practice communities are less well developed, but such groups as Smartgeometry have built necessary precursor networks. Vendor publications of books with worked examples partially fill the need for such models and code.

1.3.4 Search for Form: Parametric modeling opens new windows to design. Nowhere is this more evident than with curves and surfaces. These are naturally parametric objects; mathematically they are defined as parametric functions over sets of control points. Conventional systems provide these mathematically motivated controls. In contrast, parametric systems enable a new set of controls to overlay the basis controls. This creates endless opportunities to explore for forms that are not practically reachable otherwise. To the technically minded, such exploration can appear as play that is both aimless and ungrounded. A broader and longer perspective reveals serious purpose in the play. The history of design can be read as a constantly changing process of exploring for new form-making ideas, using whatever tools and intellectual concepts are at hand. New languages and styles of design require such exploratory play, especially at their early stages.

1.3.5 Use Mathematics and Computation Understanding mathematics (especially geometry) and computation can bring some design concepts into sharp focus. Working with such formal descriptions restricts the range of forms that can be expressed, but links them in a common logic that may be worth the cost paid. For example, taking sections of a toroidal surface yields a surprisingly rich language of form, with the benefit of planar faceting and a limited set of edge lengths for facets.

Sometimes you need to understand the underlying mathematics to effectively create a model. Hierarchy is a time-honoured architectural design strategy, yet has limited support in most CAD systems. The intellectual key to hierarchy is recursion, which occurs when a program invokes itself. With recursion, parts can be made to directly resemble the wholes they compose.

A geodesic curve is the shortest path on a surface that joining two points $\dot{p}$ and $\dot{q}$ also on the surface. For spheres, the geodesic curve between $\dot{p}$ and $\dot{q}$ is the shortest arc linking the two points taken from the *great circle* defined by the two points and the sphere centre. Discrete points along a sphere geodesic curve can be found by projecting points on the 3D line between $\dot{p}$ and $\dot{q}$ to the sphere's surface. Geodesic meshes can be generated by subdividing polyhedral faces and then projecting the new vertices onto the sphere. On the other hand, subdivision can be cleanly understood as a recursive operation. Even such a qualitative understanding of geodesic concepts enables complex form making.

Many contemporary parametric designers are exploring mathematically based design strategies. I cannot help but notice a pattern. They browse the web and their social networks for math, picking ideas and playing them into design work. The reasoning chains (from pigeon hole principle to permutations to binomial theorem to permutation cycles . . .) that structure classical mathematics learning and understanding are seldom part of the game. Designers mostly enter above the foundations, understand something of mathematical mechanism and move on to use it in design. Of course, there is co-evolution here. The web enables casual access (try doing it in a physical library of mathematics texts) and itself is conditioned by such use. It should come as no surprise that the constructive, recursive definition of the Bézier curve is much more common on the web than the Bernstein basis definition, in spite of revealing less mathematically. Visual construction trumps mathematical inference for design. As with algorithms, designers exhibit a copy-and-modify style in using mathematics. Even more quickly, they encounter limits. Just as a program may not even compile in the face of a minor coding error, a mathematical formula or theorem may break down completely with a seemingly minor change. There are no Pythagorean triplets for cubes, that is, there are no integer solutions to $a^3 + b^3 = c^3$. (This is an instance of Fermat's Last Theorem, proved only in 1995, that is, there is no integer solution to $a^n + b^n = c^n$ with $n > 2$.)

The mathematical knowledge available in libraries, especially those of research universities, staggers the mind. Much of this material can be accessed only by physically visiting, and relatively little can be understood without concentrated and sustained study of mathematical foundations. The World Wide Web and interactive software for working with mathematics have thrown open doors through which come a large crowd unfamiliar to the mathematically astute.

Online resources such as Wolfram's MathWorld (Weisstein, 2009) and many university courses provide immediate access to (sometimes carefully constructed) explanations that can help bridge to mathematical under-standing. Packages such as Mathematica® and Maple™ are to mathematics what parametric modeling is to design – by making math active, they enable exploration and discovery.

1.3.6 Defer Decisions: In design, accuracy measures how the design relates to the thing being designed. Precision measures how design parts relate to each other. Conventional systems require geometric precision and provide tools such as snaps to help achieve it. Without precise size and location, models look messy. They do not have the ambiguity and appropriate refine-ment of a sketch; they are just messy. I argue that, more than anything else, this need to commit to specific locations at the outset of modeling is what is least sketch-like about computer-aided design. A clear exception is the implicit modeling toolset widely used in animation and gaming. Implicit surfaces lie "somewhere near" their generating objects and provide rules to merge "nearby" surfaces together. Implicit modeling removes both the need for precision and the possibility of accuracy.

Parametric modeling introduces a new strategy: *deferral.* A parametric design commits to a network of relations and defers commitment to specific locations and details. The system maintains the prior decisions made. Deferral pervades parametric practice. Those new to parametric modeling often ask how to locate their initial points and lines. Those teaching delight in the answer: "It doesn't matter; you can change that later."

One of the earliest (and most effective!) demonstrations of parametric modeling in architecture was the International Terminal Waterloo by Nicholas Grimshaw & Partners (see Figure 10.10). Lars Hesselgren crafted the original model in the I_EMS system. More than 15 years later Robert Aish used a similar model to demonstrate the CustomObjects system (which later became GenerativeComponents™). A salient site condition is that the train track curves through the station. A parametric model need not be initially constrained by this curve; fitting it to location can be deferred. Changing the order in which modeling and design decisions can be made is both a major

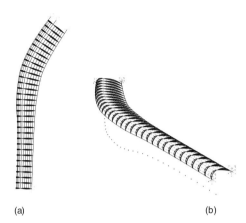

(a)   (b)

Figure 10.10: Two views of Waterloo Station: (a) plan, (b) perspective. Using parametric modeling, the exact location of the structure can be changed at the very end of the modeling process. Image credit: Drawings courtesy Robert Woodbury.

feature of and deliberate strategy for parametric design. Indeed, a principal financial argument for parametric modeling is its touted ability to support rapid change late in the design process.

The Eden Project also by Nicholas Grimshaw & Partners, combined parametric modeling and geodesic geometry to address an unusual problem. The site was a quarry that remained active until very late in the design process. Consequently ground levels could not be predicted in advance. The geodesic geometry made it easy to extend and rearrange partial spheres, while parametric modeling shortened revision cycles.

1.3.7 Make Modules: Propagation graphs can, and do, get big. Large size increases system update times and, more importantly, makes models hard to understand. Copying parts of a large graph and reconnecting them elsewhere in a model is prohibitively difficult. Reducing graph complexity and enabling reuse are the main reasons that systems universally provide module-making tools. The names and details of these vary from system to system, but their essence is the same. They provide a means to encapsulate a sub graph as a single node with its own set of node-independent (input) parameters. Copying and reuse then reduces to making a copy of a single node and reconnecting its inputs as needed.

It takes much effort to make a module work well and communities of practice develop surprisingly sophisticated module-making techniques. Almost always, the process iterates; through successive attempts modelers converge on stability.

1.3.8 Help Others: In *Gardeners and Gurus: Patterns of Cooperation among CAD Users,* Gantt and Nardi (1992) use the concept of the *gardener* to describe internal developers (and extenders) of CAD systems who are supported by their organization. Perhaps the peak example of gardening in architectural design in 2010 is the Specialist Modelling Group at Foster + Partners. This group employs many strategies to enable complex geometric and computational design work throughout the firm. From 2003 to the time of writing (2010) such gardening at a community scale was clearly evident in the Smartgeometry organization, in which more than 20 tutors volunteer a week of their time, year after year, to mentor students and practitioners new to parametric modeling. Of course, other rewards are at play: such events are superb places to meet peers, scout for employees and check out the latest work. From their offices and studios, some parametric practitioners (naming one or a few would be unfair – there are just too many good ones) freely share code and insight into modeling tasks. To them flow the rewards not just of fame, but more importantly, of new problems and approaches to solutions. Formalized or not, helping others is a clear strategy to at least some aspects of mastery.

1.3.9 Develop Your Toolbox: The parametric medium is complex, perhaps more so than any other media in the history of design. Using it well necessarily combines conceiving data flow; new divide-and-conquer strategies; naming; abstraction; 3D visualization and mathematics; and thinking algorithmically. These are the basics, and mastery requires more. We can expect that new technique and strategy will flow from the practices and schools that invest time and effort in the tools. Between the basics and the designs that are the focus and aim of professional work, lies a largely unexplored territory of what might be called *parametric craft*. I choose the word "craft" on purpose, to align with Malcolm McCullough's (1998) case for a developing digital craft. Some of his examples were of parametric models. Understandably, given the date and breadth of the book, McCullough merely hinted at the richness of parametric technique.

We can expect explorers in the new territory of parametric craft. Unlike the medieval sailors in whose portolanos we can see cartography slowly develop, the current explorers can learn from other fields that have undertaken similar voyages of discovery. There are numerous books on spreadsheets; some, like Monahan (2000), focus on strategies for spreadsheet design. Borrowing partly from film, computer animation has grown an extensive repertoire of technique. Software engineering has forged and polished a powerful tool. *Software Design Patterns* describe fragments of systems both functionally (by what they do) and structurally (by how they are composed of simpler structures). Their origins lie in architecture, particularly in Alexander's many works on pattern languages. In software, though, design patterns have a new and philosophically different logic and application. They have come to occupy a pragmatic place between the technical description of computer languages and the overall organization of a complex computer program. In software, design patterns record demonstrably useful ideas for system design. In *Elements of Parametric Design* (Woodbury, 2010) I have both adopted and adapted software design patterns as a basis for expressing the new parametric craft.

We can expect, as with the medieval nation-states, that some of the parametric portolanos will be kept strictly private. But practices and universities alike will come to use and value only those that are public. I devote much of my book, *Elements of Parametric Design* (2010), to a small, initial set of design patterns. My aim is to begin what I hope will be a long and fruitful process of developing an explicit, shareable and learnable craft of parametric design. Before patterns must come programming and geometry – the practical manifestations of algorithms and mathematics for much of design. Explaining particular patterns relies on a few key ideas from each of these very large fields.

Berlinski, D. (1999). *The Advent of the Algorithm: The Idea that Rules the World*. Harcourt.

Buxton, B. (2007). *Sketching User Experiences: Getting the Design Right and the Right Design*. Morgan & Kaufmann.

Flemming, U. (1986). On the representation and generation of loosely-packed arrangements of rectangles. *Environment and Planning B: Planning and Design*, 13:189–205.

Flemming, U. (1989). More on the representation and generation of loosely packed arrangements of rectangles. *Environment and Planning B: Planning and Design*, 16:327–359.

Gantt, M. and Nardi, B. A. (1992). Gardeners and gurus: patterns of cooperation among CAD users. In *CHI '92: Proceedings of the SIGCHI Conference on Human Factors in Computing Systems*, pages 107–117, New York. ACM.

Harada, M. (1997). *Discrete/continuous design exploration by direct manipulation*. PhD thesis, Carnegie Mellon University.

Kundu, S. (1988). The equivalence of the subregion representation and the wall representation for a certain class of rectangular dissections. *Commun. ACM*, 31:752–763.

Lakatos, I. (1991). *Proofs and Refutations: The Logic of Mathematical Discovery*. Cambridge University Press.

McCullough, M. (1998). *Abstracting Craft: The Practiced Digital Hand*. MIT Press.

Monahan, G. (2000). *Management Decision Making: Spreadsheet Modeling, Analysis, and Application*. Cambridge University Press.

Palladio, A. (1742). *The Architecture of A. Palladio; in four books*. Printed for A. Ward, S. Birt, D. Browne, C. Davis, T. Osborne and A. Millar.

Palladio, A. (1965). *The Four Books of Architecture*. Dover Publications, Inc.

Peters, B. (2007). The Smithsonian courtyard enclosure: a case-study of digital design processes. In *Expanding Bodies: Art • Cities • Environment: Proceedings of the 27th Annual Conference of the Association for Computer Aided Design in Architecture*, pages 74–83, Halifax (Nova Scotia). Riverside Architectural Press and Tuns Press.

Pollio, V. (2006). *The Ten Books on Architecture*. Project Gutenberg. Accessed at http://www.gutenberg.org/etext/20239 on 11 June 2009.

Qian, Z., Chen, Y., and Woodbury, R. (2007). Participant observation can discover design patterns in parametric modeling. In *Expanding Bodies: Art • Cities • Environment: Proceedings of the 27th Annual Conference of the Association for Computer Aided Design in Architecture*, pages 230–241, Halifax (Nova Scotia). Riverside Architectural Press and Tuns Press.

Ramsay, C. and Sleeper, H., editors (2007a). *Architectural Graphics Standards*. American Institute of Architects, 11th edition.

Ramsay, C. and Sleeper, H., editors (2007b). *Architectural Graphics Standards*. American Institute of Architects, 4.0 CD-ROM edition.

Weisstein, E. (2009). Wolfram MathWorld. Accessed at http://mathworld.wolfram.com on 7 December 2009.

Woodbury, R. F. (1993). Grammatical hermeneutics. *Architectural Science Review*, 36:53–64.

Woodbury, R. F. (2010). *Elements of Parametric Design*. Routledge.

This chapter provides detail about some of the turning points that helped shape my portfolio; these are not offered as formulae for others to take up, but rather as pointers to some of the creative relationships that link scripting to design.

> Design Space Between Geometry, Mathematics and Computation

Ultimately scripting is anything but rigidly formulaic in application however much scripters might flock to this or that fashionable problem-solving algorithm at any particular point of time. Scripting can be engaged purely to speculate, and even working from an historiographical perspective, future gaze. The range of techniques I describe here are limited somewhat to what I can do myself framed around what I have actually wanted to do over the years. There is an absolute connection between the two. The key message in *Scripting Cultures* is not the techniques so much as the creative inclinations at work. In looking for an umbrella to place over all five examples from my portfolio presented in *Scripting Cultures*, I have settled on 'dimensionality' in all its meanings – a long-standing interest which I will detail as I proceed. Less figuratively than the word 'dimension' might initially suggest, it is precisely the frustratingly complex and therefore difficult dimensionality of space and its associated narrative potential that has guided all the projects presented here.

Through a combination of good luck and timing, a passionate interest in Antoni Gaudí (1852–1926) led to an interview in 1979 with two of Gaudí's octogenarian successors who were directing the small team completing the Sagrada Família church (1882 – ongoing); they had been young apprentice architects during Gaudí's final years. I was requesting material for my undergraduate thesis and I had two principal questions: Where was the authority to complete the building coming from when so little of the building had actually been completed, and much of Gaudí's design models and all of his drawings destroyed during the Spanish Civil War (1936–39)? And how, precisely, were instructions given to the master masons charged with actually building so complex a construction? Their answer was to point me to boxes and boxes of model fragments with the suggestion that all the secrets lay within. I have been engaged as an architect and design researcher studying these models ever since.

My intimate introduction to Gaudí at the commencement of my career has coloured everything I have done. I hasten to add that this is not a stylistic connection – as if any pretender

Figure 11.1

could succeed with such vainglory. The attribute I discovered in Gaudí's work that captured me was his dimensional thinking, evidently one of the principal drivers for all that he accomplished. He wrote nothing at all about his architectural theory in a career spanning 48 years. In order to gain insights into one of the most creative and technically competent architects ever, we have to unravel the mysteries of his work itself, which sets us all a number of significant challenges.

Any discussion about dimensionality here in words alone will probably lack prospects, and the projects that follow will take on the main thrust of this task. Let us begin with the *Oxford English Dictionary*'s (*OED*) definition of 'dimension' – at least the one that principally interests scripters. Here is the *OED*'s third definition:

> A mode of linear measurement, magnitude, or extension, in a particular direction; usually as co-existing with similar measurements or extensions in other directions. The three dimensions of a body, or of ordinary space, are length, breadth, and thickness (or depth); a surface has only two dimensions (length and breadth); a line only one (length). Here the notion of measurement or magnitude is commonly lost, and the word denotes merely a particular mode of spatial extension. Modern mathematicians have speculated as to the possibility of more than three dimensions of space.[1]

This is the mathematical and geometrical definition. When we add the other entries for 'dimension' as a noun to the mix, we see how bountiful the word is for spatial thinkers. The *OED* includes 'The action of measuring', dividing notes in music to shorter ones as measures of time or rhythm, spatial 'extent', a measure of time, 'any of the component aspects of a particular situation' citing 'an attribute of, or way of viewing, an abstract entity' as an example. We find that the definition of 'dimension' ranges between a measure, spatial extents such as 'thickness', mathematical, geometrical and algebraic properties, and the descriptive part of a compound noun such as 'dimension line'. Designers can call on all these definitions; some are more immediate than others, but overall the dimensional language of the architect is probably much easier to work with in design than as written language. When we apply the word to what we do, however, and try to link it to mathematical concepts, we can quickly get into hot water. Here are some examples.

Facing page

Figure 11.1: Antonio Gaudí, Sagrada Familia Church, Barcelona, 1882-ongoing, view of the nave close to completion, 2011. Image credit: Photo: Mark Burry.

> Beyond 3D Space

Let us start with one dimension. Convention would have it that points lying on a straight line describe a single axis, and represent a dimension. In fact, we tend to use the word 'line' when we should say 'curve', and we do not use the word 'vector' and instead refer to a 'straight line'. By using mathematical terms freely, that is to say without precision, and not engaging with the underlying mathematical concepts, we help perpetuate the myth of space being a 3D construct: limited to the first dictionary definition of 'dimension' posited above, *'modern mathematicians have speculated as to the possibility of more than three dimensions of space'.*

My impression is that spatial thinkers are comfortable with space as an abstract concept, intuitively think spatially, but end up being the equivalent of tongue-tied when it comes to representing space conventionally rather than purely through design. Ordinarily or, more accurately, in earlier pre-digital practice, a sculptor could get away with never abstracting their work as a set of coordinates, for instance. An architect working with a simple repertoire of vertical and horizontal plans could abstract their work in reasonably simple sets of projections. Crucial exceptions, however, have always been with us whether it is Francesco Borromini (1599–1667) describing the roof of San Carlo alle Quattro Fontane (1638–41), the French mathematician Gaspard Monge (1746–1818) consolidating the principles of descriptive geometry that he had invented, or Gaudí and his hanging model for the Colònia Güell chapel (1896–1914). Whatever their elaborate methodology for successfully describing spatial complexities to their colleagues, they were geometrical, not mathematical instructions.

Our recent aspirations have tended towards designing spatially complex architecture. As an example of our new ambitions in this regard we can compare Foster + Partners' magnificent dome over the British Museum Court and around the Reading Room (completed 2000) with IM Pei's relatively straightforward glass pyramid that performs a similar function at the Louvre courtyard in Paris (1989). The British Museum courtyard roof is rapidly becoming less of the exception than previously the case, being neither simplification to a convention of Cartesian coordinates set along planes and right angles nor the elegant post-Enlightenment geometrically descriptive approach by which the museum building itself would have been made. Ironically, scripting requires us to be algebraically and geometrically explicit using spatial and vectorial calculations to negotiate digitally with the computer; yet allowing these conventions to reign removes us from mathematically exciting space-warping concepts that define the glazed canopy above. This paradox is also a mark of tension: what exactly does it *mean* to be an architect today?

Lest we persuade ourselves that complexity is a goal worth striving for, a very elegant case is made for 'Simplexity' as an antedote by Sawako Kaijima and Michalatos Panagiotis:

Simplexity is a term in system science which describes the emergence of simplicity out of intricate and complex sets of rules.

In recent years there is an increasing trend in architecture to exploit the ability of algorithmic design to produce complex forms by implementing relatively simple and easy formulas. This often results in the addition of unnecessary layers of complexity to a project just for the sake of production of seemingly more complex forms. This in turn can degenerate to computational decoration and after taking into account all the layers of information, the resulting algorithms seem little different than a complicated random number generator.

In contrast there is a whole class of algorithms that deal with simplification which are usually more complex and difficult to implement. This is partly the result of the fact that multiplication and proliferation can be easily implemented via iterative function calls and local simple operations over parts of a system.[2]

The demonstration of the strictly relative and conventional rather than absolute nature of the Cartesian coordinate system, and thus its fallibility, is a simple one. Imagine that instead of three intersecting *xy, xz* and *yz* planes, each of the planes is in fact a gently arced surface similarly oriented as the adjacent Cartesian planes and intersecting in the same sense at the same origin. Coordinate values given as *x, y, z* could be the same in both constructs and have the same meaning, but would the point be in the same location? It is therefore a touch risky referring to *time* as the fourth dimension, when mathematically it is not: I am certainly guilty of helping perpetuate this lazy little simplification. We should use the term 'Euclidean space' instead of 'Cartesian space',[3] and be aware that by the late nineteenth century mathematicians, commencing with the German Felix Klein (1849–1925), were establishing themselves for their work on non-Euclidean geometry, challenging the millennia-old hegemony (of Euclidean geometry).

We should also be aware that this is not a recent post-digital interest in the creative sector, but one that has been in the artistic consciousness since at least the early twentieth century. In 1924 the Dutch artist, writer, poet and architect Theo van Doesburg (1883–1931) was quite explicit about what he saw as new potentials for architecture, as can be seen in the following extract from his manifesto *Towards a Plastic Architectures:*

The new architecture is open. The whole structure consists of a space that is divided in accordance with the various functional demands. This division is carried out by means of dividing surfaces (in the interior) or protective surfaces (externally). The former, which separate the various functional spaces, may be movable; that is to say, the dividing surfaces (formerly the interior walls) may be replaced by movable intermediate surfaces or panels (the same method may be employed for doors). In architecture's next phase of development the ground-plan must disappear completely. The two-dimensional spatial composition fixed in a ground-plan will be

replaced by an exact constructional calculation – a calculation by means
of which the supporting capacity is restricted to the simplest but
strongest supporting points. For this purpose Euclidean mathematics will
be of no further use – but with the aid of calculation that is non-Euclidean
and takes into account the four dimensions everything will be very
easy.[4]

Is this being a little pedantic? Not if we wish to engage more seriously
with the mathematics of design, and to avoid the conceptual limitations
of computation framed around Cartesian data input scripted into the black
box. In *Shifting Cultures* I show that conceptually Gaudí was working
multidimensionally beyond Euclidian space. I also consider the futility of
tying the word 'dimension' to 1D *lines*, 2D *planes* and 3D *volumes* by demonstrating that we can derive situations with many more dimensions than
cardinal axes. Again, how relevant is all this to architects who have both feet
on the ground?

Long before I became aware of a culture clash between Euclidean and
non-Euclidean space dwellers, I was happy to consider time as a fourth
dimension, which it is if we think of dimensions as attributes rather than
absolute spatial delineators. As an example of *dimension* being an attribute
rather than a coordinate let us consider the following situation:

> *Move!* (instruction) *4 paces forward* (first dimension), *turn right at right angles!*
> (instruction), *3 paces forward* (second dimension), *grab the vertical ladder*
> (instruction), *climb 5 rungs* (third dimension), *drop off the ladder* (instruction),
> *measure how long it took to drop* (fourth dimension).

This is the essence of numerical control (NC), which is first-order cybernetics,[5]
not Cartesian geometry *per se*. Numerical control is the data stream with
which we control our fabricating machinery and is, of course, our main
currency as matters stand, as it is by these means that we can fabricate our
fantasies reasonably economically. Many complex fabrication tasks can now
be taken on that could not have been realistically undertaken until quite
recently. It is another of the several digital design paradoxes that are sprin-
kled throughout *Shifting Cultures*. In this case it is the four minimum streaming
data inputs that allow NC machines to work their magic: three instructions
around placement (forward, right, up), and one about action (displacement
in a direction) versus design computation based on mathematics and not
the limitations of machine logic. The tension between iterations of shape, for
example, without shifting location (which is animation), and iterations of
shape while moving are interesting as tests for the delineation of architecture. My interest has always been drawn to architects who embrace this
tension as part of their repertoire. For the rest of this chapter I am going to
signal key moments along my own journey where greater architectural potential has been discovered, realised, or invoked through scripting with a 'time or
displacement dimension'. In all cases, scripting has driven an important
architectural advance that would not otherwise have been made.

> Life, Growth and Granite: Sequences Through Serial Division

In 1991 I started to look at the computational logic behind the geometry of Gaudí's columns for the nave. We know from comments captured by his young colleagues on-site that he conceived the entire volume of the Sagrada Família church as being inside a forest with the nave ceiling a great canopy soaring 45 metres overhead formed from tree branches, fronds and leaves supported by great stone trunks: slender columns all leaning axially into their load paths. The crossing, the central part of the church where the main body, the nave, intersects with the transept spaces on either side, completed and finally cleared of scaffolding in 2010, appears as a woodland clearing 60 metres above the altar.

Gaudí himself never saw any of this beyond a large 1:10 scaled model of the nave, but at that scale he considered every detail, not least the columns. When the nave columns are studied closely, they appear as remarkable hybrids, or amalgams at least, referring to both Greek and Gothic column language: Doric in part due to the characteristic Greek-order fluting emerging halfway up, and organicist too especially at their bases. The term organicist is appropriate both philosophically in terms of the tree-scape metaphor being read as an organic whole, and in the biological sense when we see the base of the trees as a system rather than an artful composition. When it came to building the first column as a prototype in the 1960s, before the wonders of today's CNC machinery, the approach taken was based on a model fragment that had survived the rigours of the Spanish Civil War, when Gaudí's former studio on-site was trashed and burned. This particular 1:25 scaled model has cross section zinc templates along its length at every metre equivalent – 40 millimetres actual size, with the column surfaces interpolated between each horizontal template. Unfortunately, in my opinion, the model read in the way I have just described suggests a different explanation from what was probably in Gaudí's mind, for initially the column has been conceptually unpicked from this model, built as a prototype, and then extrapolated into a *modus operandi* for the subsequent automated cutting. This has had no adverse effect on the viability of the column as an object, but until we could script an alternative story, it proved to be very difficult for some commentators to conceptualise what was really going on. Gaudí had in fact invested the column's morphogenesis with a natural life story.[6]

Using mathematical parlance, the conceptual route to the completed column form is a Boolean intersection of two solids. Taking the main columns for instance, the two constituent solids are sticks of barley sugar, Solomonic – twisted just a few degrees clockwise for one, and anticlockwise for the other. When superimposed the columns share the same profiles at their bases. As they rise in height they rotationally twist in the opposite senses to each other until eventually their profiles intersect again. We will call this one phase. Gaudí arrests the process at half phase, a point where the columns have twisted around as far from each other's path as possible, at a point from where they start to swing back in if the rotation continues unabated. At this arrested midpoint the profile shows the characteristic Doric serrations. Here Gaudí now conceives the base profile as being directly re-implicated.

This is clearly about displacement as the fourth dimension; let us consider the description of the generation of the column slightly differently. The curvy organic profile at the base is formed from cotangent concave and convex parabolas. Conceptually, these profiles ascend the column counter-rotating with respect to each other as they rise. At any point of the displacement, the actual column profile at that position is the intersection of the two counter-rotated base profiles – the bounded surfaces common to each. At the point that the rotational symmetry is halted exactly out of phase, the two profiles now have to duplicate such that we have the two existing profiles continuing on their path, and the two new duplicates counter-rotating back in the opposite direction until the next mid-phase point: four similar profiles all exactly out of phase with each other. This occurs at half the height of the original event. The four profiles then duplicate to make eight, and so the process continues at half the last rise, a quarter of the original, at which point they duplicate to make sixteen in total. For the central nave columns (made from granite), the heights are as follows: 8 metres before the two profiles become four, a further 4 metres for the eight profiles, and another 2 metres before there are sixteen, at the top. There is no need here to labour the parallel to morphogenesis and cell division cycles. The same life game is being played higher up in the volume of the church whether the columns have a square, rectangular or any other shape as their progenitor profile.

We have to build what Gaudí has designed with unequivocal interpreted fidelity and accuracy in terms of its physicality. With no written record made by Gaudí, how we interpret this intellectually is entirely up to the individual. Joan Bergós (1894–1974), an architect and artist who collaborated with Gaudí in these last years and who subsequently wrote several influential books about Gaudí and about his own experience visiting the the Sagrada Família church, quotes Gaudí as having stated:

> Man's intelligence can only act in one plane, with two dimensions. He can solve equations with one unknown, of the first degree. The angels' intelligence is three dimensional, acting directly in space. Man cannot act until he has been presented with the whole fact: at the outset, he can only follow paths, lines on a plane.[7]

The multidimensional qualities of the column, the product of Gaudí's uniquely creative mind, would by his own definition place him in the realm of the angels. The various attempts made in print to reveal all the intellectual and spatial qualities of the column that otherwise elude ready analysis can be brought together more effectively in one single visual environment: multimedia.

Scripting the narrative outlined above seems crucial if we are to animate the sequence and afford more general intelligibility. This story cannot to be

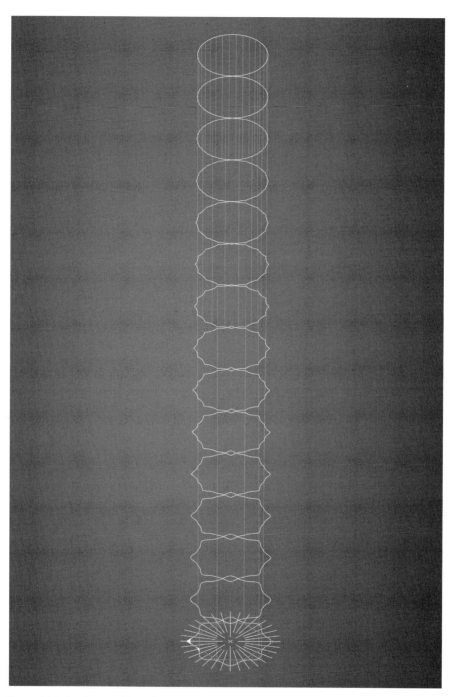

Figure 11.2: Section profiles taken through eight-sided columns at one-meter intervals for Antonio Gaudí's Sagrada Familia Church, Barcelona. Image credit: Model: Mark Burry.

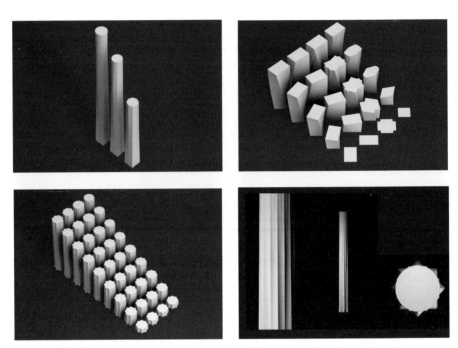

Figure 11.3: Eight-sided square and rectangular column types showing generation through intersection of two counter-rotated helical 'barley-twist' columns. Image credit: All images courtesy Mark Burry and SIAL. Models: Mark Burry. Renders: Grant Dunlop.

told any other way, and even a video of the model-making machine (invented by the model makers on-site after Gaudí's death) apparently defeats clear interpretation of the game being played by some who watch it in use.

Whether we counter-rotate two profiles made from different-coloured Perspex revealing their evolving intersections against the light, or watch master craftspeople make the column from gypsum plaster using a device of their own invention, or watch video, or interact with a computer animation, or pore over drawings, each experience can be shown to be incomplete in itself, begging for the column to be studied *in situ*.

> Paramorph: Scripting and Parametric Design Software

My adventures in the Sagrada Família church design studio have led to various probings of software for their potential to help unlock Gaudí's secrets. From 1991 I became aware of parametric design software for vehicle design through Dr Robert Aish, who worked then for Intergraph, based in Paris. Unfortunately, nothing remotely resembling this software existed in the architectural sector, and in 1992 I gained access to Computervision's CADDS5™, with its powerful parametric design engine. I was able to deploy it very successfully, and in a hybrid relationship with scripting overlays. It was a very useful medium for helping us drill down to viable design solutions with respect to Gaudí's posthumous challenges. What, I began to wonder, would be the creative spin-off from this pathway?

With the work at the Sagrada Família church, the parametric design software was being called upon to create through interpretation. I was interested in learning about creating through generation.

With 'parametricism' currently being elevated to a style and orthodoxy, I will pause briefly to explain what parametric software is, and how it differs from more typical 'explicit design' software from my perspective as 'early adopter'. With the latter, explicit design, the designer makes their model as they would in any traditional medium. Any change to the model requires erasure and remodelling whether it is with pad and pen or via CAD. With a parametric model every entity in the model (points, lines, etc.) have links between their location in the software's database and their visualisation via the monitor. Parametric software allows the user to identify a line visually, for instance, and in doing so its length will be declared such that the user can interact directly with that information. All entities in the design are logically connected when they are related, so in changing the length of a line, the ramifications of this change update the rest of the model. I suspect this is what architects thought they would be working with when they first heard about CAD, but it is only in recent years that it has begun to be accessible for those who wish to experiment with it.

In our postgraduate research studio at RMIT University's SIAL today, we now dub the parametric model the 'flexible model', because we are able parametrically to adjust its dimensions and, if there is a viable solution, a new version is born; a version of the original. To maintain the biomimetic line of thought, the flexible starting model can be taken as the genotype, and the resulting versions as phenotypes. In those days (1997), each model variant had perforce the same topology, but changing topography, as the original. In search of a name to describe each variant we came up with *paramorph* at our postgraduate research studio at Deakin University where we were based at the time, and we still use the term today.[8]

In that studio we devised *Paramorph I*, a 'dumb box' starter for a paramorph-based thought experiment, through which all 960 parametrically linked dimensions could be relaxed into all sorts of configurations at a time when such reconfiguration would have taken weeks by any other means, not just the matter of minutes our flexible model could be reconfigured in. Some very interesting implications for the use of creative parametric design software emerged from this experiment: without a scripting overlay, parametric design can be quite tedious in practice. For engineers wanting to change the size and position of a slot in a bracket, for example, being able to click on the respective parameters shown on screen as dimensions, constants or values, and change them is very appealing for its interactivity. To reform our dumb box, it was possible that we might require changing all 960 parameters and, naturally, scripting the changes came much more readily than clicking individually on all these parametric dimensions on screen, one by one. Apart from any other consideration, calculations would be useful such as bending the plan to a given curve.

From that point on, my interest in parametric design software has been contingent on how well each package allows the user to use a scripting overlay, as this seems an essential ingredient to ensure a proper insinuation of designer intent into its use. Some packages manage this better than others. This position was tested when I contributed to the early-stage design of the Swiss Re London headquarters tower in 1998. Foster +Partners had been physically modelling their concept for the tower building with its circular plan and highly original elongated egg-shaped sectional profile. Each iteration was appearing as elaborate table-high physical models, taking many weeks to prepare. I was asked to test whether a parametric model would perform the same role in searching for the optimal shape. I believe that it was a demonstration of this facility of being able to adjust the egg profile through a scripted formula that encouraged the practice to focus more on digitally based design research. Foster + Partners' Specialist Modelling Group (SMG) has been at the vanguard of intelligently scripted enquiry ever since, and they remain among the most skilled advocates of the coupled analogue and digital architectural design dialogue within mainstream practice.

Intriguingly, Gaudí used an approach akin to the paramorph as part of his strategy to explain the projects to his future unknown successors. The drawings (destroyed but surviving as published prints at least) show his schema for the remainder of the building and are clear expressions of his general intentions. As such they would not be enough to provide sufficient detail in order to proceed with the same level of confidence were it not for their vital complement: a model of a prototypical cupola. Scaled at 1:25, and with the geometry inscribed medievally on a polished slab of limestone, this model is parametrically variable in shape and size to inform all the towers and cupolas that remain to be built.

> Aegis Hyposurface: Surface Perturbation Algorithms

My collaboration with dECOi Architects also began around this time, when I met Paris-based Mark Goulthorpe (currently based at MIT) at the 1997 biennial architecture student conference hosted by my school of architecture at Deakin University in Geelong. Possibly the most demanding project of the many on which I collaborated with him was his response to an invited competition from the Birmingham Hippodrome Theatre in the UK in 1999. The competition commissioners called for an art piece to adorn a large wall that soared out from the building above the passers-by below, and Mark's response was to propose that the wall itself become the subject, rather than simply the substrate to support a sculpture. Whatever was proposed, the intervention was required to respond in some way to the theatre's interior activities. I joined the project at this point: the challenges of making the wall respond to sensors placed inside the building. Whereas an artwork with lights going on and off would minimally answer the brief, making the wall fibrillate madly in response to wild applause, or shiver in ecstasy each time the cash register rang seemed far more appropriate, inspiring a journey that still resonates over a decade later.

> What is a Surface Disturbance?

To make a convincing case for the concept, a multimedia presentation with a series of animations at its centre was composed, and the team Goulthorp assembled around the project pointed to a different kind of architectural practice ever since. First, there were the mathematician professors from UCL in London, Keith Ball and Alex Scott, who offered the perturbation algorithms that are the base function for the necessary surface displacements – the fourth dimension parameter that would make the wall come to life on cue. I was party to some extraordinary architect–mathematician dialogues where each tried to explain in plain English what they meant from the confines of their own discipline language. It turns out that there are very few types of perturbation in the front line of opportunity: circular waves as formed when a stone lands in a pond, standing waves as we see at the beach, sprites as vector-based waves such as a boat leaves in its wake, and planar tilting and folding. The individual formulae were passed on to Peter Wood, a programmer and engineer based in Wellington, New Zealand who made a series of deformation routines to be used with AutoCAD™ as AutoLISP code snippets.

My role was to assemble the snippets as a single script that would generate sufficient frames to make compelling animations of the wall in action. This I have likened to digital choreography, and it led to a fascinating set of discoveries. Principal among these was learning about the nature of disturbance, for to get a narrative to unfold I had to get each effect to propagate interactions with each other, effectively to create disturbances. The only time the placid surface arced up was when effects with completely different parameters were invoked, ran into each other and argued, sometimes strenuously, sometimes with subtlety.

At its most simple, this type of outcome could be foreseen as each effect was individually propagated, but not the vigour of the interaction between the engagements. The inspirational leap came when I discovered that if each effect was given an independent trajectory, away from one another, belief became temporarily suspended. What would otherwise not have seemed especially unfamiliar – watching a fast-flowing river, for instance – became otherworldly as the various effects failed to move in concert with an underlying current, but were, in fact, doing quite the opposite. I remember tinkering with the various scripts for many hours tuning the effects to a desired result, aware that without scripting and animation none of what I describe would have been possible.

dECOi won the competition, but Aegis Hyposurface™, as it was christened, never made it to its original destination. Various prototypes have
appeared in the intervening years, the first of which went on public display
at CeBIT in Hanover, 2001. It measured 10 metres wide by 3.5 metres high,
and responded in real time to light, movement and sound sensors. Over the
years Goulthorpe has found more sound collaborators, the mathematicians
have contributed ever more intriguing algorithms, the interface engineers
greater degrees of freedom and control, and so the project lives on.

> Digital Landscapes and Tectonics

My design research into surface disturbance reached its peak at the same
time as the more widely held architectural interest in form was at its most
intense. What had become my fascination with displacement disturbance
and disruption extended into the philosophical implications digital craft was
beginning to have on all that had immediately preceded it, not least the
Modern Movement, vestiges of which were still being referenced by the
practice giants of yore. There was a sense of being in an emerging dilemma
as it was difficult to discern the extent to which digital capability was setting
the agenda, with the tail potentially wagging the dog.

More senior practices resolutely stuck to traditional ways of working
with their tried and tested sensibilities. Others, such as Gehry Partners, led
through their design with digital capability being coaxed along only as part
of the journey. Foster + Partners responded subtly to the emerging opportunities, and relatively young practices such as Greg Lynn FORM and dECOi
made digital design thinking into sets of guiding principles. I was curious
about the situation as an academic heavily committed to the effort to
complete the Sagrada Família church. It seemed to me that almost a century
earlier Gaudí had set up many of the 'new' problems that digerati were now
engaging with, as if they were exclusively of our time; meanwhile students
were producing wild and wonderful cyberspace constructions that were
difficult to locate critically.

The 'art of the accident' came back into vogue, but it was hard not to
perceive at least part of that as a post-rationalist response to intriguing
studio outcomes rather than being a genuine philosophically argued belief.
For me, the essential digital design ingredient was to capture design intentionality. Scripting not only forces the scripter who commences with a blank
sheet to come clean (as opposed to the adopter of the script who launches
someone else's code to see what happens), it also forces a design to be logically deconstructed in order to be encoded. There may well be accidental
effects along the way, some even useful, but the essential value of scripting
appeared as the ability to pass the test of repeatability, which is why I personally have difficulty with chucking in a random function in order to spice up
the mix. In darker moments I try to image Gaudí, for instance, resorting to
the random function, but then surprisingly, he was a reactionary.

I like working parametrically to a point, because of the way the designer can move backwards and forwards. For this to happen with random intervention taking place, multiple versions need to be retained just in case the design goes irrecoverably wayward en route. Scripting offers the same authority over the design too as it can be run and rerun until a result emerges that satisfies whatever criteria are being applied or, through its use, modifications to the script are suggested in operation that can be enacted subsequently. The trouble, it struck me, was the facility with which we can now dabble in the surreal, hyperreal, and unreal arenas. While painters and trick photographers could simulate within this arena previously, they could never do so with the same facility as the digital dexterity now afforded. The same surface algorithms that had initiated the effects being sought with the hyposurface discussed above I found could be used for many other purposes. Digital terrains could be experimented with, landscapes of the subconscious could be evoked as Deleuzian perplications (by this I mean that meaningful surfaces could be simulated, hyperreal in their representation but utterly impossible to make out of materials).[9] Materials could be represented with photographic realism as being visually credible but impossible artifice in the physical world.

> Columns of the Passion Facade

Gaudí drew his design for the Passion Facade for the Sagrada Família church as early as 1917, nine years before he died. The Passion Facade is the end of the west transept, one of the two arms of the church plan that extends away from the centre of the church (the crossing), and at right angles to the main body of the building, the nave. When I say 'drew', this is a euphemism, as it was in fact a multimedia production of its day including ink, charcoal, pencil and gouache according to the accounts of his colleagues. The drawing does not survive but a fine detail photographic plate does. This has become the sole source of information on Gaudí's specific design intent, although there are highly detailed ways of working with particular geometries.

The construction of the facade proceeds today as I write, but the realisation of its design post-Gaudí has occurred in three phases: several decades of prior study by colleagues based on-site, scripted sketches as a means to develop the design rationale, and a mathematically driven fully parametricised design model. In this chapter, the story of the middle phase of 'scripted sketching' is explained in some detail.

The benefits of knowing Gaudí's complete oeuvre in fine detail, and his working practice equally well for the last twelve years of his life, have led to an excellent apprenticeship in the amalgamation of analogue and digital design practice over my three decades of involvement. Post-digitally I still start with a hand sketch with pencil on paper, even though my attitude to scripting is also resolutely in the sketching domain. Opportunities for design sketching using proprietary parametric design software are improving rapidly, but in 2001 when our design research studio began the design studies for this part of the building, such facility was not immediately apparent, and the relative facility then of the hand sketch prevailed.

In terms of finding a fourth dimension of displacement as per the nave columns described above, our starting material, the photograph of the original drawing, appeared not to offer too many clues. At best, through the powerful chiaroscuro effects that Gaudí wrought on his drawing, there was at least a 2½D story to be extracted, as he had used shadow with good effect. The facade faces west and is designed to be viewed at its most compelling during sunset, and his drawing gives a strong hint of how the effect of the low setting sun angles were to be exploited. The facade as a whole had been thought through quite extensively by former colleagues, not least because the transept to which it is attached was completed in 1978 along with the lower half of the façade, the portico formed from six soaring inclined columns. Our challenge has been the upper half, the narthex, and my account here deals only with the development of the column prototype.

Valiant efforts had been made to form the columns previously, with a quest to combine two of the three second-order surfaces that Gaudí used to complete his design, the hyperbolic paraboloid and the hyperboloid of revolution. The hyperboloid of revolution is a surface that we are familiar seeing in the form of power station cooling towers. Hyperbolic paraboloids are the doubly curved surfaces of horses' saddles and abundant in nature, for instance the webs between our fingers when we stretch them out. The characteristic that they have in common is that they can be described by a straight line moving through space following two vectors that are not coplanar. Working manually with gypsum plaster over several decades, the various versions of the columns seemed to have become ever more convoluted in an effort to match the apparent asymmetry between the 18 constituent columns that form the narthex. It seemed a good moment to attempt to simplify the arrangement.

The principal question here was focused on the art–sculpture–architecture interface: were these columns in the sculptor's court (Joan Subirach's), or the architect's? As principal architectonic components, this was not a particularly difficult question to answer. For the work to fall into the domain of the architect, however, certain of Gaudí's late working practices provided the guiding principle on how to proceed. This entailed treating the column (along with the rest of the narthex other than the associated sculpture) as an organicist system, which naturally brought scripting to the fore. The hypothetical question we asked was: 'Working within Gaudí's established procedures, what could he have done using the computer that would not otherwise have been possible?' An answer was very simple in concept and physical outcome, but very complex in between. Here is a brief account of that simplexified complexity.

The columns are an amalgam of a tall svelte hyperboloid of revolution with four hyperbolic paraboloids each at the top and bottom. Two of the

straight lines that form the boundaries of each of the eight hyperbolic paraboloids (directrices) can coincide with selected straight lines on the surfaces of
the hyperboloid of revolution (generatrices). There are an infinite number of
possibilities if we parametrically vary the characteristics of both geometries,
but only one answer for any given hyperboloid and any given hyperbolic
paraboloid. For the designer, the challenge is to find the optimal values for
all the parameters concerned such that the geometry of the combined set of
nine surfaces per column matches Gaudí's drawing. In the end we engaged a
mathematician who first defined the various simultaneous equations that
needed to be satisfied before we could seek programming assistance. The
result was a Rhino 3D™ plug-in, which since 2001 has allowed us to model 3D
circular and elliptical hyperboloids of revolution at whim completely through
graphical or direct data input. Having inputted the desired hyperboloid of
revolution, we can then define the best-fit hyperbolic paraboloid by nomi-
nating two points at the base from which two generatrices are identified or,
if we know the position of the uppermost point for the intersection of the
two geometries, the plug-in will identify the two points where the generatrices intersect with the base.

   What I have described above is fundamentally a design operation
afforded only through scripting. Answers could have been found using traditional media in conjunction with a calculator, but not only would this have
taken an inordinately long time, evidence from previous iterations undertaken on that basis had not yielded convincing material. The column design
emerging from the process I have outlined was then tested *in situ,* as three
neighbouring prototypes in order to gauge their effect.

   In the lifetime of this part of the project, the stone-cutting technology
and the expertise of the stonemason have meant that the 9-metre-high
slender columns have moved on from considering their fabrication from five
stone components to only three. The stereotomy challenge here (that is, the
art of cutting three-dimensional solids such as stone into practical shapes)
means that in moving to just three elements, the main shaft of the column is
now made up from a single piece of granite 6 metres in length. The stonemason, Jordi Barbany, considers this to be an operation impossible to undertake by hand for a piece of this length and slenderness. Furthermore, we
now parametrically design the blocks of granite from which the columns are
made, which are cut to order from the quarry face, not blasted. This reduces
the risk of fissuring, cuts back on the amount of stone being extracted, and
minimises transportation costs.

   The whole narthex has emerged as a parametric model built by Jane
Burry, mathematically conceptualised such that every single component is
inextricably linked dimensionally to its neighbours. If anything has to change,
the effect causes a ripple across the whole facade. The columns all have an
individually unique angle of lean both towards the centre of the composition
seen from the front, as well as increasingly towards the centre of the building
at the periphery of the facade. In plan the column feet splay outwards
increasingly towards the ends of the colonnade, guided by a parabola. Can

the model update itself in this way when a single-dimensional parameter is altered? Sadly, that is an answer reserved for another time and another context as it is beyond the scope of scripting at this point in time. We are always able to conceptualise beyond the limits of available computer power, but well within the potentiality of coding itself, it seems.

> Displacement as Dimension

In this chapter I have positioned scripting as a fundamental tool with which to explore dimensionality in architecture: spatially, and as a series of levels that have mathematical and philosophical implications. I have addressed both the mathematical fallacy and practical utility of considering the fourth dimension, critical within my practice described here, as a time element and instead more aptly, as suggested in this chapter, as displacement. It may appear as sophistry of the pedant, but for scripting to arrive closer to its full potential, architects might want to engage more closely with mathematicians if not mathematics.

Looking at scripting in several dimensions, for even the addition of time or displacement as a fourth dimension allows its entry on its own terms as a singularly creative design adjunct, opportunities for envisaging possibilities are born from designs that would be very hard to achieve using analogue processes.

Exciting opportunities surely await the bold.

1 'Dimension' Def. 3. *Oxford English Dictionary*, 1989, 2nd edn, CD-ROM.
2 See chapter by Sawako Kaijima and Michalatos Panagiotis in T Sakamoto, A Ferre, M Kubo (eds), *From Control to Design: Parametric/ Algorithmic Architecture*, Actar (Barcelona), 2008, p 130.
3 See definition of 'Euclidian space' in Encyclopædia Britannica Online: 'Euclidean space is a geometrical construct whereby the axioms and postulations of Euclid (3rd century BC Greek mathematician referred to as the 'Father of Geometry') apply. It is a space with any finite number of dimensions for which all points can be designated by a positional dimension, or a coordinate for each dimension. In two dimensions or more a formula can be used to calculate the distance between any two points. For over 2,000 years it has remained the essential point of departure for mathematicians to study non-Euclidean space such as that emerging from elliptic geometry and hyperbolic geometry. Cartesian space refers more accurately to a coordinate system, a convention of three planes intersecting at right angles so forming the three coordinate axes with positive and negative values, all three axes meeting as a point referred to as the 'origin'. http://www.britannica.com/EBchecked/topic/194913/Euclidean-space
4 Proposition 9: Theo van Doesburg, *Towards a Plastic Architecture,* 1924, in Ulrich Conrads, *Programs and Manifestoes on twentieth-century Architecture*, MIT Press (Cambridge, MA), 1970, p 79.
5 Cybernetics is control theory applied to complex systems. The term is associated with situations where what is actually happening to a system sampled at regular intervals is compared to the standard of what ought to be happening, with a controller adjusting the system's behaviour to meet expectation.
6 Explained in detail in MC Burry, 'Beyond the algorithm: seeking differentiated structures through alternative computational and haptic design processes', in Michael

Hensel and Achim Menges (eds), *Morpho-Ecologies: Towards Heterogeneous Space in Architectural Design,* AA Publications (London), February 2007, pp 334– 47. See also M Burry 'Re-natured Hybrid', *Thresholds Journal #26: Denatured*, MIT Press, Spring 2003, pp 38–42.

7   J Bergós, *Gaudí, The Man and His Work*, trans. Gerardo Denis, Lunwerg Editores (Barcelona), 1999, p 30.

8   'Paramorph (from mineralogy)' Def. 3. *Oxford English Dictionary*, 2nd edn, 1989, CD-ROM. A pseudomorph formed by a change of physical characters without a change in chemical composition.

'Pseudomorph' Def. 3. *Oxford English Dictionary*, 2nd edn, 1989, CD-ROM.

A false or deceptive form; spec. in mineralogy a crystal or other body consisting of one mineral but having the form proper to another, in consequence of having been formed by substitution, or by chemical or physical alteration.

9   John Rajchman, 'Perplications: On the space and time of Rebstockpark' in Judy Geib and Sabu Kohso (eds), *Unfolding Frankfurt,* Ernst & Sohn (Berlin), 1991, pp 18–77.

MORPHOGENESIS

Bio-inspired
Evolutionary
Design

**Rivka Oxman
and
Robert Oxman**

Morphogenesis is the theoretical foundation and body of knowledge related to the evolution of structure of an organism in natural phenomena. The study of the structure of organisms in Biology and Geology, the field has a rich philosophical background. Morphogenetic studies in design involve concepts and scientific research that have significant theoretical implications for form generation in design. These are particularly relevant to theories and practices of form generation in digital media, or as these type of form generative processes are frequently termed, *digital morphogenesis*.

The range of multidisciplinary sources of morphogenesis provides both a conceptual structure and a theoretical orientation that is relevant to evolving approaches to digital morphogenesis. Among the focal disciplines are developmental biology, emergence and the evolution of natural material systems, both organic and inorganic. D'Arcy Thompson's *On Growth and Form* of 1917 functions as one of the key texts of the field. Generic morphologies of nature provide models of evolutionary development that are today enlightening current work in design. Natural material forms and their evolutionary adaptation under contextual conditions of environmental forces provide precedents for the ecological orientation of current performance-based digital design.

In morphogenetic design, the emergence of material behaviors in environmental contexts provides models for the design of architecture as a complex adaptive system. Natural and architectural material systems can also be viewed as developing under conditions of self-organization. Analog and *computational form finding* exploit the experimental potential of material structures as a foundation for emergent design. Deriving from models of natural forms of self-generation and their structural behavior, novel form finding experiments were pioneered as a technique by research designers such as Frei Otto. Material computation in relation to form finding has now become a medium for the seamless integration of form and material production in a framework of performative ecological design (N. Oxman, 2010; N. Oxman, this volume).

Much of the current materials-oriented morphogenetic studies is derived from work of experimental architects and engineers such as Gaudí, Fuller, Isler, Otto, Balmond and Ban. Otto is particularly noted for identifying the relevance of natural structures, such as branching systems, and their application in contemporary advanced structural design experimentation. Form finding, or the experimental simulation modeling of structural calculations using analog models, also characterizes the experimental communality of this group of designers for whom natural form and materials have established the content of research-based design. This background may be a seen as a body of precedent for *computational form finding* today.

The contribution of theoretical sources in experimental design engineering practices has been the derivation of a taxonomy of the key concepts that provides transition between morphogenesis as a concept and digital morphogenesis. The contemporary interpretation of the concept of digital tectonics is based upon the reinterpretation of the organizational properties of form, material and structure (R. Oxman, 2010). Oxman proposed and defined tectonics as a model of morphogenetic process. Significant among these are morphogenetic evolutionary dynamics, including the relationships between phenotypes and genotypes. Topological evolution in which the phenotype can produce a multiplicity of potential solutions in digital morphogenesis may also be based upon a parametric derivational process.

Among the concepts of morphogenesis, the conditions and classes of *adaptation* and *growth* are of particular relevance to parametric design. Systems of natural material form are self-organizational and emergent. Thus the evolution and behavior of natural forms may provide models for a new material-based approach to design as well as to performative design. This relationship of theoretical and methodological sources is functioning as a general experimental model in design. This experimental model is inspired by research at the intersection of developmental biology, material sciences and complexity studies.

Digital morphogenesis is the exploitation of generative media for the derivation of material form and its evolutionary mutation. Among the key concepts of the field are topological geometries, natural models of generative design, for example genetic algorithms, L-systems and so on, parametric design, and performance analysis/design. Topology is a key underlying concept within the principle that *homeomorphic* structures are topologically similar while supporting morphological transformations. These evolutionary mutations create parametric variants in a process of generation that is potentially mediated by the data of contextual forces.

Today as architecture and architectural engineering are moving away from canonic structural types and towards emergent behaviors and non-linear organization of material structures, the knowledge of *morphogenetic dynamics* has become a fundamental component of generative design knowledge. The relationship between material structural morphologies and complex geometry must accommodate *adaptive mechanisms* that enable the adaptation of the material structure to the geometry. This significant property of biological emergence is commonly termed *differentiation*, connoting the particularization of the organizational principle of material structure through local distortion or hybridization.

Biomimetics is the research and design practice of the modeling of design principles of biological organisms as a basis for the current design of objects and systems. The field that formally emerged in the 1950s in order to exploit organic design as a basis for technological development may now be considered an emerging scientific discipline with academic research centers at various universities, particularly in the UK.

Biomimetics considered as biological design science promotes research in several fields relevant to morphogenetics in architecture and ecological design. Prominent among these is the study and modeling of the structure, organizational classes and behavioral properties of organic materials. Significant properties of material structures are their developmental characteristics, including evolutionary stages, growth and adaptability.

The *computational modeling of material structures* and their dynamics has recently emerged as a subject of interest in experimental architectural research. The materials-related simulation of material structures and adaptive behaviors may be considered important ingredients of digital morphogenesis. The design implications of material structure-related biomimetics are exemplified in the readings and suggested further reading.

The *Emergence and Design Group*, composed of Michael Hensel, Achim Menges and Michael Weinstock, has since 2004 produced a remarkable body of research and writing on morphogenesis, biomimetic design and architecture. Their presence at the AA in London during this period had an impact on experimental technology-oriented and digitally based design education at the AA as well as at other international architectural schools. Their work in the *Emerging Technologies* master's degree program also contributed to the pedagogical uniqueness of that generation of research-based graduate design education at the AA.

DeLanda, Manuel (2002), "Deleuze and the Use of the Genetic Algorithm in Architecture," in Leach, Neil, ed., *Designing for a Digital World*, Wiley-Academy, West Sussex, UK, pp. 117–120

DeLanda, Manuel (2004), "Materiality: Anaxect and Intense," in Spuybroek, Lars, *Nox*, Thames and Hudson, New York, pp. 370–377

(2004), "Frei Otto in Conversation," in Hensel, Michael, Menges, Achim and Weinstock, Michael, eds., *Emergence: Morphogenetic Design Studies*, Profile No. 169, Vol. 74, No. 3, May/June, pp. 18–25

Frazer, John (1995), "Introduction: A Natural Model for Architecture," in Frazer, John, *An Evolutionary Architecture*, AA, London

Hensel, Michael and Menges, Achim (2006), "Morpho-Ecologies Towards an Inclusive Discourse on Heterogeneous Architectures," in Hensel, Michael and Menges, Achim, eds., *Morpho-Ecologies*, AA, London, pp. 16–60

Jeronimidis, George (2004), "Biodynamics," in Hensel, Michael, Menges, Achim and Weinestock, Michael, *Emergence: Morphogenetic Design Strategies*, AD (Architectural Design), Profile No. 169, Vol. 74, No. 3, May/June, pp. 90–95

Kolarevic, Branko (2003), "Digital Morphogenesis," in Kolarevic, Branko, ed., *Architecture in the Digital Age: Design and Manufacturing*, Spon Press, New York and London, pp. 11–28

Migayrou, Frédéric (2009), "Incremental Mutations," in Andrasek, Alisa, *Biothing*, Frac Centre, Editions HYX, Orléans, France, pp. 20–29

Oxman, Neri (2010), *Material-based Design Computation*, Ph.D. thesis, MIT

Oxman, Rivka (2010), "Morphogenesis in the theory and methodology of digital tectonics," in Motro, R., guest ed., a special issue on Morphogenesis in the *Journal of the International Association for Shell and Spatial Structures, IASS*, Vol. 51, No. 3, 195–207, 2010

Weinstock, Michael (2006), "Self-Organization and Material Constructions," in Hensel, Michael, Menges, Achim and Weinstock, Michael, eds., *Techniques and Technologies in Morphogenetic Design*, AD (*Architectural Design*), Profile No. 180, Vol. 76, No. 2, March/April, pp. 26–33

> List of Key Concepts

adaptation
adaptive mechanisms
biomimetics
branching systems
developmental biology
differentiation
digital morphogenesis
ecological conditions
ecological design
emergence
environmental context
evolutionary adaptation
evolutionary dynamics
form finding
genetic algorithms
genotype

growth
homeomorphic
L-systems
material behaviors
material systems
morphogenesis
morphogenetic dynamics
morphogenetic form finding
morphology
mutation
natural computation
parametric design
performance-based design
performative design
performative morphologies
phenotype

Architecture as a material practice is predominately based on an approach to design that is characterised by prioritising the elaboration of form over its subsequent materialisation. Since the Renaissance the increasing division between processes of design and making, as proclaimed by Leon Battista Alberti (Grafton 2002), has led to the age-long development of and increasing dependence on representational tools intended for explicit, scalar geometric descriptions that at the same time serve as instructions for the translation from drawing to building. Inevitably, and with few exceptions such as Antoni Gaudí, Frei Otto, Heinz Isler and some others, architects have embraced design methods that epitomise the hierarchical separation of form definition from materialisation. In today's practice digital tools are still mainly employed to create design schemes through a range of design criteria that leave the inherent morphological and performative capacities of the employed material systems largely unconsidered. Ways of materialisation, production and construction are strategised only after a form has been elaborated, leading to top-down engineered, material solutions that often juxtapose unfitting logics. An alternative, morphogenetic approach to design unfolds morphological complexity and performative capacity from material constituents without differentiating between formation and materialisation processes. This requires an understanding of form, material and structure not as separate elements, but rather as complex interrelations that are embedded in and explored through integral processes of computational morphogenesis. It is important to note, however, that there is a crucial difference between established processes of material simulation and this design-oriented research: while material simulations require all variables of the system to be defined at the onset, the computational approach developed in this research enables the exploration of the design space established by the constraints of a material system, which leads to results that are not a priori fully determined.

12

Material Systems, Computational Morphogenesis and Performative Capacity

Achim Menges

> ## > Material Systems

While it may initially seem obvious to consider material systems more or less as the equivalent of construction systems and tectonics, we conceive of material systems as a more profound and integral concept. In this way, *material system* does not refer to the material constituents of a building alone, but rather describes, in a system-theoretical sense, the complex reciprocity between materiality, form, structure and space, the related processes of production and assembly, and the multitude of performative effects that emanate from the interaction with environmental influences and forces.

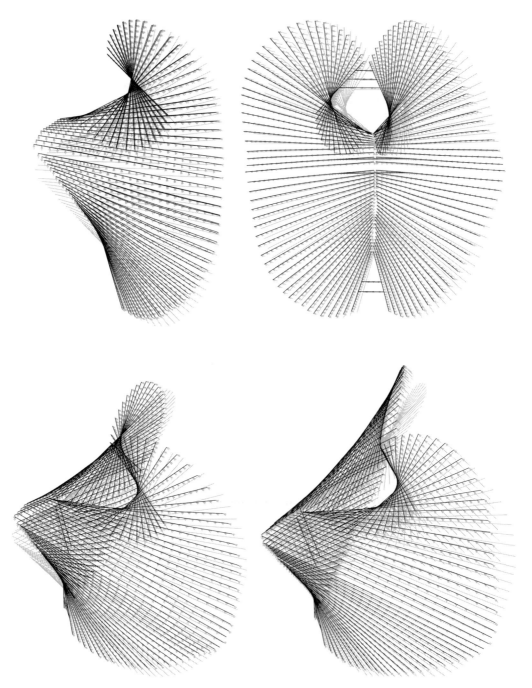

Figure 12.1

Interestingly, this conceptualisation of material systems enables the utilisation of the still latent potential of computational design processes. The ability of computational processes to simultaneously do both – to stochastically derive and systemically process complex data sets within a defined or evolving constraint space – can be utilised to explore a system's performative capacity within its materially determined limits. Furthermore, continuously informing the form generation with different modes of computational analysis enables a direct link between the ontogeny, the history of structural changes of an individual, and its interaction with external forces and energy respectively. In other words, material and morphological characteristics are derived through iterative feedback loops, which continually process the material system's interaction with statics, thermodynamics, acoustics, light, and so on. In contrast to the currently predominant modes of utilising design computation first for formal explorations liberated from all constraints of construction, and then for the economically driven rationalisation of the resultant, tectonically complicated buildings, this approach utilises computation to recognise and exploit the material system's *behaviour* rather than merely focusing on its *shape*. This enables the designer to conceive of material systems as the synergetic outcome of calibrating and balancing multiple influencing variables and divergent design criteria, which always already include the interaction with the system-external environment. The resultant environmental modulations can now be understood as highly specific patterns and in direct relation to the material interventions from which they originate. Hence they no longer rely on universal textbook principles of generalised behaviour. The design of space, structure and climate can be synthesised in one integral process rather than subdivided in a hierarchical workflow of separate actions or disciplines. Such an integral approach to architectural design based on the concept of material systems leads to considerable methodological changes and necessitates questioning some concepts deeply entrenched in current architectural practice.

In his seminal writings on morphology Goethe ([1796] 1987) draws the profound distinction between *gestalt*, the specific shape, and *bildung*, the process from which a specific shape unfolds. In this sense gestalt is a momentous snapshot in space and time. Thus the complex morphology of material gestalt always needs to be perceived in relation to morphogenesis, the continual process of becoming. Recognising that the gestalt of natural systems is always inherently and inseparably related to their processes of materialisation is of critical importance. Hence the works of the very few

---

Facing page

Figure 12.1: Displacement analysis of the viewing platform and shelter affected by seismic movement. Emergent Technologies and Design Group, 2006–2007, in collaboration with Arup and Partners. Image credit: All images courtesy of Emergent Technologies and Design Group, 2006–2007, in collaboration with Arup and Partners.

architects and engineers that pioneered a higher level integration of processes of formation and materialisation are far more relevant precedents for the work presented here than the superficially similar, yet design-methodologically fundamentally different avant-garde of contemporary digital design. Frei Otto's work is of particular interest for us, especially the synthesis of many of his investigations in his special research group *Natürliche Konstruktionen* at Stuttgart University. His realisation that 'the knowledge of the conditions under which forms develop opens up the possibility to qualify step by step the differentiation between design – the anticipation of reality in mind – and the construction of buildings – the production of objects' (Gaß 1990: 2–4), serves as a reference point in architectural research history. Frei Otto coined the term 'Selbstbildung', the process of *self-forming* that underlies most of his experiments on membranes, shells and other systems. This refers to the generation of a system's particular shape as the self-found equilibrium state of the forces acting upon it and its internal resistances determined by its material properties. In other words the designer defines a number of critical parameters and material characteristics, upon which the material system settles into the equilibrium state by itself taking on its specific shape in the process. This design method of *form finding*, as Frei Otto called it, is profoundly different from the still prevalent *form definition*.

As Frei Otto was mainly concerned with developing long-span light-weight structures with the primary objective of improving the ratio of a system's mass to its load-bearing capacity, he usually employed this method to form-find the overall shape of the structure. The work presented in this book aims at extending this research in regard to two points: [i] we have been investigating various possibilities of how form finding can also be employed on additional levels of a material system, as for example each local element; [ii] we aim for integrating a much higher number of critical design criteria, which inevitably leads to systems that no longer have one equilib-rium state, but a multifaceted and complex capacity of negotiating and balancing multiple functional and performative requirements. The related design process of *computational morphogenesis* of material systems will be explained in the next paragraphs.

> Computational Morphogenesis

Computational design lends itself to an integral design approach as it enables employing complex behaviour rather than just modelling a particular shape or form. The transition from currently predominant modes of computer-aided design (CAD) to computational design allows for a significant change in employing the computer's capacity. CAD is very much based on computer-ised processes of drawing and modelling stemming from established repre-sentational techniques in architectural design (Terzidis 2006). In this regard one of the key differences lies in the fact that CAD internalises the coexist-ence of form and information, whereas computational design externalises this relation and thus enables the conceptualisation of material behaviour and related formative processes (Hensel and Menges 2006). In computational design form is not defined through a sequence of drawing or modelling procedures but generated through algorithmic, rule-based processes. The ensuing externalisation of the interrelation between algorithmic processing of information and resultant form generation permits the systematic distinction between process, information and form. Hence any specific shape can be understood as resulting from the interaction of system-intrinsic information and external influences within a morphogenetic process (Menges 2008).

During the short history of so-called digital architecture, the notion of morphogenesis has almost become a cliché owing to excessive referencing to all kinds of design processes that operate most often merely on a metaphorical level. This has not deterred us from thoroughly investigating the powerful principles underlying natural morphogenesis and step by step transferring them into an integral computational process. As it is not possible to disentangle a material system's specificity from its morphogenetic development, we will present the most important characteristics of this design approach not in a generic manner, but along the specific example of the AA Component Membrane. This project aimed at accomplishing both, being an experiment

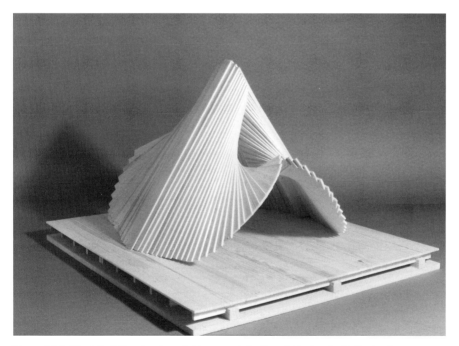

Figure 12.2: Model of the viewing platform and shelter at Hazienda Quitralco in Patagonia, Chile. Emergent Technologies and Design Group, 2006–2007, in collaboration with Buro Happold. Image credit: All images courtesy of Emergent Technologies and Design Group, 2006–2007, in collaboration with Buro Happold.

Figure 12.3: AA Membrane Canopy. Emergent Technologies and Design Group 2006–07, in collaboration with Buro Happold. Image credit: All images courtesy of Emergent Technologies and Design Group 2006–07, in collaboration with Buro Happold.

that allows exploring and synthesising a number of research topics on a relatively large scale, while at the same time resulting in the completion of a commissioned project.

In the summer of 2007 the AA Component Membrane was developed, designed and constructed with our EmTech master students in collaboration with structural engineers from the London branch of the renowned engineering practice Buro Happold. The starting point for this project was a thorough analysis of the brief to construct a canopy for the AA terrace and the careful examination of its context in terms of the actual tectonic situation of the site, its specific environmental influences and the considerable limitations for the construction process. This led to the definition of a performance profile and related fitness criteria, which significantly constrained the design space in the following way.

The contact points between the canopy to be constructed and the surrounding building were limited to three existing columns. Upon closer examination, it transpired that the columns' base points could only withstand minimal bending moments, which seemed to be at odds with the requirement that the completed canopy needed to protect the terrace from crosswinds and horizontally driven rain. On the one hand, the canopy needed to provide a sufficient rain and wind shelter, while on the other, a high degree of porosity was necessary in order to minimise horizontal wind impact pressure and to avoid blocking the view towards Ron Herron's landmark membrane roof of the Imagination building. Furthermore, the generally weak, existing substructure and the fact that the entire canopy was to be assembled without cranes or scaffolds greatly limited the overall weight and size of the individual components. Last but not least, owing to significant budget constraints, the material system to be developed needed to consist of common, inexpensive stock material and only to rely on fabrication processes operable in the school's workshop by unskilled labour. Only the membranes needed to be cut and the steel elements needed to be nickel plated by specialised manufacturers.

For the subsequent steps of initiating the development and differentiation of the system, the first critical task was to capture and embed its parameters, their hierarchies, dependencies and variable ranges in a system-defining, genotypic data set. The Danish genetics pioneer Wilhelm Ludvig Johannsen introduced the profound difference between *genotype* and *phenotype* in developmental biology in 1909 (Mayr 2002: 624). The *genotype* constitutes the unchanging genetic information, whereas the individual actual gestalt emerging from its interaction with the specific environment in which the development takes place is referred to as the *phenotype*. The possible degree of differentiation between an individual's gestalt and its genetic determination is defined as its *phenotypic plasticity*.

First the definition of the basic system constituent, the variable system component, needed to be established. Because of the aforementioned constraints, the basic component of the material system developed for this project comprises: [i] a framework of compression elements, simple galvanised steel tubes; [ii] steel wires as tension elements on the perimeter; and

[iii] the membrane assembly. In the overall structure the membrane patches contribute considerably to the structure's load-bearing capacity as the main tension elements and at the same time provide the system's skin. At this point it is important to reiterate that the material system is considered not so much as a derivative of standardised building systems and elements, but rather as the product of generative drivers in the design process. This initially requires disentangling a number of aspects that later on form part of an integral computational setup in which the system evolves.

First of all the geometric description of the material system, or rather the notation of particular features of the system's morphology, needs to be established. The designer needs to facilitate the setup of a computational model not as a particular gestalt specified through coordinates, but rather as a framework of possible formations affording further differentiations that remain coherent with the system's characteristics. Hence, for the following development steps of the membrane component system the aim was to define the material system's inherent parameters and in particular their variable bandwidth determined by the affordances and constraints of the individual elements. This generic definition allowed for each individual component to be differentiated in response to the specific requirements of the overall system's sub-location in which it is placed.

The parameterisation of the component was based on a large number of physical tests exploring the system's inherent constraints. First the self-forming behaviour of the membrane element was investigated in relation to the location of the points where it attaches to the compression framework. Depending on the relative position of the anchor points, the pre-tensioned membrane settles into different individual shapes. However, within a specific parameter range, all the individual shapes share certain characteristics: for example, they all adhere to hyperbolic-paraboloid (*hypar*) geometry with negative Gaussian curvature. In other words, the variation of the defining parameters, in this case the relative coordinates of the hypar's high and low points given by the steel framework, leads to variant equilibrium states of the acting forces and related membrane shapes. The parametric description of the tubular steel frame is hierarchically dependent on the membranes, in that its geometric variance is limited by the constraints of their self-forming processes to prevent wrinkles or more generally to ensure proper tensioning so that the membranes can become structurally active. In addition, the compression elements have their own inherent limits, for example the maximum deviation of the joint angles on both ends. Furthermore, in order to prevent local buckling, the relative maximum length of each tube is limited in relation to the compressive force acting on it as the tubes' diameter range was restricted to 16 to 22 millimetres owing to manufacturing and weight constraints.

The notion of 'component' does not only integrate the possibilities and limits of making, and the self-forming tendencies and constraints of materials, but also needs to anticipate the processes of assembly of a component collective, opening up the possibility for building up a larger system.

Similar to the definition of the elements, the definition of the relation between elements prioritises topological exactitude (Win-free 1987: 253) over the metric precision usually pursued when detailing the assembly of parts. In other words, the material system's component assembly is primarily defined through the topological relations of proximity and contiguity of its elements rather than the metric characteristics of length, angle or area as in Euclidean geometry. In Euclidean geometry the relation between elements or points is expressed as fixed length and distances that stipulate how far apart points are in relation to one another. However, in topological space distances expressed in length cannot characterise proximity as the length does not remain fixed. Such topologies can be stretched or scaled without changing the underlying characteristics of its defining points or elements. The summation of all these defining factors derived through and verified by a multitude of digital and physical test models leads to a first genotypic definition of the system's basic constituent. The relevant material properties, self-forming capacities, geometric characteristics, manufacturing constraints and assembly logics of the system elements are described as reciprocal interdependences operating within specific variable margins. Within these margins, associative computational geometry enables the differentiation of the elements' transformative behaviour, whereby more complex and adaptable interrelations across different systemic hierarchical levels can also be programmed.

> Integrative Differentiation

In computational morphogenesis the genotypic definition unfolds a performative phenotypic material system. This takes place through integrative differentiation of its elements driven by multiple functional requirements. This comprises both the ontogenetic growth process of individual systems and the comparative, evolutionary development of system populations across many generations. The technical implementation of algorithmic growth processes can vary significantly according to system type and design strategy. In any case, the common and most relevant aspect is the proliferation of the elements across several growth steps, in which each element is regenerated rather than one added to another. In this iterative *bildungs*-process each element and component adapts its morphology by calibrating its functional requirements with its particular sub-location in the overall system. This computational generation of the performative, phenotypic components is driven by a feedback with different simulation and analysis tools. These tools are not only employed for cross-checking the self-forming limits of the systems. This setup enables iterative analyses and evaluation cycles, so that the specific gestalt of the system unfolds from the reciprocal influences and interactions of form, material and structure within a simulated environment.

Both evaluative and generative modes (Sasaki 2007) of structural analysis play an important role in this process. Depending on the system's intended environmental modulation capacity, the morphogenetic development process also needs to recurrently interface with appropriate analysis applications, for example multi-physics computer fluid dynamics for the investigation of thermodynamic relations, light and acoustic analysis. It is important to mention, though, that CFD does always only provide a partial insight as the thermodynamic complexity of the actual environment is far greater than any computational model can presently handle. Nonetheless, as the main objective lies not solely in the prediction of precise data, but primarily in the recognition of behavioural tendencies and patterns, the instrumental contributions of such tools are significant.

The full exploration of the design space as defined by the variables and evolving margins of the phenotypic plasticity, as well as the related development of a system's specific performative capacity, is possible in an evolutionary process. Similar to the algorithmic growth process, evolutionary computation offers different ways of implementing such generative processes and fitness evaluation techniques. What all such procedures generally have in common is using the evolutionary dynamics of combination, reproduction and mutation of the underlying genotypic data sets through a genetic algorithm as well as selection procedures. The continuous differentiation of the system and all its elements is driven by the open-ended, stochastic search of the morphogenetic process, in combination with the selective nature of fitness rankings at the interval of each generation. This fitness evaluation always happens on the phenotypic level.

It is important to note that the fitness evaluation, as well as other aspects of the evolutionary design process, are not strictly limited to computational means. Similar to the definition of the material system through physical models and prototypes, the analysis and evaluation of the system's performative capacity may equally be cross-checked through empirical tests. The findings of analytical modes oscillating between the analogue and computational realm can lead to alterations in the weighing of evaluation criteria or even the system's underlying definition itself.

> Performative Capacities

Computational morphogenesis can be described as a process of perpetual differentiation. The increasing morphological and functional difference of elements enabling the system's performative capacity unfolds from their divergent development directions triggered by a heterogeneous environment and multiple functional criteria. For the example of the AA canopy project, this entailed the specific formation of each membrane component depending on its location within the overall system. In this case, the computational differentiation operates on three different levels: [i] the component level and its dependent elements and [ii] the level of multi-component subsystems, as well as [iii] the overall system configuration. Each level is generated in direct feedback with different analytical tools and continual cross-checks with the given constraint space. Thus the morphogenetic process enables the balancing and calibration of multiple, or even conflicting, design criteria and the unfolding of the material system's inherent performative capacity. For example, a sequence of finite element analyses conducted by the engineers from Buro Happold during the design phase evolved the structure in such a way that the pre-tensioned membrane elements became an integral load-bearing part of the system, not just a cladding on a space frame. Concurrently iterative CFD tests of the system's aerodynamic behaviour were conducted on both the level of the overall system and local components assemblies. In feedback with analytical tools simulating the system's interaction with precipitation and its related drainage behaviour, this multi-criteria evaluation derived a finely calibrated level of permeability of the porous membrane skin that minimises wind impact pressure and simultaneously prevents local accelerations of airflow due to channelling gaps between the membrane elements. A further important factor that influenced the system's development was the shading behaviour of the canopy in different seasons and at different times of day, aiming for a mix of shaded and exposed terrace zones that changes from winter to summer.

Overall it is important to note that true morphological as well as performative differentiation requires the design and evaluation criteria, as well as their hierarchies and weighing, to develop alongside the evolution of the material system. Considering multiple influencing variables, which are negotiated and balanced during the process of differentiation, and the flexible hierarchy and evolving weighing of fitness criteria, shifts the potential of computational tools significantly. Rather than aiming for rationalisation or single-objective optimisation, computation becomes the means of integration: integration of the system-inherent constraints of materials, manufacturing and assembly together with the system's interaction with a wide range of external influences and forces.

In the case of the AA membrane project, this integrative approach led to a highly differentiated, overlapping membrane structure cantilevering from three bearing points only. The information required for manufacturing forms an integral part of the derived computational data set. The 600 geometrically different steel elements were manufactured in the school's workshop, and the 150 different membranes were automatically cut and labelled by a specialised manufacturer and subsequently finished at the London College of Fashion. The resulting overlapping membrane articulation shelters the terrace while at the same time remaining porous enough to avoid excessive wind pressure or blocking the view across London's roofscape. In addition, the integrative nature of the morphogenetic process derived a high level of robustness as compared to design processes aiming for single-criteria optimisation. Since its construction, the canopy has withstood gale-force winds and excessive snow loads, both conditions that the system was originally not designed for. Considering also that the entire structure was developed, designed, manufactured and erected within the short period of seven weeks, it demonstrates the potential inherent to the integral design approach of computational morphogenesis.

> Complexity

Despite the fact that the presented design approach requires a serious engagement with technology, as may have become clear from the above description of computational morphogenesis, its use is certainly not limited to exotic materials, expensive manufacturing processes and vast budgets. The opposite is demonstrated through the following project, which is also based on the above explained computational approach, yet utilises more mundane building materials and the extremely limited manufacturing technology available in one of the world's most remote areas, Patagonia. In effect, as the main expenditure consists of the intellectual investment in an alternative conceptualisation of material systems and related computational processes, this design approach can remain operative in contexts of sparse resources. Here complexity, and related performative capacity, unfolds from the continuous evolution and differentiation of initially simple material elements and construction procedures.

The project entailed the design of a viewing platform and shelter, which was to be constructed within one week by a team of EmTech students on the land of Hacienda Quitralco in the Quitralco Fjord in Chilean Patagonia. The remote location imposed stringent constraints on the development of the material system: on-site only one kind of locally cut timber plank was available, with the only tool for further fabrication being a chainsaw. The project comprised a generic platform on a raft foundation and a shelter that consisted of two ruled surfaces made from straight equal-width timber planks. The decision of constraining the basic computational definition of the system to so-called ruled surfaces was made in response to the pre-manufacturing constraints of timber on-site, the available construction means and the local knowledge in timber construction. A ruled surface is a surface that can be swept out by moving a line in space. This implies that such a surface can be principally constructed from straight elements, such as, in this case, straight timber planks. However, the width and thickness of the planks require them to bend slightly along their longitudinal axis, which is possible as wood has the interesting characteristic of variable stiffness in relation to grain orientation. The considerable difference in modulus of elasticity in relation to fibre direction is particularly useful here, with the modulus of elasticity parallel to the main fibre direction generally being approximately fifteen times higher than that perpendicular to the fibres. This enables the ruled surface to be constructed from planks that are not all situated within parallel construction planes. Depending on the overlap and joint points with the adjacent elements, each plank can bend slightly along its longitudinal axis. This degree of deviation from coplanar plank assembly enables a specific curvature in the overall structure that is given as a function of each local plank joint.

The design space for the subsequent exploration of the system's capacity was defined by the possibility of varying both the guide curves in space, the length of each plank and the maximum angle between planks. Key design criteria for the evolutionary design process were basic functional require-ments such as the enclosed volume in relation to envelope surface, the minimum ceiling height for inhabitation and the view axis towards the fjord and the Southern Cross. Considering the exposed location of the site and the harsh climate, additional essential criteria were the wind and rain protection of the inhabitable space. Furthermore, the structural capacity, particularly in regard to frequent earthquakes, was of critical importance. The considerable constraints determined by the availability of just one material element and the performative criteria outlined above provided the key constituents of the computational design process. Various generations of ruled surface configurations were derived and each generated instance individually evalu-ated, the results of informing the subsequent generation cycles.

In the final form the rotation points of the ruled surfaces shift along a curve in space, resulting in a surface that seems to turn upon itself. This creates a raised opening where the two surfaces meet and the timber planks cantilever. The entire structure is supported by an A-shaped frame constructed from eight planks, which form an integral part of the shelter's surface. This allows minimising the contact points between platform and surface in order to avoid moisture damaging the roof planks. The two surfaces that make up the shelter are symmetrical and lean against each other. The combination of the weight of the surfaces, their flexible connection and the slightly bend-able planks enabled the resistance of the completed structure to the impact of the strong earthquakes of the region. This was put to the test the night after completion, which witnessed a number of earthquakes, with the strongest measuring 5 on the Richter scale. The shelter survived this first test without damage and has withstood a number of severe earthquakes and storms since construction was finished in spring 2007. In many ways this project demonstrates how an integral computational approach to design enables a high level of complexity and performance even in a situation where only the simplest means of construction are available. This indicates the importance of further developing the approach, as it may prove to be particularly relevant in contexts with very limited resources.

With regard to the concept of integral form-generation and materialisa-tion processes and the related methodological framework of computational morphogenesis, one concluding remark needs to be offered in view of the research presented in Emergent Technologies and Design, Hensel, Menges and Weinstock. It is important to note that computational morphogenesis is not a universal procedure or design recipe, which, once established, derives any system from basic code to fully fledged material structure given the right input. On the contrary, beyond the common technological and meth-odological framework explained above, each material system requires the development of specific techniques corresponding with the system's partic-ular composition, characteristics and performative criteria. Thus the work presented in *Emergent Technologies and Design* aims at providing an over-view of different material systems and related computational methods. Yet, one additional aspect they all share is the inherent questioning of the nature and hierarchies of currently established design processes and the promotion of an alternative approach, one that enables architects to exploit the resources of computational design and manufacturing beyond the creation of exotic shapes that are subsequently rationalised for constructability and superimposed functions, Rather, it promotes the unfolding of performative capacities and spatial qualities inherent in the material systems we construct. And this highlights the importance of the designer in an alternative role, one that is central to enabling, moderating and influencing an integral design process, which also requires novel skills and sensibilities. Exploring this challenge with the students has been one of the overarching educational aims for the research presented in the book.

Architecture is undergoing a systemic change, driven by the changes in culture, science, industry and commerce that are rapidly eroding the former boundaries between the natural and the artificial. The conceptual apparatus of architecture has always given a central role to the relations of mankind and nature. The human body has been a source of harmonious proportions and the shapes of many living organisms have been adapted for architectural use. The current widespread fascination with nature is a reflection of the availability of new modes of imaging the interior structures of plants and animals, of electron-microscopy of the intricate and very small, together with the mathematics of biological processes. New working methods of architectural design and production are rapidly spreading through architectural and engineering practices, as they have already revised the world of manufacturing and construction. The material practices of contemporary architecture cannot be separated from this paradigm shift in the context within which architecture is conceived and made. The study of natural systems suggests the means of conceiving and producing architecture that is more strongly correlated to material organisations and systems in the natural world.

Computational form-generating processes are based on 'genetic engines' that are derived from the mathematical equivalent of the Darwinian model of evolution, and from the biological science of evolutionary development that combines processes of embryological growth and evolutionary development of the species. Evolutionary computation offers the potential for relating pattern and process, form and behaviour, with spatial and cultural parameters. Evolutionary computational strategies for morphogenesis have the potential to be combined with advanced structural and material simulations of behaviour under stresses of gravity and load. This approach is part of the contemporary reconfiguration of the understanding of 'nature', a change from metaphor to model, from 'nature' as a source of shapes to be copied to 'nature' as a series of interrelated dynamic processes that can be simulated and adapted for the design and production of architecture.

The development and use of computational systems for architectural design is central to the theoretical and experimental explorations of the Emergent Technologies and Design programme. The seminar courses 'Emergence' and 'Biomimetics and Natural Systems' introduce the origins and instruments of the sciences and technologies associated with emergence, commencing with Darwin and D'Arcy Thompson, through analysis of the mathematical logics of evolution and biological development, to the experimental development of evolutionary algorithms within the limited computational environment of architectural design software.

13

Evolution and Computation

Michael Weinstock

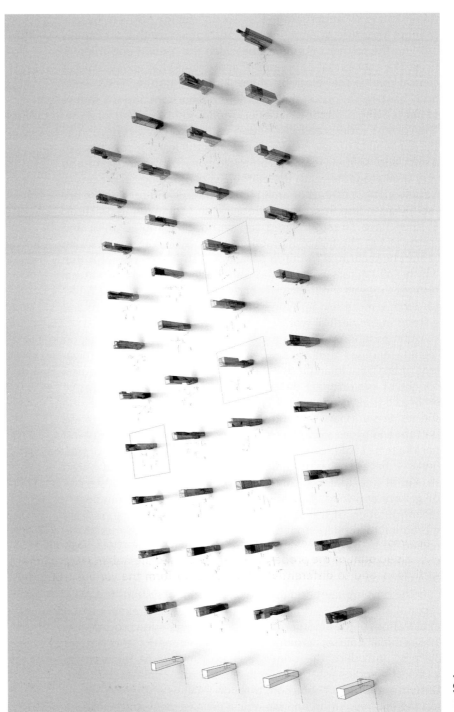

Figure 13.1

> Evolution and Development

The development of 'evolutionary' algorithms commences with an under-standing of the two distinct but coupled processes that bring about the morphogenesis, variation and distribution of all living forms. Every living form emerges from two strongly coupled processes, operating over maxi-mally differentiated time spans: the rapid process of embryological develop-ment from a single cell to an adult form, and the long slow process of the evolution of diverse species of forms over multiple generations. Fossil evidence suggests that the history of biological evolution is a sequence, from simple cell organisms to the higher complexity of plants and animals. Charles Darwin argued that all living and extinct beings were the offspring of common parents, 'descended from an ancient progenitor', and that 'all past and present organic beings constitute one grand natural system'. The diver-sification and proliferation of all living forms, the historical development of all the species of life, was driven by variation and selection. 'I have called this principle, by which each slight variation, if useful, is preserved, by the term Natural Selection' (Darwin 1859: 61). In Darwin's view variations are random, small modifications or changes in the organism that occur naturally in repro-duction through the generations. Random variation produces the raw material of variant forms, and natural selection acts as the force that chooses the forms that survive. Just as humans breed livestock and vegetables by 'unnatural' selection, methodically organising systematic changes in them, so wild organisms themselves are changed by natural selection, in a slow, steady, gradual and continuous process of change. Darwin did not, as is sometimes said, assume that selection was the only mechanism of evolutionary change. In the last sentence of the introduction to *The Origin of the Species* he wrote: 'I am convinced that Natural Selection has been the most important, but not the exclusive, means of modification' (Darwin 1859: 6).

The development of a single being from an embryo to an adult form was at that time regarded as related to but distinct from the evolutionary 'descent from ancestors'. Darwin stated that 'the early cells or units possess the inherent power, independently of any external agent, of producing new structures wholly different in form, position, and function' (Darwin 1859: 389). His account of the properties of cells included their ability to proliferate by division, and to differentiate themselves to form the various tissues of a body. Almost a hundred years later Gould published *Ontogeny and Phylogeny*

Facing page

Figure 13.1: The SSD algorithm's strength is the quick production of comparable designs given a very limited and open framework of inputs. Combined with the strategy of genetic information mapping (Fate maps), this algorithm works within the framework of genetic evolutionary strategy. Fit individuals with their related fate maps are highlighted in black frames. Emergence seminar research, 2008. Image credit: All images courtesy of Michael Weinstock, AA London. Emergence seminar research, 2008, Sean Ahlquist and Moritz Fleischmann.

(Gould 1977), in which he argued that all changes in form are the result of changes to the timing of the developmental processes relative to each other, and to the rate at which they are carried out. His synthesis of embryological development and evolution was focused on changes in the timing and rate of development.

At the end of the nineteenth century William Bateson published a substantive account of the mutations in living forms, *Material for the Study of Variation* (Bateson 1894). Bateson's interest lay in how living forms come into being, how they are adapted to 'fit the places they have to live in', and in the differences between forms, and particularly in the causes of variation. Although an admirer of Darwin, he believed that the process of evolution was not one of continuous and gradual modification, but was rather discontinuous. New forms and species could not come into being through a gradual accumulation of small changes, and distinct parts arose or disappeared rapidly. He argued that distinctive variations, entire new forms, could spring up, already perfectly adapted. His argument rests on his analysis of the morphology of living beings, observing that 'the bodies of living things are mostly made up of repeated parts', organised bilaterally or radially in series, and many body parts themselves are also made up of repeated units. The parts are already functional, pre-adapted so to speak, so that morphological changes or variations can occur by changes to the number or order of parts. Another common variation he named 'homeotic', in which one body part is replaced by or transformed into a likeness of another part, for example appendages such as legs and antennae that have similar morphological characteristics. He regarded most variations between species as differences in the spatial arrangement, number and kind of repeated parts or modules. Furthermore, he thought that these changes were initiated during the development of the embryo by fluctuations in 'force'. He described this force, to much derision at the time, as rhythmic or 'vibratory', harmonic resonances or similar wave-like phenomena capable of dynamic response to environmental changes. Discontinuity in evolution is suggested by the fossil evidence, which implies long periods of relative stasis punctuated by sudden short periods in which many new species appear (Eldredge 1995). Gould's 'punctuated equilibrium' is perhaps the best known, if not most widely accepted, version of the theory that forms tend to persist unchanged for great lengths of time, and undergo brief but rapid change to produce new species in response to severe changes in their environment.

D'Arcy Thompson agreed with Darwin's argument that natural selection is efficient at removing the 'unfit', but in his view all forms are influenced by the physical properties of the natural world, and the form of living things is a diagram of the forces that have acted on them (Thompson 1917). The physical forces act on living forms and determine the scales, bounding limits and informing geometries of the development of all adult forms. Evolution and differential growth during the process of development produce the material forms of living things. The combination of the internal forces such as chemical activities and the pressure in their cells, and the external forces of the environment such as gravity, climate and the available energy supply determine the characteristics of the field in which they act; the effect of these natural forces is expressed in different ways depending on the size of the organism. 'Cell and tissue, shell and bone, leaf and flower, are so many portions of matter, and it is in obedience to the laws of physics that their particles have been moved, moulded and conformed' (Thompson 1917). His recognition of growth as the principal means of achieving variation in inherited forms predates Gould's synthesis, but most significantly, D'Arcy Thompson proposed that 'a new system of forces, introduced by altered environment and habits' would, over time, produce adaptive modifications of forms. Living forms, like non-living forms, exist in a field of forces, and alterations in those forces will inevitably produce the response of evolutionary changes to forms. Furthermore, these changes will be systemic, to the whole being rather than to a specific part, 'more or less uniform or graded modifications' over the whole of the body (Thompson 1917).

Animals and plants that have quite different evolutionary lineages may have striking similarities in the general organisation of their body parts, their anatomical structures, and the processes of their organs. Common organisations and anatomical architectures emerge from the coupling of processes that are strongly differentiated in time and by scale: slow processes acting over multiple generations, and very fast processes acting only in the short period of embryological development (Berril and Godwin 1996). In the first process, some biological forms, structures and metabolic processes are better able than others to withstand the physical stresses of the world, the rigours of the environment and the competitions of life. Natural selection will gradually tend to produce a generalised response of adaptation to specific environmental stresses, and this will occur across many species. Over sufficient time, forms will tend to converge. In the second process, the genome acts on the construction of individual forms. The accumulated complexity of the genome manifests in a general tendency to initiate cellular differentiation along common sequences and pathways. Common sequences of development, in a stress field that all developing organisms share, tend to lead to rather generic outcomes.

Furthermore, a large portion of the genome is similar across groups of species, and the sequence of development is also similar, as is the molecular chemistry of the biological materials of which living forms are constructed. All materials experience the same physical forces, are subject to the same stresses and react in similar patterns. Small variations in the sequence of inhibition and acceleration or in the duration of either inhibition or acceleration may produce changes in the development of the embryo at many scales, through the reorganisation and recombination of biological components.

> Information and Mutation

Genetic information passing down through the generations modifies the forms of living beings and their interaction with their environment and the materials and energy that they extract from it. As each generation succeeds it ancestors, information is propagated down through time. Changes or modifications to living forms occur both by mutation or 'copy errors', and by the recombination of existing information into new sequences and patterns. This may be seen in evolution in general, in the emergence of new species, and in the emergence of social or collective behaviour and material constructions of insects, animals and humans. Energy and information produce effects that act upon the architecture of material in space and over time, and the interaction between them is neither exclusively 'bottom-up' nor 'top down'. It is clear that both the living forms of nature and the constructed forms of human artefacts emerge from complex processes that are coupled to the transmission of information.

Cultural information is also transmitted down through time, and material practices manifest that information in the social activities of humans and in the forms of artefacts and buildings they construct, from the simple pit dwellings of the first anatomically modern humans to the cities of the ancient world, and on to the built forms and 'megacities' of the contemporary world. It is clear that material culture is also inherited by descendants, that there is 'descent with modification' in artefacts, and that the forms of buildings and even cities can be grouped into morphological taxonomies in a similar manner to the grouping of species. As mutations to the known forms of organisms occur naturally, so too have the small innovations, theoretical 'errors' and design mutations of ancient architectures produced the 'populations' or cities of buildings, and driven the historical evolution of architecture, with its limited morphologies and convergent set of available forms. There are, however, significant differences between the mode of operation of material cultural evolution and biological evolution. Perhaps the most significant difference between biological and cultural evolution lies in the 'selection' of forms that survive to pass on their genes or information to their descendants. Other differences include the mode of inheritance, which in culture may be horizontal or oblique, as cultural practices concerned with material construction diffuse between distinct social groups. Information transmission has been an essential characteristic of human culture since anatomically modern humans evolved from the great apes, although the means of transmission were slower, with less immediate effects. The transmission of the information of material practices and architectural forms has been accelerated exponentially several times, with the sequential emergence of large trading networks, mathematical notation, writing and drawings systems, printing, and most recently by computation. The built forms of material cultural may also be said to have evolved, commonly producing variation more rapidly than biological evolution but still at multidecadal and millennial timescales. Computation offers a new design environment, one that has the potential to develop algorithms that mimic biological evolution, and compress the evolution of architectural designs into extremely rapid processes.

In biological evolution it is the sequential activation of the genes that 'express' the proteins and hormones needed for the construction of biological materials. The sequence of activation is regulated by a small subset of the genome, the 'homeobox'. It is thought that this regulatory set of genes emerged long before the evolution of physical complex forms, and many of the regulatory genes are similar across species. The differential growth of cells occurs in a field of stresses induced by the physics of the earth and the tendencies of biological materials to self-organise into differentiated patterns. The regulatory set of genes produce the initial spatial organisation of the embryo, by accelerating or inhibiting growth in varying sequences and patterns, and so act as differentiated feedbacks on the process of growth. Small variations in the strength of inhibition or acceleration induce a periodicity in the self-organising patterns, and that in turn produces yet more complex spatial and anatomical organisations across the range of scales.

Mutations to the forms of animal and human bodies occur naturally. Cyclops mutations, for example, are a frequent occurrence in many species. Fish may become cyclopic if their embryos are thermally or chemically traumatised, pregnant ewes grazing on corn lilies can produce cyclopic lambs, and in humans diabetes or the consumption of excessive amounts of alcohol during pregnancy dramatically increases the chances of the embryo mutating to the cyclopic form. It is a very common mutation, a deviation at the very beginning of the normal development of the embryo. The morphological characteristics of Cyclopia are similar in all species, including humans. The mutation produces an undivided brain, lacking the normal two hemispheres, and a single eye, usually with the nostrils located above the eye. Biological mutations reveal the space of morphological variation or differentiation of any given species. In evolutionary terms, they are subject to strong negative selection, but are produced in every generation by the processes of embryonic development. Morphological differentiation of the full adult form is produced by small variations that occur very early in development, and may be initiated by genetic errors or environmental changes or may be induced by experimental manipulation. The process of embryonic development determines the morphological variation or differentiation in the population of any species, the set of available forms.

Changes arise in the genome by mutation, often as 'copy errors' during transcription, when the sequence may be shuffled or some modules repeated by mutation. The changed genome in turn produces changes to physical form or phenome. Most mutations are either neutral or harmful to the living form, and beneficial mutations are rare. Differentiation during the development of an individual is controlled by the homeobox genes (originally discovered in the fruit fly *Drosophila*) that turn other genes on or off during development, controlling the order of morphogenesis and the position of different parts in relation to the body plan. In the case of the fruit fly, the mutation of a single gene, known as antennapedia, produces changes to the morphology and function of the fly's antenna, so that it develops as a leg rather than an antenna. This is possible because all cells in the fly have all of the information necessary to become leg cells or antennae. Every cell in an organism carries a complete genome, all of the information necessary for the development of the complete organism. Antennapaedia and its homologues control limb development in all vertebrates, so that the forelimbs of birds develop as wings, or the extremities of the forelimbs develop as hands in humans or flippers in seals. Homeobox sequences have been conserved throughout evolution and are controlling factors to the development of even distantly related organisms. Changes to the homeobox genes have substantial effects on the morphology of individuals, and when these changed individuals survive the rigours of natural selection, new descendant species are formed. If individual mutations offer the advantage of superior functionality in some capacity, then the mutant organism will have an enhanced reproductive fitness. If its progeny inherit the changed genome, then evolutionary change will occur. Differentiation by speciation, new species arising from a common ancestor, is normally described in phylograms, or tree-like charts. The underlying logic is to plot the sequence of morphological differentiations that lead from the 'form' of a common ancestor to the multiple differentiated forms of the whole group or taxa. For example, the common ancestor of all arthropoda, including crustaceans, centipedes, spiders, scorpions and insects, was a simple tube-like worm. The arthropoda group has over one million species alive today, with a fossil record that starts in the early Cambrian era, and it accounts for over 80 per cent of all known organisms. The sequence of morphological differentiation produced segmented bodies, exoskeletons and jointed legs.

The co-option or recruitment of existing genes into new organisations means that no new molecules are needed, so that repetition and reconfiguration produce a higher complexity within the genome. Living forms have an anatomical and spatial organisation that consists of repeated modules that vary in size, shape and number. The genome too is modular in organisation, consisting of many repeating sequences arrayed in distinct groups, each of which may contain common or multiple sequences that also occur in other groups. If small changes occur in the regulatory genes, they have the potential to produce changes to the size, shape and number of repeating modules in the living form. Over evolutionary time the genome has grown in size and complexity, but there is no apparent correlation between the size of the genome and the complexity of a living form. It has been observed that large living forms with very large genomes, such as trees in temperate climatic regions, tend to produce variant descendant species less often than other species. In the history of biological evolution, the emergence of small complex anatomical organisations made possible the emergence of ever larger and even more complex organisations. Complexity builds over time by a sequence of modifications to existing forms. There is both fossil and genetic evidence that the emergence of the general vertebrate organisation, and its subsequent modification into amphibians, reptiles, birds and mammals, occurred in this sequence.

> Experiments in Evolutionary Computation

Evolutionary algorithms are iterative processes that are structured on simplified logics abstracted from evolution, and are commonly used in many fields for solving non-linear and intractable problems. There are several different techniques, but they have in common several operations on the information or genome of each candidate form that are derived from biological evolution, including selection, reproduction and mutation. The process usually commences with the initiation of a random population of candidate forms, from which those that best match the desired criteria, the 'fittest' individuals, are selected. The use of evolutionary algorithms has been quite limited in architectural design, and algorithms that combine both growth (embryological developments) and evolution (operating on the genome) over multiple generations have not yet been successfully produced. The ambition of the experiments within the Emergent Technologies and Design seminar course is to explore the means of evolving context-sensitive and functionally specific architectural forms within typical architectural design software, such as Rhino, and with limited computational resources, typically a laptop computer.

The experiments begin with a series of geometric transformations (scale, rotate, move) that are applied to simple primitive geometries such as the cube, sphere, cone or torus. The first generations are run without scripts or code, using simple rules with parameters that allow for variation. These early generations are used to refine the relationships between 'breeding', the amount of random variation permitted in the genome, and the resultant complexity of form within the computational environment. The subsequent iterations of the process include both evolution over successive generations and the rules of embryological development of each individual within each population.

The numbers of successive generations and the number of individuals within each population of a single generation have an impact on the computational resources available and so have to be carefully calculated. The distribution of variation within each population, the percentage of deviation from the norm, has an impact on the calculation of fitness of the whole population. This is a significant point of bifurcation in the design of the algorithm, as 'fit' populations may have many very similar individuals and thus a good 'gene pool' but less fit populations may have one or two outstanding individuals within them. There are many ways of inducing environmental pressure on the populations, for example constraints on the total amount of surface 'material' available for the whole generation. The interaction of environmental constraints and population strategies are also amplified or inhibited by the kill strategy, how many if any of the parent individuals survive into the next generation, and how many individuals are bred from.

The 'growth' of each individual form within each population is manipulated by a set of actions that are designed to be the equivalent of the regulatory or homeobox genes acting on the axes and subdivisions of the 'bodyplan'. The earlier that 'mutation' or changes to the regulatory set are applied in the growth sequence, the greater the effect is on the completed or adult form. Random mutation applied to the homeobox produce changes in the number, size and shape of each of the subdivisions of the 'bodyplan'. Very significant differences in populations and individuals are produced by small changes in how much mutation is permitted in each generation, by varying the percentage of mutation in different segments of individual forms, and by constraining the differentiation of axial growth across the population. A simple example is that constraints on the ratio of lateral growth to vertical growth will tend to generate tall slender tower-like forms, whereas constraints on the range of permitted ratio of surface area to interior volume will tend to generate more rounded forms. Ratios may also be used for ranking the fitness of individual forms, such as the ratio of a linear dimension to a cross section, or the ratio of cross section to surface area.

Adding further constraints on the interactions between various modules or subdivisions of the 'bodyplan' may produce quite unexpected results. This is well known in living forms, for example in the growth of molars in mammals. Accelerating the growth of some molars will also tend to inhibit the growth of adjacent teeth, so that a great variety of different patterns and sizes of molars, canines and incisors can be achieved without having to have genes that act separately on each tooth.

The production of new and varied 'genomes' require the parameters for form generation and the analysis of how well each form matches the desired performance criteria to be made readable and calculable, to be ranked and to be recombined to create successive generations. In embryological development, the 'homeobox' is able to generate and evolve structures without itself having to continually evolve higher complexity. In computational terms, it may be regarded as a collection of switches that turn other processes on or off, at various times and in various regions during the digital growth of the specific structures. The combinations of switching, in differing sequences and at differing times and locations, is extremely powerful, capable of generating enormous variation and differentiation from a very small and computationally lean set of instructions.

> Spatial Subdivision Algorithm

This architectural algorithm derived from the study of evolutionary development was developed within the 'Emergence' seminar course by Sean Ahlquist and Moritz Fleischmann. The computational experiment explores digital mechanisms for the integration of multiple tasks and conditions. Based on the logic of evolutionary development, the algorithm is modular, non-hierarchical and uses the simplest tools, local interaction and feedback to develop higher-order structure, architectural form and behaviour. The strategy for evolving configurations of space and program is based on a

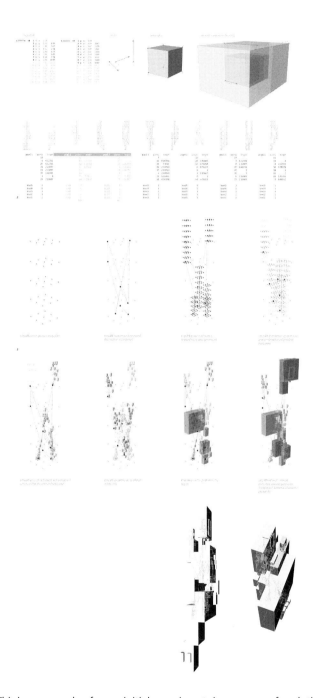

Figure 13.2: This is an example of some initial experiments in program of evolutionary-based algorithms. The method of subdivision was easily derived from a method of 10-scaling of a sample 30 polygonal shape. In this case a growth through simple iterative transform questions' was desired; leading to highly articulated results of interconnected continuous geometries. Emergence seminar research, 2008. Image credit: All images courtesy of Michael Weinstock, AA London. Emergence seminar research, 2008, Sean Ahlquist and Moritz Fleischmann.

spatial subdivision algorithm that was developed in McNeel's scripting language 'RhinoScript'. In this experiment, the algorithm begins with an overall building envelope and performs recursive steps of subdivision to distribute a series of spaces. The hierarchy of architectural programmes is determined, from which information is derived regarding the subdivision of program functions and quantities, and their particular requirements of space and organisation. The hierarchy ranks, among other parameters, the necessity of a program type to be consolidated with similar or related types or to be more widely distributed. The algorithm works only on the local level. Subdivision is triggered by the relative balance or imbalance of two conditions. The priority is to find connected volumes and insert the same or related program type. If a connected volume is too big for a program type then it is subdivided and the 'connected volume' is searched out again. Subdivision, when triggered, works with the geometry of the individual volume. The surfaces of the volume become the armatures for the subdivision of itself. This provides for varied amount of articulation, shifts in topology, and a high degree of extensibility.

TECTONICS

From Material
to Material
Tectonics

**Rivka Oxman
and Robert
Oxman**

Tectonics pertains to the generics of a theory of structuring.
Architectonics pertains to the generic conditions of the tectonic
contents of architecture. Tectonics in architecture is therefore
the culturally defined symbolic relationship between material
structure and architectural form. Architectonics particularly
relates to the experience of a "sense of structure" as well as to
the symbolic expression of the structural and material basis of
architecture. Frampton (1995) refers to this powerful theoretical
concept as "the poetics of construction," wherein a "poetics"
constitutes a general theory of the connection between a cultural
definition of the elements of architecture and their relationships.
The definition is often expanded to include tectonics as the
nature of the experience of architecture as a material culture.

The power of tectonics as a theoretical construct in design derives
from it's being an *operative theory* in the sense that defining
tectonics at a generic level enables multiple interpretations in
design. The evolution of theories of tectonic cultures is the
evolution of *tectonic paradigms* in architecture. It is the tectonic
paradigm that establishes an abstract and high-level *order* of
material components of architecture that creates a *tectonic
ethos*. The order is the symbolic definition of the generic parts as
a constructive system as well as the definition of their potential
relationships. Tectonics in architecture is the expression of the
generic material orders of architecture as a *paradigmatic order*
that supports multiple design interpretations.

The return to an interest in architectural tectonics as a productive
and generative body of theory reflects also the movement of
architectural culture in the last decades away from an emphasis
upon formal theoretical constructs such as *language* and towards a
foundational reorientation to architecture as a material practice.
The search for new paradigmatic tectonic theories has accompanied
this transition away from design generation based heavily upon the
formal and towards a revolutionary new understanding of the role
of material creation and the creation of generic *material systems* as
a central function of architectural design.

The role of digital culture in architecture is both cause and effect in
this process of cultural transformation *away from form and towards
material*. It is most appropriate to attempt to postulate the possible
meaning(s) of the term *digital tectonics*, as the interaction between
a new general theory of architectural tectonics and the evolution
over the last decade of a *digital materiality*. It is perhaps the

achievement of such a contemporary general theory of tectonics that various contemporary theories are attempting to articulate.

Tectonic theory as a medium of change was of profound significance in the transition of architectural culture from neo-classicism to modernism. Blau (2007) discusses Sigfried Giedion's attribution of the rise of a modernist tectonics to the influence of the new material technologies of steel, reinforced concrete and glass and their architectonic potential for the expression of transparency. If we can accept the equation of tectonic change with technological development, then the impact of digital media on architectural practice within the last decade would appear to be a motivating factor in a paradigm shift in tectonic theory of no less consequence than the emergence of modernist tectonics.

Modern tectonics introduced the generics of spatial experience – a *spatial tectonics* – into the traditional order of support, enclosure, separation and grounding. However, within Giedion's innovative definition of the interpenetration of interior and exterior space, the dynamics of section, and the four-dimensional order of spatial/structural experience, modern tectonics provided a paradigmatic tectonics capable of diverse generic interpretations. The significance of Frampton's exegesis of the poetics of construction in the modern age lies beyond the explication of structural logic and method of construction as the essence of architectural order. The poetics of modern tectonics is in the transcendence of the classical dictates of the concept of order and the creation of an open framework for the production of architectural mass-space relationships, each of which might be in its own way the manifestation of some cultural sensibility. The *open tectonics* produced both multiplicity of generative principles and the possibility for extension into new productive technologies. This evolutionary transition includes a chain of tectonic masterworks: the flexibility of Miesian universal space; the spatial dynamics of De Stijl's separating and surrounding planes; the structural logic of Nervi's Gatti Warehouse concrete ceiling with its isostatic ribbed structure; and the extension into the dynamic orders of masterworks such as Metabolist theory and practice and the serial orders of Safdie's Montreal Habitat.

We must be prepared to view digital tectonics as both the continuity with modern tectonics as well as an emerging radical departure from the idea of tectonics as an order of the physical component systems of architecture. Digital tectonics begins in the transition from the modernist poetics of the spatial/structural to a *new poetics of the material/structural*, or a *material tectonics*.

Concepts and computational practices of material structure and production have become one of the cultural foci of the digital presence in architecture. Material structure continues the emphasis upon continuities and dynamics that were among Giedion's indicators of modernist design. However, the material presence in digital tectonics is more complex. The complexity of material systems begins historically perhaps with the transition away from both modernist and phenomenological transparency and towards the *veiled transparency* of *Light Construction* (Blau, 2007). *Veiled transparency* as the diffused, differentiated transparency of Herzog/de Meuron's Birdsnest, or Ito/Balmond's Serpentine Pavilion signaled the emergence of a *striated tectonics*. If a smooth tectonics defines a physical ordering of tectonic components (space, structure, construction, grounding), then a striated tectonics is a complex relationship of procedures. It is a non-linear tectonics in which complexity can be generated by algorithms. The new sensibility of non-linear structuring has been characterized, *inter alia*, as *swarm tectonics* (Leach, 2004).

Material systems can be generated parametrically as non-linear structures and enclosures. Pattern is the underlying basis of the spatial structure of material. As a medium for material construction and mediation, *computational materialities* are an important class of digital tectonics. In various current material structures such as the Serpentine, the distinction between structure and surface (enclosure) is often blurred. Structure can also be created by material systems organized as arrays (Iwamoto, 2011), or in textile patterns (Spuybroek, 2006).

The design of material structure that is computationally represented and manipulated as *differentiated pattern* has become a contemporary design paradigm (Oxman and Oxman, 2010). Pattern and the spatial structure of material in natural and artificial morphogenesis has become a base of digital design knowledge. New interest is emerging regarding the classes of compositional/morphological strategies in digital tectonics (Testa and Weiser, 2006; Aranda/Lasch, 2006). The interaction of scales within natural structures is a source of knowledge for the design generation of digital tectonics.

We have attempted to present tectonics not only as a historical theory, but also as a foundational theory of design generation. As such tectonics is the core theory of contemporary digital design in architecture. Digital tectonics is not a representational order, but a network of relationships. Digital tectonics describes not physical object relationships as in modernist tectonics, but rather system contingencies as in algorithmic relationships. This is design creation not by the traditional manipulation of representations of design, but rather through the digital manipulation of numerical and geometric relationships. While the digital generation of a complex and differentiated materiality may be a characteristic contemporary medium of digital tectonics, the creation of digital effects and complexity representation may be today considered a *false tectonics*.

Parametric generation in digital tectonics abandoned the formalism of linguistically oriented form-generation systems. In the long-term evolution of a digital tectonics, digital generation attempts to supplant formal representational linguistic models of design. The open network sensibility, operativity, interactivity and procedural definition of design are among the characteristics of digital tectonics. To attempt to construe digital tectonics as a design style appears to be a misinterpretation of the evolution of a new tectonic paradigm. One way of interpreting Schumacher (2009) is as part of the discourse for the emergence of a unique tectonic paradigm. Schumacher's writings of the last decade, particularly those on the seminal role of parametric systems, parametric media and parametric design approaches, are a source for a potential interpretation of digital tectonics as a paradigmatic framework for design. Beyond the ideological affirmation of a new style, Schumacher's theoretical writings may be considered an affirmation in theory and practice of parametrics as a keystone of digital tectonics.

In any mapping of the conceptual structure of the digital in architecture, digital tectonics is a hub of all concepts related to digital design, fabrication and production processes. As such, computationally informed tectonics (N. Oxman, 2012) constitutes one of the foundation theories of tectonics in digital architecture. As digital design and production technologies continue to develop a formative role in material-based design, computationally informed tectonics may emerge as a guiding body of tectonics theory.

Kemp's writing on the epistemological significance of Balmond's conceptual production of design knowledge characterizes Balmond's revolutionary role in the production of tectonic theory and experimental digital design methodological practices. The natural philosophy of mathematics, morphology and biology are among the foundational sources of digital tectonics. This new tectonic epistemology was the basis of the design for the iconic projects that Balmond produced with the AGU (Balmond, 2006).

Spuybroek's recent publications (2009, 2011, 2012) continue his profound engagement with iconic writings of architectural and design theory. For him theoreticians such as John Ruskin and architectural experimentalists such as Frei Otto are part of the interface with the philosophical transformations of contemporary thought, and the challenges of emerging technologies. One article (Spuybroek, 2004) is seminal in his writing. His concepts and interest in "textile tectonics" introduce canonic design, theoretical, and operational issues of the digital in architecture. Spuybroek revisits and interrogates primary concepts in architectural and design theories such as configuration, classes of flexibility and their implications, as well as classes of tectonic morphologies as he articulates the theories underlying an approach to, and philosophy of, experimental design integrating analog machines and digital operations. Designer, theoretician and educator, he offers a unique model of the research-integrated digital design practitioner.

Balmond, Cecil (2004), "Geometry, Algorithm, Pattern," in Leach, Neil, Turnbull, David and Williams, Chris, eds., *Digital Tectonics*, Wiley-Academy, West Sussex, UK, pp. 128–135

Blau, Eve (2007), "Transparency and the Irreconcilable Contradictions of Modernity," in Lawrence, Amanda Reeser and Schafer, Ashley, eds., *Expanding Surface*, Praxis 9, pp. 50–59

Frampton, Kenneth (1995), *Studies in Tectonic Culture: The Poetics of Construction in Nineteenth and Twentieth Century Architecture*, MIT Press, Cambridge, MA

Fraser, Alayna (2007), "Translations: de Young Museum and the Walker Art Center," in Lawrence, Amanda Reeser and Schafer, Ashley, eds., *Expanding Surface*, Praxis 9, pp. 68–85

Iwamoto, Lisa (2011), "Line Array: Protocells as Dynamic Structure," in Spiller, Neil and Armstrong, Rachel eds., *Protocell Architecture*, AD (*Architectural Design*), Vol. 81, No. 2, March/April, pp. 112–121

Leach, Neil (2004), "Swarm Tectonics," in Leach, Neil, Turnbull, David and Williams, Chris eds., *Digital Tectonics*, Wiley-Academy, West Sussex, UK, pp. 70–77

Mertins, Detlef (2004), "Bioconstructivisms," in Spuybroek, Lars, *NOX: Machining Architecture*, Thames and Hudson, New York

Mitchell, William J. (1998), "Antitectonics: the Poetics of Virtuality," in Beckman, John, ed., *The Virtual Dimension: Architecture, Representation and Crash Culture*, Princeton Architectural Press, New York

Moussavi, Farshid (2009), *The Function of Form*, Actar, Barcelona, and the Harvard Graduate School of Design, Cambridge, MA

Reiser and Umemoto (2006), *Atlas of Novel Tectonics*, Princeton Architectural Press, New York

Shelden, Dennis R. (2006), "Tectonics, Economics and the Reconfiguration of Practice: the Case for Process Change by Digital Means," in Silver, Mike, ed., *Programming Cultures: Art and Architecture in the Age of Software*, AD (Architectural Design), Profile No. 182, Vol. 76, No. 4, July/August, pp. 82–87

Spuybroek, Lars (2004), *NOX: Machining Architecture*, Thames and Hudson, London

Spuybroek, Lars (2006), "Textile Tectonics: an Interview with Lars Spuybroek by Maria Ludovica Tramontin," in Garcia, Mark, ed., *Architectiles*, AD (*Architectural Design*), Profile No. 184, Vol. 76, No. 6, November/December, pp. 52–59

Spuybroek, Lars (2009), *Research and Design: the Architecture of Variation*, Thames and Hudson, New York

Spuybroek, Lars (2011), *Textile Tectonics: Research and Design*, NAI Publishers, Rotterdam

Spuybroek, Lars (2012), *The Sympathy of Things: Ruskin and the Ecology of Design*, NAI Publishers, Rotterdam

Tsukui, Noriko, ed., (2006), *Cecil Balmond*, a+u (*Architecture and Urbanism*) (Japan) Special Issue, November

Weinstock, Michael (2006), "Self-Organization and the Structural Dynamics of Plants," in Hensel, Michael, Menges, Achim and Weinstock, Michael, eds. *Techniques and Technologies in Morphogenetic Design*, AD (*Architectural Design*), Profile No. 180, Vol. 76, No. 2, March/April, pp. 26–33

> List of Key Concepts

architectonics
computationally informed tectonics
differentiated pattern
digital materiality
digital tectonics
informed tectonics
material tectonics
multiplicity
open tectonics
operative tectonics
pattern
performatively informed tectonics

productive technologies
soft tectonics
spatial tectonics
striated tectonics
swarm tectonics
tectonic ethos
tectonic knowledge
tectonic paradigms
tectonics
transparency
veiled transparency
virtual tectonics

The development of digital design and fabrication technologies is enabling an expanding interrelationship between technology and design. Material-based design is defined as a computational informing process that enhances the integration between structure, material, and form within the logic of fabrication technologies. The term informed tectonics is introduced as a central concept in material-based design. The current research aim is to formulate taxonomy based on a series of selected case studies embedded in the context of current knowledge. The taxonomy is derived from observations and critical analysis of case studies. Through the comparative analysis of selected case studies of material-based design in research and practice, conceptual models processes and principles have been identified and formulated.

The development of digital technologies is enabling new processes of design collaboration and a growing interrelationship between technology and design. We are currently witnessing a transition within the digital design process. The growing affinity between the interest in the role of materials in design and in the relationship to tectonics has produced a "new materiality". The emerging new synthesis of material in design is resulting in the formulation of conceptual principles of the formal, structural and material in new digital orders. Furthermore, the logic of these structural and material principles is recently becoming integrated within the rationale of emerging fabrication technologies, thus enriching the possibility of the potential integration of design with fabrication and production.

The origin of current fabrication technologies can be traced back to the evolution of computer technologies associated with automation and production of the final stages of design and to the first CAD/CAM systems (Schodek, *et al.*, 2004). Today with advances in the integration of digital design and fabrication, the designer has become directly involved with materialization technologies in both design conception and design production stages (Kolarevic, 2003; Kolarevic & Klinger, 2008). Processes of rapid prototyping (RP) employing fabrication technologies are an integral component in design and were being recognized as a significant technology that supports the full spectrum of digital design as a paperless process integrating computational models of generation and manufacturing in a single process (Sass & Oxman, 2006; Shea & Cagan, 1999). As a result, the architect and other design professions are regaining an important degree of knowledge and control of material and material processes in their designs.

The convergence of digital design, materialization processes, and fabrication technologies is breeding a shift in material-related design research and practices. According to Sheila Kennedy

14

Informed Tectonics in Material-based Design

Rivka Oxman

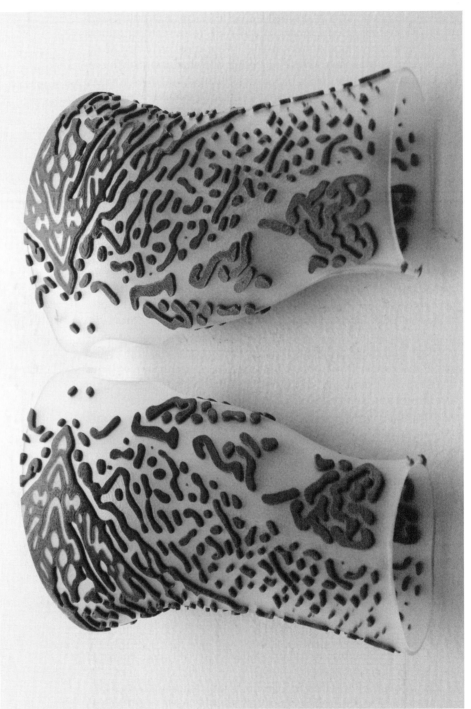

Figure 14.1

(Kennedy, 2011) there are two types of practice model: the traditional horizontal model, and a new vertical model. The horizontal model is the traditional model of design based on well-understood design models and knowledge. The vertical model emphasizes synthesis of new techniques, technologies and experimental models of design. Material-based design as the integration of digital design, materialization and fabrication is becoming a dominant emerging design model, among experimental professional practices (Barkow, 2010). Current discourse on material studies (Schröpfer, 2011) associates this material integrative design with the term, tectonic, in work related to, for example, smart materials and technologies (Addington & Schodek, 2005); in studies of responsive materials and technological processes (Kennedy, 2011); and in studies of current effects of material manufacturing and fabrication technologies in design (Kolarevic & Klinger, 2008). In this research we propose a concept termed informed tectonics as a key component of one of the dominant contemporary vertical, experimental models of design in material-based design.

Architecture is in a historic process of returning to its structural and material sources. In doing so, it is reformulating the relationships between form, structure, material, fabrication and construction. The return of design to its material sources through material-based design and fabrication is a design cultural process that raises issues related to fundamental considerations of our models of design. With this shift towards a new interest in material in design, the concept of tectonics has begun to provide important contributions to theories of material-based design. It is in the exegesis of this term and its rich cultural history that we can begin to understand the developing focal role and operative function of *tectonics* in digital technologies of material-based design.

As a means of identifying the singularities of tectonics in material-based design, we introduce the term, *informed tectonics*. It is the explication and transparency of information that provides the holistic integration of design, materialization and fabrication. In this novel integration, it is also the affinity between tectonics and digital technologies that enhances the design possibilities for the integration of form, structuring and material principles. In order to study the development of these technologies and design processes, we have undertaken research by the critical and comparative analysis of selected case studies. In this research the evolution of the concept of informed tectonics is presented; and different tectonic models and material-based design processes are identified and formulated. The contribution of these models to a new theoretical framework in design is discussed.

Facing page

Figure 14.1: Carpal Skin: Prototype for a customized carpal tunnel syndrome splint: Neri Oxman Media Lab. Image credit: Neri Oxman, Media Lab, MIT.

In a prior pilot research, first reported in the journal *Architectural Design* under the title, *The New Structuralism* (Oxman & Oxman, 2010b) a collection of a seminal body of theoretical papers and design works was documented and presented. The current research builds upon the earlier work and attempts comparative analysis of the case studies as a corpus of significant cases of material-based design selected from leading research-oriented design practices both in architecture and structural engineering.

In the following sections we first introduce the concept of the tectonic. A review of historical references and relevant concepts is presented and discussed. The second section introduces the concept of *informed tectonics* and discusses its importance as a theoretical foundation of material-based design. The third section presents a selection of case studies that illustrates principles and different models of informed tectonics. The description and demonstration of derived knowledge, including the development of novel models of integrative material-based design is presented in the fourth section. Finally, summary and conclusions are discussed with respect to the significance of informed tectonics in material-based design.

> 1 Tectonics: Theoretical Framework

As the operative design source of the new materiality in architecture and design, *tectonics* is becoming a seminal concept in design discourse. It is the emerging ontology of "digital culture", along with its technological potential that is contributing singular importance to the term and a revival of interest in its cultural history. The term tectonics was derived from the Greek word, *tekton*, meaning carpenter, or builder. Tectonics is a seminal concept that defines the nature of the relationship between architectural design and its structural and material properties. The changing definition of the symbiotic relationship between architecture and structure may be considered one of the formative influences on the evolution of this concept in different historical periods (R. Oxman, 2010). In different periods the emphasis has changed depending on the contextual content of place and culture. Contextual knowledge reflects local environmental conditions and cultural values, as well as traditional ways of building and construction (Schröpfer, 2011). In different periods throughout history, tectonic discourse has continually redefined the elements of the tectonic relationship as well as their prioritizing.

Today, due to computational processes enabling the mediation between form, structure and material properties, tectonics is again becoming a seminal and operative concept of design. Traditional tectonic relationships are undergoing a revolutionary transformation; these relationships are now capable of being explicitly *informed* and thus mediated through digital media from conception to production. This *multistage continuously informed mediation of the tectonic content* of designs is an essential component of material-based design.

The work presented below is based on a new interpretation of the concept of tectonics by introducing the idea of an *informed tectonics*. In all stages of digital design, tectonics is capable of being mediated through being 'informed' by the explicit knowledge of its making and fabrication. In the following sections the contribution of these ideas and their implications for a theory and methodology of material-based design is presented.

1.1 Vernacular Tectonics – the Origin of the Triumvirate of Form, Structure and Material in Design: The origins of tectonic expression appear to reside in vernacular building traditions. Vernacular architecture represents the essence of material technologies in providing a direct understanding and expression of the structural and constructional nature of the material. It defines the essence of the relationship between form and structural and material relationships in being a direct statement of constructional processes, where choice of local material results in the expression of form and structure. The choices of structural materials inform the construction process. Such tectonic interrelationships become highly intricate and complex in various vernacular building technologies, for example, in the dynamic temporary structures of nomadic traditions. Vernacular construction encompasses both the structural system and the constructional process that inform one another. Building construction in the vernacular proceeds essentially without design and was frequently the fruit of craft traditions such as carpentry.

In the vernacular traditional material technologies evolve to become building systems. Such systems more or less directly express both the material origins and the constructional process. In forms of traditional vernacular building material and the technologies of making are seminal factors in the culture of design (Sennett, 2008). It is this direct expression of the material content that is characteristic of the vernacular and its characteristic emphasis upon the explicit tectonic expression of the material and the making process.

In its direct expression of material, structure and construction, the vernacular is an implicit "poetics", or explicative theory. Its tectonic provides an essential, or sublime, expression of the constructional potential of the material, for example, in the traditional Japanese house, construction is an essential component of space as well as the major source of form. In this sense of a design informed by material and constructional logic, the vernacular may be seen as an analogous source of contemporary material-based design. Vernacular tectonics are also a source for a contemporary material-based design that is now finding tectonic principles in extending the logic of craft traditions such as weaving.

1.2 Tectonic as Culture: Prioritizing Building and Construction: The evolution of tectonic theory since the nineteenth century and through the modern period reflects different views of tectonic theories related to the nature of design. The Greek word *tekton* later became the *archi-tecton, or master builder* (Frampton, 1995). According to Frampton the ordering of architecture, structure, material and construction evolved from aesthetic and cultural interpretations of expressive qualities.

Historic usage adapted the term tectonics to transform the concept from that of the builder to that of an *integrated building system*, particularly in nineteenth-century interpretations of Classical architecture. Gottfried Semper (1803–1879) referred to tectonics as a phenomenon that defined the use of different materials in architecture as a cultural phenomenon thus introducing an early cultural interpretation of tectonics. He was referring to an explicit re-ordering of the physical relationships of structure and material, and the case of Semper is relevant to the tectonic re-ordering that currently occurring.

The interpretation of tectonics as the active role of structural form in the development of architectural form (Frampton, 1995) transcended the purely visual, or experiential, content of tectonics. This position considered tectonics as an essential element in the development of modern architectural form. Frampton thus emphasized a more proactive role for structure and construction in achieving a potential "poetics of construction" as a foundation of modern architecture.

For Frampton, the integration of structural and constructional contributions to architectural form, space and order is one of the unique contributions of modern architecture. He argued that modern architecture is more about structure and construction than space and abstract form. In this he departs from the position of other major theorist/historians of modern architecture such as Pevsner and Giedeon. However, his theory maintains a balance between structure/construction and space/form. This expanded interpretation also brings it closer to a contemporary definition in which fabrication and manufacturing are viewed as *digitally informed systems*.

Today, the prioritizing of materialization is a dominant theme of the cultural shift. As a design cultural phenomenon, contemporary tectonics is currently turning away from the interpretation of tectonics in the modern period. While modernism separated shape, structure and surface, tectonics in material-based design culture integration is emphasized. As a result the integrating of form, structure, material and their fabrication/construction process return material and production considerations to the definition of the tectonic.

1.3 Digital Tectonics – as Virtual and Physical Materiality: Theories and technologies of digital design (Oxman, 2006, 2008) have contributed new meaning to the term tectonics. The digital has become an informing media in its ability to *integrate, mediate and differentiate tectonic content*. The term tectonics as enhanced by computational affordance has transformed the concept of tectonics.

As a result of the enhanced tectonic capabilities deriving from digital media and computational technologies, various different approaches and definitions of the term *digital tectonics* have been proposed over the last decade.

- *Digital tectonics as virtual materiality*

The term *digital tectonics* was first introduced by William Mitchell (Mitchell, 1998). He proposed the term, *virtual materiality*, to describe a virtual computational space that accommodates the *representation of materiality*. This was seen as a counterposition to that of Frampton (Frampton, 1995). In defining the possibility and potential of a digital tectonics, Mitchell also superseded the 'earthwork' that Gottfried Semper (Semper, 1989) identified as one of the four elements of architecture.

Today the concept of digital tectonics is expanding the function of materiality in design and contributing to a new perspective of computational methods of tectonics.

- *Digital tectonics as physical materiality*

Various theoretical approaches to the term digital tectonics have been proposed as a characterization of the influence of emerging digital media and technologies upon the exploration and modification of conventional conceptions of tectonics in architectural practice. Liu and Lim (2006) have identified digital tectonics with dynamic factors of motion, information, generation and fabrication. These studies analyzed changes in traditional construction and presented the relationship between design and digital technologies, for example, the design of responsive envelopes. The role of digital tectonics is thus seen also to be formative in the exploration and production of new constructional technologies. Along with emerging technologies, there is a growing interest in motion, adaptive-responsive systems, and information embedding in building systems, all of which are dynamic characteristics. Here, digital tectonics relates to media that support design processes of four-dimensional capability, that is, the time-based and responsive dimensions.

- *Digital tectonics as fabricated materiality*

Other works (Kolarevic & Klinger, 2008) discussed the change in traditional methods of construction and the growing importance of the relationship between digital methods of design and their implications for production in computationally controlled fabrication technologies.

- *Digital tectonics as structured materiality*

Other theoreticians propose digital tectonics as a *paradigm shift of design thinking* (Leach, Turnbull, & Williams, 2004) that may be characterized as a *structural turn*. They describe the increasing importance of structure and materials in current design and the new creative synthesis of architecture and structural engineering. They also make reference to the "technological possibilities afforded by the digital realm".

- *Digital tectonics as digital form finding and morphogenetic processes*

The term morphogenesis defines the relationship between tectonic material concepts in form finding processes and in nature (R. Oxman, 2010). Numerous contemporary architectural engineering designs have employed *digital tectonics in digital morphogenesis*. Pioneering experimental and methodological processes related to *digital morphogenesis* can be found in the work, among others, of the Japanese engineer Sasaki (Sasaki, 2007) and the British engineer Cecil Balmond (2006).

- *Digital tectonics as adaptive materiality*

Adaptive buildings are associated today with the field of "smart materials" (Addington & Schodek, 2005). Adaptive behaviour is replacing mechanical principles with behavioural properties of smart materials introducing novel characteristics in responsive-adaptive architectural systems (Kennedy, 2011). The designer in such systems becomes responsible to design an adaptive material system as a set of desired affects produced by the system performance of materials with minimum material and energy.

1.4 Summary: Digital Tectonics and Materiality: In a revolutionary way digital tectonics transforms the ontology of modernist tectonics from the logic of order and aesthetics to new structuring (tectonic) processes and behavioural models of form, structure, and material. While modernism separated structure and envelope, digital tectonics tends to integrate tectonic relationships in novel ways. Modernism emphasized structural expression in the surface through structural form and performance. Current approaches to digital materiality frequently express materiality through integrating surface and material; this amplifies the role of material as part of the aesthetics of the tectonic.

Design by the digital and the material is becoming a process in which the synthesis of architect, engineer and fabricator again controls the responsibility for the total processes of conceptualization and materialization (R. Oxman, 2011). This change provides a reconciliation of digital tectonics with the arguments of Frampton (1995) and Semper (1989). The changing definition of tectonic relationship may be considered one of the formative effects of the emergence of digital tectonics.

In the following sections material-based design is defined as a computational informing process that enhances the integration between structure, material, and form within the logic of fabrication technologies. The term *informed tectonics* is introduced as a central concept in material-based design.

> 2 Informed Tectonics in Material-based Design

In order to accommodate all levels of synthesis in design and materialization processes, the term *informed tectonics* is proposed and introduced. *Informed tectonics, in material-based design, is mediated by being computationally 'informed' by explicit knowledge of its design, its making and fabrication.*

An introduction to informed tectonics and its importance as a *theoretical foundation for material-based design* is presented below. The historical background, terminological content, and basic concepts and definitions are reviewed and formulated.

2.1 Informed Tectonics: Conventional designation of the interaction between the architect and engineer has traditionally been characterized by the sequential stages. A formal concept is first conceived by the architect in early stages of design and subsequently structured and materialized in collaboration with the engineer. We have found that design collaboration is no longer *a posteriori*. All three of the design components are now involved at the earliest generative stage. This early collaboration in conceptual design also brings to the fore the design content of materialization by fabrication and manufacturing technologies.

These approaches challenge orthodox working methods of design. Now both the architect and the engineer are becoming involved at the earliest conceptual and generative stage. Classic examples of design collaborations that accommodate structural and material considerations early in the design process may be found in process descriptions of the Serpentine Pavilion, 2002, by Toyo Ito and Balmond (AGU, 2008) and the collaboration of Ito and Mutsuro Sasaki (Sasaki, 2007) on the Kakamigahara Crematorium (Xie et al., 2004).

Today, with the reintroduction of material-based design, early concepts of form finding are being revisited and providing a radical shift in experimental design. Classical works of form finding were those of the architects and engineers Gaudí, Otto, Isler and others. These experiments can be regarded as the first models of informed tectonics. While these pioneering experiments were experimental and analogical, digital media and emerging fabrication technologies are establishing novel forms of *digitally informed tectonics*.

The changing definition of the relationship between design and production may be considered one of the formative effects of digital tectonics. New concepts such as *Digital Materiality* (Gramazio, Kohler, & Oesterle, 2010) and *Digital Material* (N. Oxman, 2011) are now available for the designer as new forms of tectonic processes.

2.2 Conceptualization in Material-based Design: Material-based design is now accommodated in the early conceptual stages of design. In the work of Gramazio & Kohler, for example, computational programming of production data integrates design with the materialization process. Material conditions and assembly logic are thus integrated and can be used as the basis for design. *Digital Materiality* (Gramazio et al., 2010) is now available for the designer as new forms of tectonic representation in which design components are mutually informed in the processes of design conceptualization.

In fact, in many respects, materiality is frequently the basis for design conceptualization. Fabrication is therefore not merely a modelling technique, but a change in the generation and making of designs. The current impact of materialization concepts upon form has become one of the main influences in contemporary design.

> 3 Research on Principles and Models of Informed Tectonics

3.1 Introduction: The research methodology consisted of the selection and analysis of a case study sample of architectural and engineering design practices noted for their experiments in the integration of original computational methods of material-based design. The resulting iconic projects have demonstrated original principles and models of informed tectonics. Observations and comparative analyses have been the basis for the identification of changes in traditional design processes and the classification of concepts, processes and media that are contributing to new forms of material-based design.

Through the analysis of the case studies, we have attempted to formulate novel models of design and, in particular, to explore how the structuring, encoding, and fabricating of material systems have begun to contribute to the formation of diverse models of material-based design. A main objective of the analysis of case studies was also to identify new bodies of knowledge, models, concepts and principles in the actual practices of material-based design. Finally, we have attempted to illustrate and compare the unique contribution of each of the case studies.

3.2 Research Framework: The study and characterization of how design practitioners think belongs to a long research tradition in design studies (Cross, 2006, 2011). The pilot study was undertaken over a period of eighteen months under the sponsorship of the British architectural and design journal, *Architectural Design* which published a special issue on *The New Structuralism: Design, Engineering and Architectural Technologies* (Oxman & Oxman, 2010a). This international journal has had a long-term historical commitment to provide a professional forum for discourse in both theory and praxis.

The research underlying this publication placed an emphasis upon the impact of engineering design and emerging technologies on the design process. The original intention was to base the research upon a sample of the leading practices in design engineering that had also been prominent in theoretical discourse and publication with respect to emerging technologies. The process of sample selection was undertaken through a literature survey in the fields of recent research and theoretical studies in design engineering and material technologies. The selection process attempted to identify a body of work representative and comprehensive enough to foreground emerging theories and design models. The final selection included eight participants in design engineering and seven in material technologies. The latter group was diverse including architectural researchers in academic contexts, experimental practices, new professional specializations, etc.

Virtually all of the fifteen participants have some form of academic involvement.

The participants were approached directly. Each produced a written document relating to the issues, concepts, practices and models which defined their experience of the relationships between architectural design, design engineering and material technologies.

Major concepts and related issues are presented below:

• *Types of holistic models of material-based design (from conception to materialization)*

What types of integrated conceptual processes can be identified? i.e. initial form; form–structure; form–structure–material; form–structure–material fabrication. What diverse models of materialization processes can be defined? i.e. fabrication; material fabrication; manufacturing.

• *Information flow – supporting digitally informed processes in material-based design*

What types of knowledge, models and techniques are supporting information flow in the above models of material-based design?

• *Re-ordering of tectonic relationships*

What are the re-ordering of priorities in the relationships among form, structure, and material in material-based design and how they are achieved?

• *Integration of material fabrication and manufacturing processes in tectonic processes*

What is the role of material fabrication in the material-based design? How is it supported by information flow, and in what stage is it incorporated?

The cases studies presented in the next section were selected as significant examples of diverse models of *informed tectonics in material-based design*. Each of the cases was selected and was comparatively analysed by the concepts presented above. Each case demonstrates a unique *informed tectonic model* that is based on digital informing processes.

> 4 Informed Tectonics – Case Studies in Material-based Design

Various models that contribute to the theory of the informed tectonic were identified based on the analysis of case studies.

4.1 Informed Tectonics: The Rationalization Model: The *construction-aware design model* (Pottmann, 2010; Pottmann *et al.*, 2007; Pottmann, Schiftner, & Johannes, 2008) aims to rationalize the process of selecting optimal solutions on the basis of geometry, production, fabrication and construction. It is based on a rationalization model incorporating knowledge of a specific material used, specific panel types, sub-construction, etc. through research and design collaboration between mathematicians, designers, architects, structural and construction engineers.

- *Types of holistic models of material-based design (from conception to materialization)*

Rationalization processes for informed tectonics aim at providing digital design tools and enabling a completely digital workflow from design conception to manufacturing (developed especially for highly complex geometries).

- *Information flow – types of knowledge, models and techniques*

Information flow in rationalization processes encapsulates foundational knowledge of Architectural Computational Geometry. Research in architectural geometry (AG) and digital design has an important role in enabling a complete digital workflow from design to manufacturing. Computational models that support this kind of digital workflow incorporating structural and material properties; construction processes and manufacturing technologies that are known as "rationalization processes" (Veltkamp, 2007). Research on rationalization models can be found in the work of research groups such as the Advanced Geometry Unit (AGU) at Arup, and the Specialist Modelling Group (SMG) of Foster and Partners.

- *Re-ordering of tectonic relationships*

Rationalization processes re-compute the geometry of a given digital model attempting to make minimal deviation from the original design taking into account the integration of form, structure, material construction and manufacturing constraints.

- *Integration of material fabrication and manufacturing processes in tectonic processes*

Fabrication is not yet fully implemented as part of rationalization processes. Extensive research is currently done in order to develop a general (rather than specific) fabrication-aware design tool that can include consideration of structural constraints, material types and types of fabrication technologies.

Example: *Skipper Library conceptual design – Formtexx; consultation by Helmut Pottman Vienna University of Technology.*

The rationalization model is illustrated by the Skipper Library. In this project a *construction-aware* digital design environment has incorporated knowledge of the material used, panel types, and panel geometry options. The panelisation of the Skipper Library example issued by Formtexx is based on strips of constant width that demonstrates how a non-regular connectivity of strips can be used to structurally materialize the form computed by Evolute's (Evolute GmbH) panelisation tool (Pottmann, 2010).

4.2 Informed Tectonics: The Evolutionary Model: Evolutionary processes and types of tectonic systems that are composed of components contain design logic and are interesting in the way they inform integrated tectonics processes in design. Bollinger, Grohmann, and Tessmann (2010) present an evolutionary model in their work on the LAVA's, VOxEL, extension for the Hochschule für Technik in Stuttgart.

- *Types of holistic models of material-based design (from conception to materialization)*

In this model a design system composed of design components has a certain integrated design and tectonic logic. This logic characterizes an integrated formal-structural conceptual model that emerges from given structural and formal relationships of individual components in a bottom-up strategy in the conceptual stage.

- *Information flow – types of knowledge, models and techniques*

Computational algorithms support in this case a unique informed relationship between form and structure. Information flow related to generative and evaluative criteria that characterize the design logic; this model originates in this case from the formal and structural relationships of a particular design system. By running a computational optimization iterative process, best solutions of previous generation cycles are selected.

- *Re-ordering of tectonic relationships*

Individual components address both architectural (form) and engineering (structural) tectonic logic. The tectonic relationships are integrated and reconfigured by mutation processes generating new iterations of satisfied solutions until both architectural and structural tectonics and spatial criteria are satisfied.

- *Integration of material fabrication and manufacturing in tectonic processes*

This logic can potentially be rationalized as a driver in fabrication processes. Interactive evolutionary processes of form generation and negotiation processes between form and structure may be linked to the fabrication process.

Example: *LAVA's, VOxEL extension for the Hochschule für Technik in Stuttgart, Bollinger + Grohmann Engineers, Germany.*

The VOxEL project (Bollinger, Grohmann, and Tessmann, 2010) illustrates both the structural and the organizational principles in a conceptual model of a square-edged sponge configuration. A finite-element-method analysed the structural behaviour based on the logic of interconnected elements that presented a new typology. As characteristic of complex structural designs, the system properties are not defined by individual elements, but by sets of elements. The behaviour of the interdependent sets of elements emerges from intricately informed evolutionary computational processes without any top-down control. A finite-element-method that analysed the structural behaviour based on the logic of interconnected elements of an irregular "sponge" organization. The structural performance of the configuration becomes the fitness criteria in the evolutionary process that provides a close interlocking of the same elements for spatial and structural organization.

4.3 Informed Tectonics: The Flow Model – from Design to Production: The process of preparation for final fabrication and construction may depend upon a reinterpretation of specific tectonic properties of each individual project. This process is based on the preparation of a customized system. Specific design input is translated to production data depending on shape, surface quality, materials and fabrication methods including the logistics and assembly sequences which are project specific (Scheurer, 2010).

- *Types of holistic models of material-based design (from conception to materialization)*

The core model is "redefined" due to specific considerations of specific fabrication requirements of the final fabrication–construction–assembly stage of the design

- *Information flow – types of knowledge, models and techniques*

The integration of knowledge of structure, materials, fabrication, and construction in design is a key factor in the creation of informed design and production processes. The knowledge is incorporated in a continuous flow of information including and mapping the various types of data formats. This is a new profession which needs a new skill.

- *Re-ordering of tectonic relationships*

Individual prefabricated detailed parts and segments of intersecting girders are fabricated and assembled by CNC (Computer Numerical Control) technology.

- *Integration of material fabrication and manufacturing processes in tectonic processes*

CNC provides seamless integration of design and fabrication processes by facilitating knowledge and digital information controlled by machining data. Fabrication becomes an interface between architecture engineering and manufacturing.

Example: *Nine Bridges Golf Resort Yeoju; South Korea; Shigeru Ban, Blumer-Lehmann AG SJB Kempter-Fitze & Création Holz; consultation by Fabian Scheurer, designtoproduction, Zurich–Stuttgart.*

In this project (Scheurer, 2010) a set of canopies was composed of interwoven timber girder elements in a "craft-like tectonics". The girder elements were assembled from intricately detailed glulam prefabricated segments. The woven timber girders were assembled from 3500 intricately detailed prefabricated segments of intersecting girders that were fabricated by CNC machines (*designtoproduction*, Scheurer, 2010).

4.4 Informed Tectonics: Material Structuring and the Timber-fabric Model: The material structuring model presents designs in which material structures may have textile-like generative capability as well as adaptability (Weinand & Hudert, 2010). Traditionally, building structures have striven for rigidity whereas textiles embody the properties of elasticity and suppleness. When exposed to an increasing load, the elasticity of wood, for example, may enable deformation instead of destruction.

- *Types of holistic models of material-based design (from conception to materialization)*

Timber-fabric is an experimental approach which integrates interdisciplinary design: architecture, structural engineering and timber construction. This body of experiments is intended to explore and to demonstrate how textile principles can be applied to construction scales.

- *Information flow – types of knowledge, models and techniques*

Two planar interbreeding timber panels and the usage of particular techniques of assembly related to given material properties, have produced a structurally efficient construct by employing digital processes. Software that simulates material behaviour such as elastic deformation has been developed to integrate a textile module with digital design and material fabrication.

- *Re-ordering of tectonic principle and relationships*

This experiment is intended to explore and to demonstrate how organizational principles of one material system can be re-ordered and applied to construction scale. In this case principles of material organization of textile are transferred and tested in timber construction.

- *Integration of material fabrication and manufacturing processes in tectonic processes*

The application of textile principles to tectonic context of timber construction demonstrates an interdisciplinary approach in which architecture turns from traditional design to material-based fabrication design practice.

Example: *Timber-Fabrics; Yves Weinand, EPFL Lausanne.*

In this experiment the basic unit of a textile module is essential to the structural development of the timber fabric. This process is generic and can be applied to other materials and applications. Integrated tectonic qualities at different scales can be developed in material construction and contribute to unique tectonic properties. The application of textile principles in the context of timber construction demonstrates intrinsic contrasting physical conditions (Weinand & Hudert, 2010). The ability of a structure to adapt to a load is a significant property; when exposed to an increasing load, the elasticity of the wood enables deformation instead of destruction.

4.5 Informed Tectonics: Robotic Fabrication as a Large-scale Customization Model: Robotic fabrication can extend the scale of conventional construction methods and of craft-based fabrication methods by enabling the performance of complex and large-scale customized tasks (Bechthold, 2010). The industrial robot is a generic tool that is not specialized for any specific action. According to Bechthold, today the emphasis on customization considers the performance of industrial robots as a contribution to the production of non-standard assemblies using normative construction materials. The manufacturing machine integrates the specific material logic and can execute any combination of newly defined actions.

- *Types of holistic models of material-based design (from conception to materialization)*

The design model in this approach is based on automatic generative code that is changing the mode of design generation from top-down to bottom-up processes.

- *Information flow – types of knowledge, models and techniques*

Information flow is achieved by automating the generation of robotic code directly from parametric shape models that address the need for complexity and variability of non-standard customized parts.

- *Re-ordering of tectonic relationships*

From shape to material production: parametric shape models are driving the production of a variable sheet metal surface.

- *Integration of material fabrication and manufacturing processes in material-based processes*

Industrial robots are becoming accepted as fabrication tools. The ability to control issues of collision detection, singularities, payload restrictions and repeatability tolerances by arms and elements of robotic manipulators is becoming an essential task in fabrication environment. Development of new supportive automated programming strategies and languages is becoming a need in fabrication research and development.

Example: *Variable sheet metal surface; Martin Bechthold, GSD Harvard University.*

An early prototype of this approach is presented. It demonstrates the ability to automate the programming of a prototypical robotic sheet metal environment. The highly individualized sheet metal components in this case were cut on a robotic water jet.

4.6 Informed Tectonics: The Digital Materiality Model: This model is based on the ability to convert architectural and design representations into an explicit machine code (Gramazio & Kohler, 2008). This work (Gramazio *et al.*, 2010) demonstrates how design, fabrication, production, and manufacturing can be integrated directly in a single design process. In this work, the encoding of the assembly logic of a material system can be integrated with a fabrication machine that is capable of physically carrying out different actions of assembly. Fabrication becomes an interface between architecture, structural design and manufacturing. These novel production means negotiate between performance requirements and component-based design systems which manipulate material design systems.

- *Types of holistic models of material-based design (from conception to materialization)*

The digital materiality model provides seamless integration of design and fabrication from conception to materialization processes by facilitating a generative process of shape and form related to structure and material that is controlled by machine data.

- *Information flow – types of knowledge, models and techniques*

Information flow is achieved by facilitating a generative process of shape and form related to structure and material that is controlled by machine data. Digital design code of complex instructions is driving the production of physical and material products. Building scale elements are designed as material systems that behave and adapt according to specific materials and assembly logics. The manufacturing process consists of the data required to control the robot and the respective properties of the tool that is being used. End-effectors define the material machining process that is attached to the end of a kinematic chain. The design of custom end-effectors enables the designer to control and conceptualize the material processes. The digital design code of complex instructions drives the production of the design, e.g. in robotic brick laying.

- *Re-ordering of tectonic relationships*

The encoding of desired macro-design geometrical properties is superimposed upon the logic of a specific material system. The geometrical properties are designed according to their unique system assembly logic that represents both shape and material in specific organizational geometric pattern. Material-based components such as bricks which have certain geometrical attributes are being displayed by the machine according to a specific tectonic logic of any particular material system. These are designed according to their unique assembly-tectonic logic that represents the shape and material of a desired organizational pattern.

- *Integration of material fabrication and manufacturing processes in material-based processes*

Robotic-fabrication processes and the encoding of production data integrate design with the materialization process. This process potentially shapes both the design of structural and material elements in an encoded formal design process. In this case, both the design and construction processes may be robotically controlled. This customization potential also contributes to the function of fabrication as a generative process.

   Example: *Sequential Wall, West Fest Pavilion; Fabio Gramazio and Matias Kohle, ETH Zurich.*

In these two case studies, material-based design components such as bricks have geometrical attributes and a constructional logic. Gramazio & Kohler have demonstrated how the encoding of the assembly logic of a material system can be integrated with a fabrication machine that is capable of physically carrying out different actions of assembly. These large-scale building elements are designed as material systems that behave and adapt according to a specifically desired materials and assembly logic.

The "West Fest Pavilion" employs standard wooden battens forming columns that are transformed into large cantilevers that support a roof. The robotic fabrication allows modifying the dimensions of individual battens during the production process. The columns constitute the spatial layout as well as the carrying structure of the pavilion that satisfied the architectural organization, the structural performance and the assembly process. The coding of the assembly logic is essential in this approach. The "Sequential Wall" project presents a similar fabrication process. In this case performance requirements of an exterior wall satisfy weather conditions and thermal insulation. The physical conditions defined the arrangement and modes of variations generated by design algorithms.

4.7 Informed Tectonics: Digital Material and the Variable Property Model: In this work the digital tectonic synthesizes principles of natural design that are applied to generate a heterogeneous material structure through *digitally fabricated material*. This experimental design research has been developed and termed, *variable property design* (N. Oxman, 2010, 2011).

The following model defines the shift from *a geometric-centric design* to *material-based* design in which digital materiality is encoded as a basis for design with *fabricated digital materials* of heterogeneous behaviours. The following work, models and processes in material-based design computation were inspired by nature and by biological materials (Oxman, 2009). In this approach, the material system is informed by external performative environ-mental forces that act upon it in a similar way to nature. In nature, structural biomaterials form microstructures engineered to adapt to external constraints during continuous growth throughout their life span. This is similar to bone structures that are remodelled under structural or mechanical load. In nature, the sequence *form–structure–material* is inverted bottom-up. For example, in bones and cellular structures shape is directly informed by the materials from which they are made. In nature, in most cases, material comes first. This ability to distribute material properties by way of locally optimizing regions of varied external requirements, such as bone's ability to remodel its material structure under altering mechanical loads, or wood's capacity to modify its shape by way of containing moisture, is facilitating the variable property model.

- *Types of holistic models of material-based design (from conception to materialization)*

The variable property model provides a seamless integration of design and fabrication integrating material specification and shape giving. Where material has traditionally been regarded as a feature of form, in this model an alternative schema is presented where the properties of the material are regarded as the main driver of formal and structural expression.

- *Information flow – types of knowledge, models and techniques*

Computational algorithms of generation and evaluation along with digital design machine code are driving single information flow by facilitating a fabrication process of 3D printing machines. Various combinations of digitally informed material are printed and controlled by specified desired material properties.

- *Re-ordering of tectonic relationships*

Form–structure–material is inverted bottom-up. The encoding of material properties and the logic of specific material system is driving the formal qualities of the tectonic product. The geometrical properties are formed in response to their unique material system. Shape and variable properties are directly informed and directly produced by fabrication.

- *Integration of material fabrication and manufacturing processes in material-based processes*

3D printing in fact may become *design by fabrication*, eventually naturally shaping designs according to given specifications of any desired material system and its desired properties. Generative and materialization processes of material-based design fabrication can now be integrated in a single informed process.

Examples: *Beast, Prototype for a customized chaise lounge; Carpal Skin, Prototype for a customized carpel tunnel syndrome splint; Neri Oxman Media-Lab MIT.*

The design of the chaise lounge, *Beast* (N. Oxman, 2010) corresponds to structural, environmental, and performance criteria by adapting its thickness, pattern, density and stiffness to load, curvature, and skin-pressured areas respectively. In the chaise lounge, a single continuous surface is acting both as structure and skin that is locally modulated to provide for both support and comfort. The shape and stiffness distribution are informed by the structural loading. Variable properties are directly informed and directly produced by fabrication.

Carpal Skin (N. Oxman, 2010) is a customized therapeutic device for individualized treatment of Carpal Tunnel Syndrome (Boston Museum of Science) (see Figure 14.1). The local thickness corresponds to strategic areas across the surface area of the individual patient's wrist in cushioning and protecting it from stress.

> 5 Summary and Conclusion

The emergence of a "new materiality" as expressed by the growing interest in the role of materials in design has been viewed as a design cultural phenomenon that has motivated this research. The objective of the research was to investigate the role of digital and fabrication technologies as a force in returning fields of design to their characterization as material-based design, and, in addition, to formulate the theoretical concepts, processes and principles of a new level of digital affordance of material-based design. Within the framework of this initial definition, material-based design was further defined as a process in which *digital informing techniques enhance the integration between tectonic properties of form, structure, and material within the logic and the rationale of fabrication technologies.*

As an essential ingredient of this *theory of material-based design*, tectonics was proposed and introduced as a seminal concept, the operative power of which was enabled and supported by new digital technologies. In attempting to create a linkage between distinct traditions of discourse and to identify their newly refreshed relevance to contemporary material-based design, an exegesis of the cultural evolution of this important concept was briefly presented as the transformation of tectonic concepts. A new concept, *informed tectonics*, was introduced as a basis for the development of a theoretical framework in this research, as well as a seminal basis for the theory.

In tracing the roots of this term classical works of form finding by architects and engineers such as Gaudí, Otto, and Isler were presented as first models of informed tectonics. While these pioneering attempts were experimental and analogical, digital media and digital fabrication technologies are establishing today novel forms of tectonics.

Among objectives of the case study analysis was to identify relevant bodies of knowledge, models, concepts, and principles in the actual practices of material-based design. The methodology consisted of the selection and analysis of a case study sample of leading design practices and their application of methods of material-based design. Through the analysis of the case studies, we have explored how the structuring, encoding, and fabricating of material systems have begun to contribute to the formation of diverse models of *informed tectonics* in material-based design.

The following is a summary of concepts and principles of models that are proposed as representative emerging models of *informed tectonics in material-based design*.

• *Rationalization model*

This model constitutes an active research area for "providing construction-aware design tools to support digital workflow from design to manufacturing, especially for highly complex geometries"

- *Evolutionary model*

This model presents negotiation processes between form and structure that represents a certain design logic. In this case the logic emerges from given structural and formal relationships of individual components in a bottom-up strategy.

- *Tectonic flow model*

The flow model is based on re-use of a project-specific digital core model reflecting form, structure, material and fabrication requirements of the final fabrication–construction–assembly stages.

- *Material structure model*

The model illustrates how organizational principles of material structure of craft scale can be re-ordered and applied to construction scale. Integrated tectonic qualities at different scales are demonstrated to contribute to unique tectonic properties. This is particularly relevant to the investigation of *analogous tectonic systems*, such as textile and weaving.

- *Robotic-fabrication model*

The robotic-fabrication model extends the scale of conventional construction methods and current craft-based fabrication methods, performing complex and large-scale customized tasks. This process shapes both the design of structural and material elements in an encoded formal design process.

- *Digital materiality model*

Information flow is achieved by facilitating a generative process of shape and form related to structure and material that is controlled by machine data. Construction scale elements are designed as material systems that behave and adapt according to any specific materials and assembly logics.

- *Digital material: variable property model*

In this model, form, structure and material play equal roles in performance-based material design. They promote the application of material subsequent to form. This model is a significant in the shift from a geometric-centric design to a material-based design. Fabrication, in this case, 3D printing, becomes *design by fabrication* shaping designs according to given specifica-tions of any desired material system and its desired properties.

To conclude, there currently exist the conditions for change in traditional design processes as well as the emergence of concepts, processes and media that are contributing to the evolution of new forms of design. From the point of view of the relationship between design and technology as well as from the charac-terization of architecture as a material practice we are at a great watershed in design. We have found that *informed tectonic models of material-based design* are challenging orthodox design processes and providing innovative working methods of design. Material-based design is providing impetus for the reintegration of technology and engineering in design as well as providing a new role for digital design beyond its form-generative potential.

All three of the design components: form, structure and material, are now involved at the earliest generative stage. This new paradigm of the early inclusion of material factors in conceptual design is a profound historical transition from the form-centric domination of the last century. These changes also bring to the fore the design content of materialization by fabrication and manufacturing technologies.

Fabrication is redefined today as an integral part of the design conceptual process. In fact, in many respects, materiality by fabrication logic is frequently the basis for design conceptualization. Fabrication is, therefore, not merely a prototyping technique, but a change in the generation and making of designs. The current impact of materialization concepts upon form generation has become one of the main influences in contemporary design.

The control and the flow of digital information is now available to the designer as a new form of guidance, or driver, of tectonic process in which form–structure and material are *mutually informed* in the processes of design. These may inform one another at all stages of design, from conception to fabrication and construction. It is the computationally 'informed' content of material-based design that supports the explication of these complex tectonic relationships.

The terms, concepts, models and empowering technologies of material-based design is a design cultural field that is transforming the culture of architecture as well as other fields of design. Beyond these important historical and cultural considerations, material-based design is strengthening interdisciplinary, collaborative, and research-oriented design. The emergence of *experimental research in academia and in practice* has introduced a growing level of engagement between design and technology. This has become an area of design study in which expanded knowledge is shared among architects and structural engineers as well as industrial designers and other design fields.

How do we educate designers to function as *material practitioners*? Obviously there is the profound influence of the definition of the requisite knowledge base. Many of the research processes and subjects described above require the acquisition of knowledge and skills that are relatively new. This cultural shift within design culture is beginning to profoundly transform the cultural institutions of design. Not only are these changes challenges to practice, but they proffer a new territory for knowledge and education.

> Acknowledgement

The paper was written during my sabbatical stay at the GSD in Harvard University. I would like to express my gratitude to Professor Martin Bechthold for providing a stimulating environment and acknowledge his students in particular Rachel Vroman, Justin Lavallee, and Yahir Keshet. I would also like to thank Helen Castle, the editor of *Architectural Design* (AD) for her invaluable contribution to the publication of our prior pilot research: Rivka Oxman and Robert Oxman (Eds), The New Structuralism: Design, Engineering and Architectural Technologies, *Architectural Design* (AD), July 2010.

Addington, M. and Schodek, D. (2005). *Smart materials and new technologies for architecture and design professions*. Amsterdam: Boston Architectural Press/Elsevier.

AGU (Advanced Geometry Unit, Arup). (2008). In T. Sakamoto and A. Ferré (Eds.), *From control to design: Parametric/algorithmic architecture* (pp. 34–67). Barcelona: Actar.

Barkow, F. (2010). Fabricating design: a revolution of choice. In R. E. Oxman, and R. M. Oxman (Eds.), *Architectural design: The new structuralism: Design, engineering and architectural technologies* (pp. 94–101). John Wiley & Sons.

Bechthold, M. (2010). The return of the future: a second go at robotic construction. In R. E. Oxman and R. M. Oxman (Eds.), *Architectural design: The new structuralism: Design, engineering and architectural technologies* (pp. 116–121). John Wiley & Sons.

Bollinger, K., Grohmann, M. and Tessmann, O. (2010). Structured becoming: evolutionary process in design engineering. In R. E. Oxman and R. M. Oxman (Eds.), *Architectural design: The new structuralism: Design, engineering and architectural technologies* (pp. 34–39). John Wiley & Sons.

Cross, N. (2006). *Designerly ways of knowing*. London: Springer.

Cross, N. (2011). *Design thinking: Understanding how designers think and work*. Berg Publishers.

Frampton, K. (1995). *Studies in tectonic culture*. Cambridge: MIT Press.

Gramazio, F. and Kohler, M. (2008). *Digital materiality in architecture*. Lars Müller Publishers.

Gramazio, F., Kohler, M. and Oesterle, S. (2010). Encoding material. In R. E. Oxman & R. M. Oxman (Eds.), *Architectural design: The new structuralism: Design, engineering and architectural technologies* (pp. 108–115). John Wiley & Sons.

Kennedy, S. (2011). Responsive materials. In T. Schröpfer (Ed.), *Material design e Informing architecture by materiality* (pp. 118–131). Birkhauser Basel.

Kolarevic, B. (2003). *Architecture in the digital age: Design and manufacturing*. Taylor & Francis.

Kolarevic, B. and Klinger, K. (2008). *Manufacturing material effects: Rethinking design and making in architecture*. Routledge, Taylor & Francis.

Leach, N., Turnbull, D. and Williams, C. J. K. (2004). *Digital tectonics*. Chichester, UK: Wiley.

Liu, Y. U. and Lim, C. K. (2006). New tectonics: a preliminary framework involving classic and digital thinking. *Design Studies, 27(3)*, 267–307.

Mitchell, W. (1998). Antitectonics: the poetics of virtuality. In J. Beckman (Ed.), *The virtual dimension*. NY: Princeton Architectural Press.

Oxman, N. (2009). *Material-based design computation*. PhD thesis. Massachusetts Institute of Technology, MIT Cambridge.

Oxman, N. (2010). Structuring materiality. In Oxman., and Oxman (Eds.), *Architectural design: The new structuralism: Design, engineering and architectural technologies* (pp. 78–85). John Wiley & Sons.

Oxman, N. (2011). Variable property rapid prototyping. *Virtual and Physical Prototyping, 6*(1), 3–31.

Oxman, R. (2006). Theories and design in the first digital age. *Design Studies, 27*(3), 229–265.

Oxman, R. (2008). Performance-based design: current practices and research issues. *International Journal of Architectural Computing, 6*(1), 1–17.

Oxman, R. (2010). Morphogenesis in the theory and methodology of digital tectonics. *IASS: Journal of the International Association for Shell and Spatial Structures, 51*(3), 195–207.

Oxman, R. (2011). *Conceptualization by materialization – Design and material technologies*. Netherlands: IASDR, Association of Societies of Design Research (IASDR) and Delft University of Technology, Faculty of Industrial Design Engineering of TU Delft.

Oxman, R. E. and Oxman, R. M. (2010a). New structuralism: design, engineering and architectural technologies. In R. E. Oxman, & R. M. Oxman (Eds.), *Architectural design: The new structuralism: Design, engineering and architectural technologies* (pp. 14–23). John Wiley & Sons.

Oxman, R. E. and Oxman, R. M. (Eds.). (2010b). *Architectural design: The new structuralism: Design, engineering and architectural technologies*. John Wiley & Sons.

Pottmann, H. (2010). Architectural geometry as design knowledge. In R. E. Oxman, & R. M. Oxman (Eds.), *Architectural design: The new structuralism: Design, engineering and architectural technologies* (pp. 72–76). John Wiley & Sons.

Pottmann, H., Asperl, A., Hofer, M. and Kilian, A. (2007). *Architectural geometry*. London: Springer & Bentley Institute Press.

Pottmann, H., Schiftner, A. and Johannes, W. (2008). Geometry of architectural free-form structures. In *ACM symposium on solid and physical modelling* (pp. 15–28).

Sasaki, M. (2007). *Morphogenesis of flux structures*. London: AA Publications.

Sass, L. and Oxman, R. (2006). Materializing design: the implications of rapid prototyping in digital design. *Design Studies, 27*(3), 325–355.

Scheurer, F. (2010). Materializing complexity. In R. E. Oxman and R. M. Oxman (Eds.), *Architectural design: The new structuralism: Design, engineering and architectural technologies* (pp. 86–93). John Wiley & Sons.

Schodek, D., Bechthold, M., Griggs, K., Kao, K. and Steinberg, M. (2004). *Digital design & manufacturing: CAD-CAM applications in architecture and design*. Wiley.

Schröpfer, T. (Ed.). (2011). *Material design – Informing architecture by materiality*. Birkhauser Basel.

Semper, G. (1989). *The four elements of architecture and other writings*. (H. F. Mallgrave, & W. Herrmann, Trans.). Cambridge University Press.

Sennett, R. (2008). *The craftsman*. New Haven: Yale University Press.

Shea, K. and Cagan, J. (1999). The design of novel roof trusses with shape annealing: assessing the ability of a computational method in aiding structural designers with varying design intent. *Design Studies, 20*(1), 3–23.

Tsukui, N. (Ed.) (2006). *Cecil Balmond, special issue, A + U architecture and urbanism*. Tokyo, November 2006 Special issue.

Veltkamp, M. (2007). *Free form structural design: Schemes, systems & prototypes of structures for irregular shaped buildings*. In: *Research in architectural engineering series*. IOS Press.

Weinand, Y. and Hudert, M. (2010). Timberfabric: applying textile principles on a building scale. In Oxman., & Oxman. (Eds.), *Architectural design: The new structuralism: Design, engineering and architectural technologies* (pp. 102–107). John Wiley & Sons.

Xie, Y. M., Felicetti, P., Tang, J. W. and Burry, M. C. (2004). Form finding for complex structures using evolutionary structural optimization method. *Design Studies, 26*(1), 55–72.

To one who has watched the potter at his wheel, it is plain that the potter's thumb, like the glass-blower's blast of air, depends for its efficacy upon the physical properties of the medium on which it operates, which for the time being is essentially a fluid. The cup and the saucer, like the tube and bulb, display (in their simple and primitive forms) beautiful surfaces of equilibrium as manifested under certain limiting conditions. They are neither more nor less than glorified "splashes".

(D'Arcy Wentworth Thompson, *On Growth and Form*, 1917)

15

Cecil Balmond

The Natural Philosopher as Builder

Martin Kemp

We can recognise Cecil Balmond's fellow explorers over the years. Leonardo creating his miraculous syntheses of theory and observation in his drawings of turbulent water in balletic motion. Copernicus intuiting that the apparent order perceived by Ptolemy could be extracted with even more cogency by an observer on a moving planet. Kepler adducing a *vis formatrix* (formative virtue) that governed the six-cornered snowflake no less than the structure of the cosmos. Hooke marvelling at the little geometrical machines disclosed by his microscope. Newton positing laws of motion that challenged common sense but produced such beautifully cogent fits to the phenomena that they must be true. Lambert showing that the ratio of the radius to the circumference of a circle was an irrational number yet full of reason. The Reverend Henry Moseley delighting in the ways that the spirals of turbinated seashells followed a logarithmic progression. Mendeleyev having the courage to leave gaps in his periodic table of the elements because his conviction of orderliness said it should be so. D'Arcy Thompson expounding the manifold geometries arising from the growth of natural forms, whose complexity relied upon a simplicity that remained elusive in origin. Jean-Pierre Luminet recently proposing a dodecahedral model of the cosmos, curved and multi-dimensional in a way that lay beyond the reach of Kepler's Euclidian mathematics. And those pioneers of the mathematics of complexity (chaos theory, fractals and so on) who have revealed the very patterns of unpredictability that shape so many of the natural phenomena within which and by which we live.

None of the greatest travellers respected the territorial boundaries of the disciplines. Not for them the constraints of mathematics, chemistry, physics, engineering, medicine and biology (even less of molecular biology, cell biology, environmental biology). What we call physics fell under the embrace of "Natural Philosophy" (still the name of the "physics" department in Glasgow University when I arrived there in the late 1960s). This potentially limitless territory was ruled by those whom Leonardo called the *matematici*, those who brought all natural phenomena under the

Figure 15.1

embrace of mathematical analysis – which for Leonardo really meant geometry. I have called them the "mathematickers". As Leonardo wrote on one of his sheets of anatomical studies, "Let no one who is not a mathematician read my principles". He was in awe of natural design, where nothing was lacking and nothing superfluous. In the light of such fittingness of natural form to natural function, it was accepted by Leonardo, by Hooke, by Wren, by Blondel and by anyone who thought profoundly about such matters, that human design was an artificially contrived facet of natural orders.

There is of course a long tradition of mathematics in architecture, connected in equal measure to both beauty and structure. For followers of Le Corbusier no less than Palladio, proportion ruled supreme. Generations of post-war architectural students skimmed through Rudolph Wittkower's *Architectural Principles in the Age of Humanism* (1949), and came away with some grasp of commensurable and incommensurable ratios. But it was a proportional theory tied to the harmonics of the architectural box, constrained by the rectilinear ghosts of the lintel and post, typically spaced with plodding regularity. Balmond absorbed proportional theory (with characteristic penetration) at the same time as working through the marvels of the new mathematics of complexity. The kinds of systems being expounded by Mandelbrot, in which the "ugly" Julia equations were revealing their unpredictable beauties through countless iterations on a computer, gave a flavour to our understanding of the music of natural design quite different from that available to earlier generations.

Balmond's great and continuing intuition rests not so much with the technicalities of the new mathematics and its immediate applications but with its holistic potential across natural and human engineering. A conversation on these matters with Balmond becomes a dizzying journey through a vast range of phenomena that we now compartmentalise in our myopic disciplines. He is a supreme master of what I have called "structural intuitions", outlined in my *Seen / Unseen* (2006). This refers to the interplay of perceptual and cognitive structures in our brains with the innate and immanent patterns behind natural form and process. The prize for him is no less than a human system of design that omits none of the potential inherent in the manifold structures "invented" by nature.

He probes the orders that welled up within the "primaeval soup", however elusive they may prove, and however apparently random the surface phenomena. The orders may be numeric or geometrical, periodic or aperiodic, predictable or unpredictable. They may be expressed in dynamically unfolding processes or in the frozen music of fixed form. Like Leonardo, Thompson and others, the sciences of dynamics and statics are not rent apart. A shape is not merely a shape. It is the result of an unfolding process that has embedded in it all the organising imperatives of the

---

Facing page
Figure 15.1: Cecil Balmond: Organism. Image credit: Cecil Balmond, Balmond Studio.

physico-chemical parameters of its own material and of the external forces that have shaped it – in what is now called (in somewhat misleading shorthand), "self-organisation".

He casts his net wide. Just a few examples will have to suffice here. The tangible and tactile intricacies of weaving and knot theory provide insights into mathematical topologies of beguiling symmetry. The organic interplay of plastic curves in his sketches and models (physical and digital) parallel the "sinks" and "saddles" that mathematicians characterise in their multidimensional topologies. He looks to folded sheets or membranes for configurations that are not crumpled and disorderly but perfectly resolved in their static complexity. Branching systems set standards for structural integrity that arise from dynamic processes of growth. The incredible symmetries in Islamic tiling reveal tessellations that seem to rival nature herself – only to be surpassed by modern masters of aperiodic tiling like Penrose, Danzer and Ammann.

Not content with merely adopting Ammann's already intricate aperiodic tiling (consisting of three basic tiles) for Liebeskind's planned extension to the Victoria and Albert Museum, he stopped the subdivision of certain tiles with the result that a new fractal structure emerged across widely different scales, together with ghosts of the sets of parallel lines inherent in the Ammann system. Remarkably, but somehow unsurprisingly, the dimensions of the parent tiles relate to those of the subdivided tiles via the golden ratio.

Danzer's tiling takes him into the third dimension. The Danzer system comprises four tetrahedral units that divide fractally, again relating via the golden ratio. Similarly, a flat Voronoi tessellation, in which a cellular structure organises itself around a set of points that exercise centripetal attraction, can be extended into a 3-D foam, refracting back into the issues of packing and cell structure that had fascinated Thompson. Classic, age-old problems of natural geometry are not far away. A *locus classicus* was the honeycomb, the hexahedral delights of which exercised some major mathematical minds of the baroque era. Only recently has the complex problem of the 3-D packing of the rows of waxen cells at their bases yielded to precise mathematical equation. It has now been posited that the galaxies are disposed as if along the cell walls of a Voronoi foam. Whether this is right or wrong, it bears witness to the enduring modes of visualisation that we adopt to structure our perceptions of nature across all possible scales.

Balmond's procedures of design flow from such fundamental insights. His retrospective "memory books" of the stages in a design bear witness to a repeated recourse to basic concepts. Rather than taking the given form that might be assigned to a building and "engineering" it, he goes back to the rudimentary patterns of force that govern its very nature. The small, succinct diagrams have a relevance that only becomes apparent to us in retrospect. It is much as when Thompson is discussing "The Forms of Cells", he explores what happens to the focuses of the various conic sections when they are imagined to roll along a straight line (Thompson, 1917, p. 218, fig. 61). Thompson then passes on to soap bubbles and viscous fluids as analysed by Plateau and through a wonderful variety of "Figures of Equilibrium" before

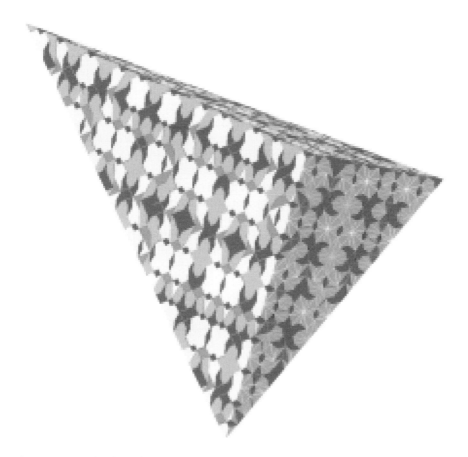

Figure 15.2: Cecil Balmond: 3D Tiling. Image credit: Cecil Balmond, Balmond Studio.

reaching the engineering of the cell. Along the way, the straight recurrently manifests itself in curves, and *vice versa*.

Balmond proceeds in a genuinely "scientific" manner – providing we mean by science that inventive process that is pursued by passionate people using their powers of observation and visualisation to probe nature in their minds or in their laboratories. The basic concept is scrutinised. Or, even more radically, the definition of the relevant concept is questioned. Thought experiments are performed, sometimes courtesy of scribbled diagrams. Physical experiments are devised to test the material behaviour that sets the parameters for the phenomenon. Interwoven with this process is the modelling of ideas on the computer, encouraging algorithms to play themselves out to their logical conclusions. The results feed back via a continuous loop into the conceptual framework. Finally, the hypotheses, qualitative and quantitative, gel in terms of precise expressions that are either technically mathematical or share in the precision of mathematics. Then a model of the phenomenon (or the engineered building) can be built. The difference with science is not one of means but of ends. The scientist is modelling the phenomenon that exists. Balmond is creating an "organism" that nature has not actually constructed.

An example of the conceptual questioning at the heart of the process is what Balmond does to the grid – or in its 3-D form the Cartesian system of coordinates. He laments its dominance over our built environment, above all in the Bauhaus modernism that still implicitly governs most of the buildings we erect. Yet the smallest perturbation can let its potential blossom. For the integrated wall and roof structure of the pavilion that he and Toyo Ito devised for the annual pavilion at the Serpentine Galley in 2002, he derived the pattern of diagonally inscribed squares not from the routine bisection of the side of the generating square but from its division into two-thirds and one-third. The result of this simple move is a fractal design of amazing complexity and structural rigour. At its heart stands the original generating square and the last undivided square. A single, unbroken square winked at us from an off-centre position in the roof. It seemed to be saying, "look what I can do if you give me the chance".

Balmond's designs are a form of "Natural Magic" – taking this term from the collective title that Sir David Brewster, the nineteenth-century physicist, gave to his set of published letters to Walter Scott. The gist of "Natural Magic" is that simple arrays of cleverly contrived causes can create wondrous effects. The reciprocal network that allows three overlapping

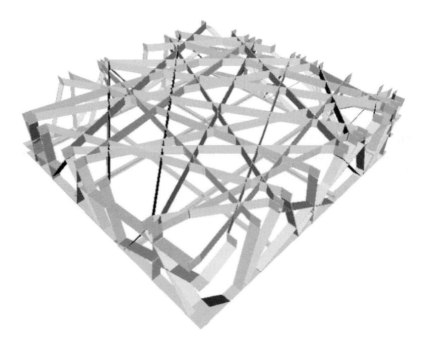

Figure 15.3: Serpentine Pavilion, Toyo Ito and Cecil Balmond. Image credit: Cecil Balmond, Balmond Studio.

knives improbably to bridge the gap between three glasses appears in Balmond's special issue of *Architecture and Urbanism* in 2006, but it would sit with equal comfort within the covers of Brewster's book. Balmond's use of a magic number square to determine the relative placement of the columns on the three floors of his S-Project for Glasgow in 2002 is entirely consistent with his unabashed delight in the mysterious and complex powers of numbers when they are disposed within patterns. The nine numbers – 4, 9, 2 / 3, 5, 7 / 8, 1, 6 – are arranged in 3 x 3 rows. In any straight-line sequence, including the two diagonals, they add up to 15.

On the wall behind Dürer's cosmically depressed *Melencholia* is a magic number square on a four-part base, yielding the constant sum of 34. Analysing how such number squares work remains a non-trivial task, particularly as they come to embrace larger numbers of rows. Complementing Dürer's magic square is the mysterious and much-discussed geometrical solid that has resulted from the truncation of a rectangular solid – oddly akin to the manipulated square in Balmond's pavilion roof. Faced with fathoming the rationale of such arithmetical and geometrical complexities, Dürer's heavy-limbed woman is paralysed into inaction, like the wasting dog and somnambulant putto. The accoutrements of practice, the architect's compasses and woodworker's shaping tools, remain impotent. The trick, as Dürer knew from the Platonising philosophy he studied, was to translate the profound mysteries into a programme of productive analysis and creative action under the influence of spiritual inspiration.

The interlocking glories of number and geometrical form have fascinated investigators of nature from the time in ancient Greece when mathematical analyses of the terrestrial and celestial worlds first came to be attempted on a sustained basis. It is interesting to note that Euclid remains on the reading lists that Balmond issues to students. I recall at school wondering how it was that the inscribed angles of a triangle always added up to 180°. However short I made one of the sides, and however much I skewed the overall shape, the result remained obstinately the same. Later I found that there were triangles where the sum was not the authorised 180°. These were drawn on the surface of a sphere and resided in the arcane world of non-Euclidian geometry. Eventually I struggled with multi- or n-dimensional geometry that did unimaginable things to triangles. This range of old and new geometries is all potent grist to mill of Balmond and the Advanced Geometry Unit he set up during his years in Ove Arup in London.

The Non-Linear Systems Organisation that Balmond has directed at the University of Pennsylvania School of Design is in one sense about design but its basic ways of thinking could be transposed into any area of experimental thought that is seeking to apply the new computer-enabled mathematics of complexity to actual systems in the material world. Its underlying principles are as relevant to cutting-edge studies of business systems as to self-organising mechanisms in biology. His vision is that we should be able to speak to each other at levels more fundamental than those that define the professional specialisms of our inherited disciplines.

Figure 15.4: Dürer, Melencolia I, 1514. Staatliche Kunsthalle, Karlsruhe, Germany. Image credit: From the collection of the Staatliche Kunsthalle, Karlsruhe, Germany.

Balmond and his collaborators are producing extraordinary computer-generated "organisms", using non-linear algorithms to invent images that are at once consistent with complex natural forms and not precisely paralleled by anything that nature has created. Just as the understanding of the five Platonic solids and their semi-regular variants provided an essential underpinning for Leonardo's architectural designs, so these organic fantasies

Figure 15.5: Cecil Balmond, Organisms: Serial. Image credit: Cecil Balmond, Balmond Studio.

provide a generating field for a new vocabulary of form, as well as being self-sufficient "sculptures" in their own right.

In the first work that carried Cecil Balmond's own name as the lead designer (rather as the designated engineer acting on another designer's behalf), we can see the kind of delicious surprise he can generate. It is a sweeping bridge near the historical Portuguese city of Coimbra, constructed in 2006 in collaboration with Adão Fonseca. As it departs from one shore of the River Mondego, the deck is cantilevered laterally from its support, which consists of an inverted curved triangle. It is an elegant motif in itself. However on the opposite shore the cantilevering is orientated in the opposite direction. At the centre, as the two halves reach out towards each other, the decks swerve or fold to unite in a way that creates a kind of musical punctuation. The pedestrians and cyclists, for whom the bridge was designed, are invited to pause, mentally and physically at a kind of *praça* or *piazza*, as their passage across the river reaches its central apogee. The rails that form the balustrade are designed fractally in an endlessly varied spectrum of skeletons and colour.

Engineered through sophisticated mathematics on a computer, the structure has become a romantic symbol, christened by the Portuguese as the "Pedro e Inês Bridge". Pedro was heir to the Portuguese throne but fell in rapturous love with Inês de Castro, a lady-in-waiting, who was deemed by the King to be an unsuitable match. Inês was eventually assassinated near

Figure 15.6: Cecil Balmond, Perdo e Inês Bridge. Image credit: Cecil Balmond, Balmond Studio.

Coimbra by the King's agents. On assuming the crown in 1357, Pedro subsequently claimed that he had married Inês in secret, and the exhumed corpse
of his lover was enthroned next to him. The emotional trajectory of the
lovers, finally united, is seen as matching the trajectories of the two arching
halves the bridge. Maths has fused with love.

As he moves out on his own, having left Ove Arup, Cecil Balmond is
forging new means and ends for architectural design, much as Bauhaus
modernism was once new. His mode of design is more than just another new
fashion or style in the oscillating historical progression of changing needs
and tastes. It all looks very new, and in one sense is. But it has been waiting
for us all the time under the skin of nature, if we only have the eyes to see it
and the tools to realise it.

> Analog Computing

16

**The Structure
of Vagueness**

Lars
Spuybroek

Within the history of methodologies in architectural design, the usage of empirical techniques has been somewhat obscured and hidden. Design methods tend to be based on historical references, canonical buildings, laws of proportion, symbolic language, or simple experience and tradition. Though it is common knowledge that architects make scale models, often in wood or plaster, we must keep in mind that these models are mere representations and as such don't inform the built result. I would like to look here at special cases in which the models' materiality itself generates form and structure. It is not very well known that engineers have used material models to actually generate forms and structures rather than to imitate them on a smaller scale. From the eighteenth century to the 19th, engineers in England and Germany used so-called catenary techniques to test designs by architects; for instance, Robert Hooke used suspended chains to see if arches designed by Christopher Wren actually fit within the desired curvature. Of course, the catenary curve hangs downward, which means the chain's links are all in tension, while in an arch all bricks are in compression. Such an inversion is a discovery of considerable magnitude. What remains unclear, however, is how, for instance, Antoni Gaudí came to use these techniques for the design of the Colonia Güell Church[1], the unbuilt predecessor of the much more famous Sagrada Familia in Barcelona. Though Gaudí didn't actually use metal chains to create catenary curves – he used yarn with tiny sandbags – it is no small modification from engineering to design, from using the tool afterwards in order to establish structural validity to using the tool during the design process itself. Since the latter is necessarily generative, the hanging chains have to form a system of multiple interacting catenary curves that relate directly to the design of (in this case) a church. The formula for a single catenary curve – which looks a lot like a parabola but isn't one – had already been worked out by Euler, and the design of a simple element like that wouldn't need the analogy of a model; an architect could simply use the formula to draw the necessary curve. The Güell Church, however, consists of many brick arches in various complex hierarchies, and such a system cannot be drawn by simply adding up a number of perfect catenaries. It needs both a systemacy and a procedural order, with decisions on which ropes to hang first. Since the chains are flexible, we must realize that the first is constantly transforming – and all subsequent ones are continuously transforming – as we reposition and add new curves and weights. Anyone who has seen the famous hanging model with the hundreds of ropes and tiny sandbags will note the striking resemblance to a typical computed

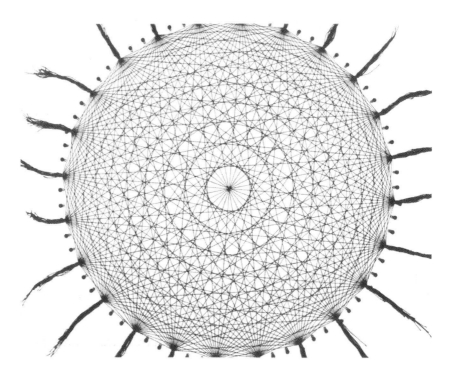

Figure 16.1a

wireframe model. I think we can safely call Gaudí the first computer architect.

In the 30 or 40 years after the late 1950s, Frei Otto and his team at the Institute for Lightweight Structures in Stuttgart experimented with material systems for calculating form, which were similar to the chain modeling technique Gaudí used for the Colonia Güell Church but used a much larger variety of materials. Each of these machines was devised so that, through numerous interactions among its elements over a certain time span, the machine would restructure, or as Otto says, "find form"[2]. This manner of *Formfindung* is directly opposed to "giving form," *Formgebung*, the German word for design, which implies the forcing of passive matter into shape. Most of Otto's analog machines consist of materials that process forces by transformation, which is a special form of *analog computing*. Since the materials function as agents, it is essential that they have a certain flexibility, a certain amount of freedom to act. It is also essential, however, that this freedom is limited to a particular degree set by the structure of the machine itself. In classic analog computing, most movement is contained in gears, pistons or slots, or (often) in liquids held by rigid containers, but in Frei Otto's machines, almost all materials are mixtures of liquids and solids or else start out liquid and end up solid. The material interactions frequently result in a geometry based on complex material behaviors of elasticity and variability. Some of us still tend to think materials act like Cartesian billiard balls, with full linear causality, but elasticity alone introduces much more complexity than that. Moreover, the involvement of so many agents generally shifts a system's dependency to feedback, i.e., nonlinearity, where effects change causes, rather than only causes having effects. These agents include sand, balloons, paper, soap film (which guided the design of the famous minimal surfaces for the Munich Olympic Stadium), soap bubbles, glue, varnish, and those I will discuss here: the wool-thread machines[3]. Though Otto used this technique less than, for instance, his soap film techniques, he used it specifically to calculate the shape of two-dimensional city patterns, as well as that of three-dimensional cancellous bone structure and branching column systems. Otto called these structures optimized path systems. All are similarly vectorized systems that economize on the number and length of paths, meaning they share a geometry of mergence and bifurcation.

For our purposes, we shall take a closer look at the wool-water technique, which follows an algorithmic three-step procedure:

Facing page

Figure 16.1a: Frei Otto, Wool Thread Models, Stage 1 (dry and taut) produced at the ILS Institute for Light-Weight Structures, University of Stuttgart. Image credit: Images courtesy of ILEK Institut für Leichtbau Entwerfen und Konstruieren Universität Stuttgart.

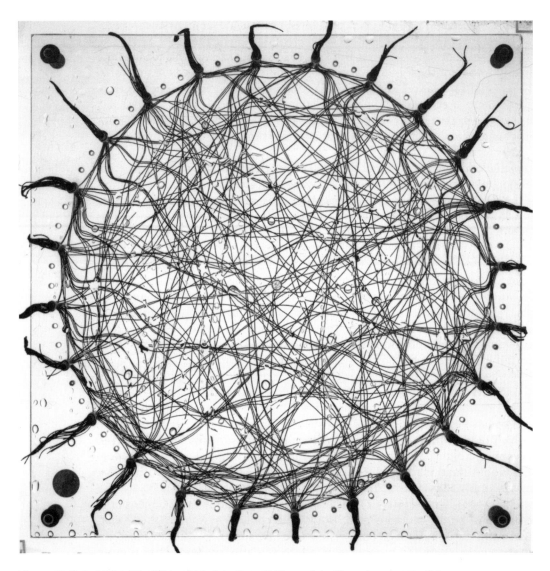

Figure 16.1b Frei Otto, Wool Thread Models, Stage 2 (dry and slack) produced at the ILS Institute for Light-Weight Structures, University of Stuttgart. Image credit: Images courtesy of ILEK Institut für Leichtbau Entwerfen und Konstruieren Universität Stuttgart.

a. Step 1 (figure a): Map all the targets of the system (in this case, houses) on a board. For demonstrative purposes and the sake of simplicity, the targets are arranged in the shape of a circle, but there can be any number of targets in any configuration. The points can be mapped on a supporting surface or merely on an open ring, which will give the clearest result. To ensure the basic connectivity of the system, you must connect each point to every other using wool threads. In this case, this simply means each house is connected to every other by a road. This stage of the system consists only of crossings; it is a typical surface model, a wire-frame of lines that neatly make up a surface.

b. Step 2 (figure b): Since we are always forced to take detours in cities, no single road ever leads straight to a single house. So in step two, it becomes necessary to give each wool thread an overlength, or slack. In this case, Otto's team decided on 8 percent, a random figure but also a generalized one, since the amount of detouring need not be averaged down to a single figure for the whole but can be differentiated throughout the system.

c. Step 3 (figure c): Now, dip the whole system in water, shake it carefully underwater, and take it out, slowly bringing it above the surface. The wet threads will tend to stick together, and as they begin to merge, they will lose this capacity at other points, since merging means elimination of available overlength. All overlength is processed out of the system by a surplus of cohesiveness. Since the paths come from all directions, the mergences do too, resulting in a system organized by gaps, or rounded holes, and surrounded by thick mergences of threads (sometimes more than eight) and smaller fields of crossings.

The first step contains only geometry and no materiality; then materiality takes over during a reshifting stage; and the procedure comes to a halt in a state of full geometry again, but this time, a geometry that is not imposed on the material but results from material interactions. It starts out explicitly Euclidean, but it doesn't end that way, because at the end there is no longer any clear division of dimensions. While we could call the first stage of the system a geometrical surface – a system in which all directions are equally present – the final stage of the model is much more complex, consisting of patches of crossings, mergences and holes. The crossing patches have two dimensions, which means that in these areas many directions are still available in the system – many lines keep crossing each other, as they do in the initial state. The merging patches consist only of one dimension, where the system takes on a single direction – multiple lines stick together to form a main artery. And the holes, of course, are areas where we lose all dimensions and no directions are available. While the first stage consists of homogeneous tiling, as in a lattice, the last stage consists of heterogeneously nested patching, as in an aggregate. The end result (figure c) is based on looseness but is itself not loose or weak but rigid and tight (when attached on an open ring, the threads come out of the water straight and horizontal!). It is a strategy of flexible, individually weak elements cooperating to form strong collective configurations. What emerges is a complex or *soft rigidity* that is very different from the top-down, simple and *frozen rigidity* of the first stage. We should therefore resist the idea that the first stage is a rigid order and the end result just a romantic labyrinth or park. The arabesque order of the end result is as rigid as the grid of the first stage but much more intelligent, because it optimizes between individual necessities and collective economy. Actually, if one were to draw lines on the photographs of the respective stages, one would find the total length in the first stage to be 100

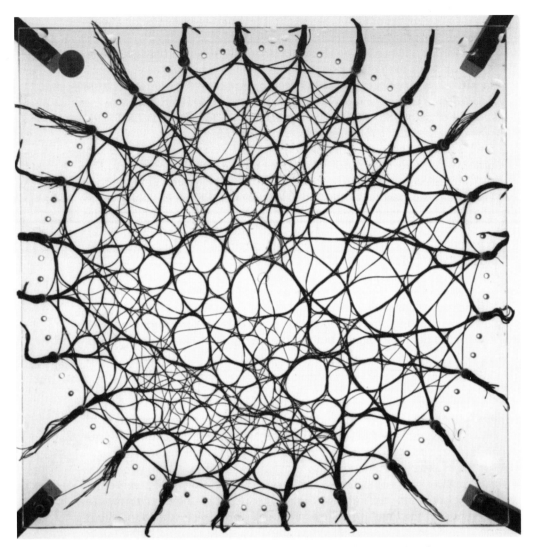

Figure 16.1c: Frei Otto, Wool Thread Models, Stage 3 (wet and merged) produced at the ILS Institute for Light-Weight Structures, University of Stuttgart. Image credit: Images courtesy of ILEK Institut für Leichtbau Entwerfen und Konstruieren Universität Stuttgart.

units; the second stage, of course, would measure 108 units, but the last would measure only 85. So the reorganization results in a considerable tightening and shortening of the system. We tend to think orthogonal systems perform best, or most economically, but this is incorrect.

Frei Otto has done similar experiments with glue threads. When two sets of parallel threads, separated in two orthogonal directions, x and y, are made to touch, they don't form an orthogonal grid, as one would expect; rather, all four-legged nodes transform immediately into three-legged nodes, and the whole surface shortens considerably. Ergo, the total length of the elements in a grid of hexagons and pentagons is much shorter than in one consisting of squares. It's simply the quality of the order that precedes the quantity of the elements. Yet this is not a clear and easily legible form of order but a *vague order;* in the final wool-thread model, it is hardly possible to distinguish between surface areas, linear elements and holes. Surfaces can function as linearities, lines can cooperate to form surfaces, and holes can exist on all scales. Everything between the dimensions is materialized. And though the dimensions are clearly singularities arranging the system (the mergences into thick lines are like the ridges of dunes, which orient the sand's surface to the wind's forces), it is continuity that makes them emerge. And though the order is vague, it should nonetheless be considered very precise, because nothing is left out. There is no randomness; there is only variation.

The truly amazing feature of this system is that it is in fact structured by holes; the nesting of holes is the driving force behind its formation, though architects are trained to think that holes are, in the end, subtracted from a system. This machine does not operate on subtraction or addition but on multiplication, in the classic sense of early systems theory, which states that a whole is always larger than the sum of its parts. Here, porosity is an emergent property. The first stage (figure a) is basically *drawn*, contrary to the end stage (figure c), which is processed by a machine, *calculated*. All the singularities that coexist in the final result – all the curves, all the mergences, all the holes – are interrelated; nothing can be changed without affecting the arrangement of the whole. All the lines are mobilized simultaneously, in parallel, whereas drawing is serial, with one line drawn after the other. A drawing is always created in the visual field, while the analog machine follows a partly blind and informational logic in which the image is the end product of the process. And though this technique should be considered as a hybrid of the top-down and the bottom-up, the drawn and the generated, its intelligence lies in the fact that nothing is "translated": the drawn is not "translated" into the real. In itself, it works at full scale. In this sense, it is not even a model. This *direct proportion* is one of the main features of analog computing, which simulates not through numbers but through an empirical rescaling of the real. This brings us to an important distinction between size and scale. A model is normally a matter of *size*: it is smaller and therefore a representation of a real object. Our system is in itself real and built; its transformation into a building, city or park is purely a matter of *scale*. Scale is topological and organizational, while size is purely numerical and geometrical. In our case of the optimized path system, it is the materialization of the ink as wool *beforehand* that makes it work. The organizational and informational stage is material, not immaterial, as is so often assumed. It is the material *potential*, the material, distributed intelligence, that sets the machine in motion, in a transfer of water turbulence to wool curvature. Then it is the stickiness, the hairiness, and the curvability of the wool thread together with the cohesive forces on the water surface that bring it to a halt again and inform the end result. It is simply impossible to do this in ink. It is

an intensive technique within an extensive system, and though the quantities (surface area, number of houses, etc.) are given beforehand, the quality
emerges through the interaction and multiplication of different parameters.
Generally, intensiveness is a deformational property (like heating), but here
it also becomes a transformational property (like boiling): the threads restructure and reorganize to "find form." The system as a whole passes a critical
threshold. The degrees of freedom of deformation, which are more like
extensive movements within an internal structure, become intensive, qualitative changes in the structure through transformation.

> Wet Grid vs. Frozen Grid

The classic Greek lattice grid is a system that separates infrastructural movement from material structure. Simply put, the structure is that of a solid, while
the movement is that of a liquid. We must consider the orthogonal grid as a
frozen condition, because its *geometrical* state of homogeneity relates directly
to a *material*, crystallized state of frozenness. Frozen states are simple states,
and of course these were the first to be mastered by the geometricians, but to
understand complex states we need to develop complex geometries. We are
generally taught that geometry is the higher – the more abstract and pure –
form of materiality, which is a misconception, because though geometry urges
the necessary exactitude, it is totally imprecise. Any geometrician arrives after
the event, when everything has dried up, and can therefore deal only with the
extensive state of the material, measuring length, width and height. The wet
grid, Otto's aggregational grid, is one in which movement is structurally
absorbed by the system; it is a combination of intensive and extensive movement, of flexibility and motion. The geometry does not follow the event; it
coevolves with materiality, is generated through analog, wet computing. One
could call the organization of the final stage wet and its structure frozen, since
it has come to a halt. Though it is no longer moving, it has attained an architecture of movement. In this sense, movement must be viewed as information, as
pure difference, because we all know that "information," if it does not cause
change, is superfluous. It simply has not in-formed, has not entered the form.
This means movement in itself cannot be called information: it must be internally processed as a (temporary or permanent) transformation. Physical displacement through movement must be processed as a structural change. Basically,
my argument here is that all movement as deformation is merely indexical and
meaningless if it does not result in structural transformation. Movement freezes
are merely *traces*, momentary stoppages of a bygone present: they are not
structured through time, are not *paths* that allow movement to be repeated
over and over again and slowly condense and evolve. Traces can never form a
system; they are individual. Paths are collective. But paths are not *roads* either;
roads are collective, all right, but not emergent, since they lack the capacity for
reconfiguration. With state-controlled roads, the distinction between the field's
surface material and the road's prevents the system from adapting.

Each phase of path formation should function as an analog computer for the next one. There should be enough solidification to record and enough plasticity to enable changes. This makes Otto's optimized path systems similar to contemporary multi-agent computing programs based on ant colonies with their pheromone distribution. Ants have no idea they are building a complex road system around their nest; they are simply foraging, finding food and bringing it back, and meanwhile excreting pheromones. The secret behind the emergence of a path system, however, is that the pheromones evaporate within a certain period. In this way, the trails of the ants that return soonest to the nest are selected out for path usage, since their trails are the freshest and still have enough pheromones for the next group of ants to detect. Over time, we can observe an abundance of initially zigzagging radial patterns sprouting from the nest turning into a complex but optimized path system that self-tightens. This can be either a straight highway between a single food source and the nest or a more complex forking morphology with multiple foraging points. Similar multi-agent systems have been translated into software packages truck drivers can use to calculate the shortest route between multiple addresses in a day's delivery schedule.

A real-time, analog computing model requires two things: a system that is internally structured (otherwise it cannot process information) and external flows of information. This simply means there are always two states coexisting, simple states and complex states, in gradation. Higher states of information can only occur within lower states of information; the two coexist hierarchically but on a continuum. They do not exist next to each other; rather, the generic and the specific share the same continuous, topological space. One always engulfs the other. We must start from a state of equilibrium that already contains information in its structure; then we need disequilibrium to increase the amount of information, and then we need equilibrium again to memorize it.

The brilliance of Frei Otto's model is that flexibility is taken literally and materially: the real movement of the water flow becomes the abstract movement of the wool structure, resulting in a coherent language of "bending," "splitting," "curving," "nesting," "aligning," "merging" and the like. All the arabesque figures in the final state of the model immediately relate to complex configurations. To understand this complexity, however, one must understand the nature of a curve. For Aristotle, any curve could be described as a mixture of straight lines and circle segments arranged in different orders. The later curve of differential calculus virtualizes both the straight line and the circle respectively as the *tangent* and the *approximative circle* that today is still an important indication of curvature[4]. In seventeenth-century shipbuilding, however, control of curvature was based wholly on material intelligence and not on geometry. The curves needed for a ship's hull were "lofted" at full scale using splines, thin slats of wood bent into shape with the help of lead weights. The spline is still present in all 3D modeling software, and though it now exists in many different forms, it is always based on that very important notion of materiality. Modern-day splines are the Bézier spline, the

B-spline, and NURBS – it is no accident that Pierre Bézier worked for car manu-facturer Renault. After shipbuilding, splines were transferred to the even more complex technology of building automobile chassis, and since car manu-facturing is completely industrialized, the spline had to attain mathematical precision. A digital spline starts out straight and becomes curved as informa-tion is fed to it. The initially straight spline has an internal structure of "control vertices," or CVs, and when these are moved sideways, it takes on curvature. Therefore, the number of CVs on a line indicates the type of curvature: how far it is from straightness and how close to circularity. In short, a *geometrical* straight line going from A to B doesn't have enough structure to be moved into a state of higher complexity: moving either A or B only results in a rota-tion of the same straight line. The spline's pre-structuring through the range of control vertices makes it *parametrical*. The only difference between a mate-rial spline and a digital one is that in the material version the overlength is external and in the computerized one it is internal. In Frei Otto's model, the wool thread going straight from A to B in the initial state (figure a) is charged in its final state (figure c) by a whole field of other influences and directions, from C to D and from F to G, etc.; the line is taken up in a field of potentials that make it an intensive line, which is simply a curve. *A curve is an intelligent, better-informed straight line.* Keeping in mind that Frei Otto's model is a path system, this curve should be read as a road with a variable openness on which one can partly retrace one's footsteps, change one's mind, hesitate or forget. It is not labyrinthine, causing you to lose your way completely; rather, it complicates your way, makes it multiple and negotiable. A curve is a compli-cated straight line: it still goes from A to B, has an overall direction and takes you somewhere, but it manages many other subdirections (tangents) along the way. It negotiates difference; it is differential precisely through connecting, through continuity. The frozen grid is always segmented and Euclidean, while the wet grid is always a continuous network, topological and curved.

> Vagueness vs. Neutrality

In architecture, flexibility has always been associated with the engagement of the building with unforeseen events, with an unpredictable or at least vari-able usage of space. During modernism, this flexibility often resulted in an undetermined architecture, in an averaging of program and an equalization, even a generalization, of space – in short, in the transformation of an archi-tecture of compartmentalization into one of generality and openness, seen in halls like Mies' Neue Staatsgalerie in Berlin. But we should ask ourselves: How does such generality affect the emergence of events? General, Miesian open-ness is only suitable when all desired events are fully programmed in advance by strictly organized bodies, as in the case of a convention center, fair or museum – when the organization of events is tightly controlled, not by the architecture but by management. A generalized openness in itself always has the effect of neutralizing events and being unproductive, because the type of space is not engaged in the emergence of events. It is flexible, of course; it is open, yes; but it is totally passive. All activity is assigned to the institutional body. The architecture itself does not engage with the way events and situations emerge; it is indifferent, neutral, with respect to this. It states that life is merely the effect of decisions already made behind the scenes, of acts that are repetitions of previous acts, with intentions that are completely transparent. The Cartesianism of the grid applies not just to its geometry but even more to the neuropsychology of the homunculus, which decrees that decisions necessitate an internal control mechanism. In its ambitions, the frozen, orthogonal grid is not very different from, say, the Miesian box or hall in architecture: it aims to find a structure that enables life, chance and change and can itself last and endure over time, spanning the unforeseen with the foreseeable. The strategy of the grid and the box has always been to average out all possible events, to be general enough for whatever happens. Now, certainly a lot of what we do is planned, and a lot of what we intend is transparent; we script and schedule ourselves all the time. But engaging with the unforeseen does not mean events are just accidents befalling our calendars.

The whole question here comes down to a study of the relationship between flexibility and movement: how does the body's flexibility relate to that of architecture? I want to argue here that extensive bodily locomotion is only possible when it is intensive first, both in the body and in the system. There is always a direct relationship between the system of motion and the internal mapping of movements in the body. Consequently, in the frozen grid, the body must act as if it is in an archive, constantly picking movements off the shelf, every act a re-enaction – the body itself is a frozen grid. The wet grid views the body as a complex landscape of tendencies and habit chreodes that form grooves (lines) in less defined areas that are surfaces. All modern neurology describes the body as a wet computer, constantly evolving, adapting, practicing, managing, coping and scripting. If one follows this line of thought, the problem of flexibility is not so much "opening up space to more possibilities," as is always stated, but the concept of the *possible* itself. An event is only ever categorized as possible afterwards. The possible as a category lacks any internal structure that can relate the variations to one another; it does not produce variation by itself – it is without *potential*. The choice has always been between determined functionalism and undetermined multifunctionalism, between early and late modernism, between the filled-in grid and the not-completely-filled-in grid. But potential is something else: "Potential means indeterminate yet capable of determination . . . The *vague* always tends to become determinate, simply because its vagueness does not determine it to be vague . . . It is not determinately nothing" (Charles Sanders Peirce)[5]. Vagueness comes before the situation and actively engages in the unforeseen, while generality neutralizes the forces making up the situation. *Architects must replace the passive flexibility of neutrality with an active flexibility of vagueness*. In opposition to generality, vagueness operates within a differentiated field of vectors, of tendencies, that allow for both clearly defined goals and habits for as yet undetermined actions. It allows for both formal and informal conduct. But more importantly, it also relates them through continuity, puts them in a tense situation of elasticity. The informal doesn't come out of the blue; it emerges precisely from the planned, but only because of intensive elastic planning. It is a structural Situationism that allows for *dérives* and *détournements* as structural properties. The transparent intentionality of planning and habit is stretched by the sideways steps of opaque intentionality. It does not mean the unforeseen has been successfully tamed and reckoned with: things are precisely left unplanned, but the foreseen is now structured so that it can produce the unforeseen and the new. How? Since all linearity is embedded within fields of nonlinearity, there is an enormous surplus of information in the system, a *redundancy* that allows behavior to develop in multiple ways. This redundancy is opportunistic and pragmatic, offering multiple routes toward a goal, but it doesn't afford anything to happen at any place.

At the level of design, this might be close to what J.J. Gibson has theorized as affordance[6]: a form affords certain actions and creates opportunities but doesn't determine them. Nonlinearity doesn't mean a breaking of the line, or even a relaxation that can stretch infinitely; it means a more fundamental bendability, a looping or a feeding back of the line. This means there is enough definition to allow a range of behaviors, but not so much definition as to single out one form of behavior (to be subsequently categorized as a function), nor so little definition as to make everything possible. So vagueness is not some state of amorphous indeterminacy; it is structured by singularities, by transformations in a larger field of deformations. And this applies to all architectural issues, not only the ones that relate to activity but just as much to the ones that relate to structure, since it is structure in all directions (vertical as much as horizontal) that evokes activity, be it of loads or of people. In the realm of vagueness, structure and infrastructure are continuous. Charles Peirce developed a radical rethinking of vagueness, which has been an important philosophical issue since the time of the ancient Greeks[7]. For Peirce, it all revolved around a logic of continuity. "The principle of continuity is the doctrine that our knowledge is never absolute but always swims, as it were, in a continuum of uncertainty and of indeterminacy," he wrote. "Now the doctrine of continuity is that *all things so swim in continua*"[8]. Or – even more confidently – "continuity is the great evolutionary agency of the universe"[9]. Continuity, or vagueness, understands things in the opposite way to what we know as elementary, not as prior to relations but as a posterior result of relationality. It is a universe where relationality is a given, and things – objects, beings, events – emerge from it. It accepts dimensions as much as Euclid's elements; it just doesn't accept them as discontinuous, only as generational, as sprouting from one another.

> An Architecture of Continuity

The techniques invented and suggested by Frei Otto have been diverse, varying from the application of already invented techniques to ongoing projects and more fundamental research into material form finding. Not surprisingly, his optimized path system machine is unique within his body of research, because he has hardly ever had to bother with horizontal structures. Essentially, his research has been into the complexity of the elevation, the structure, not the plan. He has always been invited to cooperate with architects who had already developed plans, and his contribution has been in the subsequent engineering stages. We should try to develop a different agenda. Patterning effects, configurational emergent effects, happen at all stages, in both the plan and the elevation. Instead of following the plan-floor/extrusion-wall method, we should opt for a method in which elevation and plan become more inter-twined and coevolve into structure. How interesting it would be to let the catenary technique generate a plan as well as an elevation, rather than merely hanging chains from pre-fixed points on a plan. For centuries, the order of the design process has been: first the plan (action), then structure at the corners (construction), which is finally filled in with walls (perception). Such an order, we must note, is completely Semperian, since action is the plan, or what he calls the earthwork, construction the tectonic wooden frame, and perception the woven textile walls. This must be finalized with the fire, or the hearth, which in our terminology would constitute a fourth category of sensation. Our agenda should be to short-circuit action, perception and construction – which is precisely what constitutes an architecture of continuity. Getting weak textile threads to team up into rigid collective configurations is a direct upgrade or inversion of the Semperian paradigm. But they should be three-dimensional from the start: plan threads should be able to twist and become wall threads. All these techniques already exist in textile art: complex interlacings occur in crochet, weaving and knitting. The art of the arabesque is as old as architec-ture; it has just never been conceived at the scale of structure. And this certainly has technological reasons – the arabesque has always been accommodated by manual labor, while the straight extrusion was necessarily associated with standardization and industrialism. We should be careful, though, not to mistake the vague for "free-form architecture," or for the streamlined or the amorphous. We should strive for a rigorous vagueness, rethinking repetition within sets of variability, rethinking structures within ranges of flexibility and redundancy. The more we move towards the vague, the more articulation has to become an issue. If there is no technology of design, a technology of manu-facture becomes nonsensical. With machines under numerical control, we also need the design process itself to be an informational procedure; it needs clearly stated rules and scripts to generate a structure of vagueness.

I have argued here and elsewhere that starting with the soft and ending with the rigid will offer us much more complexity in architecture. And here I am not referring to Venturi's linguistic complexity (one of ambiguity) but to a material complexity (one of vagueness). Obviously, the science of complexity has produced many diagrams of the vague, and these have often been dropped onto rigid architectural structures or typologies. That is not the way to go. Though *deconstructivism* proved successful in breaking down most of the top-down ordering tools we were used to in architecture (contour tracing, proportion, typology, axiality, etc.), it proved totally incapable of instrumentalizing complexity itself as a material, architectural tool. It understood every act of building as an implicit counteract, a negation – and meanwhile, the engineers silently repaired it. We should, however, understand all objects as part of a process of emergence, *the made as part of the making, not the unmade*. Our goal must be *constructivism*, or emergence, and anything that emerges should co-emerge. The way we see is emergent, the way we move around, the way we act in relation to others, to our habits, to our memories – all these emergent patterns should coemerge with a building's material structure. This makes our agenda one of a postindustrial constructivism, a vague constructivism. All behavior is material; all structure is material. All three constructivisms must run simultaneously, intertwined: a constructivism of form, a constructivism of seeing and feeling, and a constructivism of structure. The loads and forces working through our bodies to create social patterns are no less real than those running through columns and beams. There have been many attempts to borrow images of complexity and feed them into either circulational, formal or structural diagrams – Klein bottles, weather maps and so on – which were interesting, but not interesting enough. We should create complexity by feeding these modalities into each other through continuity. We should feed circulation into structure, feed structure into perception, and feed perception into circulation. It doesn't matter where we start, as long as we loop vagueness of action into vagueness of structure into vagueness of perception.

1   Jos Tomlow. *Das Modell, The Model* (Institut für Leichte Flächentragwerke, Stuttgart IL 34, 1989). Also in: Mark Burry, *Gaudí Unseen* (Jovis, 2007): 98–101.
2   Frei Otto and Bodo Rasch. *Finding Form: Towards an Architecture of the Minimal* (Menges, 1995).
3   Ibid., pp. 68–70. Also in: Frei Otto, *Pneu und Knochen, Pneu and Bone* (Institut für Leichte Flächentragwerke, Stuttgart IL 35, 1995): 174–182.
4   To better understand lines and their curvature, one can compare them to the way a car moves. A straight line, with its first-degree ("linear") curvature, holds the wheels in position. Second-degree ("squared") curvature, as in a circle, ellipse or a parabola, rotates the wheels. The third-degree ("cubic") curvature of differential calculus adds to that rotation a change in speed: during acceleration or deceleration, changing the direction of the car turns curvature into something completely different from the circles and ellipses we have been used to in architecture. After Gauss, these lines could be made into double-curved surfaces, which could be analyzed using so-called Gaussian analysis. The approximative circles (the biggest circle that fits on a point on the line without intersecting it) that fit in the cubic curves can be multiplied with one another: a sphere or balloon gives a positive Gaussian curvature, a saddle negative curvature.
5   Charles S. Peirce. *The Essential Peirce: Selected Philosophical Writings* (Bloomington, 1992).
6   James J. Gibson. *The Ecological Approach to Visual Perception* (LEA, 1986): 127–143.
7   See, for instance, Rosanna Keefe and Peter Smith. *Vagueness: A Reader* (MIT, 1999): 58.
8   Charles S. Peirce. *Collected Papers of Charles Sanders Peirce, Volume 1: Principles of Philosophy* (Cambridge, 1932): 1.171.
9   Charles S. Peirce. *The Essential Peirce: Selected Philosophical Writings* (Bloomington, 1992): p. xxii.

MATERIALIZATION

Materialization
Processes
and Design
Technologies

**Rivka Oxman
and
Robert Oxman**

In architecture considered as a *material practice*, materialization as a concept is transformed from its traditional meaning as the translation of an *a priori* design representation to its material condition; it is now transformed to become one of the sources of *the inception of designs*. The rediscovery that we can design in material has been a source of the reformulation of a *digital praxis* in the last decade. What traditionally was the material terminus of the design process has become a new beginning. This new primacy of material design brings architecture close to its engineering collaborators, and returns the architect to a position of centrality in the control of the total process of design, fabrication, manufacturing and the construction of building.

Materialization newly conceived as the *design of materialities* is among the seminal components of the transition towards an integrated and comprehensive digital praxis. Despite the centrality of this concept, there currently exists no general theoretical foundation for the role of material design in architecture. In the micro-history of what has been referred to as a "new materialism" in design, there is a complex network of relations. Prominent among these is the invention of new materials through material science, engineering and design including composite, hybrid and gradient materials. In Paola Antonelli's *Mutant Materials in Contemporary Design*, MOMA, 1995 the creative potential of new materials is seen as beyond the bounds of nature. No longer must designers respect "the nature of materials" in the modernist sense; rather materials innovation has become a process of mutating form and performance through the manipulation and mediation of materials.

There is emerging from this experimentalism in the relationship between design and material design the sense that we are beyond the constraints of being faithful to natural models. There is now the possibility for a *second nature*, a synthetic nature. This idea of creative materialization implies that we are now capable of synthesizing materials in order to guide performance, appearance or other material attributes. This conceptual breakthrough appears to be the fountainhead of *materialization* as a new material order in architecture.

Material structure is the geometric-structural field relationships of the material. Materialization can be mediated in order to vary material properties relative to behaviors such as structure, energy and information. It is this material structure that is generally considered *digital material* or *digital materiality* and underlies the micro-representation of the material structure from design to fabrication.

Materialities are the morphological properties of a material structure. Designing the emergent properties of a materiality require the representation of its material structure in order to mediate its variable properties. *Performative materiality* is a transmutation of material morphologies in order to achieve desired behaviors under environmental stress conditions.

This relationship of form and behavior, in fact, approximates natural morphogenesis. In the context of natural material behaviors DeLanda (2004) references Deleuze and Guattari's concept of "hylomorphic materialities" and "hylomorphic schema" as a paradigm of form genesis in which force-induced stress-driven operations lead to self-organizing formation/modifications of the material structure.

The relationship between materiality and environmental force conditions is a characteristic of design today in most cutting-edge engineering practices. Design of structure is emergent as compared to the attempt to achieve an *a priori* formal objective in design. For example, in evolutionary design, instead of imposing a form or canonic preexisting structural order upon a structural design problem, evolution processes are guided by optimization. See, for example, Bollinger, Grohmann and Tessmann's article, "Structured Becoming: Evolutionary Processes in Design Engineering," in this volume.

Material structures, for example textile or network structures, are experimented with for the optimization of their mechanical, structural or energetic properties. Much of what is referred to as material design research in architecture studies parametrically controlled topological transformation of three-dimensional structural patterns (*tectonic patterns*) and their resulting behaviors. This may be considered as an example of experimentation of *material form finding* in experimental design research.

Materialization has become a prominent subject of research in digital design. Such research includes the study of *parametric matter*, the exploratory research of innovative classes of material structure. The pavilion series produced yearly by the Architectural Association in London over the past decade has explored innovative forms of materialization and investigated classes of structural problems as *topo-tectonics*, such as the structural properties of continuous networks of elements. For further reading on parametric design research of classes of materialities, see also the article by Lars Spuybroek in this volume and in other writings that have explored the potential of *Textile Tectonics*.

Just as in nature, differential stress conditions can result in *differentiation of the material structure*. This property of differentiated and/or hybridized orders is one of the hallmarks of contemporary design. Differentiation is one of the major characteristics of natural design. In architecture, it is a theoretical subject underlying the departure from a repetitive architecture to one that enables non-standard and differentiated architectures. Morphological multiplicity and diversity characterizes the topological mediation of material structures. We must begin to develop, through research, the knowledge of performative material design as a theoretical/methodological foundation in an age of environmental consciousness and sustainable design.

Due to the open-ended and interdisciplinary nature of this young field, its relationship to computational design systems, and its centrality in various fields of design, there has been a burgeoning literature in the past decade. We have given preference to a selection of research and design that focus upon subjects of the professional and theoretical discourse.

SHoP's (2002) introduction to the *Versioning* issue of AD exemplifies a position of professional experimentalism with respect to accommodating pragmatic material research within an innovative approach to professional, industrial and constructional relationships. Their exploitation of various approaches to technological experimentalism and research-driven material design is characteristic of the ways in which younger offices engage in material-based design of prototypes while also experimenting with new professional relationships within the institutions of the building industry. Leveraging the conservative institutions of the building industry towards the technological frontier of rapid manufacturing is a broad objective of experimental offices.

Scheurer's article deals with the continuities and changes that characterize transitions and refinements between stages of the materialization process. Developing from the work of designtoproduction, the case studies of this article include references to the problematics of carrying into production works that have been conceived materially, but must inevitably be adapted to unexpected conditions of construction. While, in principle, the various stages of the process employ the same digital core model, structuring complexity frequently requires the evolution of a new tectonics (i.e., of production/construction) to be superimposed upon the tectonic structure of the main parametric model.

Martin Bechthold (this volume) in speaking about his definition of design robotics emphasizes the implications of the understanding of *materialization processes and technologies* as an integrative basis for innovation in design. In his definition, "Design robotics describes creative, material-focused automation approaches from conceptual digital design to robotic fabrication and construction" (p. 295). This presents material technology as a foundation of research and education in contemporary architectural design.

DeLanda, Manuel (2004), "Material Complexity," in Leach, Neil, Turnbull, David and Williams, Chris, eds., *Digital Tectonics*, Wiley-Academy, West Sussex, UK, pp. 14–21

Van Duijn, Chris (2004), "OMA Rotterdam: Material Research," in Ferré, Albert, Kubo, Michael, Prat, Ramon, Tomoko, Sakamoto, Salazar, Jaime and Tetysas, Anita, Verb 2, *Matters*, Actar, Barcelona, pp. 80–91

Garcia, Mark (2006), *Architextiles*, AD (*Architectural Design*), Vol. 76, No. 6, November/December, pp. 5–7

Kolarevic, Branko and Klinger, Kevin, eds. (2008), *Manufacturing Material Effects: Rethinking Design and Making in Architecture*, Routledge, New York and London

Lawrence, Amanda Reeser and Schafer, Ashley (2007), *Expanding Surface*, Praxis 9

McQuaid, Matilda (2005), *Extreme Textiles: Designing for High Performance*, Princeton Architectural Press, N.Y.

Menges, Achim (2010), "Form Generation and Materialization at the Transition from Computer-aided to Computational Design," *Detail*, Vol. 4, July/August, pp. 330–335

Schröpfer, Thomas (2010), *Material Design*, Birkhäuser, Basel

Taylor, Mark, Editor (2003), *Surface Consciousness*, AD (*Architectural Design*), Profile No. 162, Vol. 73, No. 2, March/April

> List of Key Concepts

composite materials
computational form finding
differentiation
digital fabrication
digital material
digital materiality
gradient materials
hybridized material
   structure
hybrid materials
hylomorphic
hylomorphic schema
material design

materialities
materialization
material prototypes
material structure
material system
mutant materials
network structures
new materialism
performative materiality
tectonic pattern
tectonic system
textile tectonics
topo-tectonics

Everything that's worth understanding about a complex system can be understood in terms of how it processes information
– Dr Seth Lloyd, Professor of ME, MIT

'Versioning' is an operative term meant to describe a recent, significant shift in the way architects and designers are using technology to expand, in time as well as in territory, the potential effects of design on our world. A 'second generation' of digital architects and theorists are emerging who have placed an emphasis on open models of practice where the application of technology promotes technique rather than image. The content within the 2002 issue of *AD*, titled *'Versioning Evolutionary Techniques in Architecture'*, is meant to be direct and straightforward, although versioning is an open, gestural idea and the range of contributions should signal the pluralistic nature of the concept. Versioning can be seen as an attitude rather than an ideology. It allows architects to think or practise across multiple disciplines, freely borrowing tactics from film, food, finance, fashion, economics and politics for use in design, or reversing the model and using architectural theory to participate in other problem-solving fields. Versioning is important to architects because it attempts to remove architecture from a stylistically driven cycle of consumption.

The computer has enabled architects to rethink the design process in terms of procedure and outcome in ways that common practice, the construction industry and conventional design methodologies cannot conceive of. This, in turn, has had an equally profound impact on legal practices, insurance liabilities and design/production partnerships, thereby initiating a restructuring of the traditional relations of power, responsibility and accountability in design. Versioning implies the shifting of design away from a system of horizontal integration (designers as simply the generators of representational form) towards a system of vertical integration (designers driving how space is conceived and constructed and what its effects are culturally).

Versioning relies on the use of recombinant geometries that allow external influences to affect a system without losing the precision of numerical control or the ability to translate these geometries using available construction technology. It advocates the use of vector-based information over pixel-based simulation and representation:

representation: modelling :: modelling: versioning

While simulation remains a useful formal estimate of future organisational strategies, versioning of vector-based information allows immediate results to be transformed and refined as the previous tests feed additional data through the framework of

17

Introduction to Versioning

SHoP/Sharples Holden Pasquarelli

Figure 17.1

intentionality. Both the desired design objectives and methodology thereby become simultaneously accelerated and adaptive.

Traditionally, the term implies the copying of a type or original. Yet, in this context, versioning should not be understood as originating from a singular identifiable model, prototype or master form in which all variations or evolutions can be measured by, or traced to, one specific source. In fact, versioning no longer relies on the necessity of the archetype to be manipulated and changed over time with the end goal of producing a master type for eventual mass production. Instead, versioning can be characterised by a set of conditions organised into a menu or nomenclature capable of being configured to address particular design criteria. The primary source is constructed from a set of detail types comprising a menu, and organised around a collection of specific detailed actions capable of evolving parametrically to produce specific effects or behaviours.

For example, the nomenclature of automobile highways offers a model to help illustrate this point. There is no original source highway or correct proportional system based on the image of road or speed. Most highways are made up of components such as 'loops', 'spurs', 'plains', 'bifurcations' and 'crossovers'. These highway menu types change their position relative to desired traffic behaviour in order to optimise movement efficiencies across changing terrains. No base prototype exists, nor is there an image-based set of relationships underlying the design. Instead, design decisions are based on an organisational strategy capable of responding to the effects of speed, turning radius, gradients, congestion and the landscape, to create a fluid behaviour of variable movement. The highway can be regenerated continuously to adapt to changing manufacturing techniques, yet maintains its clarity as an object-space-time construction.

The question of what is original or a copy is no longer of any relevance. By not relying on a formal apparatus or protoform, the practice of versioning is capable of responding in a nonlinear manner to multiple influences. By developing an elemental vocabulary of conditions in the planning stages for each project or project type, the practice of architecture becomes less about a search for a specific overriding form and more about a specific formal means of production to address variable conditions.

In the work of Office dA, we can see their use of the brick as a building component to test the notion of aggregation and seriality of construction much in this way. In their Tongxian Arts Centre project, the potential of the exception to the singular element creates possibilities for new resolutions of surface, edge, corner, circulation and tectonics. The geometry of the structure moves past the simulation of folding and pliancy in image and towards a method of design and execution. Ingeborg Rocker places the argument of

---

Facing page

Figure 17.1: 290 Mulberry Street, Elevation study SHoP architects. Image Credit: Image courtesy ShoP.

originality, difference and emerging technologies within the context of the corporate identity machine to question versioning's role in the production of form. She questions the desire, or plausibility, of design's relationship to representation when new models of practice are allowing architecture to become an informed result of differentiated effects. Another key element of versioning is its ability to question time and its relationship to other cultural processes. In his essay, Ed Keller firmly positions recent technological advances in fields as disparate as biotechnology and DJ remixing, and links them to a discussion of 'new forms of time' which emphasise the potential effects versioning can have on the city/machine and the speed at which a self-regulating mechanism for temporal/cultural control emerges. In this way, Keller argues that versioning advances the 'genetic substance' of architectural design.

Versioning also extends to methods of practice where nontraditional use of architectural theory is appropriated by other disciplines. Anna Dyson discusses the advances in the field of industrial ecology, where methods for disassembly and reuse can be built into the design process through techniques of versioning. She continues with a projection of emerging advances in biotechnology that shift the economic paradigm for the development and gestation of materials. Panelite's materials-research work exposes the process of making new building products from a singular technique while allowing for difference at multiple scales. Its products seamlessly integrate both theory and technique to create an aesthetic that is not image based. Similarly, the work of inventor David Levy suggests how design solutions are discovered by using the external actions which will act upon the device while allowing for continuous feedback from both the manufacturing and organisational requirements. The ability to see the device, understand it without using directions and fabricate it quickly, drives a resultant aesthetic that is highly specific yet more inclusive.

If versioning operates at different scales within a design it should also operate at different scares of practice. Helen Castle's interview with three partners of Buro Happold Consulting Engineers begins to examine how a 700-person design consulting firm uses new technologies and theories of versioning to operate on multiple continents and on projects ranging in size from 2000 to 200 million square feet. At the same time, Vishaan Chakrabarti writes an essay on the political manifestations surrounding the notion of the sole practitioner and the corporate practice in this new climate. How can these new techniques allow smaller firms to take on larger projects, and what types of alliances are the result of these shifts of scale and responsibility? And, if versioning allows small firms to perform large, can the corporate behemoth suddenly act lithe and tactical?

Rick Joy, William Massie and SYSTEMarchitects present some of their recent work, projects in which they are heavily involved in the building of their structures, allowing them to control all aspects of the work. Versioning here is instrumental in allowing the practice of architecture and design to return to a vertical organisational structure similar to the 'master builder' of the Renaissance. Their invention of new forms of digital drawing and manufacturing is closer to Brunelleschi's systems of variable brick models than it is to the image-generating machines of the architects of the 'dot-blob bust'. When building the Duomo in Florence, Brunelleschi modelled multiple brick shapes and sizes using wooden moulds constructed from versioned templates to respond to specific loading conditions when assembled in different combinations. No singular or master brick form is used to address the overall static behaviour throughout the structure. The work of the architects can be local or international, but the designers use the technology to create a true integration of the process of construction no matter what space/time conditions exist. They are using innovating building materials and construction techniques to expand the possibilities of design and effect, and to keep all aspects of construction under their control. In contrast, when the blob is left in its rendered state it leaves us flat, no matter how sophisticated are the continuous recalculation of the NURBS geometries. The form may use every data-crunching animation technique to process multiple variables, but the result is too often all image. The texture maps cloaking them are similar to the banal skins of consumption architecture. Without making the intentional connection between the digital geometries on the screen and the execution of a technique to produce that geometry at building scale, the work seems limited.

Can versioning alter the distinction between the 'aesthetic object' and the 'theoretical text' and collapse this distinction where the object and the text are one and the same with the technique of manufacturing? Can the forces that make the object, both in the generation of the broad strokes and specific resolutions, combine with an intelligence of fabrication to become a 'process product'? Here the form, the forces that shape it, and the assemblage of materials in which we execute the ideology are part of the same gesture. This is not a call to replace the human act of design with algorithms, but a critical search for a common language between design and execution. The resulting control of these processes empowers the architect to take on the role of the translator of unforeseen relationships simultaneously in imagined and real space. The techniques and processes are not far off in the future, but available right now. Are you ready?

> What Are We Doing?

From the start of designtoproduction in 2006 we have been searching for a single term that would explain the central core of our services to architects, engineers, and fabricators. But even branding experts were not able to boil our lengthy explanations down to a single sentence. Oddly enough, despite this marketing void our enterprise was satisfactorily successful. Obviously, a niche had opened up in the building workflow, which lacked a name, but was nevertheless full of opportunities. Where did it come from? Let me speculate. . .

> Regular to Non-regular

One decade earlier, an innovation had finally found its way from the French car industry into the CAD software used by designers. Splines and Non-uniform Rational B-Spline Surfaces (NURBS), developed at the laboratories of Renault and Citroën as mathematical definitions for curves and curved surfaces in the 1950s, suddenly appeared in the program menus of designing architects in the 1990s. And they apparently liked it. The curvy, non-orthogonal, non-regular, "blobby" results can be visited all over the world. But it quickly turned out, that those designs would pose completely new challenges, once they had been sold to a sufficiently extroverted client and entered the construction design and building phase. What had started as a happy trip away from repetitive, industrialized, orthogonal boredom became a labor-intensive nightmare. Suddenly, façade-panels had to be either curved (expensive!) or the panelisation had to be meticulously optimized to approximate the curves with planar facets (difficult!). And where the panels met, there were no repeating details anymore, which could be drawn once and multiplied over a whole building. Thanks to the non-regular shape, every panel and every joint had a slightly different geometry. The convenient set of standard detail drawings got replaced by hundreds and thousands of individual workshop drawings.

> Concrete to Abstract

Fortunately, some CAD systems even at that time had programming interfaces (APIs), which allowed "remote control" of the drawing tools from an algorithm. Lazy but smart architects, like designtoproduction partner Arnold Walz, immediately took the chance and started to program drawing algorithms instead of

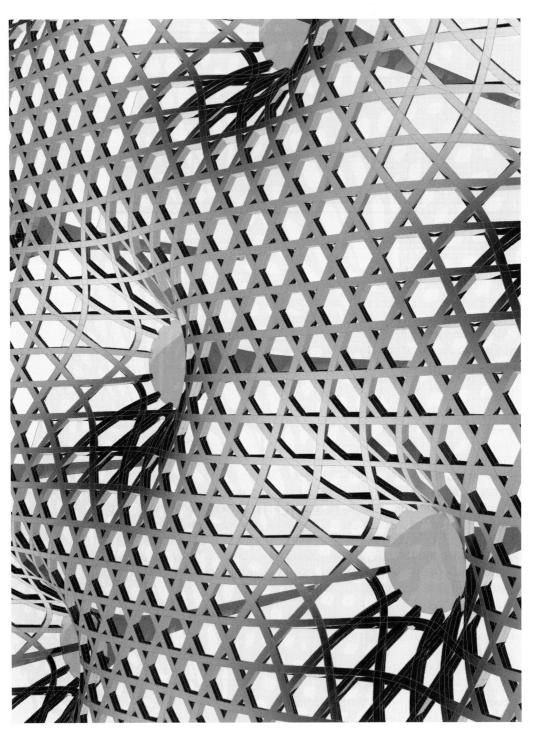

Figure 18.1

drawing countless variants of the same thing by hand (or mouse). Such an algorithm takes the defining properties of a component or joint as input parameters and delivers a perfect drawing or 3d model as output. The information of a thousand drawings can thus be reduced into one well-defined algorithm and a thousand small sets of only a few parameters. But again, this trick posed new challenges: First, you need to know how to program. Designers, especially well-prepared to deal with ambiguous, ill-defined problems, suddenly had to come up with unambiguous, well-defined, formal descriptions, syntactically correct to the last semicolon. Second, you need to abstract the problem. Finding an elegant common definition for all the different details of a curved façade was even more difficult than to solve the problem for just one, nicely orthogonal situation. And finally, you have to know about geometry. All the mathematics, so comfortably hidden behind the CAD-software's buttons, suddenly had to be dealt with in the form of normal-vectors, curvature-measures and coordinate-transformations.

> Parametrics and Complexity

But apart from that, parametric modeling makes things considerably easier. At first sight, even the notion that parametric models "reduce" the complexity seems be true, at least in terms of Kolmogorov's definition of descriptive complexity[1]: a printout of the program code together with a table of all parameter-sets still needs less paper than all the workshop-drawings. But this is misleading: both descriptions define the same degree of complexity, only in different languages. The algorithm is much easier to handle than the set of drawings – especially when it comes to changes – but it is just a translation of the same description. This translation, however, does not come for free. It takes energy in the form of brain action to come up with a clever algorithm. And even though the current development of parametric modelers – from Grasshopper to CATIA – removes a bit of the programming hassle, the two main tasks remain the same. First, to abstract from a mass of individual problems to a generic "class" of solutions and a minimal set of parameters that open a solution space just big enough to accommodate all necessary variants. And second, to instantiate all the individual variants with the right parameter-values. Thus, the work did not simply vanish, it just shifted to a higher level of abstraction: programming instead of drawing. Or in other words: once the complexity has been introduced into the system by making it curvy and non-regular it will not go away anymore. It can only be handled in better or worse ways.

Facing page

Figure 18.1: Shiguru Ban, Haesley Nine Bridges Golf Resort, Reference geometry view from above. Image credit: Digital images courtesy Fabian Scheurer, DESIGNTOPRODUCTION.

> Mass customization

All the parametric planning effort would be largely useless without digitally controlled (CNC) fabrication tools that allow the production of individual components at almost the price of mass production. Those tools are widely available by now, but they are neither small, nor cheap, nor will they respond to the file-to-factory buzzword – at least if you want to build something on a one-to-one scale and not just small gypsum models. Owning and running such equipment is a business on its own and requires a lot of investment and specialist knowledge. Ideally, this knowledge is available at early design stages, in order to optimize the design towards the fabrication method. Usually, it isn't. Simply because no one knows who is going to be the fabricator and which technology he is going to use, before the tender is completed. And even worse, almost every CNC machine reads a different data format and every fabricator uses a different CAM software, which makes generating the machine data for all the individual parts from the parametric geometry model all but an easy task.

> So, What Are We Doing?

Obviously, the recent evolution of parametric CAD systems and digital fabrication technologies has left its traces in contemporary architecture. It opens new prospects, but at the same time generates new challenges, mainly due to the immensely increased amount of information that needs to be handled in the planning phase. The integration of knowledge about structure, materials, fabrication, and construction into the design is key to the creation of efficient planning and production processes – but let's be honest: this is nothing completely new. Actually it should have always been the lodestar for every good design. What maybe has changed is the fact that all this knowledge has to be incorporated into continuously digital production chains, which connect design and fabrication and ensure the efficient and frictionless flow of all the information, including all necessary translations between different data formats. That is, what designtoproduction is offering, and it will be interesting to see where the ongoing development takes us and – in the end – how our profession is going to be named.

---

1   In algorithmic information theory, the Kolmogorov-Complexity of an object is defined by the shortest description of the object in a given language.

Figure 18.2: Shiguru Ban, Haesley Nine Bridges Golf Resort, View from below. Image credit: Digital images courtesy Fabian Scheurer, DESIGNTOPRODUCTION.

After a decade-long hiatus robotic construction is back, now driven by design – speculative, confident, and complex. The current shift from digital fabrication towards *design robotics* has been enabled by the sinking cost of industrial robots, and by the academy's increasingly sophisticated digital design culture.

This networked culture has generated a digital infrastructure that readily supports design to production approaches in newly integrated modes. The development of design robotics parallels the emergence of CNC technology in the 1990s, except the driving forces have changed. Fabricators implemented CNC fabrication methods originally in order to improve productivity and quality. Integrated steel, concrete, or heavy timber building systems are a prime example. Today it is the academy's insatiable appetite for design novelty that is driving technological innovation. Contemporary academic research has produced new instances of robotically fabricated prototypes that are beginning to shift fabricators towards integrating robotics in their workflows. New robotic work cells are emerging at most major schools of architecture. Robotics, once an interdisciplinary engineering discipline, has been absorbed by the architectural design community: it is the new era of design robotics.

Design robotics describes creative, material-focused automation approaches from conceptual digital design to robotic fabrication and construction. Work at the Graduate School of Design (GSD) at Harvard University has focused on customization approaches for architectural production in the quest for new design knowledge. Projects include one-off installations as well as research studies that strategize on the deployment of robotics in the industrial production context. Customization has been a persistent challenge for architectural construction that, at its core, is a commitment to site and program specific responses of space and form. The materialization of buildings inevitably involves custom components in combination with standard parts. With their typically low production volumes for custom elements ranging from a single one to several thousand at best, architectural construction requires fabrication responses that are agile and distinctly different from mass production (significant capital investments are justified through high production volumes, e.g. automotive production) or mass customization (limited design variations enabled by modular component systems produced in lean, high-volume manufacturing environments).

Deep understanding of the processes that relate to a specific material technology is fundamental to innovating on the design level. Work at Harvard University's Design Robotics Group (DRG)[1] has shown that thoughtful and strategic automation from design to fabrication is a key enabler of low-volume customization in

Figure 19.1

architecture. Before presenting a sampling of research projects it is worthwhile to look back at the beginnings of automation approaches in construction. Indeed, robotic systems for construction have a long history, with the most developed examples being the nearly 200 Japanese construction robots of the 1980s and 1990s. Technologically at the forefront at the time, their development was driven by a perceived shortage of construction workers who could find safer and cleaner jobs in other sectors of a then thriving Japanese economy. The construction industry further feared the effects of the aging population that produced fewer young people physically able to work on-site. Obayashi, Kajima, and other large Japanese construction firms invested millions of dollars into specialized robots that replaced humans on-site. Custom robots sprayed fireproofing, poured and leveled concrete floors, welded steel, and performed many other tasks previously done by people. The culminations of this development were largely automated and remotely controlled construction systems that literally 'extruded' high-rise buildings using robotic technologies in lieu of construction workers.

Material was supplied to weather-sealed workspaces in a just-in-time manner using automated gantry cranes and other equipment. Automated, laser-based surveying systems provided quality control in real time. Member connections were redesigned to facilitate robotic assembly and robotic welding. The construction process was managed based on 3-D digital models and complex workflow management systems.

But this ambitious endeavor to substitute people with robots on site never paid off economically – and it severely limited design choices to highly repetitive, uninspiring buildings. The added value was slightly higher productivity and reduced need for construction workers – it never justified the vast effort needed to develop and build customized robotic technology. These systems, although technically brilliant, ultimately lacked the ability to embrace the need to customize components and construction in order to produce buildings suitable for twenty-first-century societies that despise the monotony of industrialized modernity. The complexity present in contemporary buildings simply could not be accommodated – the mindset behind Japanese construction automation was the automation of existing tasks, and it excluded the pursuit of design excellence. When the 1990s economic crisis hit Japan these early automation systems disappeared quickly, and only occasionally has interest in this approach led to similar applications in the Netherlands or in South Korea.

The re-emergence of automation approaches as design robotics today seeks entirely new design expressions as original representations of the digital age. Rather than customizing the robotic device – inevitably time consuming and risky – it is the design itself that pursues customized

Facing page

Figure 19.1: Robotic tile placement. Image credit: Photo courtesy Professor Martin Bechthold, Harvard Graduate School of Design.

expressions. Standard robots, ubiquitous, interchangeable, cost effective, are the perfect way to pursue design robotics. It is not the tool, but what we do with it that matters.

Today's digital tools and workflows allow even novices to engage in prototyping rapidly and without lengthy learning curves. Three-dimensional sketching with robotic devices is becoming a reality. A Design Robotics Group (DRG) research study by Andy Payne and Prof. Panagiotis Michalatos (both Harvard GSD) has produced a prototypical input device which, via inexpensive parametric design software, communicates directly (and in real time when desired) with an off-the-shelf 6-axis industrial robot. In a workshop conducted by Harvard's DRG at the 2012 Smartgeometry workshop students without prior knowledge were able to produce original ceramic components, using a range of digital tools based on the popular Grasshopper platform, within only four days. The workshop was based on prior student work in a class "Material Process and Systems" taught by the author. The narrowing of the gap between digital inputs and robotic outputs allows material issues only evident in actual physical prototyping to feed back more rapidly than ever into primarily digital exploration. While there remains room for improvement in this new, design-centered sketching process, it does represent a significant step in moving towards newly hybridized ways of designing, merging digital with physical layers.

The customization research at Harvard's DRG further illustrates the focus on process-based design. The following two projects both look at architectural ceramics as a microcosm that allows broader understanding on how to strategize on the use of robotics in industries that have long relied heavily on the mass production of standard elements – in this case ceramic tiles.[2] Architects today are increasingly seeking individualized architectural forms and surface expressions, and end users are less likely to find satisfaction in off-the-shelf products. Given these new conditions for design – and understanding the ease with which highly complex and varied building forms and elements can be designed – a revision of conventional high-volume production techniques and their related marketing and installation procedures is needed. The projects presented below address this challenge in different ways, albeit both through a design driven re-conceptualization of robotic material processes. Three-dimensional printing of ceramic elements, the first project, pushes the limits of part customization in order to broaden design scope in the conception of highly performative shading systems for architectural facades. Robotic tile placement, on the other hand, revisits the installation of modularly sized tiles – an aspect disregarded by the ceramic industry that is exclusively focused on production. Tile installers are currently disconnected from the production environment. Design innovation, on the other hand, can only emerge when looking at both aspects – production and assembly – of a material system.

Rapid prototyping, 3-D printing, solid free-form fabrication – these terms have been widely used to describe the additive manufacturing of small prototypical parts initially geared towards facilitating design development of product designers. As parts produced on commercially available 3-D printers are beginning to be used in real-world applications the building industry has not been standing by idly.

Contour crafting, a technology developed by a team led by Berokh Khoshnevis at the University of Southern California, can produce entire building structures through layered application of concrete. While technically sophisticated, the approach risks a similar fate to that experienced by Japanese construction robots of the '90s – the automation of existing processes does not produce novel design instances that inspire architects and fabricators to follow suit.

The DRG approach to 3-D printing differed in that an entire process was re-envisaged, from conceptual digital design to robotic fabrication. The ceramic 3-D printing project took as its starting point the need to optimize the forms of shading louvers on sunlight facades, while still permitting architects to pursue individualized design expression. Working with Prof. Christoph Reinhart's team of environmental technologists, a set of integrated environmental design tools was developed to facilitate a performance-driven optimization of shading geometries, while allowing the seamless integration of the physical constraints of materials and structure. This type of performance-driven parametric design approach can only succeed if the ability for digital parametric variations is equally present in the robotic production environment. The key here is to automate the generation of individualized robotic code, in this case through a newly scripted environment developed by the DRG team.

The scale of the ceramic components produced is in between a consumer product and a full-size building element, and largely limited by constraints of the firing kilns typically used by the ceramics industry. A prototype was constructed as a proof of concept for the integrated workflow and the related, novel robotic work cell.[3] Newly developed equipment such as a novel, robotically actuated, adaptive support mold is inexpensive. It is geared towards an industry that can only rarely support the sorts of expenses common in the aerospace industry, where the use of costly 3-D printed parts is quite common. Approaching the challenge of part customization from the perspective of design robotics allowed the development of a new technical process that opens up new opportunities for performance-based design. Combining principles of efficiency with ambitious design is likely the only way to move sustainable design principles into the mainstream!

A second customization strategy takes a seemingly more pragmatic attitude in that existing production processes remain unaffected. Robotic manipulation is designed to efficiently install tile patterns that are not economically feasible to implement in developed economies with comparably high labor costs. The digital pattern generator, created by Prof. Panagiotis Michalatos (Harvard GSD), allows any image to be converted into a complex tile pattern, with the ability to accommodate industry standard or custom tile sizes.

Grayscale tones are created through tonal differences between grout areas and tile. A cost-effective robotic placement is made possible through automating the code generation for a standard industrial robot (Figure 19.1). The installation cost is comparable with industry average installation costs in the Northeast of the United States, assuming certain changes in sequence and material support technologies.[4] The technical solution is feasible – the main challenge is to reconnect an industry that has split producers and installers, and create new distribution strategies that link clients more directly to producers. Design robotics as an approach is broad enough to question current industry paradigms, and devise new strategies for robotic systems as an integral part of a larger network of constraints and opportunities.

Robotic fabrication, despite some historic debacles, remains a promising technology. Designers now need to drive the development of ideas, and show how robotic systems can help promote design as an agent of change for a better future. Design robotics, not construction automation, will drive the future of architectural design.

1   The group, headed by Prof. Martin Bechthold, supports student work and conducts research projects in collaboration with industrial and other academic partners.
2   The research was supported by ASCER Tile of Spain.
3   More information on the project can be found in Bechthold, M. et. al.: "Integrated Environmental Design and Robotic Fabrication Workflow for Ceramic Shading Systems" in *Proceedings of 28th International Symposium on Automation and Robotics in Construction (ISARC2011)*. Seoul. 2011.
4   The quality adjusted cost of industrial robots in the year 2000 was approximately 20% of the cost in 1990 (United Nations Economic Commission for Europe, Press Release, October 30, 2001).

MATERIAL FABRICATION

Design
Technologies
of Digital
Materiality

**Rivka Oxman
and
Robert Oxman**

Material fabrication is the generic term for digital materialization. It is an emerging body of concepts and technologies. The relationship between parametric design tools and the growing sophistication of materialization, fabrication and construction technologies is the incipient revolution of *fabricating design* (Kieran and Timberlake, 2004; Hopkinson, Hague and Dickens, 2006; Gershenfeld, 2007; Barkow, 2010; Deamer and Bernstein, 2010). Most of the iconic buildings of the last decade are the result of highly advanced computationally related fabrication and construction processes. Our focus here is to attempt to map the body of concepts, processes and technologies that constitute the term *material fabrication of design*. If architecture is to truly return to its sources in material practice, it will be via the high level of integration between design and materialization that advanced technology has begun to mediate.

The operative change is the integration between design, fabrication and construction. The degree of digital information flow has implications for all phases and characteristics of architecture as a practice, from the requisite knowledge of an evolving discipline to the institutional connections and nature of its traditional partnerships. Research and education are two institutions that are significantly caught up in this process of cultural transformation so strongly driven by intellectual liberation suddenly realized by the new technologies. Theories of *mass customization* are proving realistic as advances in the *new materiality* in integration with its counter-form, *material fabrication*, are becoming the driving forces of digital design innovation.

We will attempt to distinguish the most significant of the streams of development and their conceptual sources as they have emerged in the relationship between design, materialization, fabrication and construction. The transition from high-tech to digital-tech has become a *raison d'être* of a generation of the profession. To varying degrees, the continuity between design and materialization has become a central theme and design characteristic in practices such as Barkow/Leibinger in its close relationship with the digital machine tool producer, Trumpf; Heatherwick, in its inventive conception of material expression; and SHoP, in its development of an architecture based upon the adaptability and variability of existing industrial potential. Digital interfacing between design and production has also become an important function of research practice in larger offices such as Gehry Systems, Foster Associates and Zaha Hadid. This interfacing has also become the purview of engineering offices such as Arup, Buro Happold, AKT, Bollinger + Grohmann, and others. However, fabrication-based design is distinctively architectonic and represents a knowledge base shared by both the architect and design engineer.

Fabrication, from the Latin for making by assembly, is a concept that has undergone an epiphany in the last decade and has rediscovered itself as "making through computation." Generically, fabrication, or *computer-controlled machine fabrication processes*, consists of a series of technologies. Among these are *cutting* (by laser or water jet) and *3-D printing* (SLS, selective laser sintering) which is a process of construction by layers. In distinction to SLS, which is an *additive process*, fabrication also involves *subtractive processes.* Computer-controlled routers are examples of subtractive processes of fabrication.

There are three additional terminological distinctions that are relevant. While all fabrication processes are essentially *CNC*, or *computer numerical control*, certain of these technologies, primarily 3-D printing, are considered *rapid prototyping*, in which RP technologies are generally limited to prototyping rather than manufacturing. *Robotic fabrication* employs robots to perform additive fabrication (e.g. brick laying), or subtractive fabrication (e.g. routing), or other forms of processing (e.g. folding) in cases in which the process requires the geographic mobility and/or geometric flexibility of the robot. Finally we can distinguish between workshop scale devices and numerous larger-scale CNC manufacturing devices that are employed in contemporary integrated fabrication and construction (Emergence and Design Group and Sischka, 2004; Menges, 2006).

Fabricating design, or *fabrication design*, may be considered the derivation of design formation processes through the design potential of the tool. This *joy of tooling*, or the derivation of design formation in a logical *sequence from tool to process to form* has been one of the major impacts upon design of the past few years. Tooling design by fabrication means that *the form generative potential of the tool to materialize form* can be exploited as a generative paradigm. With respect to design education this idea has proved to be revolutionary in its impact; it has also created a situation in which instrumentality, or instrumental capability, has often exceeded the understanding of truly creative potential.

While several years ago it was a rarity to find a fabrication lab in architectural and design schools, today the absence of such a lab is a rarity. Despite the possibility of a new *formalism of fabrication*, particularly in the schools, when it is good, it is very good, as in the case of the series of pavilions designed and built by students of the Architectural Association (AA) in London over the last decade. Iwamoto (2009) has classified and cataloged the *form-generational affordances* of fabrication processes at the scale of furniture, installations and exhibitions. Jürgen Mayer's *Metropol Parasol* in Seville exploits the irregular planar segmented-rib grid structure that has become perhaps one of the most well known formal paradigms in design as a byproduct of the formal potential of the laser cutter.

We have seen that in understanding fabrication there is an important distinction between the CNC fabrication of industrial scale components and systems on the one hand, and the workshop scale modeling of material structures on the other. In the first case, this is part of the industrial shift from the *mass production* of standardized elements and systems to the *mass customization* of differentiated building elements and systems. This historical transition is now being accelerated by the growing ubiquity of digital manufacturing processes.

The support for the materialization and construction of complex and highly variable geometries is also characteristic of workshop scale RP. While the growing emphasis in architectural processes in digital manufacturing is upon the seamless *integration of design data* from design to production, the focus of workshop scale RP is upon experimentation in the relationship between form and technique. The first approach of fabrication has been presented in the work and writings of Scheurer (designtoproduction), Shelden (Gehry Systems) and Ceccato (Zaha Hadid). The second approach of fabrication has been presented and classified in the writing of Iwamoto.

Another formative distinction exists between the fabrication of recognized component product systems and assemblies (e.g. structural elements, curtain wall assemblies) versus the *fabrication as design*, that is, the design of material systems, or of materials themselves. This distinction touches upon a seminal set of concepts in the future of fabrication.

Digital materiality in the work and theoretical writings of Willmann, Gramazio and Kohler relates to the interrelationship between digital and material processes in design and construction. In their new work on performative materiality they engage issues related to interactive complexity and control of space (this volume). This is a design technique in which programming and data, and materials and construction are interwoven in a complex, continuous, integrated process. The idea that materialization process can become *informed* or enriched with digital information begins to enable the formulation of certain *orders of design*. The results of these internal computational logics is that materials and material systems can be *grown* through methods and in forms that are highly organic. Here design and programming become closely integrated through the *mediation of material*. This introduces a new interpretation of *digital craftsmanship* that integrates the digital with the material.

In digital materiality there is complete coordination between design and construction with the idea of knowledge and data processes of construction as part of the origin of design. Much of the work involves robotic processes that are transforming our concepts of the boundaries of serial repetition. As digital programming begins to provide the instrumental basis for design, the objective of design is transformed from the visual representation of form to the design of material processes.

If digital materiality enriches material with digital characteristics, *mediated materiality* offers the potential for the complete integration of form, material structure and performativity within the design of the material itself. The research and design of Neri Oxman (2010) extends the potential of fabrication to mediate the behavior and properties of materiality on a heterogeneous and differentiated basis in conformance with ecological conditions. The ability to achieve continuous heterogeneous materiality at both model and construction scales opens the potential of totally new methods of design and production. Inspired by natural forms and processes of design, *Material Ecology* presents computational ways of designing and making through material fabrication (N. Oxman, 2011, 2012).

Material ecology transforms the design sequence of form–structure–material to material–structure–form through material fabrication. Material fabrication design provides new approaches to *performative form finding* (e.g. in design of the performative chaise, *Beast*, and the therapeutic glove for relief of Carpal Tunnel Syndrome; N. Oxman, 2010).

Fabrication is one of the most exciting frontiers of digital design with profound social and industrial implications (Gershenfeld, 2007; Hopkinson, Hague and Dickens, 2006). We can anticipate the evolution of design rationale through the formative integration of design and its media of production (Carpo, 2011). As emerging technology drives the transformation of media we can also expect that we will discover new frontiers of knowledge that will impact both upon the culture of praxis and the education of the designer.

Barkow, Frank (2010), "Fabricating Design: A Revolution of Choice," in Oxman, Rivka and Oxman, Robert, *The New Structuralism: Design, Engineering and Architectural Technologies*, AD (*Architectural Design*), Profile No. 206, July/Aug, pp. 940–101

Barkow/Leibinger (2009), *An Atlas of Fabrication*, AA, London

Beorkrem, Christopher (2013), *Material Strategies in Digital Fabrication*, Routledge, Oxford

Ceccato, Cristiano (2010), "Constructing Parametric Architecture," *Analogue and Digital*, Detail, Vol. 4, July/August, pp. 336–340

Corser, Robert, ed. (2010). *Fabricating Architectures: Selected Readings in Digital Design and Manufacturing*, Princeton Architectural Press, New York

Deamer, Peggy and Bernstein, Phillip G., eds. (2010). *Building (in) the Future: Recasting Labor in Architecture*, Yale School of Architecture, New Haven, and Princeton Architectural Press, New York

Dunn, Nick (2012), *Digital Fabrication in Architecture*, Lawrence King, London

Emergence and Design Group and Sischka, Johann (2004), "Manufacturing Complexity," in Hensel, Michael, Menges, Achim and Weinstock, Michael, eds., *Emergence:*

Morphogenetic Design Strategies, AD (Architectural Design), Profile No. 169, Vol. 74, No. 3, May/June, pp. 72–79

Gershenfeld, Neil (2007), Fab – the Coming Revolution On Your Desktop – From Personal Computers to Personal Fabrication, Basic Books, New York

Glynn, Ruairi and Sheil, Bob (2011), Fabricate: Making Digital Architecture, Riverside Architectural Press, London

Hopkinson, N., Hague, R.J.M. and Dickens, P.M., eds. (2006), Rapid Manufacturing: An Industrial Revolution for the Digital Age, John Wiley & Sons, West Sussex, UK

Iwamoto, Lisa (2009), Digital Fabrications: Architectural and Material Techniques, Princeton Architectural Press, New York

Kieran, Stephen and Timberlake, James (2004), Refabricating Architectures: How Manufacturing Methodologies Are Poised to Transform Building Construction, McGraw-Hill, New York

Menges, Achim (2006), "Manufacturing Diversity," in Hensel, Michael, Menges, Achim and Weinstock, Michael, eds., Techniques and Technologies in Morphogenetic Design, AD (Architectural Design), Profile No. 180, Vol. 76, No. 2, March/April, pp.70–77

Menges, Achim (2008), "Manufacturing Performance," in Hensel, Michael and Menges, Achim, Versatility and Vicissitude: Performance and Morpho-Ecological Design, AD (Architectural Design), Profile No. 192, Vol. 78, No. 2, March/April, pp. 42–47.

Oxman, Neri (2011), "Variable Property Rapid Prototyping," Journal of Virtual and Physical Prototyping (VPP), Vol. 6, No. 1, pp. 3–31

Oxman, Neri (2012), "Programming Matter," in Menges, Achim, ed., Architectural Design, Material Computation: Higher Integration in Mophogenetic Design, Vol. 82, Issue 2, March/April, pp. 88–95

Reeser, Amanda and Schafer, Ashley, eds. (2004), New Technologies/New Architectures, Praxis, No. 6

Schodek, Daniel, Bechthold, Martin, Kimo Griggs, James, Kao, Kenneth and Steinberg, Marco (2005), Digital Design and Manufacturing: CAD/CAM Applications in Architecture and Design, John Wiley and Sons, Hoboken, NJ

Sheil, Bob, ed. (2005). Design Through Making, AD (Architectural Design), Vol. 75, No. 4, July/August

> List of Key Concepts

computer-aided manufacturing (CAM)

computer numerical control (CNC)

differentiated materiality

differentiation

digital craftsmanship

digital form finding

digital material (digital materiality)

digital materialization

digital orders

fabrication

fabrication design

fabrication form generation

form-generation affordances

heterogeneous material (materiality)

informed materiality

mass customization

mass production

material ecology

material fabrication

mediated matter (materiality)

new materiality

rapid prototyping

robotic fabrication

selective laser sintering (SLS)

serialization

serial repetition

standardization

variability

The synthesis of data and material, which decisively failed to develop in the early digital age, is being realized – enticingly, playfully, and sensually – in today's architecture. This becomes apparent in various medial, spatial and structural manifestations, whereby one premise persists: in the moment in which two seemingly separate worlds meet through the interaction between digital and material processes, data and material can no longer be interpreted as a mere complement but rather as an inherent condition and thus an essential expression of architecture in the digital age. A *Digital Materiality* is emerging, where the interplay between data and material is seen, then, in a new light, as an interdependent structuring of architecture and its material manifestations.[1] *Digital Materiality* is thus not incidental, nor supplemental, nor is it a process of embellishment; instead it corresponds to an extensive collaboration, which can be analytically developed and implemented on an architectural scale. This leads as well to a new form of architectural expression and its material sensuality.

Today, at the threshold between the mechanical and digital age, it appears that a large part of contemporary architecture is determined by algorithmically established design procedures in which the constructive and building implementation is of insufficient significance and appears secondary; it is resolved only upon completion of the architectural design. With *Digital Materiality* something entirely different is introduced: instead of realizing a design, an image, or a drawing, a comprehensive design and building process is conceived. Here, the central issue is not the design of a form; rather it is the design of a production process that is informed essentially by the constructive organization of the material. Thereby conceptual commonalities between the construction of a building component and the programming of a computer become apparent; just as a computer program that conducts different operations in sequential order, constructive principles can be determined that define the production of architectural components as interrelated production steps.[2]

The architectural creative intention is expressed in the setting of essential parameters and dependencies as well as by the actual design of a comprehensive building system. It unfolds fully through the constructive collaboration of highly diverse parameters of the design and its materialization. Thus *Digital Materiality* is characterized by material precision and clarity; it is uncoupled, however, from formal guidelines and relocated to another (constructive) level. It is a design and construction process controlled in all its details by the architect, a fundamental balancing or weighing of real possibilities, so to speak, during the process of making. Conversely, we are not talking about building systems that can be configured endlessly in the virtual space of a computer.[3] Rather

20

Towards an Extended Performative Materiality – Interactive Complexity and the Control of Space

Jan Willmann, Fabio Gramazio and Matthias Kohler

Figure 20.1

the constructive logic of programming and material formation are linked to each other. The digital construction process reveals itself to be a constructive structuring, disengaged from the formal, the result of a "demystified" understanding of digital technologies and a freer, more autonomous use of the computer.[4]

Consequently, *Digital Materiality* allows one to combine the abilities and deficiencies of human beings and machines to deliberate advantage. In the digital age this means that while the machine with its numerical logic can rule over an infinitely large quantity of numbers, only human beings with their cognitive abilities and intuitive approaches can recognize meaning in them. The result is an added architectural value through the "interactive connection" of the human and the machine, who are not equal but rather "equivalent" partners. The added value points the way to completely new possibilities for a future constructional reality – not just quantitatively but also qualitatively. Thus *Digital Materiality* is far more than a mere rhetorical figure in the digital discourse; it represents an architectural vision.[5]

> New Modular Capacities in Space

The central problem is to what extent the difference between data and material, or digital and analogous realities, can be maintained, since *Digital Materiality* would seem to dispense with the frequently discussed dichotomies of programming and construction, of human beings and machines. Thus it recalls what Gottfried Semper pointed out long ago – the constructional requirements of architecture can be deduced primarily from different cultural and material models. According to Semper, the architectural result is formed by its own history, that is, by the process of its origin, the process of its making. It appears relieved of its original characteristic style of form and appearance, nearly emancipated. As Semper puts it, despite all these influences and transformations, in the end the different characteristics should remain recognizable and "owe their origin to the combined engineering arts in a primitive architectonic installation."[6]

As do many other projects by Gramazio & Kohler, the project *The Fragile Structure* also demonstrates these principles.[7] It makes apparent that *Digital Materiality* develops its greatest potential whenever the number of single components that stand in relation to one another is particularly high.[8] In *The Fragile Structure* a robot freely stacks more than one thousand identical wood elements without additional fasteners, so that the issue of inherent stability takes on a decisive role in the design. As the dimensions of *The Fragile Structure* exceed by many times those of the working area of a

Facing page

Figure 20.1: View inside the architectural vision of the Flight Assembled Architecture installation. Image credit: Gramazio & Kohler and Raffaello D'Andrea in collaboration with ETH Zurich.

conventional industrial robot, the installation was assembled by a mobile robotic unit making use of caterpillar tracks.[9]

The project *The Fragile Structure* was built in a parking garage because it closely resembles a construction site; the slanted floor, freestanding columns, and limited ceiling height demanded continuous adaptations of the design towards the specific physical reality of the surroundings. Through the mobile robotic unit equipped with sensor technology, it was possible to scan the environment and quantify the geometric deviations to the idealized computer model and thus adapt the building process in real time.

In *The Fragile Structure*, curved planes seamlessly merge into each other and span the distance between ceiling and floor; an interaction is set up between the rhythmic repetition of the additively assembled wood elements and their delicate dissolution into the spatially adapted, self-supporting entirety. Because of the porous assembly of the wood elements, a complex visual effect appears depending on the viewer's perspective and on light conditions. Of course this is evident only at a certain distance; if one steps closer the illusion dissolves, leaving only a multiplicity of geometrically discrete elements. This means that one is dealing not only with the appearance of a material compound structure, but also with a visual and, in the original meaning of the word, a "virtual" event, that is, with a kind of "virtual materiality." Consequently, in reference to *The Fragile Structure*, it can be stated that such an architectural structure and its effect do not just inform each other, rather a further architectural potential of this structural and visual interdependency becomes tangible.

The Fragile Structure was initially developed by means of physical prototypes. Early on, numerous robotically assembled scaled models were built, which allowed distinctly different building systems to be developed and validated in very rapid sequences – in an "evolutionary physical way." Moreover, the specific objective of an "untethered" structure that approaches a state of equilibrium made it difficult to accomplish this development work by hand. Through its constructional clarity and differentiated articulation, *The Fragile Structure* shows how concrete materialistic-empirical research is granted an important place in the digital age. Its value accrues because this kind of architectural experimentation with programming and constructing not only forms complex compounds, linkages and aggregations; but also, within such a connection of data and material, these can now be implemented in a controlled way within a specific spatial environment.

> The Extended Operationality of Architectural Utopia

As becomes apparent in *Flight Assembled Architecture*, this strategy can go far beyond the scale of building components. The project for the Fonds régional d'art contemporain (FRAC) Centre in Orléans is the first architectural installation in the world that has been built by flying robots.[10] In this case, several "quadrocopters" developed by Raffaello D'Andrea put together more than 1,500 elements to create a six-meter-tall complex vertical structure. The flight behavior of the quadrocopters is based on the algorithmic translation of digital design data, according to which they land on a platform where they pick up individual elements and assemble them, following an assigned construction sequence. Thus a geometrically differentiated structure is created where the individual building layers are mutually offset to present a six-hundred-meter-tall building that paves the way for entirely new scales of digitally fabricated architectures.

Flight Assembled Architecture is not only an architectural installation, but rather a vertical urban utopia – a *Vertical Village*.[11] With 180 floors and a usable space of 1.3 million square meters, the *Vertical Village* provides living space for more than 30,000 inhabitants. With its porous structure it creates the largest possible diversity of urban living.[12] Consisting of vertical core structures and staggered-module chains, the *Vertical Village* employs a grid-like organization that allows a great degree of freedom to vary the arrangements of the modules. However, the grid does not run horizontally as in a conventional city; rather it is turned vertically and is closed to form a circular unit. This results in a geometric compound that is the basis for the

Figure 20.2: Flight Assembled Architecture installation, assembled from 1500 building modules at the FRAC Centre Orléans. Image credit: Gramazio & Kohler and Raffaello D'Andrea in collaboration with ETH Zurich. Copyright: François Lauginie, Gramazio & Kohler owns all rights of use.

particularly constructive, self-stabilizing properties of the entire structure. Moreover, in the transition from an ideal urban plan to a spatially differentiated and highly condensed urbanity, it also strives for nothing less than a revision of the organizational scheme of a city in the twenty-first century. The monotonous and often unbearable density of earlier times becomes an engine for a newly discovered urbanity.

Flight Assembled Architecture also represents a technological "intensification." Here the use of flying robots not only provides for the architectural implementation of design data, their accumulation and processing, but also results in the implementation of an actual, built installation. Far beyond that, the "quadrocopters" correspond to a model of thinking; they are a kind of "conceptional door opener" that can free one from the constraint of the present and facilitate instead a radical architectural utopia that excludes neither the possibility of material experiments nor a possible built reality of the future. Similar to the case of the industrial robot, which underwent a breakthrough in industrial automation several decades before its first application in architecture, the flying "variation" also represents an already established device that has been the focus of many research endeavors and is available on the commercial market. Similar to the industrial robot, the quadrocopter has a "generic nature."[13] It is important to stress, however, that the quadrocopter has the capacity to leave the conventional work area of an industrial robot; the airspace not only corresponds to an architectural environment, it also becomes an all-determining design paradigm.[14]

From its essential tendency to combine different technologies, perspectives, and potentials *Flight Assembled Architecture* generates – for the visitor – a near "state of hovering" between a real architectural installation and a utopia. Thus the installation – although on a scale a hundred times smaller than the projected *Vertical Village* – calls into question the supposedly distinct border between utopia and realities. Beyond that, the focus on the creation of a parallel reality, which is recorded with matching precision in *Flight Assembled Architecture*, thus becomes a systematic expansion of both the imaginable and the real.[15]

At the same time, the boundaries between installation and building process, between architecture and robotics, increasingly dissolve here and themselves become an instrument that fathoms anew the "borders between the real and that which is conceivable" and present *Digital Materiality* in a new architectural "perspectivity." This indicates how we may understand and investigate robot-based design processes in the digital age of architecture. It registers that empirical and at the same time "speculative" character, without which the relation to architectural research would remain disengaged and distanced from both reality and future of building. Thus *Flight Assembled Architecture* is not restricted to a pure "projection or imagining of the future," rather it is propelled by a concrete "logic of making." In the history of architecture there has always been an impetus to tame the new and thus to transform a multiplicity of possibilities and risks into concrete realities. Consequently, utopia in architecture – beginning with ancient descriptions of ideal states and cities, biblical approximations, the first architectural theory by Vitruvius, the idealized medieval representations of cities, the ideal city, architecture of the revolution up to the early socialists, modernists, and postmodern subversity – has its firm place in the history of the built and planned environment.[16] With this premise, the installation *Flight Assembled Architecture* shows that – as in all projects by Gramazio & Kohler – it is not a distinct architectural drawing or a pure picture-like vision that stands in the foreground; above all, it is a matter of pointing out, comprehending, and implementing an architectural process with all its spatial, functional, and aesthetic consequences. Thereby *Flight Assembled Architecture* opens up a radical material practice and comprehensive interdisciplinarity; at precisely this moment utopia becomes research into the future.

> The "Interactive Connection" of Man and Machine

In navigating through the world of digital design and fabrication, the question always arises as to why these tasks cannot be accomplished without a robot. Indeed, if viewed from a global perspective one must concede that it is easier for human beings than for a robot to produce a brick wall based on a simple, repetitive bond. What might be called the "operationality of the robot"[17] pertains in situations of a certain complexity. This means that every material entity that can only be built precisely and efficiently with the help of a robot becomes at the same time the reason why the robot facilitates what human beings cannot do. A robot unfolds its potential precisely where an increasing number of complex spatial and tectonic relations as well as individual requirements justify its use.[18]

As the following project, *Spatial Aggregations*, demonstrates, the question arises of how to fundamentally deal with architectural complexity; that is, the problem of the relation of spatial differentiality and functional performance. Initially this corresponds less to the efficiency, precision, and flexibility facilitated by the robot, than to the possibility of monitoring and controlling complex material processes. These can be sequentially developed and implemented on a larger scale and thereby targeted for particular architectural purposes.[19] Only there, where these artifacts are materialized does the possibility emerge for an extended performative materiality in architecture. For the implementation of the project *Spatial Aggregations*, simple rod elements were used. These are connected point-like with each other, and a large quantity are assembled in a geometrically differentiated manner. This results in statically redundant, spatially differentiated load-bearing structures, which – in contrast to traditional framework constructions – are individually adaptable and capable of assuming diverse configurations. Through robot-based fabrication, it becomes possible to produce these rod structures without additional measurement or auxiliary structures; that is, the robot grabs a generic rod element, shortens and marks it before positioning it in space, according to the data describing the overall geometric layout as well as the assembly sequence. In this sense, the assembly sequence exerts a decisive influence on the architectural design and building process; essential here are both the spatial accessibility and the structural stiffness generated by the connection of the individual elements.

This process requires new decision-making mechanisms; most of all it requires an intensive collaboration of human beings and machines because the assembly of the rod elements is in no way a fully autonomous procedure. On the contrary, human beings become part of the mechanical process by inserting individual rod elements and installing them according to the previously applied markings. In this instance the robot merely positions them in space. The tolerances introduced through the human intervention are in the meantime compensated for by the other elements put in place by the robot. This example demonstrates the potential for future adaptive and recursive processes in digital design and construction procedures. The individual elements of *Spatial Aggregations* fit adaptively as described to form a coherent, differentiated and nevertheless harmonious whole so that even more unique and highly resolved spatial structures can be built. The goal therefore is not so much the pure, automatized materialization of a concrete, previously defined scheme, as rather a procedural investigation into the cooperation between the human and the machine during a complex constructive assembly process.

While experimental research in architecture in the 1970s was still entirely concerned with "natural,"[20] self-organizing or purely industrial-modular

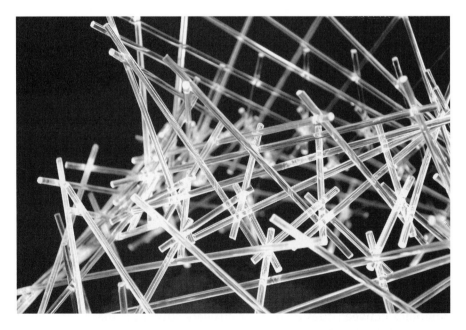

Figure 20.3: The robot made, complex structures "Spatial Aggregations", assembled from a large number of straight rods. Image credit: Gramazio & Kohler, ETH Zurich.

building systems, a very interesting shift emerges here: *Spatial Aggregations* is probably an important trial not least of all because the interaction between human intervention and digital fabrication procedures can be directly connected – what emerges from *Spatial Aggregations* are highly resolved, spatially complex formations, the results of which can be predicted or simulated only conditionally; they become accessible only through real experiments and actual materialization processes.

In this, it must be stated that human beings will in no way be relativized by the robot; instead they will establish themselves as leading figures in a constructive reality between programming and fabrication.[21] The implied turn towards the connection of digital fabrication and human intervention could prove to be so far-reaching that the central issue of our debate would consequently be the opposite; that is, through the use of the robot, the human experiences a far-reaching re-conceptualization in the "force field"[22] of the architectural information age.

> The Return of the Machine

It is perhaps this conceptual connection of human beings and machines that imbues *Digital Materiality* with its expression and makes possible the introduction of the robot into the architectural discipline. As "multiple tool," the robot allows one to execute diverse applications in a rapid and precise way, but above all, to work directly at the immediate interface between digital and material spheres and thus to exert decisive influence on the physical world through programming. Since the beginning of the 1990s, the robot has indeed become a primary tool of industrial and standardized forms of production, which throughout the entire twentieth century have been influential in our understanding of contemporary society and its stimuli for the design disciplines. However, the development towards an increasingly reflexive, individual and global "stratification"[23] of cultural forms paradoxically represents an additional, almost complementary "turning point."[24] This explains why, in the future, the robot will be granted more rather than less significance: because the robot masters not only the language of unity but also that of diversity.

Unquestionably, the hardly noted dispute about the division of labor in the digital age of architecture belongs in this context; that is, the transformation of labor and its implications for architectural building processes.[25] Particularly here, the use of the robot makes clear that instead of perceiving the robot in the context of industrialization or unleashed capitalist production of goods, it rather must be seen as an expression of a more fundamental process of the digital age: as an expression of a new digital "workability" that is, as a fabric of diverse relations that has not only dispensed with the difference between authorship and the actual producer, the production of an original and its copy, but it has also materialized in an architectural reality, which has already begun.

As if this potential had always been present in the "DNA" of the robot, now comes a breakthrough that makes the robot the suitable tool, not only of a standardized but also of an individual and global world of production. Its "generic" properties handle the most diverse tasks with consistent efficiency, precision, and flexibility while always remaining open for additional adaptations, extensions and tasks. The same is true for architecture: the robot attains significance for the architectural discipline because it allows for the implementation of individual work processes instead of uniform, repetitive building sequences, and it realizes them on an architectural scale. Thereby the robot connects the (old) world of industrial logic with the (new) world of the information age, making it possible – between efficiency and precision – to technologically grant the general primacy of individualization.

The concepts of the industrial division of labor, widespread to this day, are based on individual work sequences, on spatial and temporal surveys of human being–machine systems, which build largely on empirical knowledge. Frederick Winslow Taylor was the first to aim for clear rules and instructions for dealing with complex issues of the division of labor, exchangeability of single parts, and efficient mass production. Although production processes became considerably more precise and less expensive – the same is true for standardization, distribution, and the repair of industrial artifacts that were produced in this way – one always referred to the implementation of predefined objects and sequential procedures.[26] However, in the post-mechanical age, the fixed adherence to sequential production of architectural artifacts and their limited variation have been dispensed with, so that "productivity" and "specialization" are no longer necessarily contradictory, rather they realistically depict the interconnectedness of information and technology. The sequential categorization of architectural production thus falls away, and with it the classic division of labor of the discipline. It is precisely here that the robot in architecture makes an important contribution, so that the sometimes dialectic and equally marginal influence of digital technologies on architecture now corresponds to a "reflexive" form, through which it gains considerable significance. In this process diverse influences and disciplines enrich each other and enter into a mutual connection – less because of increased sales or efficiency potentials than from an awareness of a culturally strengthened architectural production capacity.[27]

> Towards an Extended Performative Materiality in Architecture

For our present discussion, the great achievement is that the questions of efficiency, precision and flexibility can be simultaneously reinterpreted as a question of how to deal fundamentally with building. What is sometimes inconceivable in our current modes of thinking is that the robot-facilitated approach to a comprehensive technological fabrication capability corresponds in no way to a devaluation of human skills; quite the contrary, these can be considerably expanded through the "operationality" of the robot. Thus monitoring and control of complex material processes are not only improved, they can be implemented in a differentiated way and thereby targeted for architectural purposes. Within these conceptual goals, the robot no longer is tied to the making of things, it also connects with the thinking of things.

According to Mario Carpo, the consequence is that the division between the acts of designing and producing that has existed since the Renaissance dissolves. Thus, the "operationality" of the robot is not related exclusively to the material act of producing, of material operation, and of pure implementation, but rather equally to the way architecture is intellectually conceived, programmed, and designed. Carpo's thesis gains analytic acuity when it is modified to say, conversely: programming can be interpreted as an "anthropological" form of designing, constructing, and materialization, so that it is ultimately questionable whether – in the synthesis of programming and robot-based fabrication – the intrinsic "self-referentiality" of human beings and machine becomes generally visible. Thus it can be stated: the robot is a fascinating instrument in architecture, particularly because it facilitates – removed from any determinism – the discovery of new constructive and spatial worlds, which in turn provide new insights for further discoveries. It remains to be seen how the robot will develop in the future. However, one thing is certain: in no way does operationality of data and material aim merely at digital aesthetics; it is far more than a short-lived chapter of the digital age. Rather it is a "perspectivity" that facilitates – from concrete technology-based examination of computer programming to fabrication with the aid of flying robots – an open, complex and tangible asset of architecture. The thrust of digital advancement in design and manufacture can be thus investigated and included in the content of the discipline; it becomes possible to spatially and materially relate these developments and thereby to make them culturally significant.

1   The merger of the terms "digital" and "materiality" can be traced to the essay "Digital Materiality in Architecture" in Fabio Gramazio and Matthias Kohler, *Digital Materiality in Architecture*, Lars Müller Publishers, Baden, 2008. Combining seemingly ambivalent concepts – the digital and the material – architecture is enabled to generate new constructive and sensual realities where data and material, programming and construction are interwoven by the techniques of digital fabrication. This allows the designer not only to control the architectural manufacturing process through design data and therefore to "inform" material, but also to express a new sensuality in the digital age of architecture, being characterized by an unusually large number of precisely arranged elements, a sophisticated level of detail, and the simultaneous presence of different scales of formation.

2   Central to this is an additive principle, which allows the assembly of complex architectural structures from single elements, and the control and manipulation of them so that new kinds of spatial and functional configurations can arise.

3   Cache, B., Towards and Associative Architecture, in: Leach, N., Turnbull, D. and Williams C., eds., *Digital Tectonics*, Wiley & Sons, 2004, 103–109.

4   Gramazio, F. and Kohler, M., *Digital Materiality in Architecture*, Lars Müller Publishers, Baden, 2008, 8.

5   For more information, see Professorship for Architecture and Digital Fabrication, ETH Zurich, http://www.dfab.arch.ethz.ch (01.06.2012).

6   Cf. Semper, G., *Der Stil in den technischen und tektonischen Künsten oder praktische Ästhetik, Band 1*, Bruckmann, Munich, 1878, p. 7.

7   The project *The Fragile Structure* was developed 2012 at the ETH Zurich and realised with the support of Schilliger Holz AG (Project leader: Luka Piskorec; team: Volker Helm, Selen Ercan, Thomas Cadalbert; students: Petrus Aejmelaeus Lindström, Leyla Ilman, David Jenny, Michi Keller, Beat Lüdi). For more information, see Professorship for Architecture and Digital Fabrication, ETH Zurich, http://www.dfab.arch.ethz.ch/web/e/lehre/225.html (01.07.2012).

8   Interestingly, this debate is directly related to the modularity of such systems. *The Fragile Structure* demonstrates that such a modular approach on the one hand incorporates the traditional logic of serial building systems; on the other hand, however, it articulates a wholly new state of affairs where such a generic and multiple construction system increases the integration of new freedoms and complexities. This is, however, less radical as it is generally propagated within contemporary architectural discourse on mass customization since it also leads in parallel to ever new conventions, serializations, and simplifications, even when this "return of standardization" is first out of direct visibility.

9   This implies that the traditional use of industrial ground robots in controlled environments is challenged by this project, in that a mobile robot unit is made capable of manufacturing digitally informed and geometrically complex building components, to a certain extent "in-situ." For more information, see "In-situ robotic fabrication" (Echord/EU-funded research project), Professorship for Architecture and Digital Fabrication, http://www.dfab.arch.ethz.ch/web/e/forschung/198.html (01.07.2012).

10   This project is based on a collaboration of the Professorship for Architecture and Digital Fabrication (Prof. Gramazio, Prof. Kohler) and the Institute for Dynamic Systems and Control (Prof. Raffaello D'Andrea), both of ETH Zurich.

11   Cf. Gramazio, F., Kohler M. and D'Andrea, R., *Flight Assembled Architecture*, Editions HYX, Orléans, 2013.

12   The question of the diversity and accessibility of urban spaces and their contents becomes a central theme of the *Vertical Village*, in as much as the embedding of four gigantic continuous public double-rings with a combined length of 1 km each, are found not, as usually is the case, on the lowest floor, but are spread across the entire height of the building volume, creating heterogeneous city structures. The public space thus spreads across the entire height. Together with the inner courtyard – with a diameter of over 300 meters, certainly comparable with a valley in a landscape – this creates the possibility of an urban generosity and permeability, which treats public life with all it offers, less as uniform, horizontal and insular and more as an essential feature. At the same time, a completely unique form of intimacy takes place. For through the sheer size and structure of the *Vertical Village*, the inhabitants and their comings and goings are only roughly visible from outside, whilst remaining recognizable: thus an intimate presence within the *Vertical Village* is created.

13   For more information, see Institute for Dynamic Systems and Control, http://www.idsc.ethz.ch (01.07.2012).

14   Cf. Kohler, M., Aerial Architecture, in: LOG 25, New York, 2012, 23–30.

15   Tönnesmann, A., *Die Kunst der Renaissance*, C.H. Beck, München, 2007, 22–23.

16   Cf. Alison, J. and Brayer, M.-A., *Future City: Experiment and Utopia in Architecture*, Thames & Hudson, London, 2007.

17   Kohler, M., Gramazio F. and Willmann, J., Die Operationalität von Daten und Material im Digitalen Zeitalter, in: *Die Zukunft des Bauens, Detail* – Institut für internationale Architektur-Dokumentation, Munich, 2011, 8–17.

18 Conversely, it would make less sense to use robots producing standardized building components, even when this would be technically possible. For an architectural use of robots for such things, the essential complexity would be missing; quite apart from the fact that the human represents with craft skills developed over millennia, and the highly advanced technology of mass production, a far more efficient framework within which simple and similar components can be manufactured.

19 The project *Spatial Aggregations* was developed 2012 at the ETH Zurich and realized with the support of REHAU (Project leader: Luka Piskorec; team: Thomas Cadalbert; students: Petrus Aejmelaeus-Lindström, David Jenny, Gabriela Schär, Ripple Chauhan, Evangelos Pantazis, Stylianos Psaltis, Rahil Shah, Stella Azariadi, Ivana Damjanovic, Hjalmar Schmid, Lukas Mersch, Katharina Schwiete, Enzo Valerio, Andreas Kissel, Kulshresth Patel, Christian Grewe-Rellmann, Sonja Cheng, Joe Liao, Yushi Sasada, Tarika Sajnani, Janki Vyas, Bo Li, Yuji Mukaiyama, James Yeo, Eveline Job, Joséphine Simonian). For more information, see http://www.dfab.arch.ethz.ch/web/e/lehre/228. html (01.07.2012).

20 Otto, F., *Gestaltwerdung. Zur Formentstehung in Natur, Technik und Baukunst*, Müller, Cologne, 1988, 5.

21 Cf. Kolarevic, B., *Architecture in the Digital Age: Design and Manufacturing*, Spon Press, New York, 2003.

22 Cf. Bourdieu, P., *Zur Soziologie der symbolischen Formen*, Suhrkamp, Frankfurt/M., 1997.

23 Cf. Beck, U., Giddens, A. and Lash, S., *Reflexive Modernization. Politics, Tradition and Aesthetics in the Modern Social Order*, Cambridge University Press, Cambridge, 1994.

24 What has not remained unknown is that Konrad Wachsmann's *Wendepunkt im Bauen* (1959) is situated in a similar theme, as is the work of Pier Luigi Nervi or Felix Candela. Here it is essential that Wachsmann had recognized early on the conceptual effects of industrialized production processes for architecture, and taken these beforehand for the digital age. Within this "Marxist" perspective, it is Wachsmann's distinction between technology and the art of building which is essential to the debate conducted here, insofar as through the robot the "natural sense for material and joints" Wachsmann postulated appears to be newly articulated and experiences a new "turning point," in the age of the viable individual and digital production of architecture.

25 Cf. Aureli, P. V., *The Possibility of an Absolute Architecture*, MIT Press, Cambridge, MA., 2011, 251.

26 Cf. Taylor, F. W., *The Principles of Scientific Management*, Harper & Brothers, London, 1913.

27 Cf. DeLanda, M., *A New Philosophy of Society. Assemblage Theory and Social Complexity*, Continuum, New York, 2006.

That matter is secondary to shape constitutes the fallacy of design after craft. By nature, and in its rite, the material practice of craft is informed by matter, its method of fabrication, and by the environment (Semper, 1851). As in Nature, when creation *begins* with matter, *morphogenesis*, or the generation of form, is a process engendered by the physical forces of Nature (Thompson, 1942; Thom, 1975). Similarly, in the framework of this essay, *Material* is not considered a subordinate attribute of form, but rather its progenitor. Such is the story of form told from the point of view of matter, and it begins, naturally, with form's predicament.

21
Material Ecology
Neri Oxman

> Form's Predicament: a Brief History

Over the long trajectory of architectural design history, the design and production of artifacts has been characterized by a growing separation between form and matter. In contradistinction to *craft* in which material and form are organically intertwined into a tradition of making, modern design and production have historically evolved away from this integration, or in its absence, towards the compartmentalization of form making as a process independent of its sources in material knowledge (Sennett, 2008). At least since the Renaissance, with the emergence of architectural theories, form generation has become somewhat of a self-directed and autonomous body of knowledge. Within architecture and industrial design, the most culturally sensitive of the productive design fields, form has grown in both eminence and temporal precedence in the design process to the point that the condition of *form preceding materialization* has become normative and virtually intuitive in contemporary design culture. With the exception of a few pioneering cases in contemporary design, the secularization and debasement of the material realm has become axiomatic. Materiality has become, within the logic of the modernist tradition, an agency secondary to form.

The Industrial Revolution lay open the door to machine-based manufacturing and mass production. The creation of form was now to be conceived and created by the power of industrial automation, detached and independent of environmental forces and influences. The values promoted by ancient crafts (not unlike Nature's way), pronounced by the integration of material substance and construction methods, once within the province of the craftsman, were abandoned while in their place emerged a design practice based on values of mass production. Fast, cheap, repetitive and modular building types and parts were synonymous with Ford's visionary dream. Industry's victory aside, it appeared as if design's propinquity to ancient crafts and its design expressions as portrayed by vernacular forms of design was now doomed; and with it the intimate

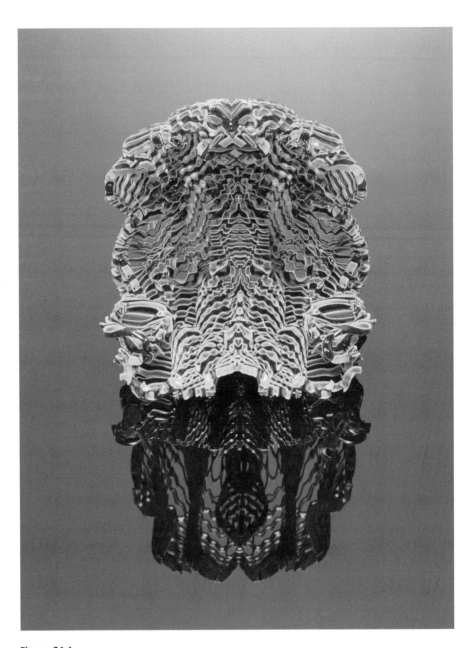

Figure 21.1

context of material technologies. Eventually, this non-material approach to the design and the automation of construction were to be reinforced under the command of computer-aided design and engineering (Jencks, 1984).

The Digital Revolution, which marked the shift from analog to digital technology, has transformed the designer's drafting board into a digital canvas. Form, it seemed, was now divorced completely from the physical reality of its manifestation. This new design space afforded much liberation in formal expression, but it has also broadened the gap between form and matter, and made the hierarchical and sequential separation of modeling, analysis and fabrication processes infinitely more pronounced.

The implementation and broad absorption of enhanced computational design tools in architectural practice has, since the early nineties, motivated a renaissance of the *formalist project* in architecture; geometrically complex shapes became emblems of creativity in digital design environments and supported the design mastery of complex geometries in form generation. This formal and geometric design orientation has also addressed "free form" design and architecture along with their enabling technologies as part of the larger design phenomenon of "non-standard" form.

> Designing (with) Nature: Towards a New Materiality

Today, perhaps under the imperatives of growing recognition of the ecological failures of modern design, inspired by the growing presence of advanced fabrication methods, design culture is witnessing a *new materiality*. Within the last decade in both industrial design and architecture, a new body of knowledge is emerging within architectural praxis. Examples of the growing interest in the technological potential of innovative material usage and material innovation as a source of design generation are developments in biomaterials, mediated and responsive materials, as well as composite materials. With the growing relevance of "materialization", new frontiers of material science and digital fabrication are supporting the emergence of new perspectives in architectural and industrial design. Thus the role of digital design research as the enabling environment of the transformation to a new age of material-based design in various design disciplines has become the cutting edge of computational design research. Here we are at the cusp of a new paradigm inspired by the *Troika* structure of craft, at the interaction of Materials Science, Digital Fabrication and the environment.

Material Ecology is an emerging field in design denoting informed relations between products, buildings, systems and their environment (Oxman,

---

Facing page

Figure 21.1: Example of Reaction-Diffusion guided 3D printing demonstrating formal variation in color, thickness, porosity and material property. Design: Neri Oxman in collaboration with W. Craig Carter, and the Mathworks. Fabricated by Objet Ltd. Image credit: Photo: Yoram Reshef, Objet.

2010). Defined as the study and design of products and processes integrating environmentally aware computational form generation and digital fabrication, the field operates at the intersection of Biology, Material Science and Engineering, and Computer Science with emphasis on environmentally informed digital design and fabrication.

> Bitmap Printing: Fabricating Nature

With the advent of digital fabrication techniques and technologies, digital material representations such as voxels (3-D pixels) and maxels (a portmanteau of the words 'material' and 'voxel') have come to represent material ingredients, for instance in the context of additive manufacturing processes. Designers are now able to compute material properties and behavior integrated into form-generation procedures.

Motivated by the prospect of designing material behavior, a novel design and technological approach for biologically inspired layered fabrication entitled *Bitmap Printing* (Figure 21.1) has been defined, implemented and explored by the author, in collaboration with Objet Ltd., Prof. W. Craig Carter, the Mathworks and in the context of new design work commissioned by the Centre Pompidou (Paris).

In this collection, 18 prototypes for the human body were fabricated, designed to augment human function such as enhancing strength, promoting flexibility, providing for comfort or exploring some functional combination. The aim was to implement material property and behavior combinations accommodating for multiple functions in the design of human armors including helmets, corsets, hip splints and various prosthetic devices. Specifically, the work explored strategies for the integration of protective functions with flexibility and comfort implementing functional gradient digital fabrication (Oxman, Keating and Tsai 2011). These experiments lay the methodological foundations for the generation of heterogeneous and functional prototype development using structural materials for humanoid armor. In order to address geometrical constraints and allow for material organization modulation, both anatomical and physiological mapping were executed during the analysis and the synthesis stages.

Anatomical and Physiological Mappings (Analysis): Combining global organismal hierarchies informed by anatomical data with local tissue composition mappings informed by physiological data (i.e. µCT scans) the aim was to achieve a fully integrated armor which varies its mechanical, chemical, environmental and thermal properties accommodating geometrical (anatomical) features and physical (physiological) properties.

Anatomical and Physiological Fabrication Strategy (Synthesis): On a global anatomical scale, basic geometrical data describing the anatomical features as transformable meshes were extracted. This network of curves and surfaces guided the distribution of material properties as behavioral patches relating to the skeletal and muscular systems. On the local physiological scale, μCT scan data converted to material distribution data informed the allocation of stiff and soft materials. A novel digital fabrication method entitled *Bitmap Printing* that facilitates the 3-D printing of 16μ physical bits was implemented to support high-resolution digital fabrication of heterogeneous functional material gradients (Figure 21.2). Each material component within the overall armor construction was designed and printed with varying physical properties informed by multi-scalar mappings.

The following example illustrates the *Bitmap Printing* concept and technique, developed in collaboration with Objet, Ltd., Neri Oxman in collaboration with W. Craig Carter (MIT) and the Mathworks and Uformia for Centre Georges Pompidou (2012).

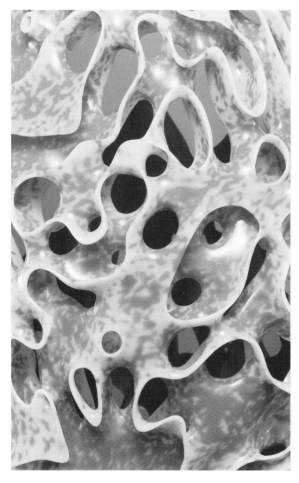

Figure 21.2: The bitmap printing technique allows for the capturing of material property data in high resolution as a collection of bitmap files. Design: Neri Oxman in collaboration with W. Craig Carter (MIT), and the Mathworks. Image credit: Photo: Yoram Reshef, Objet.

The final head shield introduces variable thickness of the shell, informed by anatomical and physiological data derived from real human skull µCT scan data. Medical scan data of a human head is selected from an open repository. Two sets of data are created and trimmed from the scan using medical imagining software simulating the hard tissue (skull) and the soft tissue (skin and muscle) (Fryazinov *et al.*, 2011). Combined, these two data sets make up the bone-to-skin threshold informing helmet thickness and material composition according to its biological counterpart such that bony perturbations in the skull are shielded with soft lamellas designed as spatial sutures (Figure 21.3).

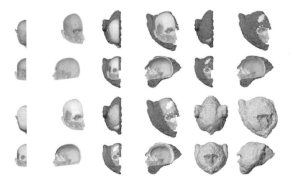

Figure 21.3: Digital images. Image credit: Neri Oxman in collaboration with W. Craig Carter (MIT), the Mathworks and Turlif Vilbrandt (Uformia).

Figure 21.4: Tissue composition data extracted from scan analysis informs geometrical and physical material properties in the design of a helmet. Design: Neri Oxman in collaboration with W. Craig Carter (MIT), the Mathworks and Turlif Vilbrandt (Uformia). Image credit: Photo: Yoram Reshef, Objet.

> What Does a Pixel Want to Be? Towards a Material Ecology

The ability to design, analyze and fabricate using a single material unit implies unity of physical and digital matter, enabling nearly seamless mappings between environmental constraints, fabrication methods and material expression (Oxman, 2010, 2011a, b). Such unity – like that found in natural bone, a bird's nest, a typical African hut or a woven basket – might promote a truly ecological design paradigm, facilitating formal expression constrained by, and supportive of, its hosting environment.

Like Kahn's brick arch (Kahn, 1969), the units of digital matter may be informed by various functions on their way to becoming and contributing to larger material organizations. The designer's voxel is equivalent to Kahn's brick, in that when combined, these material units can self-organize by way of mediating their physical properties with their external environment.

Ultimately, the faculty to author new forms of expression will depend on the craft triptych (matter, fabrication and environment) and its integration into the design practice as an undifferentiated scheme, able to process matter into shape as informed by the environment. Once achieved, architectural design will have arrived at an ecology of the artificial: a *Material Ecology*.

> Acknowledgements

This work was supported in part by an NSF EAGER grant award 1152550 "Bio-Beams: Functionally Graded Rapid Design & Fabrication." The work was also supported in part by the Institute for Collaborative Biotechnologies through grant W911NF–09–0001 from the U.S. Army Research Office. The content of the information does not necessarily reflect the position or the policy of the Government, and no official endorsement should be inferred.

The *Imaginary Beings* collection was fabricated and sponsored by Objet Ltd. (Multi-Material 3D Printing) and created in close collaboration with W. Craig Carter (Department of Materials Science and Engineering, MIT) and Joe Hicklin (The Mathworks). Other contributors include Dr. James Weaver (Wyss Institute, Harvard University), Turlif Vilbrandt (Symvol, Uformia), Kevin Cohan (The Mathworks), Sarah Zaranek (The Mathworks), and Seth DeLand (The Mathworks). The author also wishes to thank our network of colleagues and advisors at MIT including Prof. Christine Ortiz, Prof. Mary C. Boyce, Prof. Lorna Gibson and Prof. David Wallace.

Fryazinov, O., P. A. Fayolle, *et al.* (2011), "Feature-based volumes for implicit intersections." *Computers & Graphics*, 35(3): 524–531.
Jencks, C. (1984). *The Language of Post-modern Architecture*, Rizzoli, New York.
Kahn, L. (1969). *Conversations With Students*, Princeton Architectural Press, New York.
Oxman, N. (2010). *Material-based Design Computation*. Ph.D. thesis, MIT.

Oxman, N. (2011a). Variable Property Rapid Prototyping, *Journal of Virtual and Physical Prototyping* (VPP), 6(1): 3–31.

Oxman, N. (2011b). Finite Element Synthesis. Proceedings of VRAP: Advanced Research in Virtual and Rapid Prototyping, in Bártolo, P.J. *et al.*, *Innovative Developments in Virtual and Physical Prototyping*, Taylor & Francis, London.

Oxman, N. (2012). Programming Matter. *Architectural Design*, Special Issue: Material Computation: Higher Integration in Mophogenetic Design, 82(2) March/April: 88–95. Guest edited by Achim Menges.

Oxman, N., Keating, S., and Tsai, E. (2011). Functionally Graded Rapid Prototyping. Proceedings of VRAP: Advanced Research in Virtual and Rapid Prototyping, in Bártolo, P.J. *et al.*, *Innovative Developments in Virtual and Physical Prototyping*, Taylor & Francis, London.

Semper, G. (1851). *The Four Elements of Architecture and Other Writings*, RES monographs in anthropology and aesthetics, Cambridge University Press, Cambridge, UK.

Sennett, R., (2008). *The Craftsman*, Yale University Press, New Haven, CT.

Thom, R. (1975). "Introduction, Form and Structural Stability," in *Structural Stability and Morphogenesis; an Outline of a General Theory of Models*, W. A. Benjamin, Reading, MA.

Thompson, D. W. (1942). *On Growth and Form*, Cambridge University Press, Cambridge, UK.

RESPONSIVE/INTERACTIVE/ DYNAMIC

Rivka Oxman
and
Robert Oxman

The vision of a *mediated architecture*, an architecture in a symbiotic, informational relationship with both its users and its physical and cultural context, is perhaps one of the most challenging ideas of late-twentieth-century architecture. This syndrome of ideas has sources in earlier experimental projects such as the internal dynamics of the *Maison de Verre* of Pierre Chareau and Bernard Bijvoet (1928–1932) and the climate responsiveness and dynamic technology of Fuller's *Dymaxion* houses (from 1929) that begin to define and address certain of the fundamental issues of today's interest in responsiveness. To broaden this list of precedents that define the conceptual field of responsive/interactive/dynamic architecture, Le Corbusier's *Philips Pavilion* of 1958 at the world expo in Brussels was one of the first mediascapes that integrated light, sound and image in an architectural media display covering the interior hyperbolic paraboloid surfaces of the pavilion.

Later generations of architects and designers have pursued the continuation of this field of ideas as it became transformed by the growing potential for realization that derived from computation and design in the second half of the last century. Buckminster Fuller's (with Shoji Sadao and the Cambridge Seven) *US Pavilion* at Expo '67 in Montreal had a computer-controlled solar responsive envelope built into the skin of a three-quarter geodesic dome. Experimental architecture of the early 1960s included dynamic and responsive environment in the work of the British visionary Cedric Price, as well as in the works of the Archigram group. These ideas were in part realized in Rogers and Piano's competition-winning entry for *Centre Pompidou* (1971–1977), the main urban elevation of which illustrated a media façade that was not actually built in the final project.

These precedents for the integration of advanced building technologies of electronics and mechanics with the control capability of the computer enhanced the steady evolution of new practices of responsive/interactive/dynamic architecture. Toyo Ito's *Tower of the Winds* (1986) in Yokohama and the later *Egg of the Winds* (1991) employed sensors for local wind-speed and sound levels and translated the data into dynamic light and color displays; while the *Egg of the Winds* also added image displays. In Jean Nouvel's *Institute du Monde Arabe* in Paris (1987–1988) the main façade is constructed with a dynamic lens-like system of apertures which open and close in response to solar radiation. This clockwork mechanics also resembles the traditional *mashrabiya*, the latticework screen patterns and geometries of wooden screens in Arab cultures.

Between 1999 and 2001 the architectural firm dECOI (Goulthorpe, 2008) in collaboration with Mark Burry designed the first mechanically dynamic interactive and responsive mechanical wall for a competition for an interactive artwork for a theatre façade in Birmingham. Displayed in the *Non Standard Architecture* exhibition of 2003–2004 *Aegis Hyposurface* became another of the canonic precedents for mechanically dynamic, digitally controlled, interactive environments realized at architectural scale. Its smooth textile-like movement and transitioning and its infinitely reconfigurable surface forms have made the *Aegis Hyposurface* one of the most significant examples of digitally mediated interactive information environments.

The *Blur Building* (2002) by Diller and Scofidio in Yverdons-les-Bains, Switzerland for Swiss Expo 2002 was a media pavilion. The pavilion produced a fog-like spray of water in response to changing climatic conditions such as temperature, humidity, wind direction and wind speed. Visitors wore provided raincoats that stored personal data, enabling the fixing of their location within the *Blur* environment. The computer compared data of visitors, signaling by color the degree of their compatibility/incompatibility.

The Kunsthaus Graz, which opened in 2003, was designed by Peter Cook and Colin Fournier. It has a media façade, the *BIX* façade, that was designed in collaboration with the Berlin architectural media design firm, *realities:united*. *BIX* was intended to provide a dynamic visual communications medium for artistic displays. Together, these prototypes: a media façade (BIX), an interactive pavilion (Blur), and an infinitely dynamic and reconfigurable interactive surface (Aegis Hyposurface) have opened a new era of digitally responsive/interactive and dynamic architecture.

Responsiveness is the first of a cluster of interrelated concepts that constitute the theoretical background and technological territory of *responsive systems* in architecture. Responsiveness is the ability of a system to receive and react to data input from its environment. Thus responsiveness always implies an active two-way interrelationship with contextual stimuli as well as the *reactive capacity* to respond, or to change state. For example, the exterior diaphragm of the Institute du Monde Arabe was designed to mechanically adjust the degree and ambient quality of openness of the wall screen in order to control solar penetration and light quality. In the technical sense, responsiveness implies *sensitivity* to selective *stimuli* by *sensors* and some form of translation of that input into a *reactive response*.

Responsiveness is thus the central concept of responsive/interactive/dynamic systems. All such systems are, by definition, interactive. Interactivity in the generic sense is the linkage between stimuli and form of response that the stimulus engenders. Interactivity implies some degree of awareness on the part of an agent or user of how a stimulus creates a response and how the agent can control or otherwise manipulate the system in order to achieve the desired type of response, or output. Interactivity is thus both the self-awareness of the role of active agency and knowledge of the means of control, or operation, of the mechanisms. Interactive computer controlled systems are well known in recent decades due to the prevalence of *interactive art*.

The third of the central concepts of responsive systems is dynamism. Responsive systems are *dynamic systems* in that they are designed to change state, usually physically, or chemically, or otherwise in response to input. This mechanism for change of state such as the degree and fineness of the water jets in the Blur pavilion, or the dynamism of projecting/ receding in the Aegis Hyposurface are in themselves complex systems that require sensing in order to dynamically interact with the system of sensing of contextual inputs. Oosterhuis has eloquently formulated this notion of *intrinsic reciprocity* in responsive systems (Oosterhuis, 2003, 2011).

Dynamic architectural systems is a fascinating field of design which is growing in importance with the increasing ability to enhance responsive "behaviors" through parametric control mechanisms. These truly produce the "subtle technologies" of Beesley, Hirosue and Ruxton (2006). We can briefly introduce certain of the seminal concepts of dynamic architectural systems through the Aegis Hyposurface, one of the iconic dynamic architectural systems of the last decade (Goulthorpe, 2008). The first variable is the existence of a *dynamic mechanical principle*. In the Hyposurface the principle is that of lateral mobility (hinging) of a faceted surface operated by modular zones; the *operating mechanism* being pneumatically operated pistons that control the extension and recession of the faceted panels. Other well-known dynamic principles are folding and sliding panels. The architect/engineer Santiago Calatrava is among the noted designers of architectural scale dynamically transformable architecture. The designer Chuck Hoberman is well known for his original design of dynamic mechanisms.

The remarkable subtlety of response of the Hyposurface is due both to the mechanical behavior of the *dynamic material system* of faceted panels and to the underlying parametric models of sequenced movement of the panel sectors. Goulthorpe (2008, p. 96) has stated that the system is "capable of registering any pattern or sequence that can be generated mathematically." These mathematical models of distortion of the surface manipulate parameters of speed, amplitude and direction in modulating the sense of movement of the surface in an organic fluidity.

In a general sense responsiveness may be considered as "how natural and artificial systems can interact and adapt" (Beesley, Hirosue and Ruxton,

2006). Biological systems are models for responsive systems design in the operation of feedback mechanisms of control, in the relationship between contextual conditions and performative response, and in the detailed subtlety of responsive behaviors. D'Arcy Thompson traced and modeled such ecological relationships of genotypes to phenotypes and morphogenetic adaptive phenomena over long periods of time. We are rapidly growing capable of designing and modulating artificial ecosystems in relationship with natural ecosystems such as climatic, wind and acoustic conditions.

We are now witnessing a convergence of digital concepts. With "smart surfaces," "intelligent building skins" and "hybrid materialities" we are growing capable of digitally controlling building performance behaviors as well as the creation of ambience, or atmosphere.

Beesley, Philip, Hirosue, Sachiko and Ruxton, Jim (2006), "Towards Responsive Architectures," in Beesley, Philip, Hirosue, Sachiko, Ruxton, Jim, Tränkle, Marion and Turner, Camille, eds., *Responsive Architectures: Subtle Technologies*, Riverside Architectural Press, Toronto, pp. 3–11

Bullivant, Lucy, ed. (2005), *4dspace: Interactive Architecture*, AD (*Architectural Design*), Vol. 75, No. 1, January/Febuary

Bullivant, Lucy (2006), *Responsive Environments*, V&A Contemporary, London

Bullivant, Lucy, ed. (2007), *4dsocial: Interactive Design Environments*, AD (*Architectural Design*), Vol. 77, No. 4, July/August

Edler, Jan (2005), "Communicative Display Skins for Buildings: BIX at the Kunsthaus Graz," in Kolarevic, Branko and Malkawi, Ali M., *Performative Architectures: Beyond Instrumentality*, Spon Press, New York and London

Fox, Michael (2009), *Interactive Architecture*, Princeton Architectural Press, NewYork

Goulthorpe, Mark (2008), *The Possibility of (an) Architectures: Collected Essays by Mark Goulthorpoe/dECOI*, Routledge, New York

Guallart, Vicente, ed. (2004), *Media House Project: the House is the Computer: the Structure Is the Network*, IaaC Institut d'Arquitectura Avancada de Catalunya, Barcelona

Kennedy, Sheila (2010), "Responsive Materials," in Schröpfer, Thomas, ed., *Material Design*, Birkhaüser, Berne, pp. 118–131

Kubo, Michael and Salazar, Jaime (2004), "A Brief History of the Information Age," in Ferré, Albert, Kubo, Michael, Prat, Ramon, Sakamoto, Tomoko, Salazar, Jaime and Tetas, Anna, eds., Verb *Matters*, Actar, Barcelona

Lupton, Ellen, *Skin: Surface, Substance, and Design*, Princeton Architectural Press, New York

Oosterhuis, Kas (2003), *Hyperbodies: Towards and E-Motive Architecture*, Birkhaüser, Basel

Oosterhuis, Kas (2011), "Move That Body: Building Components Are Actors in a Complex Adaptive System,", in Oosterhuis, Kas, *Towards a New Kind of Building: A Designer's Guide for Non-Standard Architecture*, NAi Publishers, Rotterdam, Ch. 3, pp. 110–134

O'Sullivan, Dan and Igoe, Tom (2004), *Physical Computing: Sensing and Controlling the Physical World with Computers*, Thomson Course Technology, Boston

Ronan, Timothy M. (2003), "From Microcosm to Macrocosm: the Surface of Fuller and Sadao's US Pavilion at Montreal Expo "67," in Taylor, Mark, ed., *Surface Consciousness*, AD (*Architectural Design*), Vol. 73, No. 2, March/April, pp. 50–56

Spuybroek, Lars (2004). *NOX: Machining Architecture*, Thames and Hudson, New York

> List of Key Concepts

biological systems models
contextual stimuli
digitally mediated environments
digital responsiveness
dynamic material systems
dynamic systems
feedback mechanisms
interactive
interactive art
media façades

mediated architecture
operating mechanisms
parametric control
performative
performative behaviors
performative models of
   dynamic behaviors
reactive capacity
responsive mechanisms
responsive systems

In *Responsive Architectures: Subtle Technologies* (Beesley *et al.*, 2006), the project is an exploration of the *interconnectedness* of what surrounds us. The focus of this collection is on a new generation of interactive systems within science, art and architecture that are based on constantly evolving relationships. Using a wide definition of architecture that includes both built and natural realms, we examine dynamic systems and environments of scales from molecules to cities.

We want to pose the question 'What *does responsiveness mean?*' 'Responsive' speaks of how natural and artificial systems can interact and adapt. Speaking of evolution, we might think of how environments act via natural selection on diverse populations. While that traditional definition is included here, we also want to include conscious action. Responsiveness implies sensitivity. But stability and isolation – as we see it the opposite of sensitivity – are often seen as necessary for analysis of complex systems.[1] In traditional scientific method, sensitivity and exposure to the surroundings can be thought of as disruptive 'input' that interferes with traditional working methods. The impulse to create closed systems is not exclusive to science: we could say it runs wherever we hear opposing terms used to describe complex situations: *subject/object, self/other, form/function, organic/inorganic, observer/observed, static/dynamic.* We can observe art, technology and design dissolving many of these artificial distinctions.

A host of new working methods allow these boundaries to be opened. We want to find strategies for thriving in complex interconnected ecosystems. Nature continues to inspire us: for many authors nature is the fundamental teacher. Biological systems show molecular self-assembly and self-sustainability and serve as a model of the miniature mechanical parts that nanotechnology promises.[2] Organisms at every scale contain networks consisting of multiple parts that operate far outside of thermodynamic equilibrium. Examples of these complex feedback mechanisms are found in modern electronic control systems. This 'imbalance' creates a kind of charged state of readiness in which elegant mechanisms can resolve perturbations and damage.

The projects within *Responsive Architecture* transform the environment, and many draw upon the highest technology and economies available in the world. Mid-way through the past century, the American engineer Buckminster Fuller said:

> . . . man is just about to begin to participate consciously and somewhat more knowingly and responsibly in his own evolutionary transformation. I include evolution of the environment as a major part of the evolution of humanity.[3]

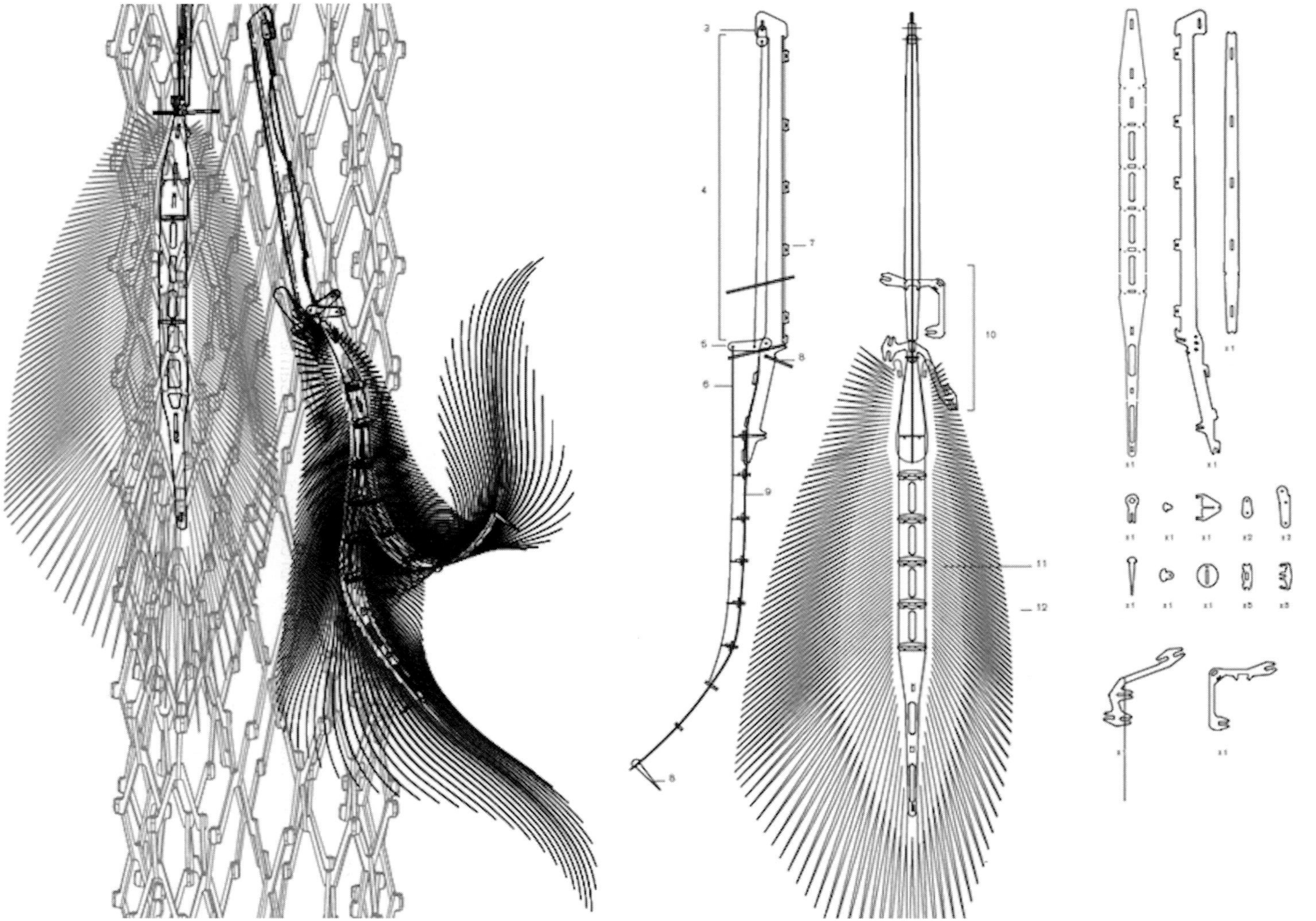

Figure 22.1

But Fuller's confidence stands in contrast to a cultural anxiety that has accompanied waves of technological advances since the Industrial Revolution. We now routinely embed devices into our surroundings that are triggered by our actions. 'Intelligent' building systems now turn on lights, lock and unlock doors and adjust heat. Data containing radio frequency identification tags[4] are increasingly standard devices attached to consumer items for point-of-purchase accounting and theft deterrence. Along with the proliferation of sensing devices comes the reality that we will be sensed everywhere we go. Who is watching?[5]

"[T]he environment touches man where it hurts. . ." said Reyner Banham, the visionary British designer.[6] Banham was speaking metaphorically, but biology confirms it is true: the soft tissues and hormonal systems immediately affected by environmental stress are closely related to the neurophysiology of emotion and pain.[7] What does it mean to create a responsive world today? We hesitate.

> Interconnectedness in Molecular Detail

At the beginning of the twentieth century, alongside the fateful discoveries that resulted in the nuclear weapons of World War Two, chemists and physicists became interested in biology.[8] The new synthesis of disciplines led to the discovery of the double-helix structure of Deoxyribonucleic Acid: DNA. That insight[9] enabled manipulation of biological structure and function at the scale of molecules.[10] The maturing field of molecular biology has again involved repeated flirtations of biology with engineering and material sciences, encouraging a systems perspective of molecular knowledge of organisms.[11]

In parallel, building upon late-nineteenth-century zoology, D'Arcy Wentworth Thompson's pioneering text On Growth and Form demonstrated that the physical forms of organisms can be understood as 'diagrams of forces' that trace physical influences within the environment over long time periods.[12] Adaptation to the environment through intimate linkages of natural forms and functions has now been described in mathematical detail.[13]

Another watershed moment was the Human Genome Project,[14] the project of creating a complete genetic blueprint of the human organism. Large arrays of experiments were processed at the same time, requiring interdisciplinary teams with specialists from robotics, quantitative image analysis, chemistry, biology, and material science. This cooperative project required processing in massive numbers, including systematic observation of hundreds of changes in activity within a cell on a single chip.[15]

Facing page

Figure 22.1: Philip Beesley, Technical Drawings for *Hylozoic Ground.* Image credit: The Office of Philip Beesley, Architect.

Looking at multiple processes encouraged moving beyond the concept that single genes are responsible for specific traits.[16] The relationship between genotype and phenotype has been traditionally thought of as 'cause and effect' where genes act as a blueprint for life. A *genotype* is a group of organisms that share a similar genetic makeup. A *phenotype* is the visible characteristics of an organism resulting from the interaction between its genetic makeup and the environment. However, it is increasingly clear that the relationship is by no means a one-way street. Organisms are influenced by their environments by selection acting on phenotypes, not on genes.[17] Ideas of genetics in evolution have been expanded by new conceptions of interconnected networks that work in concert. A convergence of dynamic 'network' thinking from information technology and computer science has contributed to this more subtle understanding. The boundary between environment and organism is indeed blurred.

In full circle from D'Arcy Wentworth Thompson's research, microscopic observations have shown that cell shapes are dictated by three-dimensional skeletons that mirror large-scale architectural space-frames. Cellular shape has been directly linked to the processes of chemical signaling, gene regulation, and development, demonstrating that form and function are intimately linked at the molecular level.[18] New approaches to three-dimensional cell culturing systems have been developed to serve stem cell research and tissue engineering. These culturing systems in turn reduce the need for animal experiments.[19] New developments in materials compatible with physiology, and miniature fabrication methods similar to those used for manufacturing computer chips have contributed to this progress.

The quantitative study of complex biological systems is a *four-dimensional* problem that includes the critical dimension of time. To effectively study the multiple dynamic processes that occur in cells and organisms, new approaches are needed. Analysis tools that support visualization and analysis in space and time are required and specimens need to be *alive*. Familiar medical technologies such as Magnetic Resonance Imaging and Positron Emission Tomography have been miniaturized to permit analysis of molecules and cells in living animals.[20] Examples of new analysis equipment include high speed microscopy featuring shutter speed timed in nanoseconds,[21] scanning confocal microscopy,[22] single plane illumination microscopy,[23] and 'non-linear' two-photon microscopy that allows imaging deeper than a single cell layer.[24] These techniques are supported by an expanding palette of 'marker' molecules that can label a specimen without interfering with its original function. Marking materials include proteins derived from jellyfish, quantum dots,[25] and super paramagnetic iron oxide.[26] These materials permit the observation of single and grouped molecules.[27] Optical tweezers[28] and atomic force microscopy allow probing and manipulating at microscopic and atomic scales.[29] This ability to probe means that mechanical properties can be measured alongside observations of spatial and chemical dynamics. The two-way street of evolutionary development often plays itself out through molecular exchanges that can be detected by using these tools. The kind of data collected in this research draws from a cluster of related disciplines, including computational algorithms and quantitative analyses from applied mathematics.[30]

Using terms of reference derived from structural engineering of buildings, Donald Ingber proposed that cells contain tensegrity structures. He suggested that they are organized as triangulated three-dimensional geodesic skeletons akin to Buckminster Fuller's revolutionary dome architecture from the past century.[31] The new tools demonstrate that these skeletal elements indeed distribute and sustain their own weight.

Molecular level biology is now poised to work with critical questions of shapes and structures at the scale of atoms, cells and organisms. By manipulating shape and structure of organisms, fundamental relationships with their communities and micro-environments are altered. It does not stop there. In the same manner, we are able to approach how organisms respond to 'macro-environmental' factors that span the scale of the galaxy, including geomagnetic and gravitational forces. Think about circadian 'clocks' that guide our own responses to the cycle of night and day,[32] or the navigational instincts that are transmitted through generations in migrating birds and insects.[33] The confluence of disciplines has created an extraordinarily effective research environment for analyzing and engineering Nature in multiple scales and dimensions. In turn, the natural world is starting to be revealed in molecular detail as a dynamic ecology of interconnectedness.

> Building Responsiveness

A wave of new industrial processes is transforming building design and construction. The next generation of architecture will be able to sense, change and transform itself. The tools and materials discussed here make this kind of *responsive* architecture possible.

Rigidity and resistance to the external environment are normal qualities in building. Traditional buildings use components of construction fabricated in a strict order. For example, a foundation and structural core in concrete might form the basis for steel columns supporting floor plates, and on these a grid of windows may be hung. The first stages of construction normally form an immovable and stable base that supports the entire assembly of building components. But new generations of buildings do not rely on completely stable foundations. Rather than relying on centralized support, they are designed to accommodate constantly shifting forces. These new systems tend to distribute their loads throughout interlinking structures that can withstand changes and deformations.[34]

New architectural projects discussed in *Responsive Architectures* explore structural systems based on tensile and 'tensegrity' systems in which stretching and pulling forces can play throughout a structure. These hybrid structures are accompanied by design methods where complex relationships can be analyzed and refined, and by a fresh palette of building elements made possible by computer-controlled prototyping and manufacturing. New fibers used in architecture include composites of glass and carbon that are stronger, more agile, and more energetically efficient than traditional steel and glass assemblies. This kind of building involves new methods of construction using continuous chains of components and distributed structures.[35]

Building Information Modeling (BIM) is a process where three-dimensional forms, engineering systems and component specifications are integrated within massive arrays of information. Similar to the fundamental implications of the Human Genome project, BIMs now have formidable influence on architecture. Systematically coded and organized components can be custom-made off-site as a building assembly kit, assembled, and then managed through the life of the building.

Computer-aided design is capturing the geometric relationships that form the foundation of architecture. Finite Element Analysis[36] is a method that breaks down a continuous structure into many simple, linked elements. This allows formerly unthinkable forms to be assessed for mechanical, material, and energy requirements and to be realized as a built structure. Form finding software supports analysis of free-form structures in order to find optimal thicknesses and arrangements of supporting elements. The practice of form finding is often enhanced by the practice of *biomimicry*,[37] design methods that follow principles from nature.

Parametric modeling is a new approach that allows designers to control variables of the design through models that can coordinate and update themselves.[38] These systems can automatically update the entire model or drawing set based on changes as small as a joint or as large as the entire floor plan. New research concepts show how parametric systems can support exploring of complex multiple alternatives. Software tools such as Bentley Systems' *GenerativeComponents* offer flexible design of deeply nested relationships. They accomplish this by organizing 'dependency' networks akin to the complex process diagrams used to express relationships in natural systems. Multiple variations can be created by manipulating digital code to create detailed individual sets of instructions for manufacturing. In much the same way that a mutating virus can generate biodiversity, individual variation can be achieved economically. The cost of making one thousand identical parts and one thousand individual parts with slight variations can be almost the same. The building design industry is in the very early stages of adoption of these tools.[39]

Computer-assisted design-to-fabrication methods are transforming what we can make. Custom cutting, shaping, and depositing tools invite new forms. Versatile modular construction systems that allow integration of diverse parts are made possible by direct-manufactured systems. Digital fabrication allows a designer to work closely with industrial production in this process. Perhaps the biggest impacts of this technology are being felt in the massive economies of traditional steel, wood and concrete construction, where automation and prefabrication have transformed the industry. The wasteful practices of solid-timber framing are increasingly a thing of the past, replaced by stranded and laminated composites that can employ almost every part of timber harvested from managed forests. Direct-manufactured steel systems allow coded and organized components to be custom-made off-site as a building assembly kit. Similarly, custom-formed concrete is now possible, no longer the exclusive province of lavish budgets. Numerically controlled fabrication machinery allows the production of prefabricated formwork for relatively economical free-form cast construction.

This increasingly fine-tuned approach to building component design and the flexibility and movement achievable in new building systems changes the fundamental behaviour of buildings. Architecture can now be operated as an instrument. Composite building structures now incorporate sensors, displays, and a range of mechanical functions much like what outfits a car today. Many of our actions trigger automatic responses in our environment. Buildings contain a myriad of sensors that detect temperature, humidity, light, fire and many other parameters relevant to the operation of the facility and the safety and comfort of their occupants. Modern public toilets have a number of sensing devices for our convenience. There are motion detectors that turn on the lights as we enter, touch sensors that turn on the hand dryers and distance sensors that determine appropriate times to flush.

The proliferation of sensing devices means that we can be sensed every-where we go. Radio Frequency Identification technology will soon replace barcodes on consumer goods. Yet unlike barcodes, these radio broadcasts also follow and identify us at home. Who should have access to all this data? The questions quickly become personal: If I am detected doing something private, do I have the right not to let other people know? Who holds the controls? The consequences of this new wave of 'making' are not simple.

> Personal Scale

Responsive systems from the point of view of an artist conjure up a world rich in both possibilities and poignant issues. Sensing devices are becoming ubiquitous. Interactive systems using sensing devices are now available as part of an artist's palette. The manufacture of these sensing devices for high-volume commercial use has provided access to artists who want to create interactive systems responding to movement, light, touch, heat, accelera-tion, and position. Because these devices are increasingly inexpensive, it becomes possible to use them in open-ended experiments. In turn, this can invite users to probe the public and commercial implications of these systems.

The proliferation of consumer-level 'gaming' computers has funded the engineering of highly efficient processors and large memory capacity, supporting manipulation of video and audio signals in real time. By inter-facing sensors with computer programs artists are able to create complex real time responsive systems that include audio and video effects. An example of an interactive system for dance is *Isadora* developed by the American media artist Mark Coniglio, of *Troika Ranch*, a dance company that presents media-rich performances. This program offers a graphic interface that allows easy programming and manipulation of video and audio compositions. Using sensors or cameras, physical action can be used as a control variable. Coniglio designed this system to be used in a performance environment. The recent performance by Troika Ranch, *16 [R]evolutions*, revealed the versatility of the system, which effectively makes the interactive system a kind of 'performer' acting in parallel with human dancers.

Many of the interactive systems currently available are the result of an artist developing software for their own use and then making it available to others. Toronto artist David Rokeby's *Very Nervous System*[40] software provides a way for artists to achieve inexpensive motion tracking using a video camera for mapping physical movement. The system is often used in dance performances where, for example, the upper body can be mapped to activate one set of sounds while the lower part of the body might activate other sounds. An entire space can be made responsive by programming sound and video to play in response to signals collected from different locations or zones.[41]

Eyes Web[42], a software package developed in the InfoMus Information Laboratory at the University of Genoa, offers the artist a sophisticated tool for analysis of physical gestures. Film production houses use motion tracking systems such as *Polhemus*[43] and *Flock of Birds*[44] that allow a point-by-point mapping from actor movements to a virtual character, yielding the realistic movements seen in popular cinema today. These devices work by measuring changes in an electromagnetic field as sensors move through space. Toronto based sound artist Darren Copeland is currently experimenting with the Polhemus system as an interface for a multi-channel sound diffusion system, showing the breadth of applications in which these sensor systems can be used. By moving sensors through space Copeland is able to control a multi-channel audio environment.

This kind of software can provide direct relationships between stimuli and actions, and it can also 'participate' by making decisions and taking random steps that add complexity to the composition. Functions can be added into the software to yield lifelike effects that simulate natural movement. For example, by including rules from natural physics in modeling software, movement that imitates the interactions of physical bodies moving within gravity can be simulated. This processing can add sensual qualities to animations within virtual performance space. These qualities can also be employed in feedback loops where automated 'outputs' are fed back into the system as new 'input', producing complex and subtle results. A particularly interesting development is in the exploration of rarely tapped dimensions such as *proprioception*, the sense of the body's position with respect to itself in space.

Wireless networking and low-cost home systems that adapt existing building power circuits allow development of interactive systems that can communicate over substantial distances. In the last decade artists have had access to small receiver-transmitter pairs that operate within an unlicensed Industrial Scientific and Medical wireless band. The recent introduction of *Bluetooth*[45] and *Zigbee*[46] technologies has given increased flexibility to wireless networking by allowing nodes to 'talk' to each other in networked configurations, opening new possibility for remote operation.

Networked compositions can involve subtle exchanges. The Toronto work "Heavy Breathing" allowed two participants in different locations to digitize their breath and send it back and forth by breathing into an apparatus while a fan recreated the transmitted breath. The recent Ku:iyashikei-net by Urico Fujii and Ann Poochareon allowed the transmission of tears over the internet.

What makes these mediated experiences so attractive? Interactive installations offer expanded powers: a small movement can be programmed to produce a world of sounds. Interactive systems can allow a performer to take control of light, sound and video within their environment. No longer reliant on sound or lighting cues, performers can find spontaneity in their actions. However, the experience likely goes far beyond 'power'. When someone enters an interactive installation, the immediate response to their presence can yield a powerful sense of personal connection. In turn, the natural world is starting to be revealed in molecular detail as a dynamic ecology of interconnectedness.[47] Artists have reacted to the proliferation of virtual meeting places and the loss of physical touch by exploring new ways of transmitting intimacy over a network. In today's mediated society, 'touch' has complex implications.

What is it that drives us to create 'responsive architectures'? Perhaps it is a sense of empowerment and involvement that drives interactive technologies forward. Is it because as a society we are becoming more cerebral that we crave increased movement around us? We rely less and less on our bodies. While children previously spent much of their time running and jumping, they now spend more time making icons and characters run and jump on a screen with a flick of their fingers. Creating more efficient structures and machines will further reduce the necessity of the human body. At the same time, this increasingly cerebral culture provides increased capacity for understanding how human bodies work. The study of nature reveals an interconnected set of mechanisms guided by structural and chemical 'intelligence'. These systems are a potent model for how we can impart sensuality and kinesthetics in buildings and machines. The importance of these qualities seems to increase as our physical bodies fade.

Seen in this way, the receding function of an original human body forms a poignant equation of loss and gain. Lost: the corporeal sensation and connection between bodies. Gained: a redefined 'body' whose expanded border embraces the surrounding environment.

The pursuit might be toward the sublime. Perhaps the sense is akin to the end of a very long period of loneliness, or a sense of returning home after an extremely long journey. We hope for a profound participation in the world around us.

1 Buckminster Fuller's definition of a system: 'A system is a local phenomenon in the universe that is geometrically definable because it returns or closes upon itself in all directions. Systems may be symmetrical or asymmetrical. I found that systems are the first subdivision of universe for they subdivide the universe into all the universe that is inside and all the universe that is outside the system.' From Utopia or Oblivion: The prospects for humanity (Bantam, New York, 1969) p. 137.

2 For an overview of biological motors, see: Fletcher, DA and Theriot, JA. An Introduction to Cell Motility for the Physical Scientist. Physical Biology 2004 1(1–2):T1–10. Synthetic Biology is a field that is inspired by biology to make and improve parts: http://synthetic-biology.org/. Nanotechnology also has its Buckminster Fuller mascot, the 'Buckeyball', a 60 carbon molecule called *fullerene* and selected by Science magazine as the molecule of the year in 1991.

3 R. Buckminster Fuller, Utopia or Oblivion: The Prospects for Humanity (Bantam, New York, 1969) p. 145.

4 RFIDs are small radio emitters that can be programmed to contain a large amount of data.

5 The Exchange 2006 project by Vancouver artist Nancy Nisbet works with RFID tags with critical perspective.

6 Reyner Banham, Architecture of the Well-Tempered Environment. Architectural Press, London (1969) p. 28.

7 Banham, who encouraged the revolution of creating environmentally controlled and 'responsive' buildings in the 1960s, sounds a reminder here of the ethical dread that Mary Shelley evoked in 'Frankenstein' two centuries before.

8 Nobelist Erwin Schrödinger's, "What is Life?" and "Mind and Matter", Cambridge University Press, Cambridge, UK. First published in 1944. The work inspired others to study biology including Max Delbrück and Salvador Luria whose studies of phage genetics also led to Nobel Prizes.

9 Watson, J. D. and F. H. C. Crick (1953a), "A Structure for Deoxyribose Nucleic Acid", Nature 171: 737–738.

10 Ernst Mayer's "modern synthesis" of C Darwin's theory of evolution by natural selection, and G. Mendel's theory of heredity gave the framework for molecular evolution. Darwin, C. The Origin of Species by Means of Natural Selection, or, The Preservation of Favored Races in the Struggle for Life (1859). Mendel, G.Versuche über Pflanzen-Hybriden (1865). For a brief historical and philosophical discussion of molecular biology see http://plato.stanford.edu/entries/molecular-biology/. For an extensive discussion see Mayer, E. The Growth of Biological Thought: Diversity, Evolution, and Inheritance. Harvard University Press, Cambridge, MA (1982).

11 Bioengineering, Biomedical Engineering: http://www.bmes.org/, Systems Biology: http://www.systems-biology.org/

12 Wentworth Thompson D. On Growth and Form (1917). Thompson drew upon structural engineering and natural science to create the new discipline of biomathematics.

13 Vogel, S. Life in Moving Fluids. Princeton University Press; 2nd Rev edition (1996). Life's Devices: The Physical World of Animals and Plants. Princeton University Press, Princeton, NJ (1988).

14 Human Genome Project and its current organization: http://www.genome.gov/

15 A 'chip' generally consists of multiple compartments segregating reactions or organisms on tailored microscope slides.

16 Folstein SE and Rosen-Sheidley, B. Genetics of Autism: Complex Aetiology for a heterogeneous disorder. Nature Reviews Genetics 2001. 2(12) 943–955. No single inheritance of genetic causes can be identified in autism, and environmental factors cannot be discounted.

17 The remarkable conservation of developmental pathways across species for millennia can be seen when ontogeny, the development of an individual from a fertilized ovum to maturity, is contrasted with phylogeny, the gradual development of an entire species.

18 Abbot, A. Biology's New Dimension. Nature 2003 424(6951), 870–872. Describes how cancer cells behave differently when grown in 2D (Petri dishes) or in 3D.

19 Griffith, LG and Swartz, MA. Capturing Complex 3D tissue Physiology In Vitro. Nature Reviews Molecular Cell Biology. 2006. 7(3)211–224.

20 Tyszka JM, Fraser SE, Jacobs RE. Magnetic Resonance Microscopy: recent advances and applications. Curr Opin Biotechnol. 2005 Feb; 16(1):93–9. Bremer C, Weissleder R. In Vivo Imaging of Gene Expression. Acad Radiol. 2001, Jan: 8(1):15–23.

21 Petty HR. Spatiotemporal Chemical Dynamics in Living Cells: From information trafficking to cell physiology. BioSystems 2006, 83(2–3) 217–224.

22 Megason SG, Fraser SE. Digitizing Life At The Level Of The Cell: High-performance laser-scanning microscopy and image analysis for in toto imaging of development. Mech. Dev. 2003 Nov; 120(11):1407–20. Graf R, Rietdorf J, Zimmermann T. Live Cell Spinning Disk Microscopy. Adv Biochem Eng Biotechnol. 2005, 95:57–75.

23 Keller, PJ. Life Sciences Require The Third Dimension. Current Opinion in Cell Biology 2006, 18(1)117–124.

24 Helmchen, F and Denk, W. Deep Tissue Two-Photon Microscopy. Nature Methods 2005, 2(12) 932–940.

25 Biepmans, B.N.G. et al. The Fluorescent Toolbox for Assessing Protein Location and Function. Science 2006, 312(5771)217–224.

26 Modo M, Hoehn M, Bulte JW. Cellular MR Imaging. Mol. Imaging. 2005, Jul-Sep: 4(3):143–64.

27 Ragan T, Huang H, So P, Gratton E. 3D Particle Tracking on a Two-Photon Microscope. J Fluoresc. 2006, Epub ahead of print.

28 Grier DG. A Revolution in Optical Manipulation. Nature. 2003, Aug 14, 424 (6950):810–6.

29 Silva, LP. Imaging Proteins with Atomic Force Microscopy: An Overview. 2005, Current Protein and Peptide Science 6(4) 387–395.

30 This includes interpretation of high-throughput data, image analyses, modeling of existing networks to test mechanistic hypotheses, and statistical inference methods such as Bayesian logic. Some examples specific to systems biology are outlined in this review. Stephens SM, Rung J. Advances in Systems Biology: Measurement, modeling and representation. Curr. Opin. Drug Discov. Devel. 2006, Mar; 9(2): 240–50.

31 Ingber, DE. The Architecture of Life. 1998. Scientific American. 278: 48–57. Ingber, DE. Cellular Tensegrity: Defining new rules of biological design that govern the cytoskeleton. J Cell Sci. 1993, Mar. 104 (Pt 3): 613–27.

32 Bell-Pedersen, D. et al. Circadian Rhythms from Multiple Oscillators: Lessons from Diverse Organisms. Nature Reviews Genetics 2005, Jul 6(7): 544–56.

33 Reppert, SM. A Colorful Model of the Circadian Clock. Cell 2006, Jan 27, 124(2): 233–6

34 This discussion is expanded in Beesley and Hanna 'Lighter: A Transformed Architecture' in Extreme Textiles: Designing for Performance, ed. Matilda McQuaid (Princeton Architectural Press, New York, 2005) p. 102–135.

35 For example, Norman Foster's Swiss Re Tower in London uses a structural skin made by placing members on a bias that dissolves the distinction between vertical and horizontal. The Seattle Public Library, designed by Rem Koolhaas's Office for Metropolitan Architecture, consists of stacked and sloped floor plates held in place by an angled 'fishnet' structure. The face of Richard Rogers' Channel Four building in London is composed of plates of glass assembled entirely without mullions, instead supported by a network of cables.

36 Finite Element Analysis originates from works by R. Courant and A. Hrennikoff. The method impacted many engineering fields when J. Argyris and S. Kelsey, and M.J. Turner et al applied solutions that made the method compatible with use on computers.

37 A term coined by American critic Janine Benyus. See her Biomimicry (Morrow, New York, 1997).

38 For example MAX, Jitter and Isadora as well as the open source program Pure Data.

39 While MAX and Pure Data are capable of creating real time interactive systems their interfaces have not been optimized for live performance. These programs accept

inputs such as sensor, audio and video signals. Objects are used to manipulate the incoming data in real time. The resulting 'output' of audio, video or data signals in turn can stimulate actuators such as lights or motors. These programs also include synthesis of audio and video signals.

40   http://homepage.mac.com/davidrokeby/home.html
41   It is not always necessary to use live performers as the stimulus in these responsive systems. For example, Willy Le Maitre and Eric Rosenzveig used VNS in an installation called 'The Appearance Machine' in which the motion of refuse and found objects stimulated the system.
42   http://www.infomus.dist.unige.it/eywindex.html
43   http://www.polhemus.com/
44   http://www.ascension-tech.com/
45   http://www.bluetooth.com/
46   http://www.zigbee.org/
47   Virtual communities include online dating sites, friendster.com, myspace.com, gaming communities. Digital communication might include chat, and IP telephony such as Skype.

> From Mass Production to Industrial Customization

23

My Nonstandard Architecture (NSA) practice, ONL, has been building a new aesthetic based on the principles of industrial customization. The principle of customization needs explaining as it is crucial for further understanding of the concept of interacting populations. Mass customization is the natural approach as seen from the perspective of CNC production methods. The logic of customization linked to CNC production requires that all building components possess unique identities, that they are individuals that can be addressed individually. In a building based on the principles of NSA not a single building component is the same as another. Each one is different, each component fits only in one place. First the building information model (BIM) and then the actual built structure are giant 3-d puzzles where each piece fits exactly in one unique location. The unique number of the component is comparable to the unique IP (Internet Protocol) address of a computer linked to the Internet. Architecture based on customization acknowledges the individuality of each component and builds a completely new aesthetic. The most obvious effect of NSA is that we no longer celebrate the beauty of repetition or a series of the same.

One must realize that all modernist architecture, from Le Corbusier to Herzog & de Meuron, is based on the outdated production methods of mass production. Although many critics think differently, deconstructivists like Morphosis and Gehry also have developed an aesthetic that still leans heavily on mass production. What they do, essentially, is start from a series of mass-produced components and then impose many exceptions, in other words they cause complicatedness. They cut out holes, they slice off, they chamfer and twist, they superimpose, they collide in collage, they build in conflicts, all as attempts to individualize the components. But creating uniqueness in this brutal old-school fashion is such a tragic mistake, such a waste of energy. What irritates me is that the deconstructivists violate their materials and production methods instead of working with them. The more logical approach, consistent with the principles of customization, is to instead synthesize architecture based on scripting and generative procedures, and to take advantage of the file-to-factory (F2F) processes and CNC production. Then each different shape is no longer an exception but one of many possible instances of the rule. The design rules are formulas mapped onto structures, surfaces and volumes, by definition open to changing parametric values. For the computer running the scripts and the computers plotting out the F2F half-products, each individual component is

Figure 23.1

treated according to the same procedure. CNC machines do not care which numbers and parameters change from one component to the next. CNC machines adjust automatically. This is the first paradigm shift.

> From Static to Proactive

The second paradigm shift leading architecture towards new horizons is the step from static to interactive architecture. Exactly the same prerequisite that allows for customized CNC production also allows for dynamic behaviour of the constructs. Once the building components possess their unique numbers, once they are tagged, they can be addressed as individuals. When the individual components are continually addressed in a streaming mode in real time, and when the building components are capable of making moves, then that component may be said to be responsive, adaptive.

From responsiveness to interaction is another step. Responding to incoming information is based on information streaming in one direction from the sender to the receiver, then the receiver responding back to the sender. But this is still far from the bidirectional dialogue that characterizes the interactivity paradigm. To have interactivity, the receiver must send back new information; it must process the received information and send it back in a slightly adjusted form. Some parameters must have changed. A dialogue is a two-way communication in which each actor is somewhat changed after having sent back its response. From ear to brain to mouth; listen, think and speak: so perfectly normal for humans; so complex for machines. But small Arduino circuits are currently being developed that can actually behave as relatively dumb actors. On a local scale they receive, they process, they send signals. When these small and locally intelligent processors are built into building components, these components can then be designed as to act and react. The jump from responsive and adaptive to the proactive can then be made. Smart building components can be provided with algorithms that allow for real time behaviour, even when there has not been an explicit demand from any human for them to respond to. Thus buildings may start to act for themselves; they may start to propose changes and thereby start a dialogue with their users.

The coming decade will show accelerating development from the static through the interactive towards the proactive. Only when information architects band together and gain control over the new paradigms of interactivity and proactivity, only when they include their fascination for interactivity and proactivity in their designs, and only when they develop the necessary

---

Facing page
Figure 23.1: Digital Pavilion, Seoul, ONL Architects. Image credit: All images courtesy Kas Oosterhuis, ONL Architects.

skills to implement interactivity and proactivity in their BIMs and in their CNC-produced building components, only then can the modern information architect claim responsibility for the fascinating field of augmented architectural working space.

> Interacting Populations

After one understands both paradigm shifts, one shift from standard to nonstandard, the other from static to proactive, it is then feasible to discuss the concept of interacting populations in the discipline of architecture. Since I have developed my buildings as information processing vehicles, it should be immediately obvious that these vehicles are not isolated objects, but are receiving and transmitting information to other such information processing systems as well, to other instrumental bodies. Just as the totality of cars on the motorway form a population of interacting mobile vehicles, these input-output (IO) instrumental bodies form a global population of interacting bodies and interacting species. Swarm behaviour forms the basis for describing and scripting the behaviour of such IO populations. The links between the IO vehicles are established locally through senders and transmitters, and globally networked through the Internet. Their behaviour is subject to local constraints (forces from within) and global constraints (forces from outside the system). What do the IO vehicles tell each other, what sort of information do they send, what information do they narrowcast?

My first truly interactive structure was the Saltwater Pavilion, built in 1997. A weather station positioned in the North Sea informed the computer running Max MSP, feeding the raw data from the weather station and in turn informing a mixing table to produce unique MIDI numbers in real time. The MIDI numbers drove the interior lights and sounds, refreshing the *massage* of light and sound 20 times per minute. The public could interact with this dynamic environment using a sensor board, pushing and pulling lights and sounds towards the extremes of the interior space. Interactive experience and architecture were both designed from scratch with similar budgets and at the same scale. In much the same way that we successfully fused art and architecture by assigning equivalent budgets and working space to both the art and the architecture, we applied this radical form of equivalent collaboration to the fusion of architecture with interaction truly a first in the history of architecture. The integration of a light-and-sound environment in architecture had been achieved before, as, for example, in the Philips Pavilion at the 1958 World Expo in Brussels, but that program was passively consumed, while the Saltwater Pavilion is a participatory environment.

Suppose we now have a swarm of water pavilions, all placed on different locations around the globe, all exchanging information with each other, with their local environment, with their local users, and also obedient to their global directives. That would then establish a hive-mind of intelligent self-aware buildings. That is the broader context I am seeking with the concept of proactivity. All IO members of the swarm would feed on data produced by other IO vehicles, all would behave in real time, all would tell the others about their behavior, and all would be self-learning entities. Self-learning capacity will only arise if the IO bodies continuously communicate with their peers as part of a dynamic swarm. Then they can begin building a body of knowledge as does the human species. It is easy to see that the human mind would be completely helpless and uninformed if it did not communicate with its peers. The human body of knowledge is not embodied in one brain; only the global hive of all connected brains has the total information and is thus able to evolve. It will be much the same with IO bodies. Their brains will feed on meaningful data from the Internet and other wireless transmitted semantic signals that they need for their metabolic operations.

> Cars Are Actors

Keeping yourself in an upright position is a precarious balancing act. If you have ever tried running with your eyes closed, you know that you are bound to deviate from a straight path; you immediately start wobbling and become unsure how to proceed. You are soon lost in space. By keeping your eyes open, however, you are continually updated via your eyes on information about the path, and thus are able to respond continuously to the incoming data, able to tell your brain to send signals to your muscles to balance your body. This is how swarm behaviour works; this is how birds adjust their trajectories in the swarms; this is how cars flock on motorways as well.

Thus cars must be seen as actors on the motorway. By analysing their flocking behaviour one can see that it is the *car* that is responding, that the car uses the driver to execute the response. It is not the driver but the system – that is, the car including the driver – that makes the decisions. The car is an intelligent agent, an actor playing the rules of the motorway game. In streaming fashion the car is informed by the signs and the lines on and along the motorway, by signals from other cars, by radio signals caught by its antenna, and above all by continually measuring distance, speed and direction of neighbouring cars. This is an ongoing computational process. Even when the flock of cars comes to a complete standstill in a traffic jam the same intelligent operations are still active. The car is still measuring, still being informed, perhaps mostly by radio signals in this case. Even the car that is stopped in the traffic jam is a still a process being executed.

This notion is important for understanding future paragraphs where I focus on the behaviour of building components being actors in the building body. The car as a participant in the motorway system is not only receiving and processing, but also sending signals to its immediate neighbours. The car blinks its lights when turning left or right, it lights up its taillights when braking to slow down. In the dark, it is even more obvious how the motorway system works: only the signs lighting up and blinking signals lead the cars, there is no landscape left to distract the car body. Driving a car at night is like flying an airplane. Planes fly through virtual corridors, visualized by 3-d software as a virtual tunnel with boundaries to stay within. Signals from clash-detection software will alert the plane if it deviates from its proper course. These advanced yet relatively simple techniques are now embedded in modern cars as well. The car reads the signs on the road, sends information to the steering mechanism, and at the same time informs the driver via signals and visuals.

It is by the social technique of empathy that I describe the motorway system in such a manner. It is this same empathic technique that I then apply to the informed building body system to describe how it works in real time, and how we can take advantage of this new awareness for the development of programmable building bodies. Now what processes does the car go through, what does it do with the incoming information? Let's assume that I am looking at modern cars in which hundreds of small computers are embedded to ensure the safe behaviour of the car. Thus I don't need to give the driver all of the credit for the proper response to incoming signals. Internally there is a complex of connected systems at work to validate the incoming data. When a car gets too close to another car in front of it, it diminishes its speed. When the car notices a continuous line at one side and the car shows an inclination to cross that line, the steering wheel adjusts the direction of the car, if only by a fraction of a degree. The car, in cooperation with the driver, continually fine-tunes its direction on the basis of incoming signals, just as the human body keeps itself upright and finds its direction along a straight path. Validating incoming data basically means that the incoming data, in the form of numbers, are compared to the bandwidth of allowed numbers. If the incoming value is higher or lower than the allowed value, then it is considered out of range and the vehicle is instructed to take action. First an out-of-range signal is sent to the steering installation to make a minor correction. It should be unnecessary to say that this is a delicate and responsive processing system. It rules over life and death. But just imagine that if you change the rotational angle of the steering wheel only a fraction of a degree yourself, you would quickly deviate from the proper path and within seconds would crash. It is amazing how subtly humans are able to operate the car to keep it on the right track. But from our empathic point of view it is similarly amazing how the car itself, by receiving wireless information, can self-correct and perform these subtle continuous corrections. The car flourishes in a flock of interacting populations of different types of cars that are interacting with their internal drivers and the external motorway system. The car has become a 'living' complex adaptive system to be admired and to serve as an ideal subject with which to investigate evolution at work.

Figure 23.2: Digital Muscle, 2003, ONL Hyperbody. Image credit: All images courtesy Kas Oosterhuis, ONL Architects.

> Buildings Are Actors

Think of the behaviour of buildings as coming from members of a flock, informed actors in a swarm. What sort of information comes in, how is it processed, and what information does it spit out? How does it behave in the context of the city? Think of buildings as they are built today in the developed countries, including their cabling, wiring, piping and plumbing, including their sense organs and wireless waves. Although the infrastructure makes up at least one-third of the building budget, the building installation is the most ignored part of the building design, which is understandable as designers usually have no power to control the infrastructure in the same way that they control the geometry and the materialization of their designs. However, designers should pay more attention to this infrastructure, especially since buildings are becoming smarter and the infrastructure budgets are rising higher and higher. The building body feeds on information of many kinds. Hooked onto the infrastructural system of the city, the building body reads many wireless signals. It inhales information, some comes in digital format, and others (such as water, gas and people) come in analogue format.

By applying the principle of empathy, we see that 'people' is just another form of data from the point of view of the building body. People are selectively admitted by the building body to give character to its existence. People are the carriers of information, the translators of ephemeral information into a physical change in the building body. People effectuate changes such as switching on the lights, opening the door, plugging into the Internet.

The door is essentially a switch in the building system. When a door is open, air travels from one room to the other so that the internal conditions and hence the performance of the building changes. The performance is felt by people, and they might act by closing the door/switch again. Thus people and buildings cooperate in the functioning of the building. People operate and interact, but it is the building itself that interacts systemically with the other members of the city swarm. Using incoming data, the building body continually adjusts its internal condition. Although unlike cars it does not move along the ground, still it does change the interior temperature, the relative humidity, the amount of direct sunlight.

The building body feeds on electricity, gas and water. The electricity could be generated by photovoltaic cells that are wrapped along the skin of the building's body, or by a series of smaller wind turbines along its external edges, where the speed of the wind is naturally accelerated.

The city contains a mix of many building types, all acting as individual information-processing members of their flock, all flocks interacting with the other flocks of other typologies, all of them connected to a central nervous and lymphatic supply and waste removal system. All the members of the city swarm follow the simple rules set by the urban designers, and as imposed by their own individual feature designers, and eventually they make up the complexity of the city as a whole. The buildings are the biggest actors in the city system, structuring the movements of the inhabitants. In this way of looking at the built environment, the inhabitants only assist in the behaviour of the buildings; the people operate on parts of the buildings by supplying parameters that are read, heard or seen by the buildings in real time. In a speeded-up movie of the cityscape the people and cars move so fast that they become almost invisible shadows, while the buildings themselves seem to make their changes at normal speed.

> What Is Interactive Architecture?

What exactly is interactive architecture? Let me first clarify what it is *not*. Interactive architecture (iA) is *not* simply a structure designed to be responsive or adaptive to changing circumstances. It is not a response to pushing a button, as when switching on the lights. It is much more than that; it is based on the concept that bi-directional communication requires two active parties. Communication between two people is interactive naturally; they each listen (the input), think (the processing part) and talk (the output). But iA is not about communication between people; it is defined first as the art of building relationships between tagged built components, and second, in the art of building relationships between people and the built components. It is the art of building bi-directional relationships in real time. In our approach, all built components are seen as input-processing output (IPO) devices. The theory of iA includes both passive and active IPO systems.

Let me clarify this once more with the classic example of the door. As I have described above, the door in the building functions as a switch. It is either open or closed. When we add the lock to the door, it is then either locked or unlocked and the one who has the key is the only one authorized to lock and unlock the door. In the building the door functions as a semi-permeable membrane for the two spaces A and B on either side of the door. The door allows people or goods to come in or go out. What about the processing part of the IPO procedure? The door can be said to process people (including the bags that are carried as backpacked information by the people), to process the airflow, the dust particles, the transport of aromatic molecules. When the door is opened the two systems on either side will find a new equilibrium with respect to number of people, goods, light, temperature, data. An actively computing door processes by quantifying what passes through the opening.

In iA it unfolds exactly like that. The iA software counts whatever changes occur in the positions, configurations and other possible characteristics of any IPO object. Each object that is defined in Hyperbody's *proto*SPACE software behaves in real time to keep track of changes of their neighbouring objects. Each object is then an IPO machine, an agent communicating with other agents, like birds communicating with other birds in the swarm. Understanding iA is not possible without having understood and adopted the rules of nonstandard architecture (NSA) in the design process. NSA

Figure 23.3: Interactive Wall, 2009, Hyperbody-Festo. Image credit: All images courtesy Kas Oosterhuis, ONL Architects.

implies that all constituent components of a built construct are unique. They each have a unique number, position and shape. If two components are the same then it is pure coincidence and *not* simplifying the structure per se. In the design process and in the mass customized file-to-factory production process all components are addressed individually. No longer is repetition the basis for production and hence design. Repetition is no longer beautiful. In NSA the uniqueness of the components is what is felt to be natural, logical and beautiful. Once all building components have a unique number, when they are tagged to be addressed in real time, the components then can instantly change their mutual positions. Floors can become *proto*DECKs, walls can become Interactive Walls, and building bodies can become Muscle Bodies. Having designed and built a dozen interactive prototypes, Hyperbody knows how realistic it is to think of a building as consisting of interacting populations of building components being informed in real time to either act slowly as if frozen to death or to act in an excited way in order to enjoy a dialogue with their users.

> Proactivity

Despite all the achievements of nonstandard architecture in the dynamic design process, the built NSA product is still static just as is the modernist building that is based on repetitive mass production. The door I took as an example is, in static architecture, usually operated by a human, although some doors are automatic. But the currently unfolding IT revolution is significantly affecting the operation of doors and locks. Doors will become self-aware IPO devices following their own local behavioural instructions, while at the same time listening to top-down authorized commands. Soon these doors will lock and unlock, open and close as they wish, and if you are authorized to do so they will also open when *you* wish them to open. Doors will themselves become aware of changing circumstances, and they will act accordingly without having to receive an additional instruction to act. Doors will become active building components, and so will each of the thousands of individual components that make up the overall built construct. Once electronics sneak into the building components the logical first step is that the doors will respond deliberately, based on a complex evaluation of many impulses. After that has been achieved, the next logical step is that they will become proactive. They will start proposing changes themselves. Nothing to get worried about, however, humans will still co-evolve just like they co-evolved with dogs and other domesticated life forms. Proactive doors will become domesticated as well. Instead of being fearful of so much action, you will like it because of its liveliness.

To summarize, iA is not just responsive and adaptive, it is also proactive. Building components that are iA-tuned are capable of a wealth of subtle actions; they constantly propose new configurations in real time, sometimes unnoticeably slowly, sometimes faster than you can move your eyes and faster than you can think. In iA software the active behaviour is built deep into the scripted code of the design, into its own DNA structure. Each component calculates its new input in real time, many times per second, and produces its new output behaviour, thereby continuously changing the state it is in. This ever-changing state acts as new input into the IPO system of other components and so on and so on, as actors in the interacting populations. The entire set of thousands of active components makes up the complex adaptive system (CAS) of the building.

The art of designing interactive architecture then is defined as the art of conceptualizing the CAS and the art of imposing style on the active building materials. A designer must keep in mind the fact that many of the constituent components are programmable actuators. This is a paradigm shift for the creative designer, as the architect thus becomes an information architect. The information architect sculpts data, designs the flow of information and constructs the IPO components to selectively transmit, absorb, transform or simply bounce back the information flow. My objective is to always make sure that iA is perceived as beautiful, that it not be experienced as merely a technical achievement. Can iA compete with conservative architecture as we have learned to appreciate it as meaningful, relevant and beautiful? My personal view is that iA naturally deals with beauty since objects in (slow) motion always get more attention than static objects. People relate emotionally more easily to dynamic structures than to static ones. It simply is more fun to watch live painting than to watch the paint dry. And when we train ourselves to not be satisfied with the initial fascinating fact that a building moves, when we train ourselves to be concerned about *how* it moves, when we focus, as we should, on the fashionable and stylish aspects of the iA design concepts, then the age of interactive architecture will have arrived, then information architects will be respected designers of proactive structures.

> There Is Only a Window When You Need One

The iWEB, the spaceship that can alternately be art or architecture, and thus is both art *and* architecture has different modes. The difference between the two was created by a giant door mounted on hinges. The iWEB building itself is a static structure, the door is positioned at a fixed place and there are only two different modes. However, our Trans-Ports project showed that a building need not be restricted to two modes. Trans-Ports can be in education mode, in lounge mode, in lecture mode, in research mode, in playtime mode, in nightclub mode. The space itself is envisioned to be able to change shape and content in real time. Trans-Ports is a multimodal design concept, physically actualized as a structure with a telescopic structure and a flexible skin. The skin material of Trans-Ports always remains the same skin, while the structure is equipped with the same set of electronic pistons but in different physical configurations. The built structure itself does not change in principle, but it has the built-in capacity to behave, to move its skeleton, to stretch its skin. Now imagine that the door is not hung from hinges but is thought of as a responsive, adaptive and proactive specialization of the skin. Suppose that the skin could change its physical properties at any place on the surface, just by reprogramming its constituting components.

The interactive prototype Hyperbody that students built during the spring semester of 2008 carries out the idea of an interactive entrance, a semi-permeable wall through which one would wade rather than enter through a specific portal. There would only be an opening in the wall when someone stood close enough to it and the wall would open only there. The entrance would not have a fixed position; it could be any place along that wall. You might compare it to the ground floor façade of a large building with thousands of small automatic doors, all responsive to sensors. The only area that would open for you would be the area of actuating components that you were closest to and were authorized to open. Thus a building façade would become something you could wade through; there would be no hierarchy in the floor plan. This sounds like a speculative thought experiment, but it is perfectly possible to do today with existing technology. My students are typically able to design and build such a façade in six to eight weeks, even without previous knowledge of interaction design. It is that simple, only needing a switch inside your brain to look at things differently.

For the process of actually making the prototype, each actuating component must be embedded with a small processor to read an RFID tag, then process the information and act accordingly. When the door knows you and trusts you, when your data matches its own data, it will let you in. When the door does not know you, you will not have the privilege of wading through the building wall, and you will have to take the lane for unidentified guests. Perhaps there could be a website where you could introduce yourself, get your tag, and get authorized to open the doors. Scary? Not at all. Something similar already happens when you check-in for your flight online and get yourself authorized to skip the check-in desk. The tag may take the form of a barcode in this instance, but much more sophisticated devices are also available on the market that can be woven into your clothes so that you do not have to show the printed version. The desk would automatically recognize your signal and let you through. Obstructive barriers would thus be dissolved, but there's nothing to be afraid of, as was suggested between the lines in the movie *Minority Report*. When watching *Minority Report* I realized that I could do exactly the same thing with knowledge developed during the first decades of existence of ONL/Hyperbody. Tagging yourself with wearable miniature IPO dust would be more reliable than any other form of identification, much friendlier than oversized passports and identification cards. Identity may even become integrated with fashion and become a matter of dressing, a daily routine.

Now suppose that you not only imagine interacting with doors but with a complete building envelope, and with all the flexible interior separation walls, and with the floors and ceilings too. These building components can be embedded in much the same way with intelligent agents and actuators that can interact with your personal profile. Thus any façade can become a truly interactive envelope, opening and closing for light and fresh air wherever, whenever and whoever may want it – you, by yourself, or the space you are in, by itself. There would only be a window when there was a locally expressed need for one.

> Versatile Time Zones

Let us perform another thought experiment. As are many other travellers, I am often disturbed by the different time zones, especially because of their irrational simplified structure. The time zones simply do not match up with high-resolution reality. Is there another solution possible to account for the passage of time, other than the low-resolution division of the world into 24 time zones? Dividing the world into just two dozen time zones is just as primitive as is a picture of 5 by 5 or 25 pixels to depict the world. The nonstandard approach (NSA), since it deals with the notion of the mathematically infinite, would naturally lead logically to an unlimited number of time zones. The NSA approach would facilitate a perfectly smooth transition from one spot on earth to another, without the rude one-hour jumps. Time would be stretched along with your own movement over the surface of the earth. Time would be real time. You can imagine having an atomic clock in your cell phone indicating the exact time on that very place where you are – just there, just then.

When you travelled in the same direction as the rotation of the earth, your watch would tick slightly slower, because you would be going faster than the flow of time. When you stop for a moment for a stop light, the watch would slow down to the general speed of the rotation of the earth again. And when you were travelling in the opposite direction your clock would speed up to compensate for the loss of time. (Remember that the USA is always six to nine hours behind Central European Time, while China is well ahead of that.) Now instead of resetting your clock manually when arriving in the USA from Europe, your clock would have done that for you during your trip in a high-resolution streaming fashion. It would keep track of the changes in real time, many times per second. That real time clock would need to be tagged to communicate its position on earth, and it would need to send, process and receive information with other tagged clocks (a swarm of satellites) in real time. The complete network of tagged watches and clocks would take care of the worldwide distribution of the proper time, as high-resolution as is technically possible, with no more time lags, paving the way for smooth (variomatic) awareness of time. Your variomatic clock would no longer be an old-school mechanical watch; it would be a computer, keeping track of the real time in real time.

Just imagine the effect it would have on the daily lives of people. If we abandoned the low-resolution division into 24 time zones, everyone and everything would have its own personal time. When making phone calls one would be able to see the exact time difference from the other end. And with devices interacting with each other, there would be a *delta t* keeping track of each individual time position. This thought experiment of versatile time zones could only become reality if everything was tagged and had a small processor embedded, exactly the condition I foresee for all building components in nonstandard and interactive architecture. The obvious advantage is that, just as the complexity of nonstandard architecture will feel natural and comfortable, having the precise time without ever having to adjust your watch will also feel natural and comfortable. We will live closer to the unfolding computation of nature, which will no longer be brutally cut into low-resolution chunks of time. That nature is, when all is said and done, a computation has been argued by Stephen Wolfram in his prophetic book *A New Kind of Science*. He proposes that nature be understood as a complex set of executing cellular automata, performing probably billions of operations per second. Nature, then, is one big transaction space, negotiating vast amounts of data.

> The Actuator

One more thought experiment, this time not on stretching time but on stretching the physical structure of a high-rise tower. This thought experiment explores the potential of programmable architecture. Imagine a one-mile-high tower – not feasible unless we apply the new technology of programmable building components. As explained before, we can apply the technique of programming embedded actuators to bring more excitement into the built structure as it changes shape in real time. Moreover, a programmable building can also be programmed to dynamically freeze into an extremely motionless crystal. Let's investigate in further detail this extreme end of the spectrum of possibilities of programmable architecture. While there is no bandwidth for static architecture since it is fixed to one particular configuration, the bandwidth of the behaviour of buildings with actuators may range from almost zero to almost endless: zero being the completely frozen situation; endless being the maximum amount of movements that is mechanically and electronically feasible.

So the position of *one* on a logarithmic scale of proactivity represents the static configuration of the inert buildings you see around you. The static reality means that conservative high-rise buildings will swing from side to side with a substantial amount of sway. The sway of the late World Trade Center towers was measured to be more than 1 m. A sway as large as 1 m is definitely not pleasant; one could easily develop seasickness. If it were possible to avoid sway caused by the stronger winds higher up in the air, then it would be possible to build much higher.

The height of buildings has always been constrained by what is technically possible. The elevator paved the road for the first generation of high-rises, innovations in steel and concrete structures stretched the upper limits to 800 m as recently seen in Dubai, the United Arab Emirates, by the high-rise structure renamed the Burj Al Khalifa in 2010 (since the ruler of Abu Dhabi, Al Khalifa paid the debts of Dubai). Frank Lloyd Wright wanted to build a One Mile High Tower, and he even made a sketch of it – a large foot that diminished in size towards the top like a vertically stretched pyramid. Basically all high-rise towers, including the Burj Al Khalifa, follow more or less that conceptual idea.

Recently a proposal was published for a one-mile-high tower in Saudi Arabia, the Jeddah Tower by Adrian Smith + Gordon Gill Architecture. Here is a quote from the designers:

> Architecture and engineering have traditionally treated structure as static – the building frame was constructed to be strong and heavy enough to resist all anticipated loads. The Mile High Tower proposes a lighter, dynamic structural system that actively responds to forces placed upon it. Controlled by wind detecting sensors, stabilizing aileron-like fins run the length of the tower frame and modulate their position to control resonant motion and building drift.

To me, this accurately describes the kind of architecture society is heading for in the coming decades. Buildings will become lighter and structural systems will respond to changing loads. Such a one-mile-high tower could theoretically be frozen into a perfectly upright position, without any deviation from its upright position as caused by winds or other disturbances. However, the Jeddah Tower still follows the old aesthetic of the super high-rise; it is still basically a stretched pyramid. I would rather have opted for a tower that increases in size towards the higher levels, perhaps taking advantage of the strong winds higher up in the air by capturing the power with wind turbines, meanwhile securing its uprightness by a substantially dense diagrid web of actuators on the exterior load-bearing skin. I would have also opted for a swarm of actuators to ensure that if one or more actuators failed the others would take over that function, emulating a robust network of thousands of cooperating players, like birds in a swarm.

EPISTEMOLOGY

Disciplinary Knowledge of Digital Design in Architecture

Rivka Oxman and Robert Oxman

The rapid evolution of design media and architectural technologies over the last decade and a half are actively producing a revolution in the disciplinary practices of the field (Kalay, 2004; Lynn, 2004; Burry, 2011). The transformation of the tool set beyond its origins as a drafting medium and productivity tool is the manifestation of a far more profound transformation that has taken, and is taking place in *design thinking*. This new logic of design thinking has now come to affect the existence of a new epistemology of design in architecture. While a previous generation sought the epistemological foundations of architecture as a discipline in history and formal language, a new generation of digitally resourceful young designers has transcended the lure of formal content in favor of espousing, with the aid of emerging technologies, new research-oriented processes of design. It is this orientation to design as research in the context of the digital in architecture that is enabling us again to view design as a medium of knowledge production.

Beyond the transformation that "being digital" has enabled in the computational logic that we now employ in representing our designs, digital fabrication technologies are also re-enabling the architect to gain control of material processes. The redefinition of the linkage of design and production has been supported directly by the emergence of *digital materiality*. While here too, it is the new architectural technologies that are motivating cultural change in architecture, it is again the foundational significance of computational systems in their symbiotic relation and linkage to both design and production that is among the sources of the material shift.

Parametric design (Aish and Woodbury, 2005; Woodbury, 2010; Burry, 2011) provides an exact medium for representation and control of relationships between parts and wholes in both a numerically precise and highly flexible manner. In order to provide such associative descriptive facility, the parametric model requires a unique form of design logic in constructing the associative modeling that is characteristic of most parametric systems. This logic creates the complex relation sets as a network of associations. Building such sets of relationships between the elements of a building form, or structure, may be considered the logic *schema* of the model. The clarity of the structure of this logical schema of the parametric model that defines the relationships between functions and parameters is very significant and may frequently be improved by modularizing the schema

(Davis, Burry and Burry, 2011). As such algorithmic models become open source and generic in parametric architecture, they may constitute a new form of disciplinary knowledge. Woodbury (2010) has developed a set of fourteen generic *patterns* for parametric modeling, while various designers are attempting to build sets of generic design patterns for architecture within popular parametric software applications such as *Grasshopper*, a graphical algorithm editor integrated with Rhino 3D's modeling tools.

By setting up a system of rules, or dependencies (for example, a graph structure underlying Grasshopper's representation of the model) the model, in effect, builds a design space of solutions that can be varied infinitely by the variation of the parameters. Thus parametric variations can be achieved while preserving the schematic structure of the model. Parametric variability (guided by dimensional and geometric constraints of the model) exploits the topological integrity of the model in order to enlarge the design space of solutions.

There are three additional unique attributes to current parametric systems in architecture that relate directly to questions of *research-based design* and knowledge production through experimental modeling in architecture. Ultimately these issues also relate to the need for the redefinition of disciplinary knowledge for design education.

The first of these attributes is the ability to experiment through analytic media while systematically modulating the parameters of the model. Thus parametric models enable performance-based design; see for example, Sasaki, *The Morphogenesis of Flux Structures* (2007). The second attribute is the integrated connection between the 3-D model and the ability to more or less directly produce *fabrication designs*. Here the close integration between design and production, at least in the sense of model production (if not full scale building) creates a means for parametric design generation of experimental modeling. Experimental modeling + fabrication becomes a medium for form finding; see for example, Steele (2008), on the role of modeling and full-scale modeling as one of the substantive foundations of experimental design at the AADRL in London's AA.

The AADRL has consistently constructed its multi-year research programs around the exploitation of typical problems in design modeling as the subject matter of research. The experimentation derives from the systematic exploration of new technologies in processes that typically involve material design and prototyping or large scale/full scale model building. Model making is here construed less as a form of representation and more as research-based experimentation with characteristic problems of design modeling and with large scale/full scale prototyping and materialization.

An additional attribute of parametric systems that strongly affects material-based design is their ability to achieve *differentiation* (heterogeneity) in the mathematical orders that underlie parametric schema. Just as in natural design, generic schema are one way to support differentiation, materially, structurally, formally and dimensionally on the basis of ad hoc contextual conditions of loading and so on. This attribute of instantiating uniqueness, for example creating a gradient within the otherwise repetitive cell structure of the system, is part of the unique formal and spatial components of a generic model. *Parametricism* – coined by Patrik Schumacher in a series of articles recently published, including his contribution to this volume – constitutes one of the contributions of parametric systems to digital design and enables unique formal, structural and material responses to contextual forces.

Pottmann represents a traditional area of architectural knowledge that has now become particularly relevant to rationalization processes in architectural design. Pottmann (this volume) points to the significance of training in mathematics, geometry and computer science as architects and designers become more engaged in research. He addresses how these subjects are essential in contemporary design and describes the present lack of educational programs in these areas. In projecting the significance of this knowledge in future developments in architecture, Pottmann illustrates the emerging role of architectural geometry and computational design as foundational knowledge in design.

Knowledge and digital skill in the creation of architectural form with code has now become a basic part of the architectural tool set for the current generation of young designers. The ability to couple these skills with generic architectural structural problems of digital modeling is the foundation of experimental architecture today (see Lynn, 2004). Reas, McWilliams, LUST (2010) define "procedural literacy" as an essential form of knowledge for the designer. The understanding and control of basic operations such as recursion and transformation (numerical, geometric and topological transformations) are among the foundational concepts underlying digital modeling today.

The ability to specify, construct, model and modulate form through a matrix that potentially provides an unlimited population of designs has become a new form of design thinking. Burry (2011) refers to this new approach to design as *scripting culture*. Scripting is generally considered the writing of shorter programs within the framework of existing well-known modeling packages. Examples are MEL in Maya and Rhino Script in Rhino and Grasshopper. Burry defines at least three distinctive scripting cultures: scripting for productivity; scripting for experimentation in coding as research; and scripting for creative discovery.

Much of the experimental work in architecture of the last few years is the result of joint work with computer scientists and engineers who act as collaborators to provide expertise in programming while the designer provides the design knowledge. Burry dates the beginning of architectural scripting to around 2002 when several packages provided interactive modeling environments with the presence of a scripting facility. This highlights the condition that many of today's architectural digerati have acquired their skills by chance and that scripting education is perhaps only recently and only rarely a known part of the architectural education program.

As we seek to address sustainability issues through performative design, as we begin to explore nature's principles of self organization, all of which now appear relevant to architecture, scripting and the related mathematical and morphological knowledge are emerging as significant ingredients in the tool set, logic and knowledge of the designer. This obviously also relates to the building of prior knowledge in thinking algorithmically. All of this touches upon larger issues of design education such as creative thinking and innovative design that emphasizes the need for a broad reorientation of design education.

Mathematics and geometry are among theoretical and knowledge foundations of architecture. Jane Burry and Mark Burry (2010) have published a study of the how the sources of new non-Cartesian, non-linear mathematical concepts have contributed over the last decade to the production of a series of iconic and geometrically complex architectural works. The book is constructed around six architectural/mathematical themes (Mathematical Surfaces and Seriality; Chaos, Complexity, Emergence; Packing and Tiling; Optimization; Topology; Datascapes and Multi-Dimensionality). It is in the combination of mathematical/geometrical knowledge with digital design knowledge that creativity is emerging. Here again, we find a new imperative for design education.

> We have reached the end of a decade and a half in which digital computation has given architects new creative opportunities with which to access the geometrical space opened up by post-17th Century mathematicians. The resulting new wave of interest in the relationship of mathematics to space-making has been aesthetically driven, and yet its expression has transcended the metaphorical. It has found expression from within the process of making as a new species of architecture and has infiltrated architectural process in ways that have forged radical change.
>
> (Burry and Burry, 2010, p. 8)

Design intelligence (see Speaks, 2007), a concept explicated by Speaks in various articles, promotes a new agenda for architecture, "after theory." The pragmatic, material-based, digital and performative orientation of this new architecture is evolving rapidly in the wake of the media revolution. New forms of design intelligence are coalescing in the impact of new technologies. All of this radical transformation has occurred in less than a decade and a half, and we have barely begun to recognize the nature of its impact.

Aish, Robert, and Woodbury, Robert (2005), "Multi-level Interaction in Parametric Design," in, *Lecture Notes in Computer Science*, Berlin, Springer, pp. 151–162

Burry, Mark (2011), *Scripting Cultures: Architectural Design and Programming*, AD Primer, John Wiley and Sons, West Sussex, UK

Burry, Jane and Burry, Mark (2010), *The New Mathematics of Architecture*, Thames and Hudson, London

Kalay, Yehuda E. (2004), *Architecture's New Media*, MIT Press, Cambridge, MA

Lynn, Greg (2004), "Constellations in Practice," in Reeser, Amanda and Schafer, Ashley, eds., *New Technologies, New Architectures*, Praxis 6, pp. 8–17

Pottmann, Helmut, Asperl, Andres, Hofer, Michael and Killian, Axel (2007), *Architectural Geometry*, Bentley Institute Press, Exton, PA

Reas, Casey, McWilliams, Chandler and LUST (2010), *Form and Code in Design, Art and Architecture*, Princeton Architectural Press, New York

Speaks, Michael (2007), "Intelligence After Theory," in Burke, Anthony and Tierney, Therese, eds., *Network Practices: New Strategies in Architecture and Design*, Princeton Architectural Press, New York, pp. 212–216

Steele, Brett (2008), *DRL Ten: A Design Research Compendium*, AA, London

Terzidis, Kostas (2006), *Algorithmic Architecture*, Architectural Press/Elsevier, Oxford

Verebes, Tom, Spyropoulos, Theodore, Obuchi, Yusuki and Schumacher, Patrik, eds. (2008), *DRL Ten: A Design Research Compendium*, AA Publications, London

> List of Key Concepts

architectural geometry
associative geometry
dependencies
design intelligence
design knowledge
digital design thinking
digital materiality
disciplinary knowledge
mathematical knowledge
modular design of code

parametric design
parametricism
parametric logic of design
parametric schema
performative design
procedural literacy
scripting
scripting cultures
scripting languages
variable parametric representation

Geometry has always constituted basic knowledge in the architectural design process, especially as a design language in the form of drawings based on the rules of Descriptive Geometry, but it has hardly ever formed an area of research. The advent of free-form shapes in contemporary architecture has completely changed this situation. The geometry of architectural designs is rapidly becoming more complex and challenging. Architects today exploit digital technology originally developed for the automotive and airplane industries for tasks of architectural design and construction.[1] This leads to a number of problems, since architectural applications differ from the original target industries in many ways, including aesthetics, statics and manufacturing technologies. The advent of numerically controlled machining and other digital production technologies in the automotive and aviation industries has resulted in a significant body of research on appropriate mathematical representations and algorithmic solutions. Its main findings form the backbone of state of the art 3D modeling software. A similar development for architectural applications has just started; the resulting area of research may be called *Architectural Geometry* (AG). For an overview of research groups working in this area, we refer to the Conference Proceedings[2] of "Advances in Architectural Geometry."

Research in Architectural Geometry aims at the development of new tools for the creation of digital models for architecture which meet the requirements in the shape-creation and design phase and already incorporate basic aspects of the actual construction including material, manufacturing technologies and structural properties. AG also plays an important role in enabling a completely digital workflow from design to manufacturing, especially for highly complex geometries. Moreover, AG provides tools to transfer standard digital models into a form suitable for the architectural application and fabrication; this process is referred to as "rationalization" and discussed below in more detail.

Construction-aware geometric design vs. rationalization. A *construction-aware design approach* incorporates knowledge on the material used, panel types, sub-construction, and so on in the shape-creation process via customized geometric modeling tools. As AG is not yet at the stage of design sophistication to deliver powerful software for accomplishing this approach, one often has to enter a kind of redesign phase after the original geometry definition; this is known as *rationalization*. Rationalization has to re-compute the geometry by minimally deviating from the original design and, at the same time, meeting requirements on panel types, smoothness of the skin, aesthetics of panel layout, cost of production and other aspects. From a mathematical perspective,

24

Architectural Geometry as Design Knowledge

Helmut Pottmann

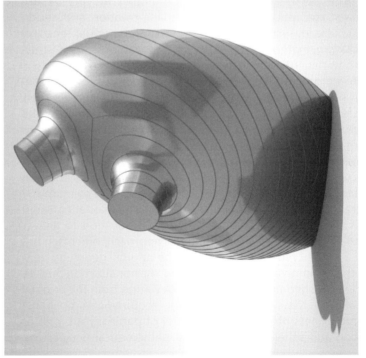

Figure 24.1

rationalization amounts to the solution of often highly nonlinear and computationally expensive optimization problems. The development of efficient optimization algorithms and the incorporation into user-friendly rationalization software tools are substantive research challenges in AG. Methodology developed for rationalization also opens up new avenues for the creation of novel construction-aware design tools. AG research has strong roots in applied mathematics, computational science and engineering and can only meet its ambitious goals in close cooperation with architects, structural engineers and construction companies. In the following, these general claims and thoughts are illustrated by selected research results and by geometry consulting work of Evolute GmbH.[3]

The trend towards a high level of geometric complexity also has strong implications for geometry in architectural education. The effective use of powerful geometric design software already requires further knowledge of geometry than is traditionally taught in drawing or descriptive geometry courses, and an even deeper understanding of geometry is necessary to excel in the exploitation of parametric design technology. The book *Architectural Geometry*[4] provides support for meeting the resulting challenges in education and also leads the way from basic high school geometry to research in AG.

Architectural free-form structures from single-curved panels. Frank Gehry has been one of the first to employ free-form surfaces in architecture. Examples include the Guggenheim Museum in Bilbao (1991–1997), the Experience Music Project in Seattle (1999–2000) and the Walt Disney Concert Hall in Los Angeles (1989–2004). The research performed in connection with his work is described in the PhD thesis of Dennis Shelden, chief technology officer of Gehry Technologies.[5] This is also one of the first contributions to AG in the sense of the present article. Gehry used mostly developable surfaces. These surfaces, also known as single-curved surfaces, can be unfolded into the plane without stretching or tearing. They are characterized by a family of straight lines, along each of which they possess a constant tangent plane. This implies various positive properties for fabrication. Recent research relates the coverage of a free-form surface by developable surface strips with work on quadrilateral meshes with planar faces.[6] A technique composed of subdivision (refinement) and optimization towards developability provides a direct (construction-aware) modeling approach. The process of rationalization of a given free-form surface with developable panels (strips) follows related ideas.

Facing page

Figure 24.1: Formtexx, Skipper Library, Conceptual design, 2009. Image credit: Image courtesy of Alexander Schiftner, Heinz Schmiedhofer, and Formtexx.[7]

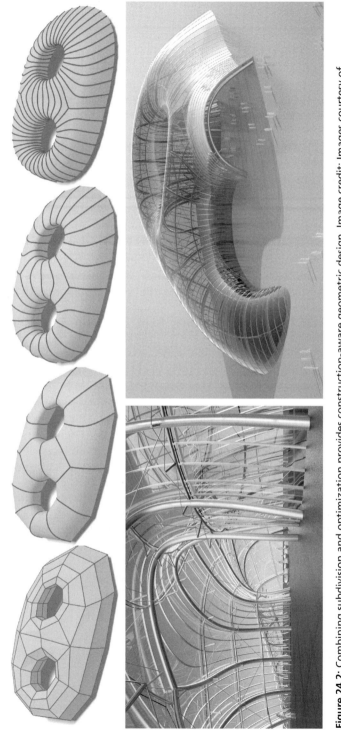

Figure 24.2: Combining subdivision and optimization provides construction-aware geometric design. Image credit: Images courtesy of Alexander Schiftner, Pengbo Bo, Johannes Wallner, and Heinz Schmiedhofer.

Rationalization by ruled surfaces and relation to manufacturing technologies. Ruled surfaces are formed by a family of straight lines and therefore possess advantages in fabrication. To give an example, ruled panels from GRC (glass fibre reinforced concrete) can be produced more efficiently than general double-curved panels, since the rapid and inexpensive hot-wire cutting technique can be used to manufacture their styrofoam molds. Generically, ruled surfaces possess negative Gaussian curvature K, which means that they are locally saddle shaped; they may also be single curved ($K=0$). Hence, designs which contain large areas with non-positive K are promising candidates for rationalization with ruled panels. Software for performing this task has recently been developed by Evolute. An example of its application is given by the Cagliari Contemporary Arts Centre (Zaha Hadid Architects).

Panel layout. Recent developments in manufacturing technology for doubly curved metal panels suggest that large-scale free-form metal façades will be buildable in the near future. This technological advancement will eventually simplify the rationalization of a metal façade surface, but splitting the surface into panels of maximum manufacturable size is still required. State-of-the-art design tools do not yet efficiently support the design of such panel layouts for complex free-form surfaces. In the paradigm of parametric modeling this often leads to free-form surfaces being replaced by simple parametric surfaces at an early stage. Recent research therefore tries to close these gaps, treating arbitrary free-form surfaces as parameters themselves and fully parametrizing their panel layouts.

Conclusion and future research. Architectural Geometry constitutes a new and challenging research area which aims at providing construction-aware design tools and enabling a completely digital workflow from design to manufacturing, especially for highly complex geometries. Simple fabrication-aware design tools like the generation of planar quad meshes or surfaces composed of single-curved strips via subdivision and optimization are now ready for use in practice. However, a lot more research has to be performed in connection with the development of tools for an effective and user-friendly exploration of the variety of design options under given constraints imposed by material, fabrication technology, production cost, structural considerations and other aspects one wants to take into account already in the shape-creation phase.

We have shown how advances in architectural geometry start to influence architectural practice and are about to change digital architectural design. It is foreseeable that in the near future we will have specialized tools that effectively integrate important aspects (such as structural properties, material behavior, fabrication cost, energy efficiency, functionality, etc.) into the shape-design phase. One may say that we will directly manipulate nearly optimized designs and hopefully also have tools for a more effective navigation in the usually high-dimensional space of feasible designs. Certainly, we will have to solve a number of outstanding difficult research problems before reaching this state.

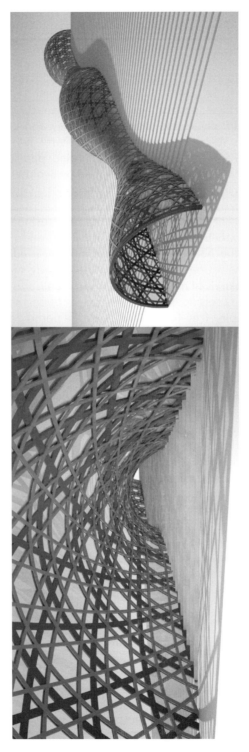

Figure 24.3: Three curve families which are close to geodesics (shortest paths) are arranged in a trihexagonal pattern. Image credit: Images courtesy of Alexander Schiftner, Johannes Wallner, and Heinz Schmiedhofer.

The new tools which are currently being developed have some built-in detail knowledge in AG, but their efficient use requires a very solid basic understanding of geometry which goes beyond the content of the traditional geometry curriculum in architecture. Future academic developments will have to address these new challenges in order to recognize the emerging significance of geometry as architectural knowledge.

1   CATIA is one of the first and most prominent examples of software transferred from the automotive and aircraft industries into architecture, namely by Frank Gehry. NURBS-based modelers, for example Rhino, are mainly based on technologies originally developed for other applications than architecture.

2   H. Pottmann, M. Hofer and A. Kilian, eds., *Advances in Architectural Geometry*, Vienna University of Technology, 2008; see http://www.architecturalgeometry.at/aag08. C. Ceccato, L. Hesselgren, M. Pauly, H. Pottmann and J. Wallner, eds., *Advances in Architectural Geometry*, Springer, 2010; L. Hesselgren, S. Sharma, J. Wallner, N. Baldassini, P. Bompas and J. Raynaud, eds., *Advances in Architectural Geometry*, Springer, 2012.

3   Evolute GmbH is a spin-off from the research group of the author at TU Vienna, which performs research, software development (EvoluteTools PRO) and consulting in geometric computing for architecture and manufacturing technologies; see http://www.evolute.at

4   H. Pottmann, A. Asperl, M. Hofer, A. Kilian, *Architectural Geometry*, Bentley Institute Press (Exton), 2007.

5   D. Shelden, Digital surface representation and the constructability of Gehry's architecture. PhD thesis, MIT, 2002.

6   H. Pottmann, A. Schiftner, P. Bo, H. Schmiedhofer, W. Wang, N. Baldassini and J. Wallner, Free-form surfaces from single-curved panels, ACM Trans. Graphics 27 (2008). Ongoing related research has been funded via Project 230520 of the FP7-IAPP framework; project partners: TU Wien, Evolute and RFR (http://www.rfr.fr).

7   Formtexx manufactures double-curvature free-form metal façades for the architectural sector; see http://www.formtexx.com

Working with parameters is an exciting way of thinking about visual form. In this capacity, the designer is no longer making choices about a single, final object but creating a matrix encompassing an entire population of possible designs. This is a move from thinking about an object to thinking about a field of infinite options. This involves searching for and exploring a population of designs that meet certain requirements, behave in particular ways, or fit the desires of the designer.

Defined broadly, a parameter is a value that has an effect on the output of a process. This could be something as straightforward as the amount of sugar in a recipe, or as complex as the activation threshold of a neuron in the brain. In the context of architecture and design, parameters describe, encode, and quantify the options and constraints at play in a system. A common constraint might be the budget available for a project, while a configuration option might control color, size, density, or material.

Identifying and describing the variable elements in a process— be it a section of code or the rules of a Dadaist poem—is called parameterization. This multi-step process requires that the designer decide both what can change and the range of possible values for each parameter. For example, a designer can explore the effects of different color palettes on a logo design. In this case, the colors of the elements within the logo are the parameters, and the list of possible palettes defines the value range. Parameterization creates connections between the intention of the designer and the system he or she is describing.

As a greater number of parameters are identified and incorporated into a process, the number of possible outcomes also increases. Imagine each parameter as defining an axis on a graph, and a parameterized system as defining a space populated by potential design states (resulting from a combination of specific values being assigned to each parameter). As a simple example, consider a rack of T-shirts. Each shirt on the rack is a different size and color, and we can say that the "large, green shirt" is the design state when the size parameter is large, and the color parameter is green. But it is just as easy to imagine a "large, red shirt," as being exactly the same as a "large, green shirt," just in a different color.

Thinking about parameters provides a bridge between repetition and transformation, as well as visualization and simulation. While transformation describes a parameter's effect on form, repetition offers a way to explore a field of possible designs for favorable variations. Both visualization and simulation require the use of parameters to define the system, and they describe how data or other inputs will influence the behaviors of that system.

25

Parameterize

**Casey Reas,
Chandler
McWilliams
and LUST**

Figure 25.1

> Composition Systems

The desire to construct a system for composing images, rather than making a single image, has a long history in modern art. Marcel Duchamp's 3 Standard Stoppages, 1913–14, is an early and fascinating example. To create this series of objects, he dropped a string, measuring 1 meter, from a height of 1 meter to define a curve. Defined by gravity, this ephemeral curve and the twisting of the string as it fell was then cut out of wood and used as a template for other images. For example, the curves were used within his Large Glass to define the shapes of the bachelor figures. A contemporary of Duchamp, Jean Arp, produced collage works, such as Untitled (Collage with Squares Arranged According to the Laws of Chance), by scattering the elements onto a page. Perhaps the clearest, most iconic pre-software examples are the mobiles of Alexander Calder. In these sculptures, shapes relate to one another through fixed connections, under the weight of gravity, but they are so well balanced that the wind can move the elements to shift their positions. Umberto Eco wrote of these objects:

> Each of his works is a 'work in movement' whose movement combines with that of the viewer. Theoretically, work and viewer should never be able to confront each other twice in precisely the same way. Here there is no suggestion of movement: the movement is real, and the work of art is a field of open possibilities.[1]

Experimental writers Tristan Tzara and William S. Burroughs introduced innovative, unpredictable operations as methods of writing, and John Cage used randomness as a fundamental technique for musical compositions.

While it's clear that these early compositional systems relied heavily on chance, these artworks are important within the context of parameters in that each of their creators defined a set of rules where some elements were selected by themselves and others resulted from events outside of their control. They invented systems from which an infinite number of unique works could (and did) emerge. This way of working is summarized well by Sol LeWitt's statement: "The idea becomes a machine that makes the art."[2]

More carefully determined systems include grids for composing pages in books, magazines, websites, and for posters. They allow each page to be unique, while still relating to every other page. For example, the Unigrid System, designed for the U.S. National Parks Service (NPS) in 1968 allows each park (Yellowstone, Yosemite, etc.) to have a unique brochure suited to its needs while also allowing the NPS to maintain a strong organizational

---

Facing page

Figure 25.1: Greg Lynn Form, Flatware set for Alessi: overall view of set. Image credit: Image courtesy, Greg Lynn Form.

identity. The Unigrid System is a flexible, open framework that allows indi-vidual designers to make their own decisions about layout while working within a larger system. Subtraction.com, which is the website and blog of Khoi Vinh (the art director of NYTimes.com) is a more contemporary example. A grid system applied to a website allows for hundreds, even thousands of pages to be generated based on a single structure. Vinh cites Josef Müller-Brockmann and Massimo Vignelli as influences, and he makes direct links between the history of the grid within print design and how it transfers to the web. Speaking about grids in an interview, he said:

> A grid system is not just a set of rules to follow . . . but it's also a set of rules to play off of—to break, even. Given the right grid—the right system of constraints—very good designers can create solutions that are both orderly and unexpected.[3]

> Variables

In any system or set of rules, there exists the potential for variation. Though the primary variation of form present in a Calder mobile comes from the unpredictable interaction of natural forces, it is still possible to get an even wider field of possibilities by changing other parameters in the system. These include the lengths of the rods, weights of the objects, and positions of the connections. A compositional system built out of 1-foot (0.3-meter) rods will look and behave very differently than a system made of 1-meter (3.3-feet) rods.

When the value of a parameter can change, we call this a variable. Variables can be distinguished from constants, whose values cannot change, such as the force of gravity; or constraints, which are fixed in response to the requirements of the project, such as cost or available materials, and provide boundaries that define the edges of a design space. The creation of a mobile, for example, may be constrained by the size of the room it will hang in and the need for it to be light and strong enough to hang from the ceiling. Though all three of these parameter types will effect the range of possible forms, the variables can be considered as the primary axes of variation. The artist changes the variables, either by hand or with code, in search of interesting outcomes.

Sometimes the variable's value will only makes sense within a certain range. Consider the tuning knob on a radio; only frequencies within the range shown on the dial are valid. It is conceivable that a radio could use values outside of this range, but the results will be unexpected, and certainly won't sound like radio. Defining the range of values is one way that designers can assert their aesthetic sensibilities in a parameterized system. Perhaps not all values will look good or create interesting results. Much like the dial on the radio, the range can be refined to produce a narrower, but more pleasing field of variations.

As with the compositional systems in use prior to the invention of the personal computer, randomness is a useful tool for finding interesting variations in a parameterized system. Random values can be used to emulate unpredictable qualities of our physical reality and to generate unexpected compositions. Though not as random as a toss of the dice, code provides a more flexible way to create random values. Sequences of random numbers can be generated in such a way that each number in the sequence differs only slightly from the last; this technique aids in the simulation of natural effects like wind, waves, and rock formations.[4] Although using random numbers to find interesting variations Is not an efficient way to discover every possible form, it does provide a way to explore an exhaustively large parameter space in order to get an idea of possible outcomes. Even in a small system that uses only three parameters, each of which has a value from 0 to 100, there are a million possibilities—far more than one can explore methodically.

> Control

Parameters are often used to create a system that generates optimal variation within a given set of constraints. These constraints can be semi-fixed, meaning that they provide a boundary for the field of variations, but the constraints themselves can be changed when necessary. The most common example of this type of constraint is the cost of producing a variation. For example, a CNC-milling machine is a cost-effective digital fabrication technique, but most machines are not capable of producing shapes with undercut areas. The CNC bit sits on a computer-controlled arm that descends onto the material, so it can only remove the material on top. A parametric design system might take this into consideration by eliminating any design model that requires this type of cut. The constraint is semi-fixed, because it is always possible to use a different, more costly fabrication technology if necessary, or if the budget allows.

When the architecture firm SHoP Architects was commissioned by the Federal Emergency Management Agency (FEMA) to design a bridge in Lower Manhattan to restore a vital pedestrian connection that was lost after September 11, they used a combination of ready-made structures and parametric design techniques to quickly create an interesting, cost-effective form. The architects wanted the exterior cladding of the bridge to let light in during the day and allow it to shine through at night, but also to discourage sightseers from stopping on the walkway. These programmatic constraints were combined with time and budgetary concerns, as well as the fixed geometry of the ready-made bridge structure. Taking all of these elements into consideration, they were able to create a pattern using only a small number of unique pieces that gave the feel of a much more complex system.

In contrast to using random numbers to explore a field of possible designs, parametric systems can be controlled to determine the final form and to meet specific needs. In something akin to turning the knobs of an old television set to tune the picture, in this model, the designer first creates the system and defines the parameters, then inputs and adjusts specific settings to control and optimize the final output. Taking this one step further, it is possible to quantify and encode the designer's preferences or certain outcomes into the system. Less strict than a constraint, this allows flexibility in the range of possible variations, while encouraging the system to generate solutions that the designer likes.

Though parametric control is often understood in terms of numbers and variables, complex and unpredictable forms can be achieved by linking the parameters of multiple elements together. For example, an architect designing a staircase might want to connect the height of the staircase to the height of the ceiling, so that if the ceiling height changes, the staircase will adapt to the new values. The space of possible staircases is coupled to the properties of a single variation of the ceiling. This type of controlled coupling allows the designer to experiment and explore a field of possibilities, while simultaneously controlling related forms. In this way, parameters can be used to control things like proportion and scale without giving up the freedom to try different permutations.

> PARAMETER TECHNIQUE: One-of-One

Using parameterized algorithms to generate form involves an exploratory process of searching through a field of designs to find interesting variations. As a result of this process, each variation is likely to appear related to but different from other possible versions. Depending on the number of parameters and the range of possible values, these resemblances can be subtle or extreme. When used in conjunction with repetition, these techniques allow artists and designers to straddle the boundary between creating serial editions and one-of-a-kind pieces. By presenting multiple versions, one-of-one works operate as singular pieces, but at the same time provide a window into the complexity of the system used in their creation.

> PARAMETER TECHNIQUE: Variable Fonts

Since their invention, systems of writing have always been implicitly parameterized; the introduction of software has increased these possibilities. In ancient cuneiform writing, each symbol was made from a pattern of wedges impressed in clay. Changing the parameters, such as the quantity or size of the spaces between wedges, defined which character was written. This parameterization persisted to some degree in contemporary typefaces, but the Univers type family designed by Adrian Frutiger in 1954 was a landmark in this respect. Univers is a system of twenty-one related fonts, designed around the parameters of width, weight, and slant. The fonts range from Univers 39 Thin Ultra Condensed to Univers 83 Heavy Extended, with Univers 55 Roman as the base font. Programming legend Donald E. Knuth's Metafont language from 1979 is a logical extension of Frutiger's plan. As the first fully parameterized software typeface, Metafont was capable of generating letters of every width and weight, because each was defined by a geometric equation. This idea was further commercialized by Adobe, with their Multiple Master (MM) technology. Like Metafont, an MM font such as Myriad or Minion could generate any width or weight according to the parameters set up by their designers. It remains an open question as to whether this kind of typographic flexibility is needed or even feasible, given that Adobe stopped producing MM faces in favor of the Open Type format. Nevertheless, this typographic quest was continued by LettError's Superpolator.

> PARAMETER TECHNIQUE: Console

A console is a set of controls for electronic or mechanical equipment, such as cars, airplanes, radios, and milling machines. The structure of the console has migrated to software interfaces. For example, many computer games have a dense set of controls at the bottom of the screen, allowing players to monitor and control the status of the game. The values controlled through a software console are linked to variables within the program; they allow the state of the program to change without rewriting the code. Users can manipulate the program, even if they don't know how to program; and programmers can view changes immediately without stopping the program, changing variables in the code, and restarting. Consoles are used as interfaces for a wide range of tasks, including for designing buildings, flying a simulated airplane, or building avatars for online communities.

1   Umberto Eco, The Open Work (Cambridge, MA: Harvard University Press, 1989), 86.
2   Alexander Alberro and Blake Stimson, eds., Conceptual Art: A Critical Anthology (Cambridge, MA: MIT Press, 2000), 14.
3   Interview   with   Khoi   Vinh: http://www.thegridsystem.org/2009/articles/ interview-with-khoi-vinh/.
4   Ken Perlin greatly impacted the computer graphics world with his invention of Perlin Noise in 1985. This method for generating textures is widely used in computer graphics to create visual effects like smoke, fire, clouds, and organic motion.

Where are we now in terms of a dominant paradigm in respect of 'movement'? On the one hand we have a position promulgated as 'anything goes' by a leading practitioner Cecil Balmond,[1] and on the other 'the next major movement is . . .' from (Patrik Schumacher).[2] It is possible that both practitioners are arguing for the same thing from a slightly different trajectory, but what of the individual designer not necessarily at the height of their powers?

Every design scripter scripts design for the first time – but what are they joining: mainstream alternative practice, a club, a movement, a counterculture? This curiosity was sparked by my own experience: reflecting on how I myself started thinking about design and computer coding in the same thought space, it occurred to me that everyone moving into this excitingly different domain of practice might also have found themselves facing similar challenges with the same sense of joining a road without clear signposts. Certainly, when faced with students tackling scripting for the first time, there is a palpable sense of 'this could well be too difficult and beyond me, and how would I use it anyway?' It seems we are over the first hurdle – initiation – as there is considerable evidence of an emerging scripting generation with a host of committed pioneers who have trail blazed before them. Is this it: problem solved, scripting now mainstream, or near mainstream, or do we collectively still face a substantial journey? It is the combination of a personal sense of still being in *terra incognita* despite having left *terra nullius* that prompted me to correspond with a selection of current maestros and pioneers. In this chapter I lift the lid of my own experience in order to derive a series of 'questions of the day' to pose to my chosen correspondents.

26

Cultural Defence

Mark Burry

> How I Came to Script

My scripting adventure began in 1992. Investigating Gaudí's surviving plaster models for the Sagrada Família church, I had reached a point at which I seemed to be devoting an inordinate amount of time to carrying out unremittingly repetitive tasks. The alleged efficiency gains using computer-aided drafting began to seem rather far-fetched, not least the preternatural tendency for CAD software to steer towards 2D drafting, which made excursions into 3D modelling rather awkward in comparison. I had thought naively that the 'D' in CAD stood for design, not drafting, which is how the software seemed to have been prioritised to me. Specifically, there were two particular tasks that were grinding me down: drawing 2D *hyperbola* curves from which to construct 3D *hyperboloids of revolution of one sheet*, and labelling hundreds of points with unique names combined with their coordinates. For

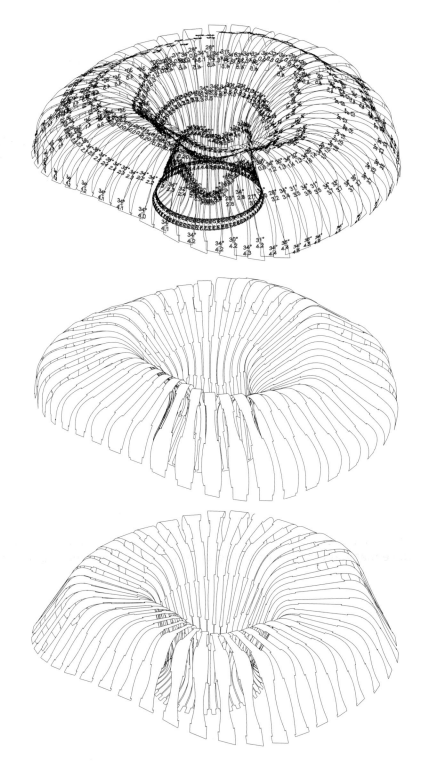

Figure 26.1

the first of such wearying tasks, the hyperbola, I needed to produce several hundred mathematically derived curves to match sections extracted from the models Gaudí had composed principally from elliptical hyperboloids. At that time I was using AutoCAD™ and this task involved computing a *polyline* through sufficient points to allow the curve to be both smooth and mathematically precise. The trouble was that each point had to be derived manually using a scientific calculator and the formula for a hyperbola. Each point, and there were 15 required for each curve, was calculated then entered into 2D space manually by typing in via the command line. At the outset, I assumed that there would be a tool within the various CAD software packages that I had access to through which I could simply type in the formula, give values to the variables and surely the curve would appear magically inside my 3D modelling environment in the correct position and orientation. There seemed to be plenty of what are now called *applets* about that could do this just as I have described, but they were the products of computer science postgraduates who generously shared them in the public domain as stand-alone 'shareware programs'. I could find no such tool within my CAD software, nor any means of interoperating between the shareware and CAD.

I was aware that in offices at that time many users of AutoCAD™, for example, had access to customised versions that had routines written in AutoLISP, a language specific to the software. These routines had been prepared to minimise routine tasks, but none of my contacts had actually written them; they had been acquired informally with consent or otherwise through the normal networks. Extensive enquiries failed to furnish any such hyperbola routine to help me draw mine so, as is often the best possible stimulant in such situations, necessity mothered a drastically innovative approach on my part: learning to program the hyperbola myself.

Like so many who were conventionally trained as architects, programming was not in my blood. I knew no one in my circle who could assist me, and I assumed it would be way beyond me: if I was to tackle programming I would have to pick it up on my own, on that basis. Once I had settled to the task two aspects surprised me. First, it was not quite as forbidding as I had expected and, second, there was no room for approximation or error: for an effective outcome that was both robust and consistent, precision was non-negotiable. Once I had succeeded in producing a routine that could be called up either in the command line or via a drop-down menu I had reduced a process that had been taking a significant fraction of an hour per hyperbola into a matter of seconds. Furthermore I could toggle each result to unique layers and names. With three points defining respectively an origin, a point where '*x*' was a minimum, and a point defining the curve's asymptote, I had all that was needed for the hyperbola to be calculated automatically and drawn in an

---

Facing page
Figure 26.1: Achim Menges and Jan Knippers, ICD, ITKE, Research Pavilion, Stuttgart, 2010. Image credit: Achim Menges and Jan Knippers, ICD and ITKE, University of Stuttgart.

instant. After having this frustration settled, I tackled the other tedious task that had also been so energy sapping: marking points in space with unique names, extracting their coordinates from the database and listing them in an associated text file, and placing this information in 3D space next to the relevant points. With both time-consuming repetitive tasks sorted, I had developed a completely different view of computer-aided drafting at least, and probably the more elusive computer-aided design that interested me far more.

Both these undertakings were highly specific to my research at the time and it is not surprising perhaps that neither were available as ready-made options within commercial software. The effect of learning to script changed my relationship with the computer. Hitherto I had regarded it as a necessary adjunct to my work as an architect moving towards the twenty-first century. I had no love for it at all, and I probably resented the enormous gulf between my thought processes and whatever was happening inside the black box. Once I had a handle on this coding caper, I could see then that I could attempt to transcend whatever limitations software might impose on me as a designer, guiding this electronic instrument with the same authority I applied to my pen and compass. At the outset, I realised that the stumbling block was not so much learning the code itself or the syntax required for its use as deconstructing the problem involved sufficiently well to represent it in code. If I could not get the logic right, no amount of syntactic precision with the code was going to compensate.

The two problems that had encouraged me to step outside my professional comfort zone of compliant passenger to become front-seat driver were stimulated by a need to rid myself of repetitive work that was not only numbingly boring, but also inclined to suffer from human error, typically induced by any manual data entry that relies on reading from the screen, writing it down, then keying it back in a different context – there was no cut and paste at that time. Very quickly, however, I could see that a prime motivation for coding on top of software was to augment my design practice by allowing me to work in ways hitherto impractical, and so scripting became a medium of experimentation ahead of productivity gains.

Within a year, scripting had infiltrated my teaching, and in 1993 I instituted an elective course in which the participants had to come up with two pieces of code: a productivity tool (this was to appease my senior CAD teaching colleagues and satisfy the school's curriculum priorities) and a design experimentation script. In many ways that period was one of my more memorable teaching and learning experiences, as we all seemed to be in the same boat on a shared voyage of discovery. We would speculate as a class and variously seek solutions together in this mutual empty territory. Seven years later, as the decade culminated, the class had progressed from working as individuals unpacking unconnected whims through coding, to collaborating on an exercise addressing the same challenge in a combined script. .

From 2001 onwards I have not scripted for myself in quite the same way, as a student base with different capabilities emerged (these I dub the 'scripting generation'), who had access to much better software environments and coding options. This combined with a shift in my professional responsibilities to confine me rapidly to the role of pioneer relic rather than hands-on scripting maestro. This is not to say that I am now remote from scripting: quite the opposite. Today's scripters are working at a fundamentally deeper level than I was able to reach a decade ago, and I am able to benefit from their input (along with contributions from the various computer scientists and software engineers with whom I have collaborated subsequently), far more effectively than I was able to do travelling alone. It seems that there is an interesting potential paradox here: for a designer to work at the right level using scripting, they probably need assistance in code writing because of the time this can take, but this necessitates a degree of handing over. The benefits gained from working with someone who is writing code all the time exceed those from direct author-applier efficiencies, yet to work effectively with a scripting collaborator the designers themselves must know how to script. To avoid this paradox the trick is being able to retire from the front line gracefully, yet continue to enhance the cultures of scripting through the injection of wisdom born of experience.

This concludes the account of my journey into scripting but my baggage does not quite end there. Originally my motivation to contribute this book came from a sense of frustration around some surprising paradoxes in addition to the one I outline immediately above. The first is the prevalence of scripting universally in exhibited and published experimental work during the past 10 years yet it is still largely absent from architectural education programmes – with certain exceptions. The second is that despite the surge in opportunity with both hardware and software along with more user-friendly and more powerful scripting tools, the originality of the output has hardly kept up. Third, instead of such powerful new media further pluralising the creative community, there seems to be a tendency to swarm towards particular approaches such as generative design using genetic algorithms, or agent systems, or some other 'system', usually from the same stable. Designers are appropriating scripting 'systems', not making them. Fourth, the preternatural instinct of the senior designer is to be secretive, quite the opposite of the scripting generation, who willingly share their booty on the Internet. Such levels of generosity may mean that while wheels are not being reinvented everywhere as they were in the closeted ateliers of yore, young designers are more inclined to mash up each others' code rather than struggle away from first principles, which could potentially stunt creative growth. Finally, the fifth paradox is that of the potentially reduced level of creative free-flow, with the former reliance on the emergence of ideas, concepts and designs from the sketch at risk of being compromised through the application of the cold hard logic in a script. Such logic is required to distil the route to an answer to the problem, perhaps yet to be fully identified, using scripted code that foregrounds discovery rather than pre-empts 'the answer' that ought to emerge through its use. For me it is this paradox that is the most stimulating, for it pits the non-scripters against the scripters if we accept emergence as a principal opportunity within any design process. In digital design it seems obvious that if one scripts in a way that avoids painting the designer into a corner and, instead, provides opportunities for new bifurcations to be encountered along the way, far richer outcomes will be possible for the same investment of time than that which will be arrived at using software merely at face value.

> Some Alternative Views

Looking through my own lens there are at least three scripting cultures, distinctive and not necessarily immiscible. The first is scripting for productivity, the second is experimentation by scripting a path to 'the answer', and the third is scripting for a voyage of discovery. Coming from a single commentator my view that there are several scripting cultures could nevertheless be seen as a single culture of simply 'scripting as I know how'. It is for this reason that I consulted widely among a group of young and not-so-young pioneers, practitioners and thought leaders. I have titled this chapter 'Cultural Defence', as I was interested in investigating whether there might be any risk that scripting cultures are, in fact, tending towards a single trajectory. A scripted outcome forcing design authorship in directions that might threaten its richness such as the dilution of ideas, too much external machinist agency, or just being straitjacketed through code.

What follows is a distillation of a wider set of opinions that go beyond my own. I found the responses surprising in many respects, but very positive, and I imagine the care that every correspondent took to answer my enquiry, and the thoughtfulness of their replies will come across as extremely encouraging to the novice scripter. I believe that there is a strong shared sense that we are on the cusp of something different, and that the way in which we will work together as designers in the future, while still a little indistinct, is rapidly becoming clearer and therefore more tangible. I will first summarise my general impressions framed around my enquiry followed by quotes in answer to specific 'questions of the day'.

Correspondents consulted

Acconci Studio (Vito Acconci), Francis Aish (*Foster + Partners*), Robert Aish, *AKT (Adams Kara Taylor)* (Sawako Kaijima and Panagiotis Michalatos), *Biothing* (Alisa Andrasek), *CEB Reas* (Casey Reas), *CITA* (Mette Ramsgard Thomsen), Pia Ednie-Brown, Cristiano Ceccato, Paul Coates, Evan Douglis, John Frazer, Mark Goulthorpe, Michael Hensel, Tom Kvan, Axel Kilian, Neil Leach, *Kokkugia* (Roland Snooks), Kyle Steinfeld, *labDORA* (Peter Macapia), Achim Menges, *MESNE* (Tim Schork and Paul Nicholas), *MinusArchitecturestudio* (Jason Johnson), *Mode* (Ronnie Parsons and Gil Akos), *MOS* (Michael Meredith), Neri Oxman, Brady Peters, Nick Pisca (*Gehry Technologies*), *Proxy* (Mark Collins and Toru Hasegawa), *SOFTlab* (Michael Szivos), *SPAN* (Matias del Campo), *Supermanoeuvre* (Dave Pigram and Iain Maxwell), Denis Shelden, Martin Tamke, *THEVERYMANY* (Marc Fornes), Hugh Whitehead.

> Initiation to Scripting

Some of my sample group have been introduced to programming as early as primary school, others at senior school, but it appears that almost all did not begin scripting in earnest until college. The clear majority are autodidacts too, which is encouraging news for any reader concerned that only nerds can enter the fray. I was interested in an in-depth enquiry into the personal circumstances of the scripters ranging from expert amateurs to creators of scripting 'languages' that have subsequently been widely taken up by others. I enquired about the age at which they first scripted and which of the languages they had been drawn to.

I also enquired into whether as accomplished designers/educators/exhibiters they script themselves today or do they in fact brief others to script for them? I was curious to learn whether they have ever actually scripted for themselves or only through collaboration in the past. Were my correspondents responsible for all their own scripting, I wondered, curious about their productivity being so high given all the other demands on their time?

I had expected a veil of unshareable intimacy around this particular stream of my investigation – 'did you paint that yourself . . .?' Initially I found it odd that this question had raised itself, but this is not information that is volunteered in routine conversation I have found. An insight here, however, might reduce the timid designer's perceived degree of difficulty – those who are attracted to entering the coding terrain but are familiar only with software straight out of the box. This group can be discouraged by what they imagine to be an unbridgeable gulf to a world of impossibly high achievement. I have not found this to be quite such an issue when seeking to encourage just as tentative and equally unpractised novices to adopt more manually applied creative skills. A student who has never sculpted before can pick up a hammer and chisel and apply it to a piece of wood, for instance, taking on the challenge with enthusiasm because they can quickly assess the degrees of difficulty relative to their experience. Subsequently they can readily evaluate where their innate skill lies in comparison with the work of an expert. Where the skill being acquired appears to be deeply intellectual, as is the case with computer coding, a wall seems to place itself rudely separating the possible from the apparently impossible. Perhaps the scripting world's mysteriousness to the uninitiated suits the initiated – twenty-first-century tradecraft to be protected?

My correspondents reveal two interesting commonalities that dispel any notion that all scripters are natural born coders. The first is that they have almost all coded to a sophisticated level at some point in their careers even if they are not doing so now – they have developed their skills to a high standard of application. Some continue to work at the hands-on level, but a surprising number admit to only having enough time to *pseudocode*:[3] it seems that as careers progress, as my correspondents move forward from being struggling up-and-coming *arrivistes* to accomplished professionals, the corollary is insufficient time to indulge in coding. Many admit to coding being time consuming even when they are experienced at it. The nature of the design envelope-pusher means that they are just as energetic in scripting beyond any obvious horizons as they would be burning the midnight oil designing by any other route.

In terms of design, the principal difference between scripting oneself and briefing others to script is not clear-cut. When an accomplished designer-scripter is working with others who are doing the lion's share of code writing there are three alternative pathways to follow. The first is via studio teaching where the give-and-take arrangements are quite clear: the maestro shares knowledge and, in some cases, pieces of code with their protégés who, in turn, work on a project with a complexity beyond what they would be likely to address on their own. The studio along with the project benefits from the insight brought to the mix by the project leader's experience. This model is probably the most prevalent, but carries the danger of the 'flocking towards familiarity' syndrome – moths drawn to a bright light, or even straightforward design cloning: a shared vocabulary or a sole signature that may not offer individuals sufficient sense of shared authorship. If this is an assertion it clearly risks coming across as a polemic, given that to some cloning can be read as sharing a creative voice with others. Whether this leads to a risk of a cultural impoverishment through the suppression of individual identities will depend on how critical owning a design actually is in the age of Web 2.

The second collaboration path is working closely with an expert programmer whose background is code writing, not design. This can be fraught with unexpected issues when the computer-science-educated code writer has an outlook fundamentally attuned to an analysis of a situation or condition, and turns this distilled knowledge into a logical procedure. Unless the designer in the team can, in turn, completely attune their creative synthesis to the proposed logic, the relationship could be one of eternal disconnect with neither party feeling that they have achieved what they set out to do.

The third collaboration path is a variation of the second, where a symbiosis operates between designers and coders. In these teams the designers are experienced (usually former) scripters who can drill down within their design strategy to a logical basis. They can do this sympathetically as the code writer is sufficiently 'design aware' in terms of understanding the implications of creative synthesis not to lock their script into predefined and therefore inevitable outcomes. From experience, this represents a perfect partnership, but they are relatively hard to come by – certainly many of my correspondents describe this kind of relationship as being their ideal. Put at its simplest, 'talented designer seeks clear-headed coder writer' is not in itself an automatic success if an intellectual partnership cannot be assured.

I was interested to learn the extent to which scripting is seen by others as primarily a productivity tool compared with its potential to assist design exploration. I was motivated by my early experience in forcing a split between the two (productivity versus experimentation) in what one of my contributors described as a 'false dichotomy'. In my circumstances, and this seemed a global situation during the 1990s at least, CAD was taught as a productivity tool. The teachers of CAD were drawn from that pool of inspired individuals who had previously taught 'drafting', 'technical drawing', 'detailing', 'representation', *et al.* Relatively few teaching staff that I came across at that time tried to uncover any digital design potential and, in the main, students did not seek to experiment with software in the studio beyond visualising the completed project with obligatory fly-throughs. With the exception of Form Z™ I could see little in architectural CAD software to tempt students to be more playful. In that context to script with CAD software was to find ways to automate the mundane, as I described at the beginning of this chapter – this applied as much to my architectural practice as it did initially to my design research, and for this reason I initiated teaching scripting with both productivity and exploration as two distinct approaches.

Consulting a combination of preeminent and up-and-coming designers may not seem the most scientific means to elicit a categorical distinction between the two, but it served to establish a consensus all the same. Hardly anyone proposed that the motivation to script was founded exclusively on one or the other of the two poles – productivity and design exploration – with almost everyone describing a mix of the two, but with proportions that varied. The question obviously causes a pause for thought for many: even if design exploration via scripting is not a time saver in itself – in other words, if the same time is invested in the design as would have been without any scripting – through scripting the eventual outcome will be that much more sophisticated. Indubitably, in such terms, scripting is a productivity tool even if the scripter is more inclined to direct their coding towards a speculative investigation than simply to ensure complexity is untangled to guarantee a more manageable and affordable project.

> Software and Scripting Language Choices

There is a very long list of scripting tools available. The list in the box here is distilled from my 34 correspondents.

Adobe ActionScript
C, C#, C++
GenerativeComponents script
Html
Iron Python
Java, JavaScript
LUA
Mathematica
MATLAB
MaxScript
Maya (Maya Embedded Language (MEL) and Python)
Objective-C
Perl
PHP

> Processing (Java)
> Python
> RhinoScript (VB, Grasshopper (VB), Python)
> Rhl
> VB, VBA

Not surprisingly Maya, Adobe and Rhino appeared in the lists of at least half the group. Among my correspondents there is a cluster of initiates commencing around the year 2002, the time when several packages combined thrilling levels of 3D modelling with associated scripting languages, principally Maya™ (using MEL for scripting), and Rhino 3D™ using Rhino VB. A little more surprising is the fact that over half use languages such as C#, Python and VB, demonstrating real commitment to the task. *Processing* (shareware), written by Casey Reas (one of my correspondents) and Ben Fry, is used by half my sample. The power and simplicity of Processing point to the phenomenon of an emerging generation of scripters who wish to focus their intelligence on sorting out the logic of their design approach rather than on hitting obstacles with obscure coding syntax. Processing is a language designed by a designer to help other designers leapfrog over the lack of ease of use that characterises many programming languages.

> To Script or to Brief Others to Script

I was surprised by the admission of several correspondents that they are no longer in a position to take up any new programming environments as their careers have moved on to leadership roles with associated time constraints. Others will not relinquish their direct pivotal role in design scripting at the highest level on the basis that as designers they need to be pulling, not pushing.

Many of those consulted have had access to expertise that can vary from straightforward assistance to (as in my case) input to coding at a level I would never have reached by myself, certainly within the time frames of the projects concerned.

> Challenge or Breeze

With only a single exception everyone consulted sees programming as a hard-won skill, not acquired with ease. A few ventured that their teaching experience reveals that some students are more naturally able to assimilate the rather unusual aspects of code writing (compared with all other design activities) than others. Some suggest that on the one hand scripting is a vital opportunity but on the other, the required logical approach is challenging for designers more familiar with freer ways of thinking. There is evidence of people who, while they 'get' scripting, and despite scripting very ably, still struggle with it. With unusual candour some of my correspondents admitted to struggling themselves, all the more astonishing when their top-drawer output is compared with a self-assessed lack of facility – another instance of hope for the reader who might suspect that they too are a potential struggler. Most replied that it gets easier as they progress and, as with any high-level skill, constant practice is a necessity. The comment I enjoyed the most in this regard was that scripting is easy until you get to the first bug.

> Design Productivity and Design Exploration

I was also curious to learn the motivation of the designers I approached – what attracted them to scripting? The responses were satisfyingly varied:

- reaching beyond analogue processes;
- capturing material logic and computing performance;
- being playful;
- exploiting generative processes;
- seeking deeper access to the imagination;
- engaging with complexity;
- inducing rapid iteration and variation;
- grappling with the performative;
- toying with the unexpected and delving into the unknown;
- being forced to be explicit;
- discovering novelty;
- localising intelligence;
- investigating self-organisation principles;
- studying phenomena;

. . . and of course going for good old task automation.

Hardly two responses were the same.

I received a similarly wide and perceptive range of responses to my enquiry about potential dangers in scripting such as contributing to 'the death of the pencil sketch', 'enfranchising the amateur', or design becoming 'automated'. In some it provoked a response bordering on irritation – as if this were an absurd proposition – while others went to the other extreme, positively welcoming an end to the supremacy of design skills being framed entirely around mind–hand–eye coordination. Several made comparisons with the arrival of cheap high-definition still and movie cameras, which they noted had not necessarily reduced the quality of top photographers and filmmakers: talent always shines through. This is an optimistic view perhaps, as one considers the implications of the architectural equivalent: amateur house designers given tools to create their own home; can we really compare an album of poor photos with a landscape blighted by properties built from poorly understood design principles? Is this even a scripting consideration?

There is at least a niggle that a designer who has appropriated the use of someone else's script to create 'interesting effects' might end up with the credit for something for which they are not the complete author. Again, this is the dilemma of tool or process versus outcome. When scripting there is a further dilemma that comes from the typical need to begin encoding a design at the outset compared with new ideas emerging through intuition from the undirected sketch, as it is hand drawn or modelled along the way. But in scripting a design, a logic has to be investigated up front, which for many can be seen as an opportunity, not a hindrance. Any argument that scripting leads to standardisation can be countered by the fact that it affords highly wayward and idiosyncratic designers the opportunity to innovate in ways otherwise not possible, which segues into my next line of enquiry: new design avenues.

> Essential Scripting and its Value

When I asked my correspondents what they could design through scripting that they could not reasonably produce otherwise, and with what added value, I received a highly spirited response with as many unique suggestions as respondents. Firstly, the ability to work with large data sets, proceeding in many directions simultaneously, and working beyond our perceptual capacity were prominent responses. While scripting might veer towards the complexification of otherwise quite simple things as well as deal with still more, several pointed out that scripting can do the exact opposite, and be used to look for simplification. Others enjoy the opportunity to capture specific know-how, encoding it with tacit knowledge rendering it more declared and shared. A proportion of my correspondents also pointed to the link between scripting and fabrication.

How stuck would scripters be without the opportunity to script elicited replies ranging from not being able to do any of the things that particular individuals or practices currently undertake to do, to only being inconvenienced, forced to spend more time than would otherwise be necessary, and possibly being forced to work with a reduced set of inputs.

> Scripting Education

In this chapter I have covered the origins of my own interest in scripting, and I have opened up the subject a little by anonymously reporting the opinions of a group of experts who have responded to my request for additional insights.

One generation on, scripting seems to be here to stay. So what does this mean for the education of architects? I conclude this chapter by incorporating the views of my correspondents listed earlier to enrich what ought to be a very vigorous debate in every school of architecture and all practices still relying on traditional ways of working in the face of a wider uptake of scripting.

> The Need for Prior Knowledge

I am impressed by the way that architects' professional organisations in many countries have worked hard to ensure that a school that is highly experimental and culturally focused is professionally accredited on the same basis as a school with a strong technical focus, for example. Correspondingly, entry requirements seem to vary considerably. I have worked in schools where maths proficiency at senior school level was a core requirement and others where no such condition of entry is made. Given that almost all those I have consulted see scripting skills as being hard won, should the schools that include scripting at an elective if not fundamental level seek some computational skilling as a prerequisite to coding? If this comes across as an unusually draconian proposition, readers who have tried to involve in their scripting studio a student with no maths beyond early senior school basics in a class otherwise full of those with a good level of maths, will appreciate the dilemma that prompts this question. For anyone nervous that compulsory scripting skills for pre-university initiates is a secret agenda within scripting cultures, the selected responses that follow will help allay any such fears, while still provoking some discussion all the same.

The question does open up a broader educational issue, for instance the assertion that scripting might contribute usefully to what is taught in many disciplines well before college.

> Scripting should be taught in high-schools (will elementary schools follow) as general culture: scripting for architects & designers, scripting for mathematicians & biologists, scripting for dancers & musicians, scripting for poets & moviemakers & dramatists. (Vito Acconci)

There are also assertions that procedural literacy has an increasingly vital role to play:

> Yes, absolutely, I think the education system should start teaching procedural literacy from the beginning. Students should then build on these skills and focus them within the context of architecture. (Casey Reas)

This level of affirmation is not universal with a call for sufficient scope to accommodate the unexpected perspectives that innocence often brings to the mix:

> It is useful but not necessary at the moment. People with no skill or interest in digital media may bring a different and often needed perspective or experience. (Panagiotis Michalatos & Sawako Kaijima, AKT Architects)

Crucially, many argue the case for prior training in thinking procedurally rather than for arriving with prior coding ability:

> What is far more important than the mechanics of scripting is for students to be able to think algorithmically. One question might be: Should this be taught at high school or at University? We then might consider the subsequent issues

as to whether algorithmic thought should be taught abstractly or as applied to a specific subject (of interest to the student)? Therefore linking the algorithmic thinking to the subject of architecture might make it more attractive to some students who might not respond to the abstract form. (Robert Aish)

There are also those who are happy to work with all comers; note the bravura registered with the following two comments:

Not necessarily. They can 'mutate' very fast. It is often better to learn scripting and abstraction layers directly on design problems. (Alisa Andrasek)
       No, it's OK for them to learn it there – it's part of a culture. And those that have familiarity through another education have to retrain themselves anyhow. (Peter Macapia, labDORA)

There is potential for a debate here: the hacker and masher getting by versus the highly skilled writer of elegant code working with the benefit of thorough learning. As useful as the latter context might be for skilled grounding, it is not deemed essential by the community, nor is it likely to become the norm.

> Scripting as Part of an Architectural Education

Although there was ambivalence about prior learning, almost all my correspondents are quite emphatic about the need to integrate scripting into the curriculum, although 'learning by doing' through direct application in the studio is seen as an appropriate environment by many. As shown in the selected extracts, some proponents of the teaching of scripting in college are quite emphatic about this.

Architects are ultimately choreographers of systems, and the benefits of teaching programming in an architectural context are manifold. If architecture wants to survive as a discipline, it needs to engage the culture of innovation and computing. (Mark Collins & Toru Hasegawa, Proxy)

Scripting can be seen as offering an alternative view of creativity:

An algorithmic understanding of creativity – that the act is not a flash in the dark, a blessing from heaven but the result of hard rigorous thought which can in many parts be represented algorithmically – that is the important step. Right now, scripting is a very useful paradigm but it is not exclusively so. (Tom Kvan)

And a call for scripting education to be subsumed in a wider intellectual framework:

To the extent that it is framed within the intellectual development of language, writing, mathematics, etc. and understood for what it is, not mythologized. (Mark Goulthorpe)

These are still strange times for architectural pedagogues settling down from the previous tensions between analogue as opposed to digital design practice, who now face another unscheduled cultural shift. While we are moving well into an era of digital design acceptance, we nevertheless operate within a legacy that includes many educators who have no idea of how to do anything beyond the basics with their computers. If we obsess about the need to teach coding skills we will repeat the errors of the 1990s when CAD equalled drafting. Those who want to script need to be taught by designer scripters and not by 'computer people'. More crucial still is the need to focus beyond 'scripting' to the meta topic: an appropriate approach to learning about the emerging systems in which scripts operate; culturally, and as an emerging theory.

> Scripting Critique

Given the wealth of opportunities that scripting offers to shift design practice in new directions, can we anticipate significant shifts in architectural culture and its critique, or will scripting simply be subsumed once the novelty has gone?

Since the cultures of scripting are evolving they are not yet fully formed core design constructs, hence my investigation into cultures rather than probing into 'scripting' as if it were some kind of *Zeitgeist* movement. Two generations on, the pioneers from the 1970s and '80s might decry current output as not having met expectations that their early work had pointed to, but would this be a fair criticism? Have we truly made the best use of our opportunities, and what has been the value attained anyway? I have my own opinion on this, but here are some thoughts from others.

> Inventiveness

My perspective is that too many scripters are cloning from one another under the banner of contemporary legitimacy. Many instinctively swarm to consolidate a dominant paradigm such as the swarm itself, agent-based modelling, this particular algorithm or that, potentially fogging up the zone. Who is fundamentally inventing new strategies and approaches? Whose radars are the most highly attuned to spot emerging talent and aid in its proselytising? Who discovers then generously shares with others? And how many are plundering from here and there without acknowledging their sources, or have we arrived at a new epoch where worrying about authorship in this sense is completely old fashioned?

Had I been looking for so negative a perspective I should obviously have consulted a different group of experts and educators, as most of the responses to this enquiry were largely positive, signalling a bright new future, although some replies did carry a caveat that we could do better but need more time. I did not confine my enquiry to a group with similar interests who would talk up scripting as I also sought pioneers who would, no doubt, still consider themselves among the vanguard of design computation protagonists, progressing the cause but wondering all the same whether a sea of copyists would prove a more prominent legacy than the inventors they themselves had been. I had a variety of reactions from this group, too.

In order to capture a snapshot of where we are in 2010, I have extracted some of the more provocative and sceptical opinions. The first quote points to the means of sustaining a new cross-discipline dialogue:

> Where we see interesting work occurring is in the development of interfaces between different software applications that enable designers to further test architectural ideas that bridge across related disciplines such as engineering and construction. (MESNE)

While the next three suggest an awareness of a polarity between inventiveness and uncritical uptake:

> There's more bad scripting going on than ever before. But, at the same time, there's extraordinary innovation happening. The bar is rising. (Casey Reas)
>
> In terms of production very [inventive] – in terms of creating new models for design less so – meaning a lot is done with the same underlying models over and over again. (Axel Kilian)
>
> Still very few are truly inventive. We are at the very beginning of this process and very few designers are already virtuosic [sic] and highly creative. Many are still vertiginously propagating other people's inventions. This condition is changing with maturing of scripting cultures. (Alisa Andrasek)

John Frazer's response is absolutely clear about what he perceives as neither a lack of forward movement in much of contemporary engagement with design computation nor any tangible connection with the priorities of the pioneer years which he contends remain extant today:

> If we talk in terms of Inventors, Masters and Diluters (as Ezra Pound classifies inventive activity), then we saw most of the Inventors in the early 60s, the Masters in the early 70s and then we got the Diluters in the mid 90s – who I have to say include a significant proportion of today's scripters.
>
> Just look back to the Cybernetics Serendipity exhibition at the ICA in 1968 which celebrated an incredible array of inventive energy: Norbert Wiener, Stafford Beer, Karlheinz Stockhausen, John Cage, Edward Ihnatowicz, Gustav Metzger, Gordon Pask – poetry, music, art, sculpture, dance, film, even architecture. That exhibition set the agenda for the next 50 years.
>
> It is perhaps difficult for today's scripters to realise how difficult it was to do thing at all with a computer in the late 60s. When I struggled to generate the complex geometrical drawings for my final year project at the AA in 1967–69, I had to write all the programs myself and that included the basic graphics instructions to draw just one line, never mind a wireline perspective, and they had to be output to a flatbed plotter with no graphics preview! And when I finally had access to a graphics display device at Cambridge University in 1970 I had to write the generative instructions in Atlas Titan machine code, and if you don't know what that is then you don't know how lucky you are!

But my main point is that we went to all this effort in order to solve real social, environmental and technical problems where we believed a computer could significantly assist. But now that there is massive computer power and software cheaply available, most scripting has become nothing more than an onanistic self indulgence in a cozy graphics environment. Endless repetition and variation on elaborate geometrical schema with no apparent social, environmental and technical purpose whatsoever. (John Frazer)

Frazer's pioneering work of the 1960s and '70s was synchronous with Archigram (publication of *Archigram* I: 1961). I attended the celebration of Archigram hosted at the Bartlett in 2003. There I heard Jan Kaplicky (1937–2009) make the same observation. Kaplicky, with the absolute credibility supported by his subsequent success through his practice Future Systems, noted that if in the twenty-first century work that drew on Archigram's four-decades-old speculation was being built for the first time, who was doing the future thinking now? This was more than a 'well, in my day . . .', aggrandising of a faded golden age of innovation; rather, it is a very powerful questioning around the inventive scope of what is being done today, and the scale of its ambition. Contemporary commentators echo this concern:

Today's scripters are inventive; however, scripting is a relatively new technique for the exploration of architectural designs and designers are still figuring out new potentials for using scripting as a design tool. (Nick Pisca, Gehry Technologies)

'Invent' is a loaded word. Most young computational designers are ignorant of the history of algorithmic design and think they invent everything. If you are coding now, and you think you invented something amazing, I guarantee you someone at MIT or SIGGRAPH in the 60s, 70s & 80s has already done it. (Nick Pisca, Gehry Technologies)

This is an impossible question. I think most scripters are trying to produce effects of complexity. These effects become less and less complex and interesting as they become more and more known. Corporate offices have scripters pumping out patterns for them. (Michael Meredith, MOS)

The issue of what it means to be inventive needs to be explored, and how it might be further drawn out, too:

There is a huge range. Some rely too much on the work of others, and some develop their own scripts. I think that it is important to have people teaching scripting who can teach students to write their own scripts for themselves. (Neil Leach)

Being 'inventive' really relates to the designer's ability to consider their tools in a way that adds value to the design product or process, somewhere across this range. Today, more than ever, more emphasis should be given to the intellectual foundations of this 'know-how'. Being a scripting digerati is simply not enough. (Neri Oxman)

Today scripting is learnt through the practice of sharing code through web based platforms and open source. As such it holds the danger of being repetitive. When looking at student practice this is very evident. However,

> *I think what perhaps holds students back is a real questioning of the concepts and potentials of scripting rather than it being just a matter of copying.* (Mette Ramsgard Thomsen)
> *They can only become inventive to the extent that their scripting practice confronts other practices and processes.* (Pia Ednie-Brown)

My conclusion is that there is a reluctant acceptance that much of the fizzy work we see grabbing attention today is not seeking to innovate enough. There is a duty, surely, for all in a position to influence design education through scripting to be part of a deeper enquiry and the quest for discovery of new goals and ways to reach them.

> Variety Relative to Opportunity

With this question I am really trying to find a distinction between leaders and followers. A 'sufficient variety of outcomes' signals taxonomies of scripting; insufficient variety points to a scripting style. The majority view points to scripting within mainstream practice as being in its infancy, but there is optimism about a far more significant role for design computation as it becomes less of an exception within practice. Many referred to a need for greater computer power to realise the outcomes envisaged conceptually yet not able to be computed with existing technology. Real-time optimisation remains elusive for complex and conflicting relationships between data sets, for example:

> *Scripting is powerful, but not powerful enough. And our computers are entirely too slow to demonstrate the diversity and potential that scripting can bring. But that's not all, we're blocked conceptually as well as technically.* (Casey Reas)
> *The main challenge of the scripting generation is the move from the creation of inventive articulated patterns, and the small-scale installations to the full scale architectural projects where scripting can unleash an entire universe of opportunities for architectural space.* (Matias del Campo, SPAN)

There are concerns for the emergence of a style over substance:

> *I think the outcome is extremely varied, but unfortunately it seems like scripting has started to become a style, as a result of the use of the same ubiquitous techniques.* (Michael Szivos, SOFTlab)
> *No, not enough probably, as the underlying mathematical and computational models are too similar – the products differ of course but more based on in which context they are deployed and not so much conceptually.* (Axel Kilian)
> *Certainly not. Too many projects share the same 'wiring', and there is a tendency to perpetuate the skills-based pedagogy of the previous generation.* (Mark Collins & Toru Hasegawa, Proxy)

> Surprisingly a lot of the scripting work looks similar to me, so this cannot be an outcome of the tool itself but a desire for specific types of fantastic spectacular and wonderfully naive building forms. (Michael Meredith, MOS)
>
> Variety cannot arise by the use of scripting alone. To the contrary scripting can go viral. Meaning that once something is shown to be done easily it gets endlessly repeated. (Panagiotis Michalatos & Sawako Kaijima, AKT Architects)

New modes of operation are identified as the emerging opportunities rather than scripting itself:

> The effective employment of a broad set of computational methods is still ahead for architecture. (Martin Tamke)
>
> Our interest is in how an algorithm, loaded with design intent, emerges from the design problem rather than simply the architecture emerging from a known algorithm. (Roland Snooks, Kokkugia)
>
> The most radical way in which scripting has affected the field of design is not the outcome of a particular script or set of scripts, but rather the collateral effects of participating in such a design model. (Mode)

The extracts illustrate a 'still early days' consensus; it is interesting that no collective bombast emerges from the responses to this question, and on the contrary quite a clear challenge for design scripters to engage conceptually with greater ambition.

> A Role for Mathematics

Some aspects of design such as variety and intricacy become far more inter-esting when mathematics is engaged at a fairly high level; a mathematical background provides the computational designer with a conceptual and philosophical edge. It would be a mistake to consider mathematics only as a problem-solving ingredient, but how essential is mathematics in offering creative assistance to scripting? The dictionary definition for mathematics, however, suggests that we might use the word too loosely for situations where we are probably referring to 'computation':

> Originally, the collective name for geometry, arithmetic, and certain physical sciences (as astronomy and optics) involving geometrical reasoning. In modern use applied, (a) in a strict sense, to the abstract science which investigates deductively the conclusions implicit in the elementary conceptions of spatial and numerical relations, and which includes as its main divisions geometry, arithmetic, and algebra; and (b) in a wider sense, so as to include those branches of physical or other research which consist in the application of this abstract science to concrete data . . .[4]

There is a dichotomy between the 'modern' use of the term and how it was used originally. Programming for a computer is a text-based language (an artificial language), precise and pedantic, and for use in architecture it involves a combination of logical expression and numerical input. Strictly speaking, mathematics uses a symbolic language to form abstractions of spatial and numerical relations. Probably designers are thinking of only 'the collective name for geometry, arithmetic, and certain physical sciences' when using the term in relation to using the computer. In posing this question I was not sure at what level of significance mathematics would be assumed. Here are the opinions of others, ranging from 'essential' to 'helpful'. No one claimed that it was optional, but nor am I necessarily claiming this as an exhaustive enquiry:

> Essential. Mathematics is a necessary vocabulary – when we code we are implementing a possible universe, which can only resemble our own to the degree that we are able to describe it. (Mark Collins & Toru Hasegawa, Proxy)
>
> In our own practice we consider mathematics and geometry as a crucial point of departure for the development of a project, whether it be topology or specific forms of tessellations, it is always a core issue of the design. (Matias del Campo, SPAN)

Other commentators suggest that it is useful:

> As an intellectual rigour, very helpful, but I suspect rhetoric would be useful too if we still taught it. There is little different from the expectations of classical education – clear thinking, articulation of ideas so that others can understand them. (Tom Kvan)
>
> In pure terms Mathematics is a cerebral activity which does not have any inputs or outputs that are sensory. Potentially these connections can be provided by scripting environments but only by re-thinking the concept of interface to design tools. The ability to interactively rewire plug-and-play dependencies is just one of many possible starting points. (Hugh Whitehead)
>
> Architecture has the potential to be informed by maths, but first the university tutors have to understand the relationship between maths and design in order to help the students make the connection. (Robert Aish)
>
> If you consider logic a subset of mathematics, then math is essential. An average coder would only need to know algebra for basic scripting and trigonometry for 3D. (Nick Pisca, Gehry Technologies)

Others are not convinced at all:

> I try to keep it as simple as possible; maths is a Victorian hangover. (Paul Coates)

Computer programming can be largely logically based requiring minor numerical input, or it can be mathematically driven in the sense of a pure (conceptual) and applied (practical) mathematical input. The scripter has a choice between working with a systems approach and avoiding high-level computation, especially when they are relying on code snippets pre-compiled by others, or they can hook-in to mathematics' conceptual or abstract take on space, and roll up their sleeves. It seems we are at a time when we need to be quite clear about the distinction between computation and mathematics. The more intensive the computation enacted by the computer, the more likely that the output will be innovative. I suspect that if we seek more certainty in originality of output, the next generation of design scripters will benefit from engaging more profoundly with mathematics in its modern sense, given above.

> Likely Future Changes

I wondered whether the extraordinary developments in computers and software during the past decade had helped my correspondents predict any shifts in the next 5 to 10 years. In recent years we have seen fundamental shifts in accessibility into scripting for the architectural design arena such as the emergence of Digital Project™, GenerativeComponents™, Processing, and Grasshopper with Rhino 3D™, to name a few of the paradigm shifters. Personally, I have always been surprised by the friendliness of Max/MSP™ in the sound design and music arena, and I wondered when it would cross over into visual design as it comes across as a much more natural way for designers to assemble a logical argument through programming. I have also been surprised at the effectiveness, fluency and integration of software dealing with the physics of materials into the games and movie industries: why have the architectural software companies been so complacent in this regard? Of course, that is a question that hardly needs answering, and in part it has been the lack of opportunity for creative design within conventional software that has forced scripting to start off by being a counterculture. Successful countercultures eventually become part of orthodoxy, and judging from the relative lack of sparks by my correspondents around this question, I imagine that this could be a sign that scripting has already reached an appropriate level of usefulness and applicability.

One set of responses sums up my own view quite succinctly:

I anticipate new powerful simulation environments to grow emergent complex dynamic systems as a way of developing 3D morphologies – rather hoping to design one myself. (Paul Coates)

Languages will become more compact, expressive, and comprehensible. After a period in which the mental effort of focussing on the script may have distracted designers from focussing on the design problem, scripting will become more natural, more integrated into design process, less of a distraction. (Robert Aish)

I would like to think that in the next 10 years we will have succeeded, and we will have a new conceptual environment for creative thinking and without the need for scripting. If all we have achieved is to replace drawing with typing then we have achieved nothing! (John Frazer)

While some purists will stick to rigorous old school methods of working with code, many will want to bypass code and work through more accessible pictographic forms of automation. (Neil Leach)

A future direction is to make this library of design tools less platform dependent. The concepts contained within these scripts are general design principles and could essentially be applied in many different platforms. (Brady Peters)

I guess most of us want scripting software to be more intuitive, easier to write and more visually integrated with other software, easier to find the bugs, and with a trend to a common language not tied to any particular packages. Most look forward to harnessing the greater power of the next generation of computers, with the ability to model conflicting performative aspects of architecture in real time to assist our design decision making, and not necessarily through typing in code. Some express the hope that we evolve new languages, move from scripting to programming and, the most plaintive cry of all: that we start to write our own discipline-specific algorithms instead of 'stealing' them from other fields. I believe that particular desire, if it were fulfilled, would lead to a double-edged sword, one where originality through targeted architectural solution seeking is compromised by architectural reinvention of wheels already in use elsewhere.

> Miracle Scripting Environments

It would seem that most of my correspondents are happy enough with what we have already. I received very few suggestions for higher-order virtual reality suites for an immersive coding experience, no new tangible interfaces were called for, no yet-to-be-designed collaborative tools for shared 'what if . . .?' interaction desired. Are we broadly happy with what we have already, patiently awaiting improvements in speed and accessibility? Some indicative responses follow:

> *I would be waiting for an interface that allows the seamless integration of multiple other environments.* (Achim Menges)
>
> *An environment is missing that integrates representation and simulation based approaches. It could, for example, connect modelling with physics-based behaviour, scripted elements and the generated structure could still communicate as a whole to external environments.* (Martin Tamke)
>
> *A universal scripting language that allows me to communicate with the entire array of software in our studio, instead of having to learn a new language every now and then.* (Matias del Campo, SPAN)
>
> *Definitely not one single environment doing everything – please keep the platform multiple but as light as possible – speed is key when a large population or massive variations are involved.* (Marc Fornes, THEVERYMANY)
>
> *Ben Bratton once commented that we are still in 'the silent movies' stage of digital techniques. Of course things will improve. We have hardly started yet.* (Neil Leach)
>
> *Babel Script, vocal.* (Mark Goulthorpe)

> Design Agency

As part of a cultural defence I was curious to learn from other scripting designers their thoughts on control, or loss of it to the algorithm, and on the formulation of solution seeking by 'others' not directly implicated with the problem at hand. By cultural defence, I mean defence of scripting as culture(s), not just a fad or a style. While some views point to an ascendancy of generative processes:

> *I believe that all generative processes hold the designer to account. They should be seen as prostheses to the architectural imagination. But we need to lose the old fashioned notion of the architect as some top-down demiurgic 'designer' and reconfigure the architect as the controller of processes.* (Neil Leach)

the majority view is one of designer as driver, regardless of the tools in their hands:

> *Good question. Designer is accountable for all, and it's an important aspect of how the logic of authorship is changing. I hear a lot about networked intelligence and so on and it's there, but it isn't in my opinion going to produce, say, a great building. The cultural features behind making a building have their own forces.* (Peter Macapia, labDORA)
>
>   *The designer who wants to be completely in control of the results must be in control of the process. To be in control of the process, the designer must be in control of the tools. The tools are computation, therefore a designer who wants to be in control must also be a scripter (or suffer the consequence of the unseen influence of using other people's tools).* (Robert Aish)
>
>   *. . . the mind is versatile in evolving new media in response to its intuitive needs, and doubtless the crudity of current man–computer interfaces will increasingly become symbiotic with our evolving thinking.* (Mark Goulthorpe)
>
>   *Programming is useful in handling information beyond our perceptual capabilities.* (Panagiotis Michalatos & Sawako Kaijima, AKT Architects)
>
>   *Ultimately the designer should always be held accountable. The agency within a design process is on the side of the designer, not the other way around.* (Mode)

With this final probe we have closed the circle of this chapter. I commenced with my account of what tempted me to script in the first place – most of us come to scripting from architecture rather than the other way around, and have unique stories to tell. Mine is one of being forced out of my comfort zone to confront the inadequacies of the tools I had available relative to my tasks. In the process of doing so I found that that I had to open Pandora's black box, but the bogies fled leaving me exposed to an unexpected world of opportunity offered through creative coding. From my early incursions into computing (as opposed to scripting) in the 1970s as part of my undergraduate architectural education I was made aware of logic programming, but it did not resonate with me in any tangible way. I would admit to having almost no enthusiasm then, as the dreary examples that were meant to excite our interest in fact had the opposite effect on me. I simply had a distaste for anything that sought to dampen the influence of what I regarded as the most precious design input afforded to us as humans: our intuition. Others will argue that this is evidence of a very closed mind for which my albeit weak riposte can only be: such may be the vicissitudes of youth.

1   Cecil Balmond with Jannuzzi Smith, *Informal: the informal in architecture and engineering,* Prestel (Munich), 2002, p 14.

2   Patrik Schumacher, *Parametricism as Style – Parametricist Manifesto,* New Architecture Group (London), 2008.
    Presented and discussed at the Dark Side Club, 11th Architecture Biennale, Venice, 2008; http://www. patrikschumacher.com/Texts/ Parametricism%20as%20 Style.htm.

3   Pseudocode is natural language imitating computer programming language used as a means for a code commissioner to communicate to a coder, for instance: '*if green then make square else make round*'.

4   'Mathematics', *The Oxford English Dictionary,* 2nd edn, 1989. CD-ROM.

BIBLIOGRAPHY

Abruzzo, Emily, Ellingson, Eric and Solomon, Jonathan D., Editors (2007), *Models: 306090 Books*, Volume 11, 306090, New York

AGU Advanced Geometry Unit Arup (2008), "Geometric Algorithm: Serpentine Gallery Pavilion 2002"; "Taichung Metropolitan Opera House" (both designed by Toyo Ito), in Sakamoko, Tomoko and Ferré, Albert, *From Control to Design: Parametric/Algorithmic Architecture*, Actar, Barcelona, pp. 36–43; 54–59

Aish, Robert and Woodbury, Robert (2005), "Multi-level Interaction in Parametric Design," in *Proceedings of Smart Graphics, 5th International Symposium*, Springer, Berlin, pp. 151–162

Allen, Stan (1995), "Terminal Velocities: the Computer in the Design Studio," in Allen, Stan, *Essays: Practice: Architecture, Technique and Representation*, G+B Arts International, Amsterdam, 2000, pp. 145–161

Allen, Stan (1997), "From Object to Field," in Davidson, Peter and Bates, Donald L., Editors, *Architecture After Geometry*, AD (*Architectural Design*), Profile No. 127, Vol. 67, No. 5/6, May/June, pp. 24–31

Aranda, Benjamin and Lasch, Chris (2006), *Tooling*, Princeton Architectural Press, New York

Balmond, Cecil (1997), "New Structure and the Informal," in Jencks, Charles, Editor, *New Science = New Architecture?*, AD (*Architectural Design*), Profile No. 129, Vol. 67, No. 9/10, September/October pp. 88–96

Balmond, Cecil (2004), "Geometry, Algorithm, Pattern," in Leach, Neil, Turnbull, David and Williams, Chris, Editors, *Digital Tectonics*, Wiley-Academy, West Sussex, UK, pp. 128–135

Balmond, Cecil and Ellingsen, Eric (2007), "Survival Patterns," in Abruzzo, Emily, Ellingson, Eric and Solomon, Jonathan D., Editors, *Models: 306090 Books*, Volume 11, 306090, New York, pp. 26–32

Barkow, Frank (2008), "Cut to Fit," in Kolarevic, Branko and Klinger, Kevin, Editors, *Manufacturing Material Effects: Rethinking Design and Making in Architecture*, Routledge, London, pp. 91–102

Barkow, Frank (2010), "Fabricating Design: A Revolution of Choice", in Oxman, Rivka, and Oxman, Robert Editors, *The New Structuralism: Design, Engineering and Architectural Technologies*, AD (*Architectural Design*), Profile No. 206, Vol. 80, No. 4, July/August, pp. 94–101

Barkow Leibinger (2009), *An Atlas of Fabrication*, AA Publications, London

Bechthold, Martin (2010), "The Return of the Future: A Second Go at Robotic Construction," in Oxman, Rivka and Oxman, Robert, Editors, *The New Structuralism: Design, Engineering and Architectural Technologies*, AD (*Architectural Design*), Profile No. 206, Vol. 80, No. 4, July/August, pp. 116–121

Beesley, Philip, Hirosue, Sachiko and Ruxton, Jim (2006), "Towards Responsive Architectures," in Beesley, Philip, Hirosue, Sachiko, Ruxton, Jim, Tränkle, Marion and Turner, Camille, Editors, *Responsive Architectures Responsive Architectures: Subtle Technologies*, Riverside Architectural Press, Toronto, pp. 3–11

Beesley, Philip, Hirosue, Sachiko, Ruxton, Jim, Tränkle, Marion and Turner, Camille, Editors (2006), *Responsive Architectures: Subtle Technologies*, Riverside Architectural Press, Toronto

Beorkrem, Christopher (2013), *Material Strategies in Digital Fabrication*, Routledge, Oxford

van Berkel, Ben and Bos, Caroline (1999), *Move*, UN Studio and Goose Press, Amsterdam

van Berkel, Ben and Bos, Caroline (1999), "Diagrams," in van Berkel, Ben and Bos, Caroline, *Move*, UN Studio and Goose Press, Amsterdam, vol. 2 Techniques, pp. 18–25

van Berkel, Ben and Bos, Caroline (1999), "Techniques: Network Spin, and Diagrams," in Braham, William W. and Hale, Jonathan A., Editors, *Rethinking Technology: A Reader in Architectural Theory*, Routledge, New York, pp. 384–387

Blau, Eve (2007), "Transparency and the Irreconcilable Contradictions of Modernity," in Reeser Lawrence, Amanda and Schafer, Ashley, Editors, *Expanding Surface*, Praxis 9, pp. 50–59

Bollinger, Klaus, Grohmann, Manfred and Tessmann, Oliver (2008), "Form, Force, Performance: Multi-Parametric Structural Design," in Hensel, Michael and Menges, Achim, Editors, *Versatility and Vicissitude: Performance in Morpho-Ecological Design*, AD (*Architectural Design*), Profile No. 192, Vol. 78, No. 2, March/April, pp. 20–25

Bollinger, Klaus, Grohmann, Manfred and Tessmann, Oliver (2010), "Structured Becoming: Evolutionary Processes in Design Engineering," in Oxman, Rivka and Oxman, Robert, Editors, *The New Structuralism: Design, Engineering and Architectural Technologies*, AD (*Architectural Design*), Profile No. 206, Vol. 80, No. 4, July/August, pp. 34–39

Bullivant, Lucy, Editor (2005), *4dspace: Interactive Architecture*, AD (*Architectural Design*), Profile No. 173, Vol. 75, No. 1, January/February

Bullivant, Lucy (2006), *Responsive Environments: Architecture, Art and Design*, Victoria and Albert Museum, London

Bullivant, Lucy, Editor (2007), *4dsocial: Interactive Design Environments*, AD (*Architectural Design*), Profile No. 188, Vol. 77, No. 4, July/August

Burke, Anthony (2007), "Redefining Network Paradigms," in Burke, Anthony and Tierney, Therese, Editors, *Network Practices*, Princeton Architectural Press, New York, pp. 54–70

Burke, Anthony and Tierney, Therese, Editors (2007), *Network Practices*, Princeton Architectural Press, New York

Burry, Jane and Burry, Mark (2010), *The New Mathematics of Architecture*, Thames and Hudson, London

Burry, Mark (2003), "Between Intuition and Process: Parametric Design and Rapid Prototyping," in Kolarevic, Branko, Editor, *Architecture in the Digital Age: Design and Manufacturing*, Spon Press, London and New York, pp. 147–162

Burry, Mark (2004), "Virtually Gaudí," in Leach, Neil, Turnbull, David and Williams, Chris, Editors, *Digital Tectonics*, John Wiley and Sons, West Sussex, UK, pp. 22–33

Burry, Mark (2011), *Scripting Cultures: Architectural Design and Programming*, AD Primer, John Wiley and Sons, West Sussex, UK

Cache, Bernard (Speaks, Michael, Editor) (1995), *Earth Moves: the Furnishing of Territories*, MIT Press, Cambridge, MA

Carpo, Mario (2004), "Ten Years of Folding," in Lynn, Greg, Editor, *Folding in Architecture*, Revised Edition (original 1993), AD (*Architectural Design*), Wiley-Academy, West Sussex, UK, pp. 14–19

Carpo, Mario (2011), *The Alphabet and the Algorithm*, MIT Press, Cambridge, MA

Ceccato, Cristiano (2010), "Constructing Parametric Architecture," *Analogue and Digital*, Detail, Vol. 4, July/August, pp. 336–340

Cheon, Janghwan, Hardy, Steven and Hemsath, Tim (2011), *Parametricism*, ACADIA Regional Conference Proceedings, College of Architecture, University of Nebraska-Lincoln

Chu, Karl (2003), "Toward Genetic Architecture," in Tschumi, Bernard and Cheng, Irene, Editors, *The State of Architecture at the Beginning of the 21st Century*, Monacelli Press, New York, p. 62

Corser, Robert, Editor (2010), *Fabricating Architectures: Selected Readings in Digital Design and Manufacturing*, Princeton Architectural Press, New York

Davis, Daniel, Bury, Jane and Bury, Mark (2011), "Untangling Parametric Schemata: Enhancing Collaboration through Modular Programming," in LeClercq, Pierre, Heylighen, Ann, and Martin, Geneviève, Editors, *Designing Together*, CAAD Futures

Deamer, Peggy and Bernstein, Phillip G., Editors (2010), *Building (in) the Future: Recasting Labor in Architecture*, Yale School of Architecture, New Haven, and Princeton Architectural Press, New York

DeLanda, Manuel (2002), "Deleuze and the Use of the Genetic Algorithm in Architecture," in Leach, Neil, Editor, *Designing for a Digital World*, Wiley-Academy, West Sussex, UK, pp. 117–120

DeLanda, Manuel (2004), "Material Complexity," in Leach, Neil, Turnbull, David and Williams, Chris, Editors, *Digital Tectonics*, Wiley-Academy, London, pp. 14–21

DeLanda, Manuel (2004), "Materiality: Anexect and Intense", in Spuybroek, Lars, *NOX: Machining Architecture*, Thames and Hudson, New York, pp. 370–377

Douglis, Evan (2009), *Autogenic Structures*, Taylor and Francis, Abingdon

van Duijn, Chris (2004), "Materials Research at OMA," in Ferré, Albert, Kubo, Michael, Prat, Ramon, Sakamoto, Tomoko, Salazar, Jaime and Tetas, Anna, Editors, *Matters*, Verb, vol. 2, Actar, Barcelona, pp. 80–91

Dunn, Nick (2012), *Digital Fabrication in Architecture*, Lawrence King, London

Eastman, Chuck, Teicholz, Paul, Sacks, Rafael and Liston, Kathleen (2008), *BIM Handbook: A Guide to Building Information Modeling for Owners, Managers, Designers, Engineers and Contractors*, John Wiley and Sons, Hoboken, NJ

Edler, Jan (2005), "Communicative Display Skins for Buildings: BIX at the Kunsthaus Graz," in Kolarevic, Branko and Malkawi, Ali M., Editors, *Performative Architectures: Beyond Instrumentality*, Spon Press, New York and London, pp. 149–160

Ednie-Brown, Pia (2006), "All-Over, Overall: Biothing and Emergent Composition," in Silver, Mike, Editor, *Programming Cultures: Art and Architecture in the Age of Software*, AD (*Architectural Design*), Profile 182, Vol. 76, No. 4, July/August, pp. 72–81

Ednie-Brown, Pia (2006), "Continuum: A Self-Engineering Creature Culture," in Hight, Christopher and Perry, Chris, Editors, *Collective Intelligence in Design*, AD (*Architectural Design*), Profile No. 183, Vol. 76, No September/October, pp. 18–25

Eisenman, Peter (1992), "Visions Unfolding: Architecture in the Age of Electronic Media," in Galofaro, Luca, *Digital Eisenman: An Office of the Electronic Era*, Birkhäuser, Basel, pp. 84–89. Original publication *Domus*, No. 734, 1992

Eisenman, Peter (1999), "Diagram: An Original Scene of Writing," in Eisenman, Peter, *Diagram Diaries*, Universe Publishing, New York, pp. 26–35

Ellingsen, Eric (2007), "Illogical Leap," in Abruzzo, Emily, Ellingson, Eric and Solomon, Jonathan D., Editors, *Models: 306090 Books*, Volume 11, 306090, New York, pp. 217–227

Emergence and Design Group (2004), "Charles Walker in Conversation with the Emergence and Design Group: Engineering Design: Working with Advanced Geometries," in Hensel, Michael, Menges, Achim and Weinstock, Michael, Editors, *Emergence: Morphogenetic Design Strategies*, AD (*Architectural Design*), Profile No. 169, Vol. 74, No. 3, May/June, pp. 64–71

Emergence and Design Group (2004), "Frei Otto in Conversation with the Emergence and Design Group," in Hensel, Michael, Menges, Achim and Weinstock, Michael, Editors, *Emergence: Morphogenetic Design Strategies*, AD (*Architectural Design*), Profile No. 169, Vol. 74, No. 3, May/June, pp. 18–25

Emergence and Design Group and Sischka, Johann (2004), "Manufacturing Complexity," in Hensel, Michael, Menges, Achim and Weinstock, Michael, Editors, *Emergence: Morphogenetic Design Strategies*, AD (*Architectural Design*), Profile No. 169, Vol. 74, No. 3, May/June, pp. 72–79

Emmer, Michele (2004), "Topology," in Emmer, Michele, *Mathland: From Flatland to Hypersurfaces*, Birkhäuser, Basel, pp. 66–87

Fear, Bob, Editor (2001), *Architecture and Animation*, AD (*Architectural Design*), Profile No. 150, Vol. 71, No. 2, April

Ferré, Albert, Kubo, Michael, Prat, Ramon, Sakamoto, Tomoko, Salazar, Jaime and Tetas, Anna, Editors (2004), *Matters*, Verb, vol. 2, Actar, Barcelona

Ferré, Albert, Kubo, Michael, Sakamoto, Tomoko, Editors, in collaboration with Moussavi, Farshid and Zaero-Polo, Alejandro (2002), *The Yokahama Project: Foreign Office Architects*, Actar, Barcelona

Foreign Office Architects (2003), *Phylogenesis FOA's Ark*, Actar, Barcelona

Fox, Michael (2009), *Interactive Architecture*, Princeton Architectural Press, New York

Frampton, Kenneth (1995), *Studies in Tectonic Culture: The Poetics of Construction in Nineteenth and Twentieth Century Architecture*, MIT Press, Cambridge, MA

Fraser, Alayna (2007), "Translations: de Young Museum and the Walker Art Center," in Reeser Lawrence, Amanda and Schafer, Ashley, Editors, *Expanding Surface*, Praxis 9, pp. 68–85

Fraser, Cassandra L. (2006), "Designing Matter: Responsive Metallobiomaterials and Learning Environments," in Beesley, Philip, Hirosue, Sachiko, Ruxton, Jim, Tränkle, Marion and Turner, Camille, Editors, *Responsive Architectures: Subtle Technologies*, Riverside Architectural Press, Toronto, pp. 41–45

Frazer, John (1995), "The Nature of the Evolutionary Model," in Frazer, John, *An Evolutionary Architecture*, Architectural Association Themes VII, AA Publications, London, pp. 64–73

Garcia, Mark, Editor (2006), *Architextiles*, AD (*Architectural Design*), Profile No. 184, Vol. 76, No. 6, November/December

Gershenfeld, Neil (2007), *Fab – The Coming Revolution On Your Desktop – From Personal Computers to Personal Fabrication*, Basic Books, New York

Gershenfeld, Neil and Krikorian, Raffi (2004), "Building Intelligence," in Ferré, Albert, Kubo, Michael, Prat, Ramon, Sakamoto, Tomoko, Salazar, Jaime and Tetas, Anna, Editors, *Matters*, Verb, vol. 2, Actar, Barcelona, pp. 206–217

Gleiniger, Andrea and Vrachliotis, Georg (2008), *Simulation: Presentation Technique and Cognitive Method*, Birkhäuser, Basel

Glymph, Jim (2003), "Evolution of the Digital Design Process," in Kolarevic, Branko, Editor, *Architecture in the Digital Age: Design and Manufacturing*, Spon Press, London and New York, pp. 102–119

Glynn, Ruari and Sheil, Bob, Editors (2011), *Fabricate: Making Digital Architecture*, Riverside Architectural Press, London

Goodwin, Brian C. (2008), "Structuralist Research Program in Developmental Biology," in Lynn, Greg, *Greg Lynn Form* (Edited by Mark Rappolt), Rizzoli, New York, pp. 172–190

Goulthorpe, Mark (2008), *The Possibility of (an) Architectures: Collected Essays by Mark Goulthorpe/dECOI*, Routledge, New York

Gramazio, Fabio and Kohler, Matthias (2008), *Digital Materiality in Architecture*, Lars Müller Publishers, Baden, Switzerland

Gramazio, Fabio and Kohler, Matthias (2008), "Towards a Digital Materiality," in Kolarevic, Branko and Klinger, Kevin, Editors, *Manufacturing Material Effects: Rethinking Design and Making in Architecture*, Routledge, London, pp. 103–118

Guallart, Vicente (2004), *Media House Project: the House is the Computer: the Structure is the Network*, IaaC Institut d'Arquitectura Avancada de Catalunya, Barcelona

Guallart, Vicente, Ruiz-Geli, Enric, Müller, Willy, Gershenfeld, Neil, Ruig, Pau and Diaz, Nuria (2004), "Media House Project," in Ferré, Albert, Kubo, Michael, Prat, Ramon, Sakamoto, Tomoko, Salazar, Jaime and Tetas, Anna, Editors, *Matters*, Verb, vol. 2, Actar, Barcelona, pp. 220–238

Hadid, Zaha and Schumacher, Patrik (2003), *Latent Utopias: Experiments within Contemporary Architecture*, Princeton Architectural Press, New York

Hanna, Sean (2006), "Responsive Materials/Responsive Structure," in Beesley, Philip, Hirosue, Sachiko, Ruxton, Jim, Tränkle, Marion and Turner, Camille, Editors, *Responsive Architectures: Subtle Technologies*, Riverside Architectural Press, Toronto, pp. 122–125

Hensel, Michael (2004), "Finding Exotic Form," in Hensel, Michael, Menges, Achim and Weinstock, Michael, Editors, *Emergence: Morphogenetic Design Strategies*, AD (*Architectural Design*), Profile No. 169, Vol. 74, No. 3, May/June, pp. 26–33

Hensel, Michael (2010), "Material Systems and Environmental Dynamics Feedback," in Hensel, Michael, Menges, Achim and Weinstock, Michael, *Emergent Technologies and Design: Toward a Biological Paradigm for Architecture*, Routledge, Oxford, pp. 63–81

Hensel, Michael and Menges, Achim (2004), "Frei Otto in Conversation," in Hensel, Michael, Menges, Achim and Weinstock, Michael, Editors, *Emergence: Morphogenetic Design Strategies*, Profile No.169, Vol. 74, No. 3, May/June, pp. 18–25.

Hensel, Michael and Menges, Achim, Editors (2006a), *Morpho-Ecologies*, AA Publications, London

Hensel, Michael and Menges, Achim, (2006b), "Morpho-Ecologies: Towards an Inclusive Discourse on Heterogeneous Architecture," in Hensel, Michael and Menges, Achim, Editors, *Morpho-Ecologies*, AA Publications, London, pp. 16–60

Hensel, Michael and Menges, Achim (2006c), "Differentiation and Performance: Multi-Performance Architectures and Modulated Environments," in Hensel, Michael, Menges, Achim and Weinstock, Michael, Editors, *Techniques and Technologies in Morphogenetic Design*, AD (*Architectural Design*), Profile No. 180, Vol. 76, No. 2, March/April, pp. 60–63

Hensel, Michael, Menges, Achim and Weinstock, Michael, Editors (2004), *Emergence: Morphogenetic Design Strategies*, AD (*Architectural Design*), Profile No. 169, Vol. 74, No. 3, May/June

Hensel, Michael, Menges, Achim and Weinstock, Michael, Editors (2006), *Techniques and Technologies in Morphogenetic Design*, AD (*Architectural Design*), Profile No. 180, Vol. 76, No. 2, March/April

Hensel, Michael, Menges, Achim and Weinstock, Michael (2010a), *Emergent Technologies and Design: Toward a Biological Paradigm for Architecture*, Routledge, Oxford

Hensel, Michael, Menges, Achim and Weinstock, Michael (2010b), "Introduction: Emergent Technologies and Design: Towards a Biological Paradigm for Architecture," in Hensel, Michael, Menges, Achim and Weinstock, Michael, *Emergent Technologies and Design: Toward a Biological Paradigm for Architecture*, Routledge, Oxford, pp. 9–21

Hight, Christopher and Perry, Chris (2006), "Collective Intelligence in Design," in Hight, Christopher and Perry, Chris, *Collective Intelligence in Design*, AD (*Architectural Design*), Profile No. 183, Vol. 76, No, September/October, pp. 5–9

Hopkinson, N., Hague, R.J.M. and Dickens, P.M., Editors (2006), *Rapid Manufacturing: An Industrial Revolution for the Digital Age*, John Wiley and Sons, West Sussex, UK

Horn, Bradley (2009), "The Autopoietics of Education," in Douglis, Evan, *Autogenetic Structures*, Taylor & Francis, New York, pp. 80–89

Hwang, Irene, Sakamoto, Tomoko, Ferré, Albert, Kubo, Michael, Sadarangi, Noorie, Tetas, Anna, Ballesteros, Mario and Prat, Ramon, Editors (2006), *Natures*, Verb, vol. 5, Actar, Barcelona

Iwamoto, Lisa (2009), *Digital Fabrications: Architectural and Material Techniques*, Princeton Architectural Press, New York

Iwamoto, Lisa (2011), "Line Array: Protocells as Dynamic Structure," in Spiller, Neil and Armstrong, Rachel, Editors, *Protocell Architecture*, AD (*Architectural Design*), Profile No. 210, Vol. 81, No. 2, March/April, pp. 112–121

Jeronimidis, George (2004), "Biodynamics," in Hensel, Michael, Menges, Achim and Weinstock, Michael, Editors, *Emergence: Morphogenetic Design Strategies*, AD (*Architectural Design*), Profile No. 169, Vol. 74, No. 3, May/June, pp. 90–95

Kalay, Yehuda E. (2004), *Architecture's New Media: Principles, Theories and Methods of Computer-Aided Design*, MIT Press, Cambridge, MA

Kemp, Martin (2007), "The Natural Philosopher as Builder," in Holm, Michael Juul and Kjeldsen, Kjeld, *Frontiers of Architecture 1: Cecil Balmond*, Louisiana Museum of Art, Copenhagen, pp. 90–99

Kennedy, Sheila (2010), "Responsive Materials," in Schröpfer, Thomas, Editor, *Material Design*, Birkhaüser, Berne, pp. 118–131

Kieran, Stephen and Timberlake, James (2004), *Refabricating Architectures: How Manufacturing Methodologies Are Poised to Transform Building Construction*, McGraw-Hill, New York

Killian, Axel (2007), "The Question of the Underlying Model and Its Impact on Design," in Abruzzo, Emily, Ellingson, Eric and Solomon, Jonathan D., Editors, *Models: 306090 Books*, Volume 11, 306090, New York, pp. 208–213

Kloft, Harald (2005), "Non-Standard Structural Design for Non-Standard Architecture," in Kolarevic, Branko and Malkawi, Ali M., Editors, *Performative Architectures: Beyond Instrumentality*, Spon Press, New York and London, pp. 135–148

Kolarevic, Branko, Editor (2003), *Architecture in the Digital Age: Design and Manufacturing*, Spon Press, London and New York

Kolarevic, Branko (2003), "Digital Morphogenesis," in Kolarevic, Branko, Editor, *Architecture in the Digital Age: Design and Manufacturing*, Spon Press, New York and London, pp. 11–28

Kolarevic, Branko (2005), "Computing the Performative," in Kolarevic, Branko and Malkawi, Ali M., Editors, *Performative Architectures: Beyond Instrumentality*, Spon Press, New York and London, pp. 194–202

Kolarevic, Branko and **Klinger, Kevin**, Editors (2008), *Manufacturing Material Effects: Rethinking Design and Making in Architecture*, Routledge, London

Kolarevic, Branko and **Klinger, Kevin** (2008), "Manufacturing/Material/Effects," in Kolarevic, Branko and Klinger, Kevin, Editors, *Manufacturing Material Effects: Rethinking Design and Making in Architecture*, Routledge, London, pp. 5–24

Kolarevic, Branko and **Malkawi, Ali M.**, Editors (2005), *Performative Architectures: Beyond Instrumentality*, Spon Press, New York and London

Kubo, Michael and **Ferré, Albert**, Editors, in collaboration with **Foreign Office Architects** (2003), *Phylogenesis FOA's Ark*, Actar, Barcelona

Kubo, Michael and **Salazar, Jaime** (2004), "A Brief History of the Information Age," in Ferré, Albert, Kubo, Michael, Prat, Ramon, Sakamoto, Tomoko, Salazar, Jaime and Tetas, Anna, Editors, *Matters*, Verb, vol. 2, Actar, Barcelona, pp. 2–19

Kwinter, Sanford (1994), "Who's Afraid of Formalism," in Kubo, Michael and Ferré, Albert, Editors in collaboration with FOA, *Phylogenesis FOA's Ark*, Actar, Barcelona, pp. 96–99. Originally published in *Any Magazine*, No. 7/8

Leach, Neil, Editor (2002), *Designing for a Digital World*, Wiley-Academy, West Sussex, UK

Leach, Neil (2004), "Swarm Tectonics," in Leach, Neil, Turnbull, David and Williams, Chris, Editors, *Digital Tectonics*, Wiley-Academy, West Sussex, UK, pp. 70–77

Leach, Neil, Turnbull, David and **Williams, Chris**, Editors (2004), *Digital Tectonics*, John Wiley and Sons, West Sussex, UK

Leatherbarrow, David (2005), "Architecture's Unscripted Performance," in Kolarevic, Branko and Malkawi, Ali M., *Performative Architectures: Beyond Instrumentality*, Spon Press, New York and London, pp. 5–20

Lenoir, Timothy and **Alt, Casey** (2003), "Flow, Process, Fold," in Picon, Antoine and Ponte, Allesandra, *Architecture and the Sciences: Exchanging Metaphors*, Princeton Architectural Press, New York, pp. 314–353

Lindsey, Bruce (2001), *Digital Gehry: Material Resistance/Digital Construction*, Birkhäuser, Basel

Liu, Yu-Tung, Editor (2002), *Defining Digital Architecture*, 2001 FEIDAD Award, Birkhäuser, Basel

Liu, Yu-Tung, Editor (2003), *Developing Digital Architecture*, 2002 FEIDAD Award, Birkhäuser, Basel

Liu, Yu-Tung, Editor (2004), *Diversifying Digital Architecture*, 2003 FEIDAD Award, Birkhäuser, Basel

Liu, Yu-Tung, Editor (2005), *Demonstrating Digital Architecture*, 2004 FEIDAD Award, Birkhäuser, Basel

Liu, Yu-Tung, Editor (2007), *Distinguishing Digital Architecture*, 2006 FEIDAD Award, Birkhäuser, Basel

Liu, Yu-Tung, Editor (2009), *New Tectonics: Towards a New Theory of Digital Architecture*, 2007 FEIDAD Award, Birkhäuser, Basel

Lupton, Ellen (2002), *Skin: Surface, Substance, and Design*, Princeton Architectural Press, New York

Lynn, Greg (1993), "Architectural Curvilinearity: The Folded, the Pliant and the Supple," in Lynn, Greg, Editor (2004), *Folding in Architecture*, Revised Edition (original 1993), AD (*Architectural Design*), Wiley-Academy, West Sussex, UK, pp. 24–31

Lynn, Greg (1998), *Folds, Bodies and Blobs: Collected Essays*, La Lettre Volé, Brussels

Lynn, Greg (1999), "Animate Form," in *Animate Form*, Princeton Architectural Press, New York, pp. 8–43

Lynn, Greg (2003), *Intricacy*, Introduction in Exhibition Catalogue, Institute of Contemporary Art, University of Pennsylvania, Philadelphia, 4 pages (unnumbered)

Lynn, Greg, Editor (2004), *Folding in Architecture*, Revised Edition (original 1993), AD (*Architectural Design*), Wiley-Academy, West Sussex, UK

Lynn, Greg (2004), "Introduction," in Lynn, Greg, Editor, *Folding in Architecture*, Revised Edition (original 1993), AD (*Architectural Design*), Wiley-Academy, West Sussex, UK, pp. 8–13

Lynn, Greg (2004), "The Structure of Ornament: Conversation with Neil Leach," in Leach, Neil, Turnbull, David and Williams, Chris, Editors, *Digital Tectonics*, John Wiley and Sons, West Sussex, UK, pp. 62–68

Lynn, Greg (2004), "Constellations in Practice," in Reeser, Amanda and Schafer, Ashley, Editors, *New Technologies/New Architectures*, Praxis 6, pp. 8–17

Lynn, Greg (2008), *Greg Lynn Form* (Edited by Mark Rappolt), Rizzoli, New York

Lynn, Greg and **Rashid, Hani** (2002), *Greg Lynn and Hani Rashid Architectural Laboratories*, NAI Publishers, Rotterdam

Malé-Alemany, Marta (Edited by Christopher Junkin) (2007), "Parametric Constructions: an Exploration on Virtual Standardization," in Abruzzo, Emily, Ellingson, Eric and Solomon, Jonathan D., Editors, *Models: 306090 Books*, Volume 11, 306090, New York, pp. 185–189

Malé-Alemany, Marta and **Sousa, José Pedro** (2008), "Computation and Materiality," in Kolarevic, Branko and Klinger, Kevin, Editors, *Manufacturing Material Effects: Rethinking Design and Making in Architecture*, Routledge, London, pp. 129–144

Malkawi, Ali M. (2005), "Performance Simulation: Research and Tools," in Kolarevic, Branko and Malkawi, Ali M., Editors, *Performative Architectures: Beyond Instrumentality*, Spon Press, New York and London, pp. 85–96

Massad, Fredy and **Yeste, Alicia Guerrero** (2002), *A+A Architecturanimation*, College of Architects, Catalunya, Barcelona

McLeod, Mary (2003), "Form and Function Today," in Tschumi, Bernard and Cheng, Irene, Editors, *The State of Architecture at the Beginning of the 21st Century*, The Monacelli Press, New York, pp. 50–51

Menges, Achim (2006), "Instrumental Geometry: Interview with Smart Geometry Group: Robert Aish, Lars Hesselgren, J. Parrish and Hugh Whitehead," in Hensel, Michael, Menges, Achim and Weinstock, Michael, Editors, *Techniques and Technologies in Morphogenetic Design*, AD (*Architectural Design*), Profile No. 180, Vol. 76, No. 2, March/April, pp. 42–53

Menges, Achim (2006), "Manufacturing Diversity," in Hensel, Michael, Menges, Achim and Weinstock, Michael, Editors, *Techniques and Technologies in Morphogenetic Design*, AD (*Architectural Design*), Profile No. 180, Vol. 76, No. 2, March/April, pp. 70–77

Menges, Achim (2008), "Integrated Formation and Materialization: Computational Form and Material Gestalt," in Kolarevic, Branko and Klinger, Kevin, Editors, *Manufacturing Material Effects: Rethinking Design and Making in Architecture*, Routledge, London, pp. 195–210

Menges, Achim (2008), "Manufacturing Performance," in Hensel, Michael and Menges, Achim, *Versatility and Vicissitude: Performance and Morpho-Ecological Design*, AD (*Architectural Design*), Profile No. 192, Vol. 78, No. 2, March/April, pp. 42–47

Menges, Achim (2010), "Form Generation and Materialization at the Transition from Computer-Aided to Computational Design," *Detail*, Vol. 4, July/August, pp. 330–335

Mertins, Detlef (2003), "Same Difference," in Kubo, Michael and Ferré, Albert, Editors, in collaboration with FOA, *Phylogenesis FOA's Ark*, Actar, Barcelona, pp. 270–279

Mertins, Detlef (2004), "Bioconstructivisms," in Spuybroek, Lars, *NOX: Machining Architecture*, Thames and Hudson, London, pp. 360–369

Migayrou, Frédéric (2003), "The Orders of the Non-Standard," in *Architectures Non Standard*, Centre Pompidou, Paris, pp. 26–33. Revised with new introduction, 2012

Migayrou, Frédéric (2009), "Incremental Mutations," in Andrasek, Alisa, *Biothing*, Frac Centre, Editions HYX, Orléans, France, pp. 20–29

Mitchell, William J. (1998), "Antitectonics: the Poetics of Virtuality," in Beckman, John, Editor, *The Virtual Dimension: Architecture, Representation and Crash Culture*, Princeton Architectural Press, New York, pp. 205–217

Moussavi, Farshid (2009), *The Function of Form*, Actar, Barcelona and the Harvard Graduate School of Design, Cambridge, MA

Oosterhuis, Kas (2002), *Architecture Goes Wild*, 010 Publishers, Rotterdam

Oosterhuis, Kas (2003), *Hyperbodies: Towards an E-Motive Architecture*, Birkhaüser, Basel

Oosterhuis, Kas (2011), "Move That Body: Building Components Are Actors in a Complex Adaptive System," in Oosterhuis, Kas, *Towards a New Kind of Building: A Designer's Guide for Non-Standard Architecture*, NAi Publishers, Rotterdam, pp. 110–134

O'Sullivan, Dan and **Igoe, Tom** (2004), *Physical Computing: Sensing and Controlling the Physical World with Computers*, Thomson Course Technology, Boston, MA

Oxman, Neri (2010), "Structuring Materiality: Design Fabrication of Heterogeneous Materials," in Oxman, Rivka and Oxman, Robert, Editors, *The New Structuralism: Design, Engineering and Architectural Technologies*, AD (*Architectural Design*),Profile No. 206, Vol. 80, No. 4, July/August, pp. 78–85

Oxman, Neri (2011), "Variable Property Rapid Prototyping," VPP (*Journal of Virtual and Physical Prototyping*), Vol. 6, No. 1, pp. 3–31

Oxman, Neri (2012), "Programming Matter," in Menges, Achim, Editor, *Material Computation: Higher Integration in Mophogenetic Design*, AD (*Architectural Design*), Profile No. 216 Volume 82, Issue 2, March/April, pp. 88–95

Oxman, Rivka (2006), "Theory and Design in the First Digital Age," *The International Journal of Design Studies*, Vol. 27, No. 3, pp. 229–265

Oxman, Rivka (2008), "Performance-Based Design: Current Practices and Research Issues," *International Journal of Architectural Computing*, Vol. 6, No. 1, pp. 1–17

Oxman, Rivka (2009), "Performative Design: a Performance-Based Model of Digital Architectural Design," *Environment and Planning (B): Planning and Design*, Vol. 36, No. 6, pp. 1026–1037

Oxman, Rivka (2010), "Morphogenesis in the Theory and Methodology of Digital Tectonics," in Motro, R., Editor, special issue on Morphogenesis, IASS (*Journal of the International Association for Shell and Spatial Structures*), Vol. 51, No. 3, pp. 195–207

Oxman, Rivka (2010b) "The New Structuralism: Conceptual Mapping of Emerging Key Concepts in Theory and Praxis," *The International Journal of Architectural Computing*, Vol. 8, No. 4 pp. 419–438

Oxman, Rivka (2012) "Informed Tectonics in Material-based Design," *The International Journal of Design Studies*, Vol. 33, No. 5, pp. 427–455

Oxman, Rivka (2013) "Naturalizing Design: In Pursuit of Tectonic Materiality," in Marie-Ange Brayer and Frédéric Migayrou (eds) *Archilab: Naturalizing Architcture*, FRAC Centre, HYX Orleans

Oxman, Rivka and **Oxman, Robert** (2010), "The New Structuralism: Design, Engineering and Architectural Technologies," in Oxman, Rivka and Oxman, Robert, Editors, *The New Structuralism: Design, Engineering and Architectural Technologies*, AD (*Architectural Design*), Profile No. 206, Vol. 80, No. 4, July/August, pp. 14–23

Pearce, Martin and **Spiller, Neil** (1995), *Architects in Cyberspace I*, AD (*Architectural Design*), Profile No. 118, John Wiley and Sons, West Sussex, UK

Perella, Stephen (1998), *Hypersurface Architecture*, AD (*Architectural Design*), Profile No. 133, John Wiley and Sons, West Sussex, UK

Picon, Antoine (2004), "Architecture and the Virtual: Towards a New Materiality," in Reeser, Amanda and Schafer, Ashley, Editors, *New Technologies/New Architectures*, Praxis 6, pp. 114–121

Picon, Antoine (2010), "The Seduction of Innovative Geometries," in Picon, Antoine, *Digital Culture in Architecture*, Birkhäuser, Basel, pp. 60–72

Pottmann, Helmut (2010), "Architectural Geometry as Design Knowledge," in Oxman, Rivka and Oxman, Robert, Editors, *The New Structuralism: Design, Engineering and Architectural Technologies*, AD (*Architectural Design*), Profile No. 206, Vol. 80, No. 4, July/August, pp. 72–77

Pottmann, Helmut, Asperl, Andreas, Hofer, Michael and **Killian, Axel** (2007), *Architectural Geometry*, Bentley Institute Press, Exton, PA

Rahim, Ali, Editor (2000), *Contemporary Processes in Architecture*, AD (*Architectural Design*), Profile No. 145, June, Wiley-Academy, London

Rahim, Ali, Editor (2002), *Contemporary Techniques in Architecture*, AD (*Architectural Design*), Profile No. 155, Vol. 72, No. 1, January

Rahim, Ali (2006), *Catalytic Formations: Architecture and Digital Design*, Taylor & Francis, London

Reas, Casey, McWilliams, Chandler and **LUST** (2010), *Form and Code in Design, Art and Architecture*, Princeton Architectural Press, New York

Reas, Casey, McWilliams, Chandler and **LUST** (2010), "Parameterize," **Reas, Casey, McWilliams, Chandler** and **LUST** *Form and Code in Design, Art and Architecture*, Princeton Architectural Press, New York, pp. 93–116

Reeser, Amanda and **Schafer, Ashley**, Editors (2004), *New Technologies/New Architectures*, Praxis, No. 6

Reeser Lawrence, Amanda and **Schafer, Ashley**, Editors (2007), *Expanding Surface*, Praxis, No. 9

Reilly, Una-May, Hemberg, Martin and **Menges, Achim** (2004), "Evolutionary Computation and Artificial Life in Architecture," in Hensel, Michael, Menges, Achim and Weinstock, Michael, Editors, *Emergence: Morphogenetic Design Strategies*, AD (*Architectural Design*), Profile No. 169, Vol. 74, No. 3, May/June, pp. 48–53

Reiser and Umemoto (2006), *Atlas of Novel Tectonics*, Princeton Architectural Press, New York

Rocker, Ingeborg M. (2006), "Calculus-Based Form: An Interview with Greg Lynn," in Silver, Mike, Editor, *Programming Cultures: Art and Architecture in the Age of Software*, AD (*Architectural Design*), Profile 182, Vol. 76, No. 4, July/August, pp. 88–95

Ronan, Timothy M. (2003), "From Microcosm to Macrocosm: the Surface of Fuller and Sadao's US Pavilion at Montreal Expo '67," in Taylor, Mark, Editor, *Surface Consciousness*, AD (*Architectural Design*), Profile No. 162, Vol. 73, No. 2, March/April, pp. 50–56

Rosa, Joseph (2003), *Next Generation Architectures: Folds, Blobs and Boxes*, Rizzoli, New York

Sakamoto, Tomoko and **Ferré, Albert**, Editors (2008), *From Control to Design: Parametric/Algorithmic Architecture*, Actar, Barcelona

Sasaki, Mutsuro (2007), *The Morphogenesis of Flux Structures*, AA Publications, London

Saunders, Peter T. (1997), "Nonlinearity: What It Is and Why It Matters," in Jencks, Charles, Editor, *New Science = New Architecture*, AD (*Architectural Design*), Profile No. 129, Vol. 67, No. 9/10, September/October, pp. 52–57

Schmal, Peter Cachola (2001), *Digital Real: Blobmeister – First Built Projects*, Birkhäuser, Basel

Schmitt, Gerhard (1999), *Information Architectures: Basis and Future of CAAD*, Birkhäuser, Basel

Schodek, Daniel, Bechthold, Martin, Griggs, Kimo, Kao, Kenneth Martin and **Steinberg, Martin** (2005), *Digital Design and Manufacturing: CAD/CAM Applications in Architecture and Design*, John Wiley and Sons, Hoboken, NJ

Schröder, Peter (2008), "Digital Geometry," in Lynn, Greg (Edited by Mark Rappolt), *Greg Lynn Form*, Rizzoli, New York, pp. 146–155

Schröpfer, Thomas, Editor (2010), *Material Design*, Birkhäuser, Basel

Schumacher, Patrik (2004), *Digital Hadid: Landscapes in Motion*, Birkhäuser, Basel

Schumacher, Patrik (2009), "Parametricism, A New Global Style for Architecture and Urban Design," in Leach, Neil, Editor, *Digital Cities*, AD (*Architectural Design*), Profile No. 200, Vol. 79, No. 4, July/August, p. 17

Schumacher, Patrik (2010), "Parametric Diagrams," in Garcia, Mark, Editor, *The Diagrams of Architecture*, AD Reader, John Wiley and Sons, London

Schumacher, Patrik (2011), "From Space to Field," *The Autopoesis of Architectures: A New Framework for Architecture*, John Wiley and Sons, West Sussex, UK, pp. 421–433

Shea, Kristina (2004), "Directed Randomness," in Leach, Neil, Turnbull, David and Williams, Chris, Editors, *Digital Tectonics*, John Wiley and Sons, West Sussex, UK, pp. 88–101

Sheil, Bob, Editor (2005), *Design Through Making*, AD (*Architectural Design*), Profile No. 178, Vol. 75, No. 4, July/August

Shelden, Dennis R. (2006), "Tectonics, Economics and the Reconfiguration of Practice: the Case for Process Change by Digital Means," in Silver, Mike, Editor, *Programming Cultures: Art and Architecture in the Age of Software*, AD (*Architectural Design*), Profile No. 182, Vol. 76, No. 4, July/August, pp. 82–87

Shelden, Dennis (2009), "Information Modelling as a Paradigm Shift," in Garber, Richard, Editor, *Closing the Gap: Information Models in Contemporary Design Practice*, AD (*Architectural Design*), Profile No. 198, Vol. 79, No. 2, March/April, pp. 80–83

Shelden, Dennis R. and **Witt, Andrew, J.** (2011), "Continuity and Rupture," in Legendre, George L., Editor, *Mathematics of Space*, AD (*Architectural Design*), Profile No. 212, Vol. 81 No. 4, July/August, pp. 36–43

SHoP/Sharp, Holden, Pasquarelli, Editors (2002), *Versioning: Evolutionary Techniques in Architecture*, AD (*Architectural Design*), Profile No. 159, Vol. 72, No. 5, September/October

Silver, Mike, Editor (2006), *Programming Cultures: Art and Architecture in the Age of Software*, AD (*Architectural Design*), Profile No. 182, Vol. 76, No. 4, July/August

Simmonds, Tristan, Self, Martin and **Bosia, Daniel** (2006), "Woven Surface and Form," in Garcia, Mark, Editor, *Architextiles*, AD (*Architectural Design*), Profile No. 184, Vol. 76, No. 6, November/December, pp. 82–89

Speaks, Michael (1995), "Folding Toward a New Architecture," in Cache, Bernard (Speaks, Michael, ed.), *Earth Moves: the Furnishing of Territories*, MIT Press, Cambridge, MA, pp. xii–xviii

Speaks, Michael (2007), "Intelligence After Theory," in Burke, Anthony and Tierney, Therese, Editors, *Network Practices: New Strategies in Architecture and Design*, Princeton Architectural Press, New York, pp. 212–216

Spiller, Neil (1998), *Architects in Cyberspace II*, AD (*Architectural Design*), Profile No. 136, Vol. 68, No. 11/12, November/December

Spiller, Neil (2008), "Digital Architectures: The History So Far," in Spiller, Neil, *Digital Architecture Now – A Global Survey of Emerging Talent*, Thames and Hudson, London, pp. 6–15

Spuybroek, Lars (2004), *NOX: Machining Architecture*, Thames and Hudson, London

Spuybroek, Lars (2004), "The Structure of Vagueness," in Spuybroek, Lars, *NOX: Machining Architecture*, Thames and Hudson, London, pp. 352–359

Spuybroek, Lars (2006), "Textile Tectonics: an Interview with Lars Spuybroek by Maria Ludovica Tramontin," in Garcia, Mark, Editor, *Architextiles*, AD (*Architectural Design*), Profile No. 184, Vol. 76, No. 6, November/December, pp. 52–59

Spuybroek, Lars, Editor (2009), *Research and Design: The Architecture of Variation*, Thames and Hudson, London

Spuybroek, Lars (2011), *Textile Tectonics: Research and Design*, NAI Publishers, Rotterdam

Spuybroek, Lars (2012), *The Sympathy of Things: Ruskin and the Ecology of Design*, NAI Publishers, Rotterdam

Spuybroek, Lars and **Lang, Bob** (1999), *The Weight of the Image*, 4th International NAI Summer Master Class, NAI, Rotterdam

Steele, Brett (2006), "The AADRL: Design, Collaboration and Convergence," in Hight, Christopher and Perry, Chris, Editors, *Collective Intelligence in Design*, AD (*Architectural Design*), Profile No. 183, Vol. 76, No. 5, September/October, pp. 58–63

Steele, Brett (2008), *DRL Ten: A Design Research Compendium*, AA Publications, London

Studio Rocker (2005), *Re-Coded, Exhibition Catalogue*, Aedes East Gallery, Berlin

Szalapaj, Peter (2005), *Contemporary Architecture and the Digital Design Process*, Architectural Press, Elsevier, Oxford

Taylor, Mark, Editor (2003), *Surface Consciousness*, AD (*Architectural Design*), Profile No. 162, Vol. 73, No. 2, March/April

Terzidis, Kostas (2006), *Algorithmic Architecture*, Architectural Press/Elsevier, Oxford

Terzidis, Kostas (2006), "A Brief History of Algotecture," in Terzidis, Kostas, *Algorithmic Architecture*, Architectural Press/Elsevier, Oxford, pp. 37–64

Testa, Peter and **Weiser, Devyn** (2006), "Extreme Networks," in Garcia, Mark, Editor, *Architextiles*, AD (*Architectural Design*), Profile No. 184, Vol. 76, No. 6, November/December, pp. 42–43

Tierney, Therese (2007), "Biological Networks: On Neurons, Cellular Automata, and Relational Architectures," in Burke, Anthony and Tierney, Therese, Editors, *Network Strategies: New Strategies in Architecture and Design*, Princeton Architectural Press, New York, pp. 78–99

Tramontin, Maria Ludovica (2006), "Textile Tectonics: an Interview with Lars Spruybroek," in Garcia, Mark, Editor, *Architextiles*, AD (*Architectural Design*), Profile No. 184, Vol. 76, No. 6, November/December, pp. 52–59

Tsukui, Noriko Editor (2006), *Cecil Balmond*, a+u (*Architecture and Urbanism*) (Japan) Special Issue, November

Verebes, Tom, Spyropoulos, Theodore, Obuchi, Yusuki and **Schumacher, Patrik**, Editors (2008), *DRL Ten: A Design Research Compendium*, AA Publications, London

Vollers, Karel (2001), "Context of Twisted Constructions," in Vollers, Karel, *Twist and Build: Creating Non-Orthogonal Architecture*, 010 Publishers, Rotterdam, pp. 18–33

Weinstock, Michael (2006), "Self-Organisation and the Structural Dynamics of Plants," in Hensel, Michael, Menges, Achim and Weinstock, Michael, Editors, *Techniques and Technologies in Morphogenetic Design*, AD (*Architectural Design*), Profile No. 180, Vol. 76, No. 2, March/April, pp. 26–33

Weinstock, Michael and **Stathopoulos, Nikolaos** (2006), "Advanced Simulation in Design," in Hensel, Michael, Menges, Achim and Weinstock, Michael, Editors, *Techniques and Technologies in Morphogenetic Design*, AD (*Architectural Design*), Profile No. 180, Vol. 76, No. 2, March/April, pp. 54–59

Whitehead, Hugh (2003), "Laws of Form," in Kolarevic, Branko, Editor, *Architecture in the Digital Age: Design and Manufacturing*, Spon Press, New York and London, pp. 81–100

Wigley, Mark (2007), "The Architectural Brain," in Burke, Anthony and Tierney, Therese, Editors, *Network Strategies: New Strategies in Architecture and Design*, Princeton Architectural Press, New York, pp. 30–35

Williams, Chris (2004), "Design by Algorithm," in Leach, Neil, Turnbull, David and Williams, Chris, Editors, *Digital Tectonics*, Wiley-Academy, West Sussex, UK, pp. 78–85

Woodbury, Robert (2006), "Every Designer Is An Editor," in Beesley, Philip, Hirosue, Sachiko, Ruxton, Jim, Tränkle, Marion and Turner, Camille, Editors, *Responsive Architectures: Subtle Technologies*, Riverside Architectural Press, Toronto, pp. 142–147

Woodbury, Robert (2010), *Elements of Parametric Design*, Routledge, Oxford

Woodbury, Robert (2010), "How Designers Use Parameters," in Woodbury, Robert, *Elements of Parametric Design*, Routledge, Oxford, pp. 23–47

Zaero-Polo, Alejandro (2003), "Breeding Architecture," in Tschumi, Bernard and Cheng, Irene, Editors, *The State of Architecture at the Beginning of the 21st Century*, The Monacelli Press, New York, pp. 56–55

Zaero-Polo, Alejandro/Foreign Office Architects (2002), "Roller Coaster Construction," in Rahim, Ali, Editor, *Contemporary Techniques in Architecture*, AD (*Architectural Design*), Profile No. 155, Vol. 72, No. 1, January, pp. 84–92

Zaero-Polo, Alejandro and **Moussavi, Farshid** (2003), "Phylogenesis: FOA's Ark," in Kubo, Michael and Ferré, Albert, Editors *Phylogenesis: FOA's Ark*, Actar, Barcelona, pp. 6–18

Zellner, Peter (1999), *Hybrid Space: New Forms in Digital Architecture*, Thames and Hudson, London

INDEX

References in *italics* indicate figures.